True Faith

In fact, the law requires that nearly everything be cleansed with blood, and without the shedding of blood, there is no forgiveness.

—Hebrews 9:22

Rev. Silas Kanyabigega, DMin

WESTBOW
PRESS®
A DIVISION OF THOMAS NELSON
& ZONDERVAN

Contact information for Rev. Silas Kanyabigega

E-mail: kanyabigegasilas@gmail.com
Websites: www.movementforchrist.com
www.radiokwizera.org
Telephone: (937) 559-5862

WestBow Press books may be ordered through booksellers or by contacting:

WestBow Press
A Division of Thomas Nelson & Zondervan
1663 Liberty Drive
Bloomington, IN 47403
www.westbowpress.com
1 (866) 928-1240

Because of the dynamic nature of the Internet, any web addresses or links contained in this book may have changed since publication and may no longer be valid. The views expressed in this work are solely those of the author and do not necessarily reflect the views of the publisher, and the publisher hereby disclaims any responsibility for them.

Any people depicted in stock imagery provided by Thinkstock are models, and such images are being used for illustrative purposes only.
Certain stock imagery © Thinkstock.

Scripture quotations marked NIV are taken from the Holy Bible, New International Version. NIV. Copyright © 1973, 1978, 1984 by International Bible Society. Used by permission of Zondervan. All rights reserved.

The Authorized (King James) Version of the Bible ('the KJV'), the rights in which are vested in the Crown in the United Kingdom, is reproduced here by permission of the Crown's patentee, Cambridge University Press.

Scripture taken from the Basic English Bible.

Scripture taken from the King James Version of the Bible.

Scripture quotations marked RSV are taken from the Revised Standard Version of the Bible, copyright © 1946, 1952, 1971 by the Division of Christian Education of the National Council of the Churches of Christ in the USA. Used by permission.

ISBN: 978-1-5127-6663-9 (sc)
ISBN: 978-1-5127-6664-6 (hc)
ISBN: 978-1-5127-6662-2 (e)

Library of Congress Control Number: 2016919893

Print information available on the last page.

WestBow Press rev. date: 11/23/2016

Dedication

This book is dedicated to my wife, Venantie
Nzavugankize, and to my children.

It is also dedicated to my mother, Julie Nyirumulinga,
and my father, Thaddee Buhake.

Contents

Acknowledgments

I want to thank Andrew S. Park, PhD, professor of theology and ethics at United Theological Seminary, Dayton, Ohio, USA, for reading the draft of *True Faith* and for his encouragement in his words, "It is a very comprehensive manuscript. This book is very intriguing. May God bless you and your publication, Silas!" Dr. Andrew S. Park, my teacher, inspired me in various ways and encouraged me to sharpen the title of this book.

I would like to take this opportunity to express my deepest gratitude to my spouse, Venantie Nzavugankize, who has fully supported this project by taking care of the lion's share of the housework. I am grateful most of all for her unfailing love and patience through the long process of writing a book. I am also thankful for the understanding and patience of my seven children, Joyce Mushimiyimana, Joshua Nsengiyumva, Evanyse Manishimwe, Judith Niyimpa, Fortune Nishimwe, Samuel Silvain Sezerano, and Tite Niyonshuti. The youngest boys often wanted to play with Daddy a little longer, but when Daddy had to be alone in his room, or visiting different libraries, they understood and let him have time for this project.

Without the ardent support of Rev. Randy Griffith, senior pastor of Huber Heights Free Methodist Church in the United States, the completion of this project would not have been possible. I thank him for taking time to read the draft.

I also would like to take this opportunity to express my gratitude to Matthews Caleb, director of admissions, Northeastern Seminary at Roberts Wesleyan College of New York, who read a portion of this work sent to him as a graduate theological paper for my Doctor of Ministry degree, and advised me about formatting the biblical citations.

Excerpts from the article on Hinduism are used by permission of the Traveling Team.

Excerpts from the book *Christ-Centered Therapy* by Neil T. Anderson are used by permission of HarperCollins Publishing.

Introduction

God created us for his own glory. The sin of the first couple caused a profound change in humanity and in humanity's relationship with God (Rom. 5:12). As a result, we have the seriousness of sin as rebellion against God, the continuing responsibility for our actions, our consequent guilt in God's sight, and our liability to punishment. Sin is any failure to conform to the moral law of God in act, attitude, or nature. Sin, here defined in relation to God and his moral law, includes not only individual acts such as stealing, lying, or committing murder, but also attitudes that are contrary to the attitudes God requires of us.[1] In *True Faith*, we will discuss the problem of forgiveness in relation to the gravity of sin and the majesty of God, taking into account the reality of who we are and who he is. Propitiation is mandatory on account of the holiness of God and the sinfulness of humankind. After all, a holy God cannot look upon sin.

"For the wages of sin is death, but the gift of God is eternal life in Christ Jesus our Lord" (Rom. 6:23). We all need a Savior, because, as it is written, "All have sinned and fall short of the glory of God. ... There is no one righteous, not even one" (Rom. 3:23, 10).

God in his grace did not leave humanity to perish eternally but provided for redemption. Salvation became possible when God became the self-substitute for sinners. Humankind is reconciled when God is propitiated. The sin could not be retracted and the nature of God could not forgive the sinner without a satisfactory payment. The price for this satisfaction is the blood of Jesus Christ, and the act of satisfaction is propitiation. Christ did more than die for us; he also gave himself up to face God's wrath.

The concept of propitiation involves the satisfying of God's just wrath against sin by the holiness of Jesus Christ's death.[2]

As mentioned previously, propitiation is necessary given the holiness of God and the sinfulness of humankind. "In fact, the law requires that nearly everything be cleansed with blood, and without the shedding of blood there is no forgiveness" (Heb. 9:22).

Since the law is eternal, unchangeable, and applicable to every human being, no person can escape the demands of the law. Since a degree of criminality is attached to every violation of the law and since God will punish according to the degree of criminality (Luke 10:10–15; Luke 12:47–48), every violation of the law will be punished according to a predetermined standard. Since every human being has violated the law and will suffer its consequences, there is no hope for those who have violated the law. Nothing in human beings can help them escape the criminality of their actions. In addition, God can neither treat the violations as if they never occurred nor forgive any violation arbitrarily. Since the law is an extension of the person of God, breaking the law is an offense against God. God must be compensated before the lawbreaker can be saved.

Christ suffered in the place of humankind. Since punishment must be eternal and complete, Christ suffered ultimately for all criminality. This act of Christ's, called the vicarious substitutionary atonement, was Christ's suffering in the place of the sinner (vicarious). The death of Christ was both the substitute for our sin and the satisfaction of the law.

The symbol of this transaction is the actual blood of Jesus Christ, a symbol of his substitutionary death.

There is a double transference associated with the act of reconciliation through Jesus's death: First, our sins were imputed to Jesus Christ, "For he hath made him to be sin for us" (2 Cor. 5:21). Second, our sins were imputed to Christ "that we might be made the righteousness of God in him" (2 Cor. 5:21). In the act of salvation, the righteousness of Jesus Christ was placed on the account of the sinner, and inversely the sins of sinners were assumed by Jesus Christ when he died for the sins of the world. It is noteworthy to realize that the tense of the verb *reconciled* suggests that this work is specifically a work of God and is completed. Therefore, unregenerate humanity today is not guilty of sin under the Old Testament law. Rather, humankind's guilt and punishment stems from a rejection of Christ as personal Savior and Lord.

The blood of the God-man, Jesus Christ, is able to save all people, but this blood is effective only for those who believe in him. A person who believes in him is no longer condemned for breaking the law; rather, a person who does not believe in Jesus Christ is now condemned for rejecting him.

True Faith

To have true faith is to believe in Jesus Christ as Lord and personal Savior.

To believe in Jesus Christ as Lord means that a person repents and asks forgiveness for his or her sins. To believe in Jesus Christ as Savior means that a person recognizes the work of Jesus Christ at the cross, and believes that Jesus Christ died for his or her personal sins. The purpose of God's love is to save every one of us. Even if there had been only one person on the planet, Jesus Christ would have come and died for that person.

Propitiation focuses on the wrath of God, which was placated by the cross; redemption, on the plight of sinners, from which they were ransomed by the cross.

False Faith

False faith is a faith that does not believe in Jesus as Lord and Savior. To have false faith means to believe without God's blood being part of the salvation process, that is, to believe in a god who did not become the self-substitute for sinners. To have false faith is to exclude Christ's cross from one's beliefs. "For the message about the cross is foolishness to those who are perishing, but to us who are being saved it is the power of God" (1 Cor. 1:18). "And without the shedding of blood there is no forgiveness" (Heb. 9:22).

In reality, God exists. Human beings are already informed about God's existence through creation and consciousness. In one way or another, people know that there is a problem between God and humankind. For people of less understanding, the consequences of sin—death, suffering, and problems of all kinds—are credible witnesses to this fact.

Actually, everyone adheres to a religion in order to find a way of connecting with an extraordinary Being, commonly called God.

Each religion has a process to follow to connect a person with God. Different doctrines espousing different beliefs are put forth to succeed in this area.

According to the Bible, a price is needed to placate God. God requires the price, and human beings have to pay that price to restore the broken relationship between them and God. Adam and Eve offended God, and all descendants of Adam are guilty of the sin of their ancestors. Each individual must restore his or her relationship with God. According to the Bible, "Without the shedding of blood there is no forgiveness" (Heb. 9:22).

Blood and *sacrifice* are not uncommon words in different religions. People of different religious know that when blood is shed, there is something serious done. Especially when the blood of a person is shed, it means that the person is dead.

Even though the words *sacrifice* and *blood* are known to be used in belief systems other than Christianity, this doesn't mean that any blood or sacrifice has the ability to save humankind.

True Faith seeks to expose and analyze the beliefs of different religions in order to see which of them meet the criteria established by God for humankind's salvation. Based on scripture, we will identify what is true faith and false belief. In doing this, we will enable the reader to identify and follow the true religion with true faith.

CHAPTER 1

The Bible

Introduction

The Bible is the starting point, or the source, of our religious knowledge.[3] Christianity is the religion of a Book, as it is based upon the impregnable rock of Holy Scripture. The starting point of all doctrinal discussion must be the Bible. But this Book is no natural book, for it claims to be a divine revelation, penned by human authors. As such, the Bible has dual authorship, written by human beings in their own languages while being supernaturally guided by the Holy Spirit so that both the words and the messages were without error or mistake.

The Extraordinary Claim That the Bible is from God

Over three thousand times in scripture, the authors claim their message is from God. Expressions like "thus saith the Lord" appear approximately five hundred times in the Pentateuch and over twelve hundred times in the books of the prophets.

Old Testament prophets used expressions like "thus saith the Lord or "The word of the Lord came unto ..." These expressions are themselves among the strongest arguments for accepting that the Bible was divinely inspired. Concerning the expressions "Word of the Lord" (*debhar Yahweh*), B. B. Warfield, professor of theology at Princeton Seminary from 1887 to 1921, writes that it "is at once the simplest and the most colorless designation of a Divine communication." He then goes on to note, "Both phrases ['Word of the Lord' and 'Law of the Lord'] are used for any Divine communication of whatever extent; and both came to be employed to express the entire body of Divine revelation, conceived as a unitary whole ... and both passed into the New Testament with these implications."[4]

The various authors wrote the books of the Bible during a time span of approximately sixteen hundred years, from Moses, who began writing around 1440 BC, to John, who finished the last book of the Bible around AD 100. The Bible was written over the course of fifty-five generations, yet there remains a singular unity. Only God who transcends all time could be its source.[5]

Since God is what he is—infinite, loving, and the Redeemer—we can only expect that this loving and wise God would reveal a plan of redemption to humanity powerful enough to save human beings.

Since humanity is what it is—limited, sinful, and needy—we can only conclude that human beings need a message of help that will meet their need. Therefore, we expect the message of redemption from God that is given to meet the needs of sinful humankind to be authoritative, accurate, and reliable. If the message of redemption were riddled with mistakes, then humankind could not exercise faith in the message, and this would be counterproductive to revelation. If the message of redemption were not authoritative, then humankind could have no confidence in its claim. Therefore, we can only conclude that the Bible is a revelation that is given in a manner that produces full confidence in both its content and its transmission to humankind.

The Two Areas of Revelation

God's act of self-revelation can be divided into two areas. First, the self-revelation of God is evident in nature, or as someone has observed, "The Creator is evident in his creation." Second, God has revealed himself through the Word of God and its central message, who is Jesus Christ. This second area is called special revelation.

The claims of Jesus Christ are quite remarkable when examined thoroughly. Jesus Christ affirmed his deity:

1. He applied to himself the statement of Jehovah "I am" (John 8:24). This affirmation is taken from the root word for "Jehovah," "I am that I am" (Exod. 3:14–15; John 4:26; John 18:5–6). The Jews of

Jesus's day did not misunderstand his claim. They knew that he was claiming full deity, and they tried to stone him (John 8:59).

2. Jesus claimed to be identical to the Father (John 10:33; John 14:9).
3. Jesus asserted his omnipresence (Matt. 18:20; John 3:13), omniscience (John 11:14), and omnipotence (Matt. 28:18; John 5:21–23; John 6:19).
4. Jesus received and approved of human worship (Matt. 14:33; Matt. 28:9; John 20:28–29).
5. Jesus forgave sins (Mark 2:5–7; Luke 7:48–50).
6. Jesus made Jehovahistic statements, such as "I am," and saying that he was the Bread of Life, the Light, the door, the Way, the Truth, and the Life, and resurrection—hence identifying himself with God (John 6:37; John 8:12; John 10:9; John 11:25; John 14:6).[6]

The Authority of Scripture

We are convinced of the Bible's claims to be God's Words as we read the Bible. It is one thing to affirm that the Bible *claims* to be the Words of God; it is another thing to be convinced that those claims are true. Our ultimate conviction that the words of the Bible are God's Words comes only when the Holy Spirit speaks *in* and *through* the Words of the Bible to our hearts and gives us an inner assurance that these are the Words of our Creator speaking to us. Just after Paul has explained that his apostolic speech consists of words taught by the Holy Spirit (1 Cor. 2:13), he says, "The natural man does not receive the things of the Spirit of God, for they are folly to him, and he is not able to understand them because they are spiritually discerned" (1 Cor. 2:14). Apart from the work of the Spirit of God, a person will not receive spiritual truths and in particular will not receive or accept the truth that the words of scripture are in fact the Words of God.

The Words of Scripture Are Self-Attesting

Thus, the words of scripture are *self-attesting*. They cannot be *proven* to be God's Words by appeal to any higher authority. For if an appeal to some higher authority (say, historical accuracy or logical consistency) were used to prove that the Bible is God's Word, then the Bible itself would not be our highest or absolute authority: it would be subordinate in authority to the thing to which we appealed to prove it to be God's Word. If we ultimately appeal to human reason, or to logic, or to historical accuracy, or to scientific truth as the authority by which scripture is shown to be God's Words, then we have assumed the thing to which we appealed to be a higher authority than God's Words, an authority that is more true or more reliable.

To Disbelieve or Disobey Any Word of Scripture Is to Disbelieve or Disobey God

The preceding section has argued that all the words in scripture are God's Words. Consequently, to disbelieve or disobey any word of scripture is to disbelieve or disobey God himself. Thus, Jesus can rebuke his disciples for not believing the Old Testament scriptures (Luke 24:25). Believers are to keep or obey the disciples' words (John 15:20: "If they kept my word, they will keep yours also"). Christians are encouraged to remember "the commandment of the Lord and Savior through your apostles" (2 Pet. 3:2). To disobey Paul's writings is to make oneself liable to church discipline, such as excommunication (2 Thess. 3:14) and spiritual punishment (2 Cor. 13:2–3), including punishment by God (this is the apparent sense of the passive verb "he is not recognized" in 1 Cor. 14:38). By contrast, God delights in everyone who "trembles" at his Word (Isa. 66:2).

God's Words Are the Ultimate Standard of Truth

In John 17, Jesus prays to the Father, "Sanctify them in the truth; *your word is truth*" (John 17:17, emphasis added). This verse is interesting because Jesus does not use the adjectives *alethinos* or *alethes* ("true"), which we might have expected, to say, "Your word is true," but he uses words indicating "truth itself."

The difference is significant, because this statement encourages us to think of the Bible not simply as being "true" in the sense that it conforms to some higher standard of truth but also as being itself the final standard of truth. The Bible is God's Word, and God's Word is the ultimate definition of what is true and what is not true: God's Word is itself *truth*. Thus we are to think of the Bible as the ultimate standard of truth, the reference point by which every other claim to truthfulness is to be measured. Those assertions that conform with scripture are true, while those that do not conform with scripture are not true.

What then is truth? Truth is what God says, and we have what God says (accurately but not exhaustively) in the Bible.

Written Scripture Is Our Final Authority

It is important to realize that the final form in which scripture remains authoritative is its *written* form. It was the words of God *written* on the tablets of stone that Moses deposited in the ark of the covenant. Later, God commanded Moses and subsequent prophets to write their words in a book. And it was *written* that scripture (*graphe*), as Paul said, is "God-breathed" (2 Tim. 3:16). Similarly, it is Paul's *writings* that are "a command of the Lord" (1 Cor. 14:37) and that could be classified with "the other scriptures" (2 Pet. 3:16).

The Bible Is the Word of God

The Bible is superior to all other religious books. Another natural character of scripture erupts when it is compared to any other books: the real Author of the Bible is clearly greater than the human mind, because his message is infinite and eternal.

Prophets: Proof of Divine Inspiration

God alone is omniscient, and therefore able to predict the future. He is Jehovah; time for him does not count. Tomorrow, eternity itself, is present to him, as well as today. No false god, no other religion on earth, has never made similar prophecies to those of the Bible. "Who announced it from the beginning ... and well in advance, that we may say: That is true? ... He does ... nobody among them who prophesy ... It was I who announced, saved, predicted ... among you a strange god ... who confirms the word of his servant, and fulfills the prediction of his messengers" (Isa. 41:26, 28; Isa. 43:12; Isa. 44:26).

The Bible, the Word of God, Is Living and Active

The written Word, living oracle of the Lord, emanates supernatural strength. "Is it not my word like a fire, says the Lord, and like a hammer that breaks the rock in pieces? ... I am now making my words in your mouth a fire, and this people wood, and the fire shall devour them" (Jer. 23:29; Jer. 5:14).

After talking about the message to the people in the desert and confirming the psalms in the Holy Spirit, the author of Hebrews concludes, "For the word of God is alive and active. Sharper than any double-edged sword, it penetrates even to dividing soul and spirit, joints and marrow; it judges the thoughts and attitudes of the heart. Nothing in all creation is hidden from God's sight. Everything is uncovered and laid bare before the eyes of him to whom we must give account" (Heb. 4:12–13).

The Word of God Drives Away the Opponent

The Bible, the Word of God, is a sword of the Spirit, the offensive weapon of choice (Eph. 6:17). Christ used the Word of God to overcome Satan.

> The Scripture just quoted, without comment or development, are all that Jesus opposed against great opponent, in this mysterious and terrible day, after which the entire work of our redemption was suspended. It is written! And the tempter stops. It is written! And the tempter stepped back. It is written! And here the tempter turned his back. It is written! And by whom? Moses the messenger, the servant, the creature of the One to whom his words came to the rescue in the hour of battle and distress!

The inspiration of the Bible is proven by its works.

CHAPTER 2

Blood

Meaning of the Blood

In 1948, Alan Stibbs's excellent Tyndale monograph *The Meaning of the Word "Blood" in Scripture* was published, which should have laid this ghost to rest for ever. He makes a thorough examination of the occurrences of the word *blood* in both the Old Testament and the New Testament, and has no difficulty demonstrating that it is "a word-symbol for death."

True, "the blood is the life of the flesh." But consider the following:

> This means that if the blood is separated from the flesh, whether in man or beast, the present physical life in the flesh will come to an end. Blood shed stands, therefore, not for the release of life from the burden of the flesh, but for the bringing to an end of life in the flesh. It is a witness to physical death, not an evidence of spiritual survival.

To "drink Christ's blood," therefore, describes "not participation in his life but appropriation of the benefits of his life laid down." We cannot do better than to conclude as Stibbs does with a quotation from Johannes Behm's article on blood in Gerhard Kittel's *Theological Dictionary of the New Testament*: "'Blood of Christ' is (Like 'Cross') only another, clearer expression for the death of Christ in its salvation meaning" or "redemptive significance."

The redemption image has a third emphasis. In addition to the plight from which, and the price with which, we are ransomed, it draws attention to the person of the Redeemer who has proprietary rights over his purchase. Thus Jesus's lordship over both church and Christian is attributed to his having bought us with his own blood. Presbyters, for example, are summoned to conscientious oversight of the church on the ground that God in Christ has bought it with his own blood (Acts 20:28). If the church was worth his blood, is it not worth our labor? The privilege of serving it is established by the preciousness of the price paid for its purchase.

Remembering that Jesus Christ has bought us with his blood and that as a consequence we belong to him should motivate us as individual Christians to holiness, just as it motivates presbyters to faithful ministry and the heavenly host to worship. "You are not your own; you were bought at a price. Therefore, honor God with your body" (1 Cor. 6:18–20; cf. 1 Cor. 7:23). Not only has our body has been created by God and not only will it one day be resurrected by him, but also it has been bought by Christ's blood and is indwelled by his Spirit. Bought by Christ, we have no business becoming the slave of anybody or anything else. Once we were the slaves of sin; now we are the slaves of Christ—and his service is the true freedom.

Redemption

The word *redemption* comes from a word that means "to buy back." Christ gave his blood as a ransom for sin, hence redeeming the lost (1 Pet. 1:18–20). In the context of soteriology, the price of redemption is blood that is paid for the remission of sins (Heb. 9:12, 22). The Greek words for *redeemed* were applied to purchasing servants in the ancient slave market. The biblical use of the terms reveals the extent of redemption to all human beings.

First, the Bible teaches that Christ purchased the sinner in the marketplace. *Agorazo* is the verb, which means "to go to the marketplace (agora) and pay the price for the slave." The verb "is common in deeds of sale" and generally meant the paying of a price for a group of slaves. Similarly, those who were "sold under sin" are redeemed (Gal. 3:10). In each of the following scriptures, the term *agorazo* is used: Revelation 14:3–4 speaks of the 144,000 as those redeemed from the earth; Revelation 5:9 notes that Christ's blood was the price paid for redemption; and 2 Peter 2:1 shows that Christ redeemed (paid the price for) not only the saved but also the false Christians. *Agorazo* speaks of the aspect of redemption that is simply paying the purchase price—and the purchase price is the blood.

The next word used to mean "redemption" in the Bible is *exagorazo* (*ek* meaning "out; to buy out from"). This term refers to the fact that Christ paid the price with his blood and bought the slave "out of the marketplace" (*exagorazo*). The slave is never again exposed to sale (Gal. 3:13). Galatians 4:5 also shows that when Christ took humankind out from under the law, He placed human beings in a different relationship with God by providing them with the opportunity to become the adopted sons and daughters of God. *Exagorazo* emphasizes the removal of the curse of the law.

The third word that refers to redemption is *lutrao*. This word means "to pay the price for the slave and release him." It emphasizes the freedom that Christ makes available to those he redeemed. In Titus 2:14, the use of *lutrao* (redeemed) shows that Christ wants to completely separate us from all sin. In Luke 24:21, *lutrao* is used to describe the redeeming of Israel from Roman domination.

TABLE **2.1.** New Testament words for "redemption"

Agorazo	"Purchased"	2 Peter 2:1
Exagorazo	"Removed"	Galatians 3:13
Lutrao	"Given freedom"	Titus 2:14

A consideration of each of these terms and the verses in which they appear clearly demonstrates that Jesus Christ has provided redemption for all people, including false teachers (2 Pet. 2:1), by the shedding of his own blood (Heb. 9:12).

Redemption by Blood

Since the law is eternal, unchangeable and applicable to every human being, no human being can escape the demands of the law. Since a degree of criminality is attached to every violation of the law and since God will punish according to the degree of criminality (Luke 10:10–15; Luke 12:47–48), every violation of the law will be punished according to a predetermined standard. Since every human being has violated the law and will suffer its consequences, there is no hope for those who have violated the law. Nothing in humanity can help human beings escape the criminality of their actions. God can neither treat the violation as if it never occurred nor forgive any violation arbitrarily. Since the law is an extension of the person of God, breaking the law is an offense to God, and God must be compensated before the lawbreaker is saved.

Christ suffered in the place of humankind. Since punishment must be eternal and complete, Christ suffered ultimately for all criminality. This act, called the vicarious substitutionary atonement, means that Christ suffered in the place of the sinner (vicarious), and the death of Christ was both the substitute for our sin and the satisfaction of the law.

The symbol of this transaction is the actual blood of Jesus Christ—a symbol of his substitutionary death.

"It is *shed* blood which has always been required for deliverance, and thus it was in the type and the antitype, Christ in His crucifixion."[7] Yet, the symbol of the blood was not introduced at the time of the cross of Jesus Christ. It goes back to the pages of the Old Testament.[8]

The sin could not be retracted and the nature of God could not forgive the sinner without a satisfactory payment. The price for this satisfaction was the blood of Jesus Christ, and the act of satisfaction is propitiation. Christ did more than die for us; he gave himself up to face God's wrath.

Propitiation is necessary given the holiness of God and the sinfulness of humankind.[9]

God purchased human beings with the priceless blood of the Lamb. He ransomed the helpless sinners not with gold or silver but with the incorruptible blood of Jesus Christ. We believe that we are only justified by the blood of Christ, through which we are reconciled to God.

When we talk about Jesus's blood, we usually think of it as being shed for us sinners.

Like Abel's, Christ's blood exposes the wrong and violence of evildoers. After Abel was murdered, as it is written, "His blood cried out to God from the ground" (Gen. 4:10). The same is true of Christ's blood: his blood is not silent but incessantly cries out from the ground for justice. Jesus's blood cries not for vengeance but for vindication, exposing the violence, injustice, and evil of violators to God and to the world.

The cross of Christ directs the attention of wrongdoers to the suffering of victims. Christ's blood and the Paraclete work together to convict wrongdoers of their sins. Christ's blood is the visible symbol with which the invisible Paraclete confronts sinners or wrongdoers of their need to change, that is, their need for repentance.

CHAPTER 3

God

There are many reasons to study God, but perhaps we should start with the command, "Be still and know that I am God." There is no greater reason to study God than the fact that God invites us to know him.

But there are other reasons, such as the fact that there can only be one God. Plus, we have an inner desire to know all things, including God. Also, since we are made in the image of God, we should understand him in order to better know ourselves.

The Nature of God

We begin our discussion of God by stating that God is being. This means that God is a substantive entity, an eternal person who exists in Spirit with certain absolute attributes. As a being, God has an existence that is real, measurable, and to a certain degree, knowable. This is the opposite of those who have denied the existence of God by redefining him. Plato said that God is eternal mind, the cause of all good in nature. Aristotle considered God to be "the ground of all being." Spinoza, a pantheist, called God "the absolute universal substance." Hegel identified God as the absolute Spirit. God is also called "the first cause" or "the unmoved mover." We object to the denial of his actual and literal existence as a being. God is an essence or a substance, not an idea.

Perhaps one of the best man-made statements about God is found in the Westminster Catechism in response to the question, what is God? "God is a spirit, infinite, eternal, and unchangeable in His being, wisdom, power, holiness, justice, goodness and truth."[10] As adequate as this statement is, it leaves out the personhood of God and confuses the distinction between God's nature and his attributes.

The nature of God is his "essence" or his "substance." God's nature is what he is, and if we could take away God's nature, it would eliminate his existence. God's nature is his being, without which he would not be God.

The nature of God is singular, because God is one and has only one existence. In the next section, we will discuss the attributes of God that are plural, because God manifests himself by many duties and relationships.

The nature of God defines his existence, whereas the attributes of God reflect his nature through attitudes, actions, and points of relationship with his creation and his creatures. Each attribute is an extension of the nature of God and becomes a focus by which God is revealed. Just as sunlight is a part of the sun and emanates from the sun, so the attributes of God are manifestations of the nature of God.

Any complete definition of God's nature must include these seven aspects, for these are the nature of God, without which he has no existence. The scriptures define God as (1) Spirit, (2) personhood, (3) life, (4) self-existent, (5) unchanging, (6) unlimited by time or space, and (7) unity, the last of which means that God is one God.

Every definition must have a definitive term that gives direction to the meaning it defines. The following table gives seven definitive terms that give meaning to the nature of God. Notice that each contains a specific truth about God. Taken together, these terms reveal a more complete picture of God's nature.

God Is Spirit

The first definitive term to aid in the description of God is the word *spirit*. Some theologians use the term *spirituality* in their description of God, but by today's definition it is misleading because spirituality describes personal piety. The term *spirit* when used in description of God means that he is immaterial, incorporeal, and invisible.

TABLE **3.1.** Who is God?

God is ...	Spirit Person Life A self-existent being Unity (one God) Unchangeable Eternal and immense

Russell Byrum points out that the spiritual motive of God is implied beyond biblical Christianity. He suggests that the theistic conception of God implies spirituality. Even idolaters usually do not think of their image as their god but rather as a symbol or abode of a spirit that they worship. In some of their images is an opening to a cavity into which the spirit is supposed to enter.[11]

God Is a Spirit Who Is Invisible and Incorporeal

Who is the divine person who reveals himself in perfect intellect, emotion, and will; who is the source and personification of all material and spiritual life; who is a self-existent being; who is eternal in relation to time; who is unlimited in relation to the immensity of space; who is immutable in his nature; and who is the unity of all existence, consistent within his being and corresponding, in reality, to the manifestations of his nature and attributes? Jesus told the Samaritan woman, "God is a Spirit: and they that worship him must worship him in spirit and in truth" (John 4:24). Even though the King James Version uses the article *a* with *Spirit*, God should not be described as *a* Spirit, which means "one of many." The original language should be interpreted to read, "God is spirit" (as in the New King James Version, the New American Standard Bible, and the New International Version), which describes his nature. As Spirit, God is not limited by a physical body. *Spirit* means an incorporeal being, whereas God is a real being who does not exist in or through a physical body (Luke 24:39). Although God is said to have hands (Isa. 65:2), feet (Ps. 18:9), eyes (1 Kings 8:29), and fingers (Exod. 8:29), these are not to be understood as actual parts of God's physical body.

These statements are "anthropomorphisms," whereby human beings project onto God their own characteristics for the sake of understanding and expression.

Anthropomorphisms are commonly expressed in the Bible as authors attempt to describe God in terms understandable to humankind. The following is a summary list of those statements as compiled by West.[12]

- He has location (Gen. 4:16; Exod. 19:17–21; Exod. 20:21; Exod. 33:14–15).
- He moves (Gen. 17:22; Gen. 18:33; Exod. 19:20; Num. 12:5; Num. 23:4; Deut. 33:2; Judg. 5:4; 1 Sam. 4:7; Ps. 47:5; Ps. 68:7–8; Ezek. 11:23; Mic. 1:2; Hab. 3:3; Zech. 2:13).
- He uses vehicles (2 Sam. 22:11; Ps. 18:10; Ps. 104:3; Hab. 3:8, 15; Zech. 9:14).
- He is said to dwell on the earth (Exod. 25:8; Exod. 29:43, 44; 1 Kings 6:13; 1 Kings 8:12–13; 2 Chron. 6:1–2; Ps. 132:14; Mic. 1:2–3).
- He dwells with humankind (Exod. 29:45; Lev. 26:11–12; 2 Chron. 6:18; Zech. 2:10; Rev. 21:3).
- He dwells in human beings (1 Cor. 3:16–17; 1 Cor. 6:19).
- He has physical attributes ([a face] Gen. 32:30; Exod. 33:11, 20; Deut. 5:4; Deut. 34:10; Rev. 20:11; [eyes] 2 Chron. 16:9; Prov. 22:12; [nostrils] 2 Sam. 22:9, 16; Ps. 18:15; [a mouth] Num. 12:8; Ps. 18:8; [lips and a tongue] Isa. 30:27; [breath] Isa. 30:28; [shoulders] Deut. 33:12; [hands and arms] Exod. 33:22–23; Ps. 21:8; Ps. 74:11; Ps. 89:13; Ps. 118:16; Isa. 52:10; Hab. 3:4; [fingers] Ps. 8:3; [a back] Exod. 33:23; [feet] Ps. 18:9; [a voice] Exod. 19:19; Exod. 20:22: Lev. 1:1; Num. 7:89; Num. 12:4; Num. 22:9; Deut. 4:12; Num. 36; 1 Kings 19:12–13; Ps. 29:3–9; Ps. 68:33; Jer. 25:30, 31; Ezek. 43:6).
- His voice is spoken of as dreaded (Exod. 20:19; Deut. 4:33; Deut. 5:24–26; Joel 2:11; Joel 3:16; Amos 1:2; Heb. 12:19, 26).
- He is said to exercise laughter (Ps. 2:4).
- He appears to human beings (Gen. 35:9; Gen. 48:3; Exod. 3:2–6; Exod. 24:9–11; 1 Kings 9:2; Job 42:5–6; Amos 9:1).
- His appearance is described (Exod. 24:10; Deut. 31:15; Isa. 6:1; Ezek. 8:1–2; Dan. 7:9–10; Rev. 4:5).
- He has a human form (Gen. 18:1; Ezek. 1:26–27: Rev. 4:2–3).

As Spirit, God is a real being not limited by a human body. God is much greater than any body. Even Jesus distinguished his resurrected body from a spirit when he noted, "A spirit hath not flesh and bones as ye see me have" (Luke 24:39). Therefore, we conclude that a spirit is a real being without a body. However, on some occasions in scripture, spirits possess bodies and reveal themselves through physical form. Angels, demons, and even Satan himself are described as spirits. But remember, God is "the Father of spirits" (Heb. 12:9; Num. 16:22). Even though these spirits have the same "spirit" characteristics as God, they have neither the moral attributes nor the nature of God. They are just similar in their existence.

A Spirit Is Also Invisible

Though God was in the pillar of fire that led Israel through the wilderness, he was never visible to the nation (Deut. 4:15). There are some passages in scripture where it seems that people actually saw God (e.g., Gen. 32:30; Exod. 3:6; Exod. 24:9–10; Num. 12:6–8; Deut. 34:10; and Isa. 6:1). Actually it would be more correct to say these people saw a reflection or a result of God, as they did not see him directly.

The only people who have seen God are those who saw Christ, "the image of the invisible God" (Col. 1:15). Because God is an invisible Spirit, no one has ever seen him (John 1:18; 1 Tim. 1:18).

The First Commandment is a ban on the making of idols.

The Second Commandment prevents the use of idols in religious service. God prohibits idols for many reasons, but one of these reasons is because God is spirit.

When God is described as spirit (John 4:24; Deut. 4:15–119; Ps. 147:5), it is implied that God is absolutely pure spirit. God is perfect in all. His being and spirit are the highest form of being; therefore, we say that God is absolutely pure in kind, quality, and quantity, and he is different from every being he has created, both in measure and in kind.

Even though God is without body and physical existence, God is still a person. As such, he has personality. As a spirit who is a person, God has existence in and of himself.

Further, God is not limited by time or space, so his omnipresence is an attribute born out of his nature. According to Boyce, "To have an omnipresent and eternal mode of existence is possible for a spiritual nature, because spirit has not of necessity succession of time and specific limitation of location."[13]

God Is Person

Most of the religions of the world portray God as an impersonal being or a force. The German philosopher Hegel said that God is an impersonal being, just as a picture on the wall or a plate on the table. Others have said that God is an idea. Paul Tillich made God the ground of all being. These definitions fall short of the New Testament designation that God is a person.

That God is "the personal Spirit" is fundamental to Clarke's identification of God. According to Clarke, "A personal spirit is a self-conscious and self-directing intelligence; and a personal God is a God who knows himself as himself, and consciously directs his own action."[14] Strong suggests, "The Scriptures represent God as a personal being. By personality we mean the power of self-consciousness and of self-determination."

God is immutable. By definition, the immutability of God is his unchanging nature. All changes are for the better, or the worse. By definition, God is perfect and cannot become better. If he became less than perfect, then he would not be God. God is therefore immutable; he cannot change.

God is unlimited in time and space. He is also unlimited by time. The Bible describes him as the one who "inhabiteth eternity" (Isa. 57:15).

Paul called God "immortal" (1 Tim. 1:17). Abraham recognized "the everlasting God" (Gen. 21:33). Moses observed "even from everlasting to everlasting, thou art God" (Ps. 90:2). The psalmist wrote, "But thou art the same, and thy years shall have no end" (Ps. 102:27).[15]

Time is the measurement of events that appear in sequence. Since God created the world, he existed before the first event. As a matter of fact, God never had a beginning point; he always existed. And God will continue without a terminal point. This is why Christ is called the Beginning and the End, the Alpha and the Omega (Rev. 21:6; Rev. 22:13).

Neither is God limited by space. Space is all the area where there is physical reality and being. It is also the distance between objects. But God is greater than space and is independent of space. His existence goes beyond the furthest located object. The existence of God never ends. Paul told the Athenian philosophers, "God, that made the world and all things therein, seeing that he is Lord of heaven and earth, dwelleth not in temples made with hands" (Acts 17:24).

Solomon observed, "The heaven and heaven of heavens cannot contain him [God]" (2 Chron. 2:6).

Both time and space are results of God's creative act. But he himself exists beyond time and space. God is infinite, while time and space are limited. God alone exists in the universe without limitations. If another God did exist, then God would not be the self-existent, all-powerful, unlimited God that he is. It is axiomatic that two unlimited beings cannot occupy the same space. If another God did exist, then God could not be an unlimited God. The infinity and immensity of God are strong arguments for the sovereignty of God in the universe.

God Is One

"Here, O Israel: The Lord our God is one Lord" (Deut. 6:4). There can only be one God. To speak of more than only one supreme, absolute, perfect, and almighty being makes about as much sense as talking about a square circle. The meaning of words would become useless and truth would collapse if such were the case. "Thus saith the Lord, the King of Israel, and his redeemer, the Lord of hosts: I am the first, and I am the last; and beside me there is no God" (Isa. 44:6).

The unity of God is expressed through scripture as demonstrated in the following:[16]

- The passages that declare explicitly that God is one (Deut. 6:4; Mal. 2:10 ["Hath not one God created us?"]; Mark 12:29, 32; 1 Tim. 2:5; Eph. 4:5, 6; James 2:19)
- Those that assert that there is none else or none beside him (Deut. 4:35, 39; 1 Sam. 2:2; 2 Sam. 7:22; 1 Kings 8:60; Isa. 44:6, 8: Isa. 45:5, 6, 21, 22; Isa. 46:9; Joel 2:27)
- Those asserting that there is none like him and none to be compared with him (Exod. 8:10; Exod. 9:14; Exod. 15:11; 2 Sam. 7:22; 1 Kings 8:23; 2 Chron. 6:14; Isa. 40:25; Isa. 46:5; Jer. 10:6)

- The passages stating that he alone is God (2 Sam. 22:32; Neh. 9:6; Ps. 18:31; Ps. 86:10; Isa. 37:16; Isa. 43:10, 12; Isa. 46:9; John 17:3; 1 Cor. 8:4–6)
- Those stating that he alone is to be worshipped (Exod. 20:5; Exod. 34:14; 1 Sam. 7:3; 2 Kings 17:36; Matt. 4:10; Rom. 1:25; Rev. 19:10)
- Those forbidding that anyone else to be accepted as God (Exod. 20:3; Deut. 5:7; Isa. 42:8; Hosea 13:4)
- Those proclaiming him as supreme over all so-called gods (Deut. 10:17; Josh. 22:22; Ps. 96:4, 5; Jer. 14:22; 1 Cor. 8:4–6)
- The passages declaring him to be the true God (Jer. 10:10; 1 Thess. 1:9).

When we talk about the Trinity, we are still talking about one God, but three persons. In the nature of the one God, there are three eternal distinctions that are represented to us under the figure of persons, and these three are equal. Reason shows us the unity of God; only revelation shows us the Trinity of God, thus filling out the indefinite outline of this unity and vivifying it.[17]

The idea of a compound Trinity was common in Hebrew thought and is reflected in the very name of God, Elohim.

Polytheism teaches that there are many gods, which is a denial of the being of God. Tritheism teaches that there are three gods, which is not true for the same reason. Dualism teaches that there are two independent divine beings, which concept also fails for lack of an axiology. The multiplication of gods is a self-contradiction. There can only be one supreme, absolute, perfect, and almighty being. To say that there are two or more gods is to say that one means two or more. To do so defies logic and rationality.

Mentioning the unity of God is not the same as saying that God is a unit. The term *unit* indicates a single thing marked by mere singleness. A unit usually admits no interior distinctions, whereas the term *units* implies diversity in unity, or in other words, more than one makes up the total. The unity of God implies his Trinity.

Erroneous Views of God

Over the centuries, various people and movements have suggested views of God that are different from the description of God found in the Bible.

Because part of knowing God is knowing what God is not, the following summary of leading non-Christian worldviews is provided.

Atheism

Literally, the term *atheist* designates a negation of deity. In one sense, all non-Christian religions are atheistic in that they deny the true God, yet Thiessen suggests there are three kinds of atheism: (1) practical atheism, practiced by those who have been disappointed by Christianity and thus overreacted by describing all religion as fake; (2) dogmatic atheism, a view that espouses the nonexistence of God; and virtual atheism, which holds to principles inconsistent with belief in God.[18] In conclusion, atheism is not an affirmative position but a negative posture. As a result, when the author meets someone who claims to be an atheist, he usually asks, "What kind of god do you deny?" He further asks, "Do you deny the Christian God, Muslim god, or Shinto god?" The purpose is to show that the person is only reacting, not holding an affirmative view.

Agnosticism

To be a dogmatic atheist, one must profess to have virtual omniscience in all areas to be certain that God does not exist. Few people are so foolish to make such a claim for themselves. Those who choose to deny the existence of God will sometimes profess agnosticism. Thiessen uses this term to identify any doctrine that affirms the impossibility of any true knowledge holding that all knowledge is relative and, therefore, uncertain.[19] The agnostic, if he or she is consistent, is unsure not only of the existence of God but also of any knowledge.

Materialism

Strong defines materialism as "that method of thought which gives priority to matter, rather than to mind, in its explanations of the universe. Upon this view, material atoms constitute the ultimate and fundamental reality of which all things, rational and irrational, are but combinations and phenomena. Force is regarded as a universal and inseparable property of matter."[20] This theory, which recognizes God vaguely defined as a force, has been popularized in the *Star Wars* films. Essentially, it denies the personality of God and is a natural consequence of such a denial.

Animism

Animism is the term used in primitive religions to describe the existence of spiritual beings who "are held to affect or control the events of the material world, and man's life here and hereafter; and, it being considered that they hold intercourse with men, and receive pleasure or displeasure from human actions. The belief in their existence leads naturally, and it might almost be said inevitably, sooner or later, to active reverence and propitiation."[21]

Animistic religions tend to emphasize human efforts to pacify a deity and are based on fear rather than devotion. The worship of ancestors and fetishes is often a part of primitive animism.

Polytheism

Polytheism represents the worship of and belief in a multiplicity of gods. This was the theistic view of both Greeks and Romans at the writing of the New Testament. It was also the predominant view of Egyptians at the writing of the Pentateuch. Often, polytheism is characterized by idolatry through the making of idols and is not necessarily implied in the view. There are several varieties of polytheism, but all agree in their denial of the essential unity of God.

Henotheism

One view of polytheism recognizes that one of many gods is supreme over others. Jastrow suggests, "The monotheistic tendency exists among all peoples after they have reached a certain level of culture. There is a difference in the degree in which this tendency is emphasized, but there are distinct traces of a trend toward concentrating the varied manifestations of divine powers in a single source."[22] Henotheism, then, recognizes many gods but places them in various ranks, identifying one as supreme above others.

Tritheism

Some have abused the doctrine of the Trinity to suggest the existence of three gods who are coequal in every respect yet are distinct deities and personalities. This charge is often made against Christians by Jews, Mormons, and Jehovah's Witnesses, who claim that the idea of the Trinity denies the unity of God.

Dualism

An additional abuse of the unity of God is found in the position known as dualism. According to Thiessen, "This theory assumes that there are two distinct and irreducible substances or principles. In epistemology these are idea and object; in metaphysics, mind and matter; in ethics, good and evil; in religion, good (God) and evil (Satan)."[23] The Christian, of course, cannot recognize Satan as God's equal. Nevertheless, many Christians fall into the trap of equating God and Satan when they identify them as two opposing forces in constant struggle.

Pantheism

Robert Flint defines pantheism as "the theory which regards all finite things as merely aspects, modifications, or parts of one eternal and self-existent being; which views all material objects, and all particular minds, as necessarily derived from a single infinite substance."[24] Pantheism normally involves the recognition of gods or a god in matter, but it falls short of the denial of God, as is the case with materialism.

Idealism

Idealism equates God with the mental energy of the thinking process. According to George Patrick, Hegel thought of reality as "thought, reason. The world is a great thought process. It is, as we might say, God thinking. We have only to find out the laws of thought to know the laws of reality. What we call nature is thought externalized; it is the Absolute Reason revealing itself in outward form."[25] The view was popularized most recently in the hippy and drug culture of the 1960s.

Deism

A final erroneous view of God is that of deism.

> For deism God is present in creation only by His power, not in His very being and nature. He has endowed creation with invariable laws over which He exercises a mere general oversight; He has imparted to His creatures certain properties, placed them under His invariable laws, and left them to work out their destiny by their own powers. Deism denies a special revelation, miracles, and providence.

This view, sometimes described as an "absentee landlord" view of God, is an erroneous view of God that denies the basic attribute of God—love— which implies that God involves himself in the affairs of his creation.[26]

The Attributes of God

The attributes of God are those virtues or qualities that manifest his nature. To put it another way, an attribute of God is the extension of his nature. God's attributes are different from such things as strengths, characteristics, and qualities. These are words that identify the positive influence of a personality, whereas an attribute of God is more than the influence of God. An attribute has a distinct existence and can be separately identified, yet an attribute can never be separate from God, who is the source of each attribute.

The following is according to Boyce:

> The attributes of God are those peculiarities which mark or define the mode of his existence, or which constitute his character. They are neither separate nor separable from his essence or nature, and yet are not that essence, but simply have the ground or cause of their existence in it, and are at

the same time the peculiarities which constitute the mode
and character of his being.[27]

When we describe the attributes of God, we are not describing God as
the sum of his many characteristics. A human being may be the sum of his or
her parts, but such is not the case for God. Since God is unity, God's entire
nature is manifested in every part of his being. We cannot describe God
as a perfect balance between his parts, because that implies that one of his
parts can stand alone. If that were so, then his attributes that are different
from one another (such as love and justice) would be a contradiction of his
nature. But God is a Trinity and all of his attributes are unified in him. God
cannot suspend one attribute to exercise another, because God's nature is
working in unity at any one time. God does not divide himself to perform a
work, nor does he divide himself to think a thought. In short, God does not
divide himself to act in any way.

The key to understanding the description of God is seen in his six
attributes. Tozer defines an attribute as "something true of God ... something
that we can *conceive* as being true of him."[28] The attributes of God are those
virtues or qualities that manifest his nature. (The previous chapter discussed
the nature of God.) The Westminster Shorter Catechism lists four attributes
(holiness, justice, goodness, and truth) in its definition of God: "God is a
spirit, infinite, eternal, and unchangeable, in His being, wisdom, power,
holiness, justice, goodness and truth."

Even though we attempt to number God's attributes, we do not know
exactly how many he has. Because God has only revealed part of his nature,
we do not know all of his existence; therefore, we cannot arrive at an exact
number of attributes. One theologian said, "God has a thousand attributes."
Charles Wesley, the hymn writer, described God's attributes as "glorious all
and numberless."

Some theologians describe God as having communicable attributes,
which are those attributes that are communicated to humankind. Other
theologians call some attributes "moral attributes," that is, those involving
the moral exercise of God's nature. Also, some theologians describe the
affirmative attributes, which express his positive perfection, while others are
called negative attributes, that is, those that note his reaction to everything

outside his nature, such as the justice of God. Some theologians use the phrase *relative attributes* to speak of those that relate to the created world. In contrast, they also describe absolute attributes, which belong in and to God himself.

TABLE **3.2.** The absolute and the comparative attributes of God

Absolute	Comparative
1. Holiness	1. Omniscience
2. Love	2. Omnipresence
3. Goodness	3. Omnipotence

The Absolute Attributes of God

God manifests himself in divine attributes that reveal his nature as being holy, which is the expression of all that is right and pure; love, which is the sharing of his life with his created beings; and goodness, which is the embodiment of all ideal qualities rewarding all that personifies the law of God.

Holiness

Holiness is the first description that comes to our mind when we think of God. God is holy and apart from everything that is sinful. The root meaning of *holiness* is "to separate or to cut off." The primary meaning of holiness implies separation. As this applies to our life, it includes both separation from sin and separation from God. The holiness of God makes it impossible for God to commit sin or even to look upon sin with approval.

Love

Perhaps the most popular attribute of God that readily comes to mind is love. When children are asked to describe God, they most often respond by saying, "God is love" (1 John 4:8; 1 John 4:16). Love is basically an attribute as expressed in an act that emanates from God, its source. When God loves, it reflects his whole being.[29]

Therefore, love is not just a virtue of God; it is God himself. Also, love is not something God begins, or expends his energy to maintain. The love of God is as eternal as the nature of God. Therefore, the love of God is self-existing.

Love is basically an attitude, as expressed in an act that emanates from its source. The concept of love as an attribute of God makes Christianity a unique religion in the world. Love is the attitude that seeks the highest good in the person who is loved.

Goodness

When parents teach their children to pray, they often teach them to say before eating, "God is great, God is good." The goodness of God is another of the absolute attributes of God. In a broad sense, the goodness of God includes all the positive moral attributes of God.

The Comparative Attributes of God

The absolute attributes of God are those things humankind cannot know apart from the revelation of God to them. If any human being has holiness, love, or goodness, then this person first recognized it in God and then received it from God. The comparative attributes of God contrast human abilities and the divine nature. Every human being has presence, but only God is omnipresent. Every human being has power, but only God is omnipotent. Every human being has some knowledge, but there is only One who is omniscient. These three attributes of God may be defined by a comparison of degrees of things that God and humankind share. Psalm 139 lays a foundation for understanding the comparative attributes of God.

Omniscience

The omniscience of God is seen in Psalm 139:1–6. When we say God is omniscient, we mean he possesses perfect knowledge of all things. The prefix *omni-* means "all," and the word *science* comes from a Latin root meaning "knowledge." The omniscient God has all the knowledge in the world. God has never had to learn anything. He has never forgotten anything he ever knew. God knows everything possible. This means that he knows and understands the sum total of all the world's knowledge and even those things humankind has yet to discover.

a. God Has Not Learned

The Bible teaches that God has not learned anything from any person (Isa. 40:13–14).

b. God Accurately Knows Himself

If God knows all things, then he must know himself. This knowledge comes out of his nature and is a part of his being.

c. God Knows Everything Possible

If God knows all things, then he knows all things that happened in the past, in addition to everything that will happen in the future. But also, God has knowledge of everything that could have existed in the future (Rom. 4:17). This frightening insight ought to drive human beings to have faith in God, because he knows the outcome of every alternative. God knows what would have happened if we had not married our mate and what would have happened if we had not received his Son as Savior. All potential knowledge is bound up in the omniscience of God.

d. God Knows without Effort

God does not need to act or exert effort in order to recall an incident of the past. God is eternal; there is no past, as God is without time. Therefore, God has no need to recall, because he knows all things perfectly at all times. God does not remember, forget, or in a literal sense make an effort to memorize for future use. If we say that God had to make an effort to recall, we are saying that at one moment God does not know the facts until he recalls them to his mind. Therefore, this would be saying that God is not perfect, that he was limited at that given time. Because of this, a self-existent and unlimited God must be omniscient, knowing all things at all times without effort.

e. God Knows All Things Equally Well

The Bible teaches, "Neither is there any creature that is not manifest in his sight; but all things are naked and opened unto the eyes of him with whom we have to do" (Heb. 4:13; cf. Ps. 147:4–5).

Omnipresence

God is present everywhere at the same time. The prefix *omni* means "all," and the main root "presence" means "here, indwelling, or in the approximate location." Therefore, God is everywhere present. God is in all things and is close to everything that has existence.

a. God's Omnipresence Is a Manifestation of His Immensity

The nature of God knows no limits in space. This means that he is everywhere. But the immensity of God goes beyond space. It extends to "no space." God exists even where there is no space. There is no existence beyond God's existence. One theologian implied that God is to space as the sea is to fish, meaning that God is larger in his totality than space—everywhere there is space there is God, and he exists beyond space.

Therefore, we can say that God is over all things, under all things, enclosed within all things, and never excluded from anything. He is completely above, beneath, and within—and is the Sustainer of—all things.

b. God's Omnipresence Implies His Immensity

The immensity of God indicates that he is everywhere present at the same time. This means that the center of God is everywhere and his circumference is nowhere. The human mind is baffled by the immensity of God, which defies proper explanation. Because God is everywhere present, he is close to his created world. The Bible teaches that human beings cannot escape from God (Ps. 139:7–10; Gen. 4:16).

c. God's Omnipresence Allows for Transcendence

God's omnipresence teaches us that he exists within his created world yet is distinct from it. This means that God is transcendent over the world, because he is supreme. God exists within every part of the world as the Sustainer, but he also exists apart from the world to be worshipped by the world and one day to judge the world.

d. God's Omnipresence Teaches That He Will Manifest Himself in Some Places More Than in Others

The Bible teaches the localized presence of God. The Lord is in the heavens (Isa. 66:1), for his throne is there, as is his presence from which he speaks. But God is also on the earth and near to his people (Rom. 8:10; Acts 17:27).

Also, God is under the earth (Luke 16:23; Rev. 14:10). The institutional presence of God was in the holy of holies (Num. 7:89), and is in the midst of the churches (Rev. 2:5). Beyond this, there is the indwelling presence of the Trinity in every believer. First, the Father and Jesus Christ indwell every believer (John 14:23). Next, the Holy Spirit indwells every believer (Rom. 8:9). The fact that the presence of God dwells more in the believer than in the unbeliever reinforces the principle that God manifests himself in some places more than in others, yet the presence of God is everywhere present.

e. God's Omnipresence Implies His Omnipotence and Omniscience

Since God is everywhere present, it is to be assumed that God knows all things. Since God is omnipotent in sustaining and controlling the world, it is only natural that he is omnipresent, meaning that he is everywhere present to run the world. Finally, he must be omniscient, knowing all that is happening. Any one of the three attributes presupposes and demands the other two attributes.

f. God's Omnipresence

The perfections of God demand that he exist everywhere at the same time. Since he is perfect in knowledge and power, and because these are part of his nature, the implication is only that God's presence must necessarily exist where he is exercising his wisdom and works.

The existence of a God who has created all things logically did not begin itself; therefore, there must be a first cause who was capable of being everywhere present to create the world. Since all things came into existence at the same time, God was everywhere present at the same time in bringing the world into existence.

God is omnipresent. Throughout time, people have assumed the existence of God. The psalmist said, "Thou art there" (Ps. 139:7–9). Hagar, who languished in the desert, cried out, "Thou God sees me" (Gen. 16:13).

The fact that God is means that God is here and now. He comforts, guides, and protects the believer with his omnipresence. And the fact that God is here implies that God is everywhere.

The Omnipotence of God

God can do everything that is in harmony with his nature and perfection. Of all of the attributes of God, God has limited his omnipotence by his will. He can do whatever he wills to do, but he does not necessarily will to do everything. On many occasions, God has limited his power by deferring to the free will of his rational creatures. By this God does not force people to become Christians; therefore, he limits his power by the rejection of their will. God could have exercised his power to keep sin out of the universe, but that would have been inconsistent with the nature of his created beings. Therefore, God limited his power to allow sin to enter the world.

God's will controls his power; otherwise, his power would act out of necessity and he would cease being a free being. Berkhof suggests, "Power in God may be called the effective energy of His nature, or that perfection of His Being by which He is the absolute and highest causality."[51] By the term *omnipotence*, Byrum means, "the almightiness or unlimited power of God, or that God has power to do all things which are objects of power."[30]

God's Power Is Potentially Unlimited

Not only can God do impossible things (such as raising the dead), but also God does improbable things (such as walking on the water, as in John 6:19).

God has the potential to do anything he wills. The Bible teaches, "With God all things are possible" (Matt. 19:26).

But when we analyze the omnipotence of God, we realize that at times God is limited. He will not do those things that are contrary to his nature. For example, God cannot look on sin (Hab. 1:13), deny his existence (2 Tim. 2:13), lie (Heb. 6:18), or be tempted to sin. These things are against his nature (James 1:13). Even though God is all-powerful to do everything that is in harmony with his nature, he cannot go contrary to his nature or deny his being. God cannot make a square a circle, nor can he make a true myth.

God's Power Is Comprehensive

It does not require any effort on God's part to act in any way. The idea of exertion or labor is unknown to God. He spoke and the worlds were created. He wills and it is carried out (Isa. 59:1–2).

The Power of God Is Discernible

The Bible teaches that God's power can be seen in the created world: "For the invisible things of Him from the creation of the world are clearly seen, being understood by the things that are made, even his eternal power and Godhead; so that they are without exercise" (Rom. 1:20). The power of God is not withheld from the understanding of humankind, but it is made evident in nature. This self-disclosure of God's omnipotence is that humankind might know God and turn to him.

God's Power Holds the World Together

The Bible teaches that God "upholdeth all things by the word of His power" (Heb. 1:3; cf. Col. 1:17). The power of God keeps the comets in their paths and the planets in their orbits. The power of God keeps the atom from exploding into unlimited nuclear fission.

The omnipotent God preserves the world as he created it in the beginning. This is the greatest evidence of the person of God.

God's Sovereignty Is a Result of His Omnipotence

The one cannot exist without the other. If God is going to reign, then he must have power. And if God is going to reign sovereignly, he must have omnipotent power. When recognizing God's sovereignty, we see that it includes all things seen and known, plus the spiritual world that we do not see and experience. The sovereignty of God includes all people, all things, and all potential situations (Matt. 11:26–27; Rom. 11:33–36).

The Names of God

The study of the doctrine of God includes a study of his names, for they reveal the nature and works of God.[31]

The Primary Names of God

There are three primary names of God: Elohim (God), Jehovah (Lord), and Adonai (Lord). When referring to the strength of God, the name Elohim (God) is used. It occurs thirty-one times in Genesis 1 to reveal his creative power. When referring to God's existing nature or his relationship to humankind, the name Jehovah (Lord) is used. The title Adonai (Lord) is used when referring to God's authority, such as the relationship of master to servant.

After examining the primary names of God, we shall look at the compound names of God. As might be expected, their complexity is a reflection of his absolute attributes.

TABLE **3.3.** The names of God in scripture

I. Primary Names

Elohim	The Strong and Faithful One
Jehovah	The Self-Existent One
Adonai	Lord or Master

2. Compound Names

El-Shaddai	The Almighty God
El-Elyon	The Most High God
El-Olam	The Everlasting God
El-Gibbor	The Mighty God
El-Roi	The God Who Sees
Jehovah-Sabaoth	The Lord of Hosts
Jehovah-Jireh	The Lord Shall Provide
Jehovah-Nissi	The Lord Our Banner
Jehovah-Rapha	The Lord That Healeth
Jehovah-Shalom	The Lord Our Peace
Jehovah-Maccaddeshcem	The Lord Our Sanctifier
Jehovah-Tiskena	The Lord Our Righteousness
Jehovah-Shammah	The Lord Is There
Jehovah-Roah	The Lord Our Shepherd
Jehovah-Naheh	The Lord That Smiteth
Jehovah-Elohim	Lord God
Adonai-Jehovah	Lord God
Jehovah-El-Gemuwal	The Lord God of Recompense

Elohim-God

One of the common names used in the scriptures is the most common designation for deity, "God." The Hebrew word for *God* is "Elohim." *El* means "the Strong One who manifests himself by his Word," with *Elohim* being the plural form. Hence, the attributes of faithfulness and omnipotence are manifest by this name. Elohim is used over twenty-five hundred times in the Old Testament, often to remind the reader of the strength or faithfulness of God. Moses wrote, "From everlasting to everlasting thou art God [Elohim]" (Ps. 90:2). Elohim is the name first used of God in the scripture. "In the beginning God [Elohim] created the heaven and the earth" (Gen. 1:1). The final reference to the word *God* in the New Testament is the Greek equivalent *theos* (Rev. 22:19). Usually, the name of God [Elohim] is used in connection with the unsaved or with inanimate objects.

Elohim is a plural form used in connection with plural verbs and objectives (Exod. 20:3; Deut. 6:4). We see the implication of the Trinity in this word. However, Jewish writers speak of the "plural majesty" as used in reference to kings.

Jehovah-Lord

An unusual problem confronts the study of this second name of God. We really are not sure how to pronounce it. Some scholars say "Yahweh," but others say "Jehovah." Usually it is translated as "Lord" in our Bibles, and all four letters are capitalized. The reason we are not sure of its pronunciation stems from the reverence Jewish leaders gave to this name. No one would pronounce it out of fear of offending God. When some scribes came to the word *Lord* in copying the scriptures, they would stop, bathe, and put on clean clothes. Others would begin with new pen and ink before writing God's name. This concern for not dishonoring the name of God was also expressed in the reading of the scriptures. When the reader came to this name for God, he or she would either pause and omit it or often substitute another name for God in its place. Also, the Hebrew language has no vowels in its written alphabet, so pronunciation of words is learned orally. Because people did not speak the name Lord, it was not long before others did not know how to pronounce it.

This word *Lord* means "the Self-Existent One," coming from the verb *to be* or *to become*. It comes from the verb *to be* repeated twice. *Lord* means "I am which I am." Jehovah is the name that is used when the Creator relates to his people in an intelligent and responsive relationship. In this note, the name Jehovah does not occur until Genesis 2:4 (after the creation of humankind). Jehovah is the name with which God identifies himself at the burning bush (Exod. 3:14). This name speaks of both the self-existence of God and his eternity. God is the only one who can say "I am"; that is, "I exist by myself, independent of any other." He can always say "I am" because he always was in the past and always will be in the future.

The name Jehovah is used 6,823 times in the Bible, usually in association with God's people. It has been called "the covenant name of God," as it is often used to identify God in his covenants (cf. Gen. 2:15–17; Gen. 3:14–19; Gen. 4:15; and Gen. 12:1–3).

Adonai-Lord

The third name used for God in scripture is Adonai, usually translated "Lord" in our English Bible. (Only the first letter is capitalized with the name Adonai-Lord, whereas all four letters are capitalized in the name Jehovah-LORD). Adonai was first used by Abraham as he sought the will of God in adopting an heir (Gen. 15:2). The term, which means "Master," implies two things. First, it indicates the sovereignty of God. The master is the one who assumes control of situation. It is reasonable to assume that the servants will do the master's will. Of all the names used of God, this one associates him with the qualities of an earthly master. Hence, it gives human characteristics to God.

Second, this term implies the possibility of knowing the will of the Master. Abraham used the name as he sought to determine a course of action. If the responsibility of a servant is to do the will of his master, it is reasonable to assume that the master will make that will known to his servant.

Today, Christians often talk about the Lord but show little of allowing him to control their lives. If we recognize him as Lord, then there is no longer any question of obeying his commandments. When God told Peter to kill and eat unclean animals, three times Peter replied, "Not so, Lord" (Acts 10:9–16). As soon as Peter said, "Not so," he was no longer recognizing God as his Lord. Someone put it this way: "If he is not Lord of all, he is not Lord at all."

The Compound Names of Elohim

El Shaddai—the Almighty God

The primary names of God are sometimes used with other names to identify a specific characteristic of God. The name El Shaddai means "the Almighty God." This name speaks of God's all-sufficiency. When Abraham was ninety-nine years old and still without an heir, "the Almighty God" renewed his covenant with him (Gen. 17:1–2). This was the God who was able to overcome any obstacle to keep his promise.

The term *Shaddai* means "rest or nourisher." It comes from a root word that means "breast or strength given, or Sustainer." Though translated "the Almighty God," it also means "the All-Sufficient God." Today, we can claim the psalmist's promise, "He that dwelleth in the secret place of the Most High shall abide under the shadow of the Almighty [El Shaddai]" (Ps. 91:1).

El Elyon—the Most High God

This name is used to identify God particularly to polytheistic Gentiles. The idea in this name is that the true God of Israel is above all false gods of the Gentiles. This title is first used in the scriptures to identify Melchizedek's priesthood as "the priest of the most high God" (Gen. 14:18). At that time, Melchizedek attributed Abraham's recent military victory to El Elyon (the Most High God). God is also said to be "the possessor of heaven and earth" (Gen. 14:22).

El Olam—the Everlasting God

In his experience with God, Abraham also came to know him as "the everlasting God" (Gen. 21:33). This name indicates that God is not limited by time. He is eternal. Moses wrote, "From everlasting to everlasting, thou art God" (Ps. 90:2). The name El Olam personifies all that is true about the eternity of God.

El Gibbor—the Mighty God

Isaiah uses this designation for God when prophesying the birth of the Messiah. Translated "the Mighty God" (Isa. 9:6), this name of God lays emphasis on the omnipotence or power of God. Christians have often been accused of limiting God by thinking of him in a limited way. In contrast, God has revealed himself in his omnipotence.

El Roi—the Seeing God

This name of God literally means "the Strong One Who Sees." The name appears only once in scripture, after the angel of the Lord appears to Hagar as she flees from Sarai. After realizing God is aware of her situation, she identifies God with the words, "Thou God seest me" (Gen. 16:13).

The Compound Names of Jehovah

Jehovah-Sabaoth—the Lord of Hosts

This name emphasizes the power and glory of God. The word *hosts* is used in the Bible to refer to heavenly bodies (Gen. 2:1), angels (Luke 2:13), saints (Josh. 5:15), and sinners (Judg. 4:2). It implies the power of the heavenly beings who serve the Lord. As the Lord of Hosts, God is working through all these "hosts" to fulfill his purposes.

The Christian can be encouraged today as he or she claims the promise, "The Lord of hosts is with us" (Ps. 46:7). In discussing the Second Coming of Christ, David asked and answered a very important question: "Who is this King of glory?" The answer is, "The Lord of hosts, he is the King of glory" (Ps. 24:10). The expression "Lord of Hosts" is used over 170 times in scripture to identify the Lord.

Jehovah-Jireh—the Lord Will Provide

Probably the single greatest test of faith in the life of Abraham occurred when God called him to sacrifice his son. When Isaac asked his father about the sacrificial animal, Abraham responded, "God will provide himself a lamb for a burnt-offering" (Gen. 22:8). Later that same day, God honored the faith of Abraham and prevented the death of Isaac by providing a ram in his place. "Abraham called the name of that place Jehovah-Jireh (the Lord will provide)" (Gen. 22:14). In the New Testament, Paul may have been thinking of this name of God when he asked, "He that spared not his own Son, but delivered him up for us all, how shall he not with him also freely give us all things" (Rom. 8:32)?

Jehovah-Rapha—the Lord That Healeth

God always wants the best for his people. When he brought Israel out of Egypt, he wanted his people to live full and healthy lives. "If thou wilt diligently hearken to the voice of the Lord thy God, and wilt do that which is right in his sight, and wilt give ear to his commandments, and keep all his statutes, I will put none of these diseases upon thee, which I have brought upon the Egyptians: for I am the Lord that healeth thee" (Exod. 15:26). This name of God emphasizes God's concern for our good health.

God is certainly able to, and does on occasion, heal people miraculously, but that is only part of what this name teaches. The context of the revelation of this name is preventive medicine more than it is curing. No doctor has found a cure for the common cold, but the mother who bundles up her children with scarves, mittens, boots, and snowsuits on a cold winter day has "cured" her children's cold by preventing it. Here God has promised to heal us from the diseases that plagued the Egyptians by providing the resources that are available to those who obey him. Obedience will produce good health.

Jehovah-Nissi—the Lord Our Banner

When God gave Israel the victory over Amalek, "Moses built an altar, and called the name of it Jehovah-Nissi" (Exod. 17:15). The name Jehovah-Nissi means "the Lord is my banner" or "the Lord That Prevaileth." The emphasis of this name for Christians is the knowledge that we are not in the battle alone. As soldiers, we march under the banner and colors of God. The battle itself belongs to God, and victory is already guaranteed. The Christian can therefore serve the Lord with complete confidence in the outcome.

Jehovah-Shalom—the Lord Our Peace

When God called Gideon to deliver Israel from the oppressive Midianites, "Gideon built an altar there unto the Lord, and called it Jehovah-Shalom" (Judg. 6:24). The name Jehovah-Shalom means "the Lord is our peace." The building of that altar before the gathering of an army or forming of a battle plan was an act of faith on Gideon's part. The only way one can know Jehovah-Shalom is by faith. "Therefore being justified by faith, we have peace with God through our Lord Jesus Christ" (Rom. 5:1). As we seek to live for God consistently, the Bible says, "The God of peace shall be with you" (Phil. 4:9).

Jehovah-Tiskemu—the Lord Our Righteousness

When the Lord returns to this world at the end of the age, many Jews will recognize their Messiah and turn to him as Savior. At that time they will know a name of God that every Christian knows experimentally, "the Lord Our Righteousness" (Jer. 23:6). Our admission into heaven is not dependent upon our personal righteousness but rather upon the righteousness of God applied to our account. Someday this will also be the experience of the nation of Israel. The Lord Our Righteousness will be the prominent name of God on that day.

Jehovah-Shammah—the Lord Is There

As Ezekiel concludes his discussion of the eternal city, he records, "And the name of the city from that day shall be, the Lord is there" (Ezek. 48:35). This name of God emphasizes God's presence.

When God called Moses to lead Israel out of Egypt, he promised, "Certainly I will be with thee" (Exod. 3:12). As we are faithful today in presenting a greater deliverance to the lost by preaching and teaching the gospel, Jesus has promised, "Lo, I am with you always, even unto the end of the world [age]" (Matt. 28:20). The Lord is present.

Jehovah-Maccaddeshcem—the Lord Our Sanctifier

When God appointed the Sabbath under the law, he identified himself with the sentence, "I am the Lord that doth sanctify you" (Exod. 31:13). The biblical concept of sanctification does not involve the eradication of the sin nature but rather notes God's setting a person apart for some reason. Though under law, this often involves special signs such as the vow of the Nazarite. Under grace, God still expects his people to live apart from the world. Paul's prayer for the Thessalonian Christians was that "the very God of peace sanctify you wholly" (1 Thess. 5:23).

Jehovah-Roah—the Lord Our Shepherd

One of the most familiar passages of scripture is the Twenty-Third Psalm, where God is identified as "my Shepherd" (Ps. 23:1). In the New Testament, this title is ascribed to the second person of the Trinity, who is described as the Good Shepherd who gives himself for his sheep (John 10:11), the great shepherd who leads and cares for his sheep (Heb. 13:20), and the chief shepherd who is coming in glory to reign over and reward his undershepherds (1 Pet. 5:4).

Jehovah-Naheh—the Lord that Smiteth

Only once in scripture does God say, "I am the Lord that smiteth" (Ezek. 7:9). Here, God was telling the people through his prophet Ezekiel of the coming invasion by the Babylonians, but he wanted them to know it was not the Babylonians who were fighting them; it was God himself. Because of the persistent sin of his people, God was forced to judge them. Whereas the name occurs only once in scripture, the truth continues. As it was true in Israel, it is true in the church of today (cf. Heb. 12:5–11).

Jehovah-Elohim—Lord God

From time to time, Jehovah and Elohim are used together to identify a name of God. In the giving of this compound name of God, all that is true of these two names is implied. It was Jehovah-Elohim who created humankind (Gen. 2:4), sought after the human beings once they sinned (Gen. 3:9–13), and clothed Adam and Eve with animal skins (Gen. 3:21). This relationship between Jehovah-Elohim and Adam is often understood as typical of our relationship to Christ in salvation.

Adonai-Jehovah—Lord God

Jehovah also appears in scripture related to Adonai and is normally translated "Lord God." Again, the appearance of both names together reveals all the characteristics of both primary names, but this name tends to emphasize the Adonai (Master) aspect of God. This name was first used in scripture by Abraham at the confirmation of his covenant with God (Gen. 15:2).

Jehovah-El-Gemuwal—the Lord God of Recompense

Jeremiah alone uses this name of God, in his prophecy against Babylon (Jer. 51:56). Although God used Babylon to judge Israel's sins, that did not justify Babylon's abuses directed against Israel. The prophet here identifies a God of justice who will give Babylon exactly what it deserves. Throughout the scriptures, the right of judgment is possessed solely by God (cf. Deut. 32:35; Prov. 20:22; and Rom. 12:17–21).

True God

The Bible starts with God. "In the beginning, God …" (Gen. 1:1). God of the Bible is the only one true God, the invisible, the Spirit, the Creator, the Sovereign Master of the universe, glorious, Lord, saint, absolutely wise, unknowable in his essence—with perfect justice and an unfathomable love springing from our Father's heart.

God is self-sufficient, immutable, eternal, omnipotent, omniscient, omnipresent, holy, almighty, and incomprehensible. In all his ways, he is sovereign, gracious, righteous, just, long-suffering, and merciful. And he is approachable only through Christ.

God is love, and therefore all his counsels and actions proceed from love, his main nature.

The God of the Bible is a God who speaks. From the Creation and throughout the history of his people, he reveals himself by speaking.

He said, "And nothingness arises the universe" (Gen. 1:3, 6, 9, etc.). John talks about Christ, who incarnates to save us by revealing the Father: "In the beginning was the Word … And the Word was made flesh" (John 1:1, 14).

Our God does not remain silent, like the idols of ancient pagan or the idols of modern times (1 Cor. 12:2).

The natural attributes of God are as follows:

- God is Spirit (John 4:24).
- God is invisible (1 Tim. 1:17).
- God is revealed by Jesus Christ (John 1:18). Who has seen Jesus, has seen the Father (John 14:9).

- God is Lord (Deut. 33:27; Rom. 16:26).
- Time for God is not the same as it is for us (2 Pet. 3:8).
- God is supreme (Ps. 95:3).
- God is all-powerful (Job 42:2–3; Mark 10:27).
- God knows everything (i.e., he is omniscient) (Ps. 139:1–4). The infinite greatness of God is in his ability to know everything.
- God is everywhere (i.e., he is omnipresent) (1 Kings 23:24; Deut. 26:15).
- God is eternal (Gen. 21:33; Deut. 33:27).

Another indication of the infinite greatness of God is that he doesn't have a beginning.

CHAPTER 4

The Trinity

The word *trinity* means "triunity," or "three-in-oneness." It is used to summarize the scriptural teaching that God is three persons yet one God.[32]

One of the most difficult and yet most important things to understand about God is that he is triune. God is referred to as three distinct persons in scripture, yet at the same time we are taught that there is only one God. The concept of one God in three persons has baffled Christians for centuries as they have sought to understand the complete teaching of the persons of God in scripture. The Trinity has been compared to water: it exists as a solid in ice, as a liquid in water, and as gas in the atmosphere.

The Father, the Son, and the Holy Spirit are each distinguishable from the other, yet everything that is true about God is true about the Father, the Son, and the Holy Spirit. Ignoring this simple doctrine can lead to error. When understood, the doctrine of the Trinity forms a foundation to all doctrine we believe.

God eternally exists as three persons, Father, Son, and Holy Spirit; each of these persons is fully God; and there is one God.

Definition of the Trinity

The Trinity is the designation of God as a unity yet existing in three eternal persons. The members of the Trinity are equal in nature, distinct in person, and subordinate in duties. As Son, Jesus is eternally begotten by the Father. So Jesus is submissive to do the work of the Father yet is equal in nature to him. "The Lord hath said unto me, Thou art my Son; this day have I begotten thee" (Ps. 2:7).

Then the Son sends the Holy Spirit: "the Comforter whom I will send unto you from the Father" (John 15:26). Later Jesus prayed to the Father, saying, "I have finished the work which thou gavest me to do" (John 17:4). The Father is the source of authority, the Son is the channel, and the Holy Spirit is the agent whereby authority is exercised.

The oldest existing identification of the Trinity is the Athanasian Creed written about AD 250. "We worship one God, in Trinity, and Trinity in unity, neither confounding the persons, nor dividing the substance." Nearly two centuries ago, John Dick put the same truth this way: "While there is only one divine nature, there are three subsistences, or persons, called the Father, the Son, and the Holy Ghost, who possess, not a similar, but the same numerical essence, and the distinction between them is not merely nominal, but real."[33]

The word *Trinity* is not found in scripture, but the idea and doctrine are its foundation. Many heretical groups have gone off into their doctrinal error by denying the existence of the Trinity or explaining the Trinity wrongly. Part of understanding what the Trinity is, is knowing what it is not.

The Trinity Is Not Three Gods

The Trinity does not teach the existence of three distinct Gods, which is called tritheism. Often, evangelical Christians are charged by Jehovah's Witnesses and Jews with believing in three Gods. This charge is founded upon their misunderstanding of what is meant by the term *Trinity*.

Christians are monotheists, meaning they believe in one God. "Hear, O Israel: The Lord our God is one Lord" (Deut. 6:4). When we acknowledge that the Father, Son, and Holy Spirit are each part of the triune God, we still hold to the unity of God. The Bible teaches the existence of only one God in three persons.

The Trinity Is Not Three Manifestations of God

One of the heretical groups in the early church taught what was known as Sabellianism or modalism. They held that the Trinity was three different manifestations of the same God. They explained "person" to mean a representation of God, just as a man could be father, husband, and brother at one time. According to this view, there was only one God, but he revealed himself as the Father and the Creator in the Old Testament. Next, they taught that the same person revealed himself as Redeemer. Finally, they taught that the same God reveals himself as the Holy Spirit. "The unchanging God is differently revealed on account of the world's different perceptions of him."

The basic error of modalism is that it denies the eternity and distinctiveness of the three persons of the Trinity. As we will see later, the Father, Son, and Holy Spirit were all involved in the work of creation. All three have existed and worked together since before time began. All three, however, coexist separately in the Godhead.

The Trinity Does Not Teach That the Father Created the Son or Holy Spirit

One of the hottest doctrinal controversies of the early church was Arianism. Arius taught that only the Father was eternally God from the beginning. He taught that both the Son and the Holy Spirit were created out of nothing by God before anything else. Because they were created beings, they could not be considered divine or seen as possessing the attributes of the Divinity.

The Bible, of course, does not teach the creation of the Son or Holy Spirit. Instead, it recognizes the work of both in the creation of all things (see John 1:3; Col. 1:16–17; and Gen. 1:2). Historically, Christians have recognized the error of Arianism and taught the biblical doctrines of Christ and the Holy Spirit.

The Trinity Does Not Teach That Christ or the Holy Spirit Is a Power or Attribute of God

A fourth wrong view of the Trinity teaches that the deity of Christ is merely the result of power or influence of God. According to Monarchianism, Christ had a personality as a historic person but sacrificed his essential deity after death.

This error misunderstands the truth that Jesus is God. The Bible teaches, "The Word [Jesus] was God" (John 1:1). Then, in the same context, we are told, "The Word was made flesh, and dwelt among us, (and we beheld his glory, the glory as of the only begotten of the Father)" (John 1:14). John describes the return of Christ: he "saw heaven opened, and behold, a white horse; and he that sat upon him was called ... The Word of God" (Rev. 19:11, 13).

The above-mentioned erroneous view of the Trinity continues to persist in theology to the present date. Clarke argues, "God the eternal heart of love, Christ the rational expression of the eternal heart, and the Spirit the accomplisher of the work of both, make up the Godhead."[34] Barth concludes his discussion, "Thus, to the same God who in unimpaired unity is Revealer, Revelation, and Revealedness, is also ascribed in unimpaired variety in Himself precisely this threefold mode of being."[35]

The Old Testament Points to the Trinity

There is an element of mystery in every Old Testament doctrine, particularly before it is more completely revealed in the New Testament. The Trinity is most clearly taught in the New Testament, yet throughout the Old Testament there are continuous signposts that point to the existence of the Trinity. These are seen in the names of God, the worship of God, and the distinctions made within the Godhead.

The Names of God Imply the Trinity

God reveals his nature in part through his names. The first name of God used in scripture is Elohim. Even in the first verse of the Bible, a hint of the Trinity is given, in that the word *Elohim* is plural. Even though it identifies one God, it is a plural unity. This plurality of God is further manifested in the use of plural personal pronouns for God. "And God said, let us make man in our image, after our likeness" (Gen. 1:26). When humankind gained a knowledge of good and evil, God said, "The man is become as one of us" (Gen. 3:22). Before God judged at Babel, he said, "Let us go down" (Gen. 11:7). Isaiah "heard the voice of the Lord saying, whom shall I send, and who will go for us" (Isa. 6:8)? Commenting on the term *Elohim*, Andrew Jukes notes the implications of this name.

> He is One, but in him also, as his name declares, there is plurality; and in this plurality he has certain relationships, both in and with himself, which, because he is God, can never be dissolved or broken. Thus, as [John] Parkhurst says, this name contains the mystery of the Trinity. For

the perfect revelation of this great mystery, humanity had indeed to wait until it was declared by the only begotten Son of the Father, and even then only after his resurrection from the dead, to those whom he had called to be his disciples.[36]

Isaiah records a second name of God that is plural: Maker (Isa. 54:5), which is plural in the Hebrew language. This verse then names three who are God. "For thy Maker is thine husband; the Lord of hosts is his name; and thy Redeemer the Holy One of Israel; the God of the whole earth shall he be called" (Isa. 54:5). These plural names of God suggest what is known as a "plural unity."

The Worship of God by Use of a Trinitarian Formula

A second indication of the Trinity is seen in the worship of God. Isaiah's vision of God included the threefold designation, "Holy, holy, holy" (Isa. 6:3). When Jacob blessed his son Joseph in the name of God, three times he identified God differently (Gen. 48:15–16). The Aaronic benediction given by God for recitation by Israel's first priest was also threefold in nature: "The Lord bless thee, and keep thee; The Lord make his face shine upon thee, and be gracious unto thee; The Lord lift up his countenance upon thee, and give thee peace" (Num. 6:24–26). While these are not conclusive in themselves, most biblical theologians agree that this threefold emphasis in the worship of God reflects the triune nature of God.

All Three Persons Are Distinguished As God

A third inference of the Trinity in the Old Testament is the practice of distinguishing between God and God.

The judgment of the Lord on Sodom and Gomorrah distinguishes between the Lord who judged with fire and brimstone and the Lord who sent it from heaven (Gen. 19:24). More specifically, the Old Testament teaches that Jehovah has a Son (Ps. 2:7) who is called God (Isa. 9:6). The Spirit of God is also distinguished in the Old Testament from God (Gen. 1:2; Gen. 6:3).

A Clear Statement Points to the Trinity

Probably the clearest statement on the Trinity in the Old Testament is Isaiah 48:16, which demonstrates an Old Testament belief in the three personalities of the Trinity. God the Son is speaking in this verse. He identifies the Father (Lord God) and "his Spirit" as having sent him. In the next verse, the Son is more clearly identified as God.

Therefore, this verse identifies three who are God, yet it does not deny monotheism. Missionaries to the Jews often use this verse when challenged by Jews who claim that Christians believe in "three Gods." Christians believe in one God in three persons, just as the Old Testament teaches.

Direct Teaching of the New Testament

What was hidden in the Old Testament is clearly revealed in the New Testament. Specifically, the doctrine of the Trinity is clearly taught in the New Testament.

Trinity Revealed at the Baptism of Jesus

The early church fathers used to say, "If you want to see the Trinity, go to the wilderness beyond the Jordan." By this they meant that one of the clearest revelations of the triune God is recorded in the account of Jesus's baptism. The most vivid illustration of the Trinity is found at the beginning of the earthly ministry of Jesus when he was baptized by John the Baptist in the Jordan River (Matt. 3:16–17).

As God the Son was raised from the water, the onlookers saw God the Holy Spirit "descending like a dove." The Bible also records the voice of God the Father breaking the silence of heaven to acknowledge his delight in his Son.

Jesus Taught the Truth of the Trinity (John 14:16–17)

Jesus believed in and taught his disciples the doctrine of the Trinity. When attempting to prepare them for their life of service after his resurrection, he told them he had asked the Father to send the Comforter, which is God the

Holy Spirit. By this point in Jesus's ministry, the disciples were well aware that he was God the Son. In his instruction concerning the coming of the Holy Spirit, he taught in a way that assumed they understood the doctrine of the Trinity.

Later the same evening, Jesus made the same allusion to the Trinity to the same group when he said, "But when the Comforter [God the Holy Spirit] is come, whom I [God the Son] will send unto you from [God] the Father" (John 15:26). Jesus would have had only to say something once to make it true, but the repetition of this teaching in this context suggests that not only was the teaching true, but also the learners (disciples) could relate to that truth. They were familiar enough with the doctrine of the Trinity to be able to learn new truth built upon old truth.

The New Testament Church Recognized the Trinity (2 Cor. 13:14)

The doctrine of the Trinity was taught in the early church. Two practices of the church revealed that the first Christians were Trinitarians. The first is seen in the practice of greetings and benedictions. Christians often greeted one another in the name of the Lord. Even today some Christians will comment, "God bless you," as they part company. When the apostle Paul pronounced his final benediction upon the Corinthian church, he did so in the name of the three persons of the Trinity. "The grace of the Lord Jesus Christ, and the love of God, and the communion of the Holy Ghost, be with you all" (2 Cor. 13:14).

A second practice in the New Testament church that recognizes the Trinity is baptism. Jesus instructed his disciples to baptize converts "in the name of the Father, and of the Son, and of the Holy Ghost" (Matt. 28:19). In obedience to Christ's commandment, this was done in "the name of Christ."

The Distinct Work of Each Person of the Trinity Points to the Trinity

Much of the work of God is attributed to all members of the Trinity. Hebrews 9:14 illustrates the cooperative efforts of each member of the Trinity in the atonement: God the Son offered his blood through God the Holy Spirit to God the Father for our atonement. In this way, an understanding of the Trinity is foundational to an understanding of the atonement. The author of Hebrews felt this was important when reminding Hebrew Christians in Jerusalem of what God had done for them.

The Attributes of the Trinity

One of the strongest proofs of the triune nature of God is the Bible's revealing that each member of the Trinity possesses the same attributes of God.

In the corporate identification of God, the Trinity is called holy. The Father is called holy (Isa. 41:14; John 17:11), the Son is called holy (Acts 3:14), and the Holy Spirit is called holy (Eph. 4:30). Table 4.1 reinforces the doctrine of the Trinity by showing that each person of the Godhead is equal in attributes.

TABLE 4.1. The attributes of the Trinity

Attributes	Father	Son	Holy Spirit
Omnipresence	Jer. 23:24	Matt. 28:20	Ps. 139:7–12
Omnipotence	Rom. 1:16	Matt. 28:28	Rom. 15:19
Omniscience	Rom. 11:33	John 21:17	John 14:26
Immutability	Mal. 3:16	Heb. 13:8	Hag. 2:5
Eternality	Ps. 90:2	John 1:1	Heb. 9:14
Holiness	Lev. 19:2	Heb. 4:15	name "holy"
Love	1 John 3:1	Mark 10:21	name "Comforter"

The Work of the Trinity

Table 4.1 shows that the Trinity are equal in attributes and, since the attributes are absolute, the persons of the Godhead are equal. Two absolute forces would conflict with each other if in fact they were not a unified whole. Table 4.2 shows that all three persons of the Divinity are involved in works that only God can do.

TABLE **4.2.** The work of the Trinity

Work	Father	Son	Holy Spirit
Creation of the world	Ps. 102:25	John 1:3	Gen. 1:2
Creation of humankind	Gen. 2:7	Col. 1:16	Job 33:4
Death of Christ	Isa. 53:10	John 10:18	Heb. 9:24
Resurrection of Christ	Acts 2:32	John 2:19	1 Pet. 3:18
Inspiration	Heb. 1:1–2	1 Pet. 1:10–11	2 Pet. 1:21
Indwelling believers	Eph. 4:6	Col. 1:7	1 Cor. 6:19
Authority of ministry	2 Cor. 3:4–6	1 Tim. 1:12	Acts 20:28
Security of believer	John 10:29	Phil. 1:6	Eph. 1:13–14

God Is Thrice Holy: Trinity

There is only one God. In the unity of the Godhead, there are three persons of one essence: God the Father, God the Son (Jesus Christ), and God the Holy Spirit.

It gets difficult when we think of those persons as human beings. So we have three persons: $1 + 1 + 1 = 3$. But there is only one God, not three gods.

If the word *persons* may be commonly in use for the Father, the Son, and the Holy Spirit, that doesn't mean it has the same meaning as attributed to us humans.

The Father, the Son, and the Holy Spirit are so closely linked that somebody suggested to represent them by this equation: $1 \times 1 \times 1 = 1$.

Certainly any attempt to explain the doctrine of the Trinity is bound to meet with extreme difficulties.

There are ten unsolved mysteries of science. Three of these are the nature of electricity, light, and the atom of life. Scientists have made great progress, yet they have not yet explained these mysteries. Why then are we surprised when we fail to grasp the nature and personality of God?

But also consider this: how could human beings worship a being that they can understand and analyze everything about, down to the smallest details?

No doubt, God in his wisdom created us to have limited knowledge of him. What God expects of us is our homage and worship. It is better to know what the Bible says of God than to seek to try to explain everything about him.

Blessed be the Lord. Let us worship our God. Certainly one day we will understand all these mysteries.

CHAPTER 5

The Father

The concept of fatherhood comes from the first person of the Trinity, who is addressed as "Our Father which art in heaven" (Matt. 6:9). The Bible teaches that we have a heavenly Father. While the doctrine of the Trinity is foundational to biblical Christianity, the three persons of the Godhead do not receive equal emphasis in the experience of the average Christian. Certainly the emphasis of teaching in contemporary pulpits is on the Son, though many pastors also spend time teaching about the Holy Spirit. But the fatherhood of God remains a vastly neglected doctrine. Wilmington doubts the average Christian could list more than a half dozen statements concerning the first person of the Trinity.[37]

Careful thought and observation reveal a surprising lack of reference to God as Father in the speech and prayers of Christians today, although there is constant reference to Jesus Christ as the Savior. Saviorhood is much emphasized, whereas the fatherhood of God is given comparatively little attention. Few of our hymns are addressed to God the Father or even describe his essential character and grace. It is sometimes painfully embarrassing to be unable to find a hymn setting forth the fatherhood of God.[38]

The Fatherhood of God

Some teach that the fatherhood of God means that everyone is a child of God and, hence, everyone is going to heaven. This doctrine of universalism denies the basic fundamentals of the Word of God. It denies the necessity of the vicarious substitutionary atonement, implying there is no need for salvation. Because of the abuse of these humanistic teachings, many conservative Christians will not use the phrase *the fatherhood of God*. However, the Bible teaches that God is the Father of the universe and all its people—but that does not mean everyone is a Christian and that everyone will go to heaven (cf. Gal. 3:26).

The Father of Creation

When the general public describes God the Father, they often use the phrase *the universal fatherhood of God*. This phrase makes God the Father of all living things, including people, by virtue of the fact that he is their Creator. We prefer to use the phrase *the Father of creation*, because it identifies God with the reason that he is Father. The best verse to identify "the Father of creation" is James. 1:17: "Every good gift and every perfect gift is from above, and cometh down from the Father of lights."

When we study the history of an organization or a nation, we find the term *founding fathers*. The person who invents or develops some new product is often called the father of that product. We use the term *father* to identify its source. Since God is the Creator of all things, he is the Father of the universe.[38]

The National Father of Israel

God has a unique relationship with the nation Israel; he is called its Father. Although the doctrine of the Father is fully developed in the New Testament, we have noted that it exists in embryonic form in the Old Testament. Jeremiah put it this way: "I am a father to Israel, and Ephraim is my firstborn" (Jer. 31:9). Israel was a special son to God because he was its Source; Israel was loved by Jehovah and he was their teacher, giving them the law to instruct them in the way they should live.

The Unique Father of Jesus Christ

In an extremely unique way, God is the Father of Jesus Christ, his Son. Jesus was miraculously born of a virgin with no human father. Actually, he existed from before the beginning and simply became a man, while retaining his divinity at his birth. God claims to be the Father of Christ when he says, "Thou art my Son; this day have I begotten thee" (Ps. 2:7). This does not mean that Jesus Christ was begotten at a point in time. The phrase *this day* means God's eternal day, or a day without time.

God the Son was always in the process of being begotten by the Father; both Father and Son are eternal. At the baptism of Jesus, the Father himself spoke, saying, "This is my beloved Son; in whom I am well pleased" (Matt. 3:17). Jesus declared his sonship by telling the Jewish leaders, "My Father worketh hitherto, and I work" (John 5:17). This statement looks innocent to us because we do not see the implication of the original language. The Greek word for "my" is *idios*, by which Jesus meant, "My Father, to whom I am identical." When Jesus called God his Father, he recognized himself as equal in deity.

Paul related Jesus to God the Father by saying "his dear Son" (Col. 1:13). John called Christ "his only begotten Son" (John 3:16). Jesus recognized his unique relationship with God. He used the title "Father" more than any other when referring to God. He distinguished between "my Father" and "your Father." Though he instructed his disciples to pray to "*our* Father," he never used the term, as he recognized the uniqueness of his relationship with the Father.

A Protective Father

"A father of the fatherless, and a judge of the widows, is God in his holy habitation" (Ps. 68:5). God is a father to those oppressed who need a father. This verse does not teach that all poor orphans and widows are saved, but rather that God is concerned about those for whom no one else cares. Even among Christians there is a tendency to ignore those who are less fortunate. But God is the Defender of those unable to defend themselves.

This aspect of the fatherhood of God was a major motivating factor in the life of the evangelist George Mueller. As he considered renting a building for his first orphanage, God confirmed his leading in Mueller's life by speaking through Psalm 68:5. Mueller was prepared to believe that God would provide as a father, if he were to gather the orphans. God honored Mueller's faith and proved himself to be "a Father to the fatherless."

Redemptive Father

The major emphasis in New Testament doctrine is the Father's relationship to redemption. All who are saved are born "of God" (John 1:13). God becomes our Father when we trust Christ as our Savior, which gains admittance into the family of God (John 1:12). We immediately, upon salvation, have an intimate relationship with God, "whereby we cry, Abba, Father" (Rom. 8:15). We cannot know God as our redemptive Father until we are known by him as his redeemed children.

CHAPTER 6

Humankind

Human Beings' Humanity

The biblical creation accounts in Genesis 1 and Genesis 2–3 portray humans as part of the natural world but also as specially related to God (Ps. 8:3–5). Humankind is of two types, male and female, and both are made in the image of God (Gen. 1:26; Gen. 5:1–2). As created beings, humans are not divine; rather, they stand under God's authority. As uniquely created in God's image, however, they are God's agents in ruling other creatures and caring for the earth (Gen. 1:26; Gen. 2:15). Thus, throughout the Bible, the term *humans* is often used in contrast to divine beings (humans are distinct from God and the angels—e.g., Gen. 32:38; Matt. 15:9; Matt. 16:23; and John 10:33) as well as in contrast to animals (humans are distinct from the beasts—e.g., Exod. 8:17–18; Matt. 12:12; but see Eccles. 3:18–21). Humans are also portrayed as disobedient to God in a way that damages their relationship with God and necessitates their punishment. Still, the life of a human being is sacred because humankind was made in God's image (Gen. 9:6).

The Bible offers no systematic view of the human constitution, but there is a general sense that humans have visible and invisible properties. Thus, the visible or physical aspect of humans may be described with such terms as *flesh*, *body*, *members*, and *outer person*, or with reference to individual body parts or organs. The invisible aspect of humanity is often described by references to the soul, spirit, mind, or inner person. For the most part, these terms are interchangeable and do not indicate separate aspects. Furthermore, such terminology is not consistent; the heart, for example, can be a physical organ (the one that pumps blood), but most of the time it refers to the inner person and is essentially synonymous with spirit, mind, or soul. When the breath of life departs a human body, that body returns to dust; the person survives only as an unsubstantial shade. The hope of resurrection as portrayed in the New Testament involves the creation of new bodies for those who have died (as opposed to the Greek concept of the dead continuing to survive as immortal souls; cf. 1 Cor. 15:35–55). Paul also speaks of Christ as creating a "new humanity" in which former divisions will be done away with (Gal. 2:15; Gal. 3:28).[39]

Why Was Humankind Created?

God did not need to create humankind, yet he created us for his own glory. In the discussion of God's independence in chapter 11 (see pp. 160–63), we noted several scripture passages that teach that God does not need us or the rest of creation for anything, yet we and the rest of creation glorify him and bring him joy. Since there is perfect love and fellowship among members of the Trinity for all eternity (John 17:5, 24), God did not create us because he was lonely or because he needed fellowship with other persons. Indeed, God did not need us for any reason.

Nevertheless, *God created us for his own glory.* In our treatment of his independence, we noted that God speaks of his sons and daughters from the ends of the earth as those "whom I created *for my glory*" (Isa. 43:7; cf. Eph. 1:11–12). Therefore, we are to "do all to the glory of God" (1 Cor. 10:31).[40]

Humanity Under Sin

The sin of the first couple caused a profound change in humanity and humanity's relationship with God (Rom. 5:12). The image of God remained, but it became marred and distorted. Humanity continued to procreate as male and female, although relationships with others were deeply and immediately affected by sin (Gen. 4). Humankind remained body and soul, but their inmost being was particularly impacted by sin. A person's heart, the core of his or her being, is sinful (Gen. 6:5; Jer. 17:9; Mark 7:20–23), and his or her mind is darkened (Eph. 4:17–19). The human will is in bondage to sin (Rom. 3:10–11; 2 Tim. 2:25–26), the human conscience is defiled (Titus 1:15), and human desires are twisted (Eph. 2:3; Titus 3:3). Simply put, humanity is universally dead in sin (Eph. 2:1), in a state of hostility toward God (Rom. 5:10), and subject to physical death followed by eternal judgment (Rom. 5:12–21; Rom. 8:10; Rom. 14: 12; Heb. 9:27).

Redeemed Humanity

God in his grace did not leave humanity to perish eternally but, instead, provided for redemption. Humanity's participation in salvation begins at the individual level, when one places conscious faith in Jesus Christ. Saving faith includes a recognition of who Jesus is (fully divine and human Son of God), trust in the merits of his atoning death, and submission of the will to him. This is all made possible by God who, according to his eternal and gracious purpose, enables sinful humanity to believe (Eph. 2:4–9; 1 Tim. 1:14; Titus 3:5).[41]

Following is a list of Bible verses that speak about certain things pertaining to humankind:

- The origins of humankind (Gen. 1:1, 27; Isa. 43:7)
- The nature of humankind (1 Thess. 5:23; Heb. 4:12, Rom. 12:2)
- The free will of humankind (Heb. 1:14; Luke 24:39; 2 Pet. 2:4)
- The sin of humankind (Gen. 3; Rom. 5:12)
- The future of humankind Rom. 1:20; Rom. 2:15–16; Eccles. 12:9).[41]

CHAPTER 7

Sin

Definition of Sin

The history of the human race as presented in scripture is primarily a history of humankind in a state of sin and rebellion against God and against God's plan of redemption to bring humankind back to the Creator. Therefore, it is appropriate now to consider the nature of the sin that separates humankind from God.

We may define sin as follows: any failure to conform to the moral law of God in act, attitude, or nature. Sin is here defined in relation to God and his moral law. Sin includes not only individual *acts* such as stealing, lying, or committing murder, but also *attitudes* that are contrary to the attitudes God requires of us.[42]

Sin is a reality signifying the broken relationship between God and humanity. The occasions by which this relationship breaks, the need to recognize this rupture, and the avenues for salvation are detailed in endless situations throughout the scriptures. Ancient Israel's concern for sin reflected the basic ethical nature of the early Jewish faith and the diversity of theological approaches to the problems of evil.

The concept of rebellion, or revolt, against God's commandments appears early in the biblical narrative. After the creation of the world and the formation of Adam and Eve, Genesis 3:1–7 offers a scenario in which humanity is presented with its first common dilemma—the choice between obedience to divine will or pursuit of human desire. The occasion seems to cover both conscious decision (Eve) and unwitting participation (Adam). No specific word for sin appears here, but the seeds of separation between God and humanity are clearly sown. Curiously, this revolt against God finds no further mention in the Old Testament, yet its implications continue to dominate both the actions of history's earliest participants (Gen. 1–11) and the progression of Israel's own response to God.

Later Christian interpreters of the text, from Paul to Augustine, make specific, extended usage of this episode of the fall of Adam.[43]

Many people are unable to grasp the concept of sin as an inner force, an inherent condition, a controlling power. People today think more in terms of sins, that is, individual wrong acts. Sins are something external and concrete, logically separable from the person. On this basis, one who has not done anything wrong (generally conceived of as an external act) is considered good. This argument is false, because sins are something internal, logically inseparable from the person.[44]

Terms for Sin

Terms Emphasizing Causes of Sin

The Bible uses many terms to denote sin. Some of these terms focus on sin's causes, others on its nature, and still others on its consequences, although these categories may not always be clear-cut. The first terms are those that emphasize causes of sin, that is, predisposing factors that give rise to sin.

Ignorance

One of the New Testament words stressing a cause of sin is *agonia*. A combination of a Greek verb meaning "to know," from *gnoo* and the alpha privative, *agonia* is related to the English word *agnostic*. Together with its cognates, it is used in the Septuagint to render the verbs *shagah* and *shagag*, which basically mean "to err." Its immediate derivation is from *agnoeo*, "to be ignorant." This word is often used in settings where it means "innocent ignorance" (Rom. 1:13; 2 Cor. 6:9; Gal. 1:22). Some things done in ignorance are apparently innocent in the sight of God, or at least he overlooks them (Acts 17:30). Yet at other points, ignorant actions seem to be culpable. Ephesians 4:18 says of the Gentiles, "They are darkened in their understanding and separated from the life of God because of the ignorance that is in them due to the hardening of their hearts." In two passages, Acts 3:17 and 1 Peter 1:14, it is questionable whether the ignorance is culpable or innocent. In the former, however, Peter's immediate appeal to his hearers to repent would suggest responsibility. The one instance of ignorance is in Hebrews 9:7, referring to the annual visit of the high priest into the holy of holies in order to offer sacrifice both for himself and "for the sins the people had committed in ignorance." These errors or ignorance apparently were such that the people were liable to punishment for them. This was willful ignorance. The people could have known the right course to follow, but they chose not to know it.

Error

More abundant are references to sin as error, that is, the human tendency to go astray, to make mistakes. The primary terms in the Old Testament are *shagah* and *shagag* together with their derivatives and related words. *Shagah* is used both literally and figuratively. In its literal sense, it is used to describe sheep that stray from the flock (Ezek. 34:6) and drunken persons stumbling and reeling (Isa. 28:7).

Inattention

Another scriptural designation for sin is inattention. In classical Greek, the word *parakoe* has the meaning "to hear amiss or incorrectly." In several New Testament passages, it refers to disobedience as a result of inattention (Rom. 5:19; 2 Cor. 10:6). The clearest case is Hebrews 2:2–3, where the content indicates the meaning that we are suggesting: "For if the message spoken by angels was binding, and every violation and disobedience received its just punishment, how shall we escape if we ignore such a great salvation? This salvation, which was first announced by the Lord, was confirmed to us by those who heard him."[45]

Terms Emphasizing the Character of the Sin

In the preceding section, we examined terms emphasizing causes of sin (i.e., factors predisposing us to sin), rather than the character or nature of sin, although something of the latter is also contained within those terms. In many cases, the sins we examined involve relatively minor consequences. We now come to a group of sins, however, that are so serious in character that it makes little difference why they occur, that is, what prompts the individual to commit them. The nature of the deed is the crucial matter.

Missing the Mark

Probably the most common of those concepts that stress the nature of the sin is the idea of missing the mark. It is found in the Hebrew verb *chata'* and in the Greek verb *hamartano*. The Hebrew verb and its cognates appear about six hundred times and are translated in the Septuagint by thirty-two different Greek words, the most common rendering by far being *hamartano* and its cognates.[46]

A literal usage of *chata'* can be found in Judges 20:16. Seven hundred crack marksmen, all of them left-handed (or ambidextrous) and from the tribe of Benjamin,[46] "could sling a stone at a hair and not miss." Another literal usage is in Proverbs 19:2: "to be hasty and miss the way." Such literal usages are rare, however.[47]

The phrase *missing the mark* usually suggests a mistake rather than a willful, consciously chosen sin. But in the Bible, the word *chata'* suggests not merely failure, but a decision to fail, a voluntary and culpable mistake.[48]

Irreligion

Sin is also designated as irreligion, particularly in the New Testament. One prominent word is the verb *asebe'o*, along with its noun form, *asebeia*, and its adjectival form, *asebe's*. This is the negative of *sebo'*, which means "to worship" or "to reverence," and it is always found in the middle voice in the New Testament. *Asebe'o* is the contrary of the term *eusebeo'* and its cognates, which are especially common in the Pastoral Epistles. The verb *eusebeo'* and its cognates, together with the term *theosebes*, are used in relation to the piety of the devout. Thus the cluster of terms around *asebeo* means not so much ungodliness as irreverence. They are found particularly in Romans, 2 Peter, and Jude. "Impiety" and its cognates may be the best English rendering.

Transgression

The Hebrew word *'abar* appears approximately six hundred times in the Old Testament. It means, literally, "to cross over" or "to pass by"; nearly all of the occurrences are in the literal sense. In a number of passages, however, the word involves the idea of transgressing a command or going beyond an established limit. In Esther 3:3 it is used of an earthly king's command. In most of the parallel cases, however, it is used to depict the transgressing of the Lord's commands. There is a concrete example in Numbers 14:41–42. The people of Israel want to go up to the place that the Lord had promised, but Moses says, "Why are you disobeying the Lord's command? This will not succeed! Do not go up, because the Lord is not with you. You will be defeated by your enemies." The people of Israel were not to transgress God's covenant (Deut. 17:2) or his commandment (Deut. 26:13). Other examples include Jeremiah 34:18; Daniel 9:11; Hosea 6:7; and Hosea 8:1.

Iniquity or Lack of Integrity

Sin is also characterized as iniquity. The primary word here is *'awal* and its derivatives. The basic concept seems to be deviation from a right course. Thus, the word can carry the idea of injustice, failure to fulfill the standard of righteousness, or lack of integrity.

The idea of injustice is evident in Leviticus 19:15: "Do not pervert justice; do not show partiality to the poor or favoritism to the great, but judge your neighbor fairly."

In the former case, lack of integrity is seen in failure to fulfill or maintain the just law of God. In the latter case, lack of integrity is seen in the disunity in the individual—a discrepancy between present and past behavior or character.

Rebellion

A number of Old Testament words depict sin as rebellion, a rather prominent idea in Hebrew thought. The most common of these is *pasha'* together with its noun, *pesha'*. The verb is often translated

"transgress," but the root meaning is "to rebel." It is sometimes used to describe rebellion against a human king (e.g., 1 Kings 12:19), but more frequently it is used to refer to rebellion against God. One of the most vivid of these latter usages is Isaiah 1:2: "I reared children and brought them up, but they have rebelled against me."

Treachery

Closely related to the concept of sin as rebellion is the idea of sin as breach of trust, or treachery. The most common Hebrew word in this connection is *ma'al*, which in the majority of instances denotes treachery against God. It is used in Numbers 5:12, 27, of a woman's unfaithfulness to her husband. Achan, in taking devoted things, is said to have "acted unfaithfully" (Josh. 7:1; Josh. 22:20). An excellent example of the use of this term to denote treachery against God is found in Leviticus 26:40: "But if they will confess their sins and the sins of their fathers—their treachery against me and their hostility toward me." In Ezekiel 14:13 and Ezekiel 15:8, God affirms that any land that acts faithlessly against him will be made desolate and unbearing. One other Hebrew word, *bagad*, is occasionally used to refer to treachery against God (Ps. 78:57; Jer. 3:10; Mal. 2:11).

Perversion

The basic meaning of the word *awah* is "to bend or twist." It means, as well, "to be bent or bowed down." This literal meaning is seen in Isaiah 21:3 ("I am staggered by what I hear, I am bewildered by what I see") and Isaiah 24:1 ("See, the Lord is going to lay waste the earth and devastate it; he will ruin its face and scatter its inhabitants"). In Proverbs 12:8, the idea is transferred from the physical to the mental realm, from a twisted body (as in Isaiah 21:3) to a warped mind: "A man is praised according to his wisdom, but men with warped minds are despised." The noun forms derived from *awah* speak of the destruction of cities (Ps. 79:1; Isa. 17:1; Jer. 26:18; Mic. 1:6; Mic. 3:12) and of distortion of judgment: "The Lord has poured into them a spirit of dizziness; they make Egypt stagger in all that she does, as a drunkard staggers around in his vomit" (Isa. 19:14).

Abomination

The characterization of sin as abomination appears to have special reference to God's attitude toward sin and its effect upon him. "Abomination" is the most common English translation of *shiqquts* and *to'ebah*. These terms generally describe an act particularly reprehensible to God, such as idolatry

(Deut. 7:25–26), homosexuality (Lev. 18:22; Lev. 20:13), wearing clothing of the opposite sex (Deut. 22:5), sacrificing sons and daughters (Deut. 12:31) or blemished animals (Deut. 17:1), and witchcraft (Deut. 18:9–12). These practices virtually nauseate God. The term a*bomination* indicates that these sins are not simply something that God peevishly objects to but are something that produces revulsion in him.

Terms Emphasizing the Results of Sin

Some terms focus neither upon the predisposing factors that give rise to sin nor upon the nature of the act itself, but rather upon the consequences that follow from sin.

Agitation or Restlessness

The word *resha'*, which is usually translated as "wickedness," is believed to have originally suggested the concept of tossing and restlessness. Related to an Arabic word that means "to be loose (of limbs)," the root of *resha'* may mean "to be disjointed, ill regulated, abnormal, wicked."[49] There is evidence of the literal meaning in Job 3:17 ("There the wicked cease from turmoil, and there the weary are at rest") and Isaiah 57:20–21 ("But the wicked are like the tossing sea, which cannot rest, whose waves cast up mire and mud. 'There is no peace,' says my God, 'for the wicked'"). The wicked therefore are to be seen as causing agitation and discomfort for themselves and for others. They live in chaotic confusion and bring similar disorder into the lives of those close to them. This moral sense is always present when the word *resha* or a cognate is applied to human beings.

Evil or Badness

The word *ra'* is a generic term meaning "evil" in the sense of badness. Thus, it can refer to anything that is harmful or malignant, not merely morally evil. For example, it can be used to describe food that has gone bad or a dangerous animal.[50] It may mean "distress" or "adversity." Jeremiah 42:6 quotes the commanders of the forces as saying to Jeremiah, "Whether it is favorable or unfavorable, we will obey the Lord our God, to whom we are sending you, so that it will go well with us, for we will obey the Lord our God." The phrase "favorable or unfavorable" could have been rendered "prosperity or adversity" here. In Amos 6:3, we read of a day of calamity. This word, then, binds together the act of sin and its consequences. In Deuteronomy 30:15, God sets before the people the choice of "life and prosperity, death and destruction." They may choose to keep God's commandments, in which case good will come to them, or to disobey, in which case the result will be evil: they will perish (v. 18).

Guilt

Although some of the words examined earlier imply the idea of guilt, in the word *'asham* guilt becomes explicit. In speaking of the act of sin, *'asham* means "to do a wrong, to commit an offense, or to inflict an injury." A wrong has been done to someone, a wrong for which the perpetrator ought to be punished or the victim compensated. And, as a matter of fact, in about one-third of the passages where *'asham* or a related word appears, the meaning is "sin offering." In Numbers 5:8, it means "restitution made for the wrong": "But if that person has no close relative to whom restitution can be made for the wrong, the restitution belongs to the Lord and must be given to the priest, along with the ram with which atonement is made for him." The idea in this case and in many others is that harm has been done by the act of sin, and there must be some form of restitution to set matters right.

Trouble

The word *'aven* literally means "trouble," almost always in a moral sense. The underlying idea is that sin brings trouble upon the sinner. Thus Hosea refers to Bethel, after it became a seat of idolatry, as Beth-aven, the "house of trouble" (Hosea 4:14; Hosea 10:8).

In the psalms, the expression "workers of trouble" occurs frequently (e.g., Ps. 5:5 and Ps. 6:8, among others). The Arabic equivalent means "to be fatigued, tired"; it suggests weariness, sorrow, trouble.[51]

The Hebrew term appears to bear the idea of consequent misery, trouble, difficulty, and sorrow. This implication of the term is clearly spelled out in its usage in Proverbs 22:8: "He who sows wickedness reaps trouble."

The Essential Nature of Sin

We have seen that there is a wide variety of terms for sin, each emphasizing a somewhat different aspect. But is it possible in the midst of this bewildering variety to formulate some comprehensive definition of sin, to identify the essence of sin? We have seen that sins are variously characterized in the Bible as unbelief, rebellion, perversity, and missing the mark, but what is sin?

A common element running through all of these varied ways of characterizing sin is the idea that the sinner has failed to fulfill God's law.

There are various ways in which we fail to meet God's standard of righteousness. We may go beyond the limits imposed, or transgress. We may simply fall short of the standard set, or not do at all what God commands and expects. Or we may do the right thing but for a wrong reason, thus fulfilling the letter of the law but not its spirit.

In the Old Testament, sin is to a large extent a matter of external actions or outward lack of conformity to the requirements of God. Inward thoughts and motives are not completely ignored in the Old Testament conception, but in the New Testament they become especially prominent, being virtually as important as actions. So Jesus condemned anger and lust as vehemently as he did murder and adultery (Matt. 5:21–22, 27–28). He also condemned outwardly good acts done primarily out of a desire to obtain the approval of humans rather than to please God (Matt. 6:2, 5, 16).

Yet sin is not merely wrong acts and thoughts. It is also the state of sinfulness, an inherent inner disposition inclining us to wrong acts and thoughts. We are not simply sinners because we sin; we sin because we are sinners.

We offer, then, this definition of sin: "any lack of conformity, active or passive, to the moral law of God. This may be a matter of act, of thought, or of inner disposition or state." Sin is failure to live up to what God expects of us in act, thought, and being. We must still ask at this point, however, whether there is one basic principle of sin, one underlying factor that characterizes all of sin in its manifold varieties. Several suggestions have been made.

Sensuality

One suggestion is that sin is sensuality. This was the view of Friedrich Schleiermacher, among others. According to this conception, sin is the tendency of the lower or physical nature to dominate and control the higher or spiritual nature. This takes Paul's warnings against living "according to the flesh" quite literally, and bases sin in the physical or material aspect of the human.[52] This conception, which often assumes that matter is inherently evil, is also prominent in the thought of Augustine, in his case growing out of his own struggle with sensuality.[53]

A second view is that sin is essentially selfishness—the "choice of self as the supreme end which constitutes the antithesis of supreme love to God."[54] This view was held by Augustus Strong and, in a somewhat different form, by Reinhold Niebuhr. Niebuhr contended that pride, hubris, is the major form of human opposition to God.[55]

Displacement of God

An alternative preferable to the view that sin is basically sensuality or selfishness is that the essence of sin is simply failure to let God be God. It is placing something else, anything else, in the supreme place that is his. Thus, choosing oneself rather than God is not wrong because self is chosen, but because something other than God is chosen. Choosing any finite object over God is wrong, no matter how selfless such an act might be.

This contention is supported by major texts in both the Old and New Testaments. The Ten Commandments begin with the command to give God his proper place. "You shall have no other gods before me" (Exod. 20:3) is the first prohibition in the law. Similarly, Jesus affirmed that the first and great commandment is, "Love the Lord your God with all your heart and with all your soul and with all your mind and with all your strength" (Mark 12:30). Proper recognition of God is primary. Idolatry in any form, not pride, is the essence of sin.[56]

One might ask what the major factor in our failure to love, worship, and obey God is. I submit that it is unbelief. Anyone who truly believes God to be what he says he is will accord to him his rightful status. Failure to do so is sin. Setting one's own ideas above God's revealed Word entails refusal to believe it to be true. Seeking one's own will involves believing that one's own values are actually higher than those of God. In short, it is failing to acknowledge God as God.[57]

According to Romans 3:23, sin entails missing the purpose and failing to reach perfection, which is the experience of all human beings.

Biblical Aspects of Sin

Sin is the denial of God's law, rebellion (1 John 3:4). It arises out of moral impurity (Ps. 32:5; Matt. 5:28)

The origin of sin is made clear in Isaiah 14:12–14, whereas the results of sin are provided in Genesis 3:10.

One consequence of sin is the punishment of death (Rom. 6:23). The fallen nature of Adam is the legacy of all his descendants (Rom. 5:12–18). The sin of humankind attracted God's curse on the whole of creation (Gen. 3:14–19).

Two scriptures in particular discuss the ultimate penalty of sin:

- "The wages of sin is death" (Rom. 6:23).
- "The lake of fire is the second death" (Rev. 20:14).

To remedy sin, God sent his only Son. When a person believes in Jesus Christ, he or she is saved from the penalty and the power of sin. This does not mean that he or she does not sin, but that all his or her sins, past, present, and future, are forgiven. The judicial pardon is granted at the time of conversion. Paternal pardon is granted to the child of God

CHAPTER 8

Faith

Faith is a central theological concept representing the correct relationship to God.[58] We must have faith in the Bible, and we must trust in or reliance on God, who is trustworthy.

The New Testament and the Septuagint express the understanding of faith with two terms (*pistis, pisteuein*), which are related to the Hebrew verb "to be true" or "to be trustworthy" (*'amah*).[59]

Two Meanings of Faith

When we read the Bible, we see at least two different expressions of faith: the faith of sinners and the faith of the sinned against. The faith of sinners rests on God's mercy; the faith of the sinned against trusts in God's fairness. If sinners have faith in God, God will justify them. If the sinned against have faith in God, they can know that God's justice will be done. The faith of the sinners aims at divine acceptance and validation, whereas the faith of the sinned against points to divine verdict and vindication.

Faith in Justification: the Faith of the Sinners

The phrase *the faith of the just* surfaces in Paul's Epistle to the Romans: "For in it the righteousness of God is revealed through faith for faith; as it is written, 'The one who is righteous will live by faith'" (1:17). Paul quotes from the prophet Habakkuk, applying the quotation to his own context. To Paul, this faith means believing in Jesus; more specifically, it means trusting in Jesus's redeeming power. This faith is connected to justification. Thus, faith in Paul's theology is developed for sinners. For the sinner, faith means trusting in God's pardoning mercy through Jesus Christ. In the centuries since Paul wrote, the church has further developed this idea of faith and justification of sinners. Such faith makes the sinners righteous through God's grace (as believed by Roman Catholics) or causes them to be regarded as righteous through God's grace (as believed by Protestants). This type of faith concerns the righteousness of sinners.

Faith in Justice: the Faith of the Sinned Against

The phrase *the faith of the just* derives from Habakkuk. In the book of Habakkuk, faith means waiting. Habakkuk lived in a time when evil prospered. His main complaint was that a just God would be "silent when the wicked swallow those more righteous than they" (1:13). At his watchtower, he stood and kept watch to see what God would say to him. Finally, God answered him and said the following:

> Write the vision; make it plain on tablets, so that a runner
> may read it. For there is still a vision for the appointed time;
> it speaks of the end, and does not lie. If it seems to tarry,
> wait for it; it will surely come, it will not delay. Look at the
> proud! Their spirit is not right in them. But the *righteous* live
> by their *faith*." (Habakkuk 2:2–4)

For Habakkuk, faith meant to wait for God's vindication of the wronged. Faith is also patiently waiting for God's judgment upon the wicked. Trusting in the faithfulness of God for the restoration of justice is the gist of Habakkuk's faith. Waiting signifies trusting in God's fair treatment of everyone—the divine justice.

To Habakkuk, faith is connected to justice, not justification. His concept of faith is developed for the sinned against.

This faith concerns the rights of the sinned against. Since the church has treated the faith of the sinners, it needs to balance the view by lifting up the faith of the sinned against in the Bible.

For the sinned against, faith denotes trusting in God's grace, which reinstates God's justice by restoring human rights and civil rights.

In the New Testament, we see the faith of heroes in the Letter to the

Hebrews. By faith, Moses refused to be called a son of Pharaoh's daughter, opting to share ill treatment with his people rather than to enjoy the momentary pleasures of sin. Even the hope of resurrection derives from faith: "Women received their dead by resurrection. Others were tortured, refusing to accept release, in order to obtain a better resurrection" (Heb. 11:35).

Ultimately Jesus is "the pioneer and perfecter of our faith, who for the sake of the joy that was set before him endured the cross" (Heb. 12:2). Jesus's faith endured, not so that he might secure his own justification, but so that he might achieve the vindication of the sinned against: "Consider him who endured such hostility against himself from sinners, so that you may not grow weary or lose heart" (Heb. 12:3). The Hebrews' faith was the "assurance of things hoped for, the conviction of things not seen" (Heb. 11:1).

Like Jesus, they did not seek their own justification; rather, their faith gave them courage to trust in the verdict and justice of God. For the injured, faith in justice pursues humanization. Such a faith is the foundation of resistance for the wounded.[61]

Righteousness by Faith

When Paul, having completed the Aegean phase of his ministry, sent a letter to the Christians in Rome to prepare them for his intended visit to the imperial city en route to Spain, he judged it appropriate to devote the main body of the letter to a systematic exposition of the gospel as he understood and proclaimed it. Although he had no thought of settling down in Rome and building on a foundation that he himself had not laid, he hoped to have an opportunity to preach the gospel in Rome during his limited stay, so as to "reap some harvest" there, as well as elsewhere in the Gentile world. "For," he adds, "I am not ashamed of the gospel" (meaning, "I make my boast in the gospel"): "it is power of God for salvation to everyone who has faith, to the Jew first and also to the Greek; for in it God's way of righteousness is revealed through faith for faith, as it is written, 'He who through faith is righteous shall live'" (Rom. 1:16).[62]

The words of Habakkuk 2:4b ("the righteous shall live by his faith") had been quoted earlier by Paul, with this same emphasis, in Galatians 3:11: "It is evident that no man is justified before God *by the law*; for 'He who *through faith* is righteous shall live.'"

In Galatians Paul insists that men and women are justified in God's sight by faith in Christ, not by keeping the law, and that this justification is bestowed on them by God as a gift of grace, not as a reward of merit. In Romans, he sets this teaching in a wider context but gives it the same fundamentally important position as it had in Galatians. The argument that the doctrine of justification by faith is a "subsidiary crater" in the volcano of Pauline theology, that it is a weapon first fashioned and used by him in his polemic against the Judaizing invaders of his Galatian mission field,[63] is put out of court by his more dispassionate emphasis on it in the systematic exposition of the gospel that he now imparts to the Roman Christians.[64] Indeed, as has been said already,[65] the doctrine was implicit in the logic of Paul's conversion, which revealed to him in a flash the inadequacy of the law, to which he had hitherto been devoted, as a basis for acceptance with God. In that same flash he was assured of his acceptance with God on another basis—the basis of God's pardoning grace, blotting out the sin of one who was quite unfit for his service because, as he says, "I persecuted the church of God" (1 Cor. 15:9), and calling him into his service. Only so was it possible for him to introduce himself to the Romans as one who had received through Christ "grace and apostleship to bring about the obedience of faith for the sake of his name among all the nations" (Rom. 1:5).

The Way of Salvation

If there is to be any salvation for either Jews or Gentiles, then it must be based not on ethical achievement but on the grace of God. What Jews and Gentiles alike need, in fact, is to have their records blotted out by an act of divine amnesty and to have the assurance of acceptance by God for no merit of their own but by his spontaneous mercy. For this need God has made provision in Christ. Thanks to his redemptive work, people may find themselves "in the clear" before God; Christ is set before them in the gospel as the one who, by his self-sacrifice and death, has made full reparation for their sins. The benefits of the atonement thus procured may be appropriated by faith—and only by faith. Thus God, without abandoning his personal righteousness, accepts all believers in Jesus as righteous in his sight, regardless of whether they are Jews or Gentiles (Rom. 3:21–30).[66]

The example of Abraham is instructive: it was by faith that even he found acceptance with God. "Abraham believed God," says scripture, "and it was reckoned to him as righteousness" (Gen. 15:6). Nor is Abraham an isolated instance; David similarly proclaims the blessedness of "the man against whom the Lord will not reckon his sin" (Ps. 32:1).[67]

As for Abraham, it is important to observe that his faith was reckoned to him as righteousness long before he was circumcised. This shows that the way of righteousness by faith is in no way dependent on circumcision, but is open to Gentiles as well as Jews. Abraham is thus the spiritual father of all believers, irrespective of their racial origin. And the testimony that his faith was reckoned to him as righteousness means that to all who believe in God, whose saving power has been manifested in the death and resurrection of Christ, their faith will similarly be reckoned as righteousness (Rom. 4:1–25).[68]

In light of their spiritual position, each person is one of three types:

- An unbeliever
- A believer (i.e., a person who is saved) A retrograde believer

An Unbeliever

The unbeliever has not yet arrived to the cross and therefore has not yet touched the cross. He or she wanders into the world and does indiscriminately whatever he or she wants. The unbeliever is not preoccupied by thoughts of his or her life after this earthly life. He or she prefers not to think about the Word of God (1 Cor. 2:14).

Jesus Christ has not yet entered the life of an unbeliever. An unbeliever is one who sits on the throne of his or her life. This person is in need of receiving Christ and believing in him as Lord and Savior.

A Believer

A believer has arrived at the cross.

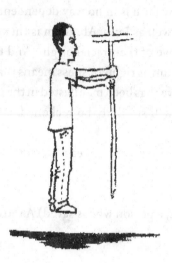

A believer knows that Christ died for him or her on the cross, and as a result he or she loves Christ.

A believer accepts that Christ leads his or her life as Lord and Savior. He or she knows that real life is not limited to earthly life. Being concerned with the things of above, a believer has Christ in his or her heart. Subsequently, this person has the power of the Holy Spirit and leads people to Christ. He or she prays and is answered; understands what the Bible says; has hope in God; and obeys God (Acts 1:8).

Jesus lives in the believer as Savior. Jesus sits in the believer as Lord. The more the believer accepts and obeys the voice of the Spirit, the more the fruits of the Holy Spirit abound in his or her life. In the believer you will find love, joy, peace, forbearance, kindness, generosity, faithfulness, gentleness, and self-control (Gal. 5:22–23).

A Retrograde Believer

The eyes of a retrograde believer are not focused on the cross. His or her thoughts are no longer dominated by the will of God. Having once accepted Jesus by faith, the retrograde believer was born again but turned back to his or her sins. He or she still believes in Jesus, but without spiritual strength. In 1 Corinthians 3:1–3, Paul complains of people who can be described as retrograde believers.

A retrograde believer does not believe fully in God. Occasionally, he or she fails to obey God. He or she does not lead people to Christ, does not read the Bible, is dominated by the negative thoughts, and may have jealousy. A retrograde believer has a consciousness that accuses him or her. He or she is often tormented, judges others, and is often angry.

Confused Unbeliever

In addition to the three types of people described above, there is another kind of person, the confused unbeliever.

A confused believer is near the cross but has not yet arrived at the cross. This person attends church, is present in the prayer rooms, gives tithes, and has repented of many sins, but (as aforementioned) has not yet arrived at the cross. He or she is similar to the person to whom Jesus said, "You are not far from the kingdom of God" (Mark 12:34).

The confused believer may have spiritual gifts, but God's Word tells us that Jesus will say to these people, "I have not known you" (Matt. 7:22-23).

As you see, the confused believer has taken many steps toward the cross but is not determined to abandon everything. He or she knows the Word of God and has tasted spiritual gifts, but he or she still has something to abandon before arriving at the cross. This individual does not yet believe in Jesus Christ. Were he or she to die in this position, he or she will be lost (see 1 John 2:19; Matt. 22:11–13).

When You Believe, Two Things Happen

The first of these things is that your relationship with God starts. The second is that you begin to commune with God.

The relationship between a person and God starts when that person is saved. At that point, he or she becomes a child of God (John 1:12). God's life is given to the person, who is now called a Christian.

Many new Christians have questions, as follows:

- "What happens when I have sinned against God or when I've done something against the will of God?"
- "Does this means that the relationship between me and God ceases to exist?"
- "In such a case, does Jesus leave my life?"

We will understand all this if we understand the meaning between our relationship with God and our communion with God. Remember that once a believer accepts salvation, he or she has already opened the door to Jesus and he has already entered the person's heart through that person's faith in him (Rev. 3:20). Jesus himself testifies that he will never leave or forsake someone who believes in him (Heb. 13:5).

Relationship

There is a difference between relationship and communion. When we talk about a relationship with God and communion with God, we mean something similar to that which exists between a son and his biological father. When the child is born, he is the child of his father, as they have the same blood, the same DNA.

Suppose that a child makes the decision to leave his father and to do things that humiliate his father. Do you think that this child will continue to be called the child of his father? Yes. The relationship between him and his father continues to exist even if the behavior of the child is bad.

Communion

What happens to the communion between God and his child because of the latter's bad behavior? The communion between God and the child becomes disturbed.

What will a child do to reestablish communion and reconcile with his father? He must approach his father, accept his sins, and ask for forgiveness from his father.

Let us use this example in our relationship with the eternal God. We are his children. This relationship will never change. But when we sin and do what is evil in the sight of God, the communion between God and us is disturbed.

To be reconciled to God, we must tell him that we have done wrong and say that we need forgiveness. Then we must accept his forgiveness. Once we do this, our communion with God is reestablished.

The throne: the authority of human life   *The cross as the symbol of Jesus Christ*

The unbeliever

Does this person have a relationship with God? No.
Does this person have communion with God? No.

A believer

Does this person have a relationship with God? Yes.
Does this person have communion with God? Yes.

A retrograde believer

Does this person have a relationship with God? Yes.
Does this person have communion with God? No.

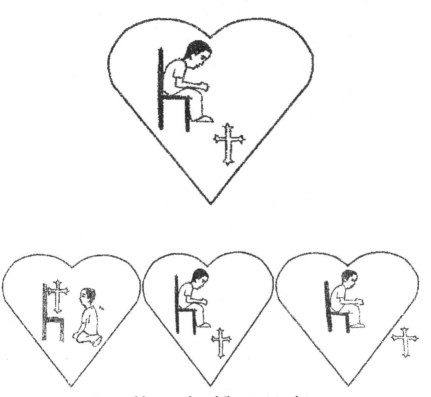

Image of three people at different spiritual stages

Which of the three pictures above would you prefer to depict you?

CHAPTER 9

World Religions Overview

Surely there is one God, only one God. The question of whether there is a supreme being, a creator of all things, is not a problem for every single person. No one can doubt that a supernatural being created the universe and human beings.

Probably for fear that after this life (that is, after death) the Creator will ask people what they have done, especially their sins, people seek to determine how they can start now in humbling themselves before this supreme being called God.

Whereas some people humble themselves before God, asking him for forgiveness for their sins, others proceed by making sacrifices to appease God's anger. These two processes are put into practice in the world religions. Actually, most every religion does the best it can to find God. Each religion establishes doctrines to follow in order to succeed at finding God.

By this, we understand that people have invented several religions to reach God and to show their submission before him.

Human beings seek and use a lot of ways to reach God, but God himself established only a single way to reach human beings and save them from perdition. This way is Jesus.

This chapter will discuss the major world religions.

TABLE **9.1.** Time line of the world religions

1500 BC	AD 1000		500 BC	0	AD 500	AD 1000	AD 1500
Hinduism (ca. 1500 BC) Judaism (ca. 1440 BC)	Sikhism (ca. AD 1469)		Shinto (ca. 660 BC) Taoism (ca. 660 BC) Buddhism (ca. 563 BC) Confucianism (ca. 551 BC)	Christianity (ca. AD 30)*	Islam (ca. AD 622)		

* On the one hand, this date is technically correct, but on the other hand, a case could be made that Christianity, which is based on the good news of Jesus Christ, was in the mind of God from before "the creation of the world" (Eph. 1:4; see also 2 Tim. 1:9) and, in particular, soon after the fall of humanity (Gen. 3:15).

TABLE **9.2.** The relationship between God's holiness and our assurance

	The Christian gospel	The way to salvation in other religions
God's holiness	Upheld as being absolute	Denied, diminished, or disregarded
Basis for salvation	God has completed the work of salvation on our behalf through Jesus Christ	Human effort
Level of assurance	Complete assurance	No assurance

69

Definition of Religion

What is a religion? The definition of religion that we will be working from in *True Faith* is that it is a set of beliefs that answer the ultimate questions: What is ultimate reality? What is the nature of the world? What is the nature of humanity? What is humanity's primary problem? What happens after death?

Such a definition means that a religion does not necessarily include a belief in God, a set of rituals, or a class of clergy or priests. Secularism and Marxism are examples of what could be called religions in that they answer the ultimate questions, but they do not teach the existence of a supernatural realm or say anything about God.

To many people, the world religions are a confusing array of beliefs, practices, and histories. Unless a person is willing to devote a fair amount of time to studying the various religions, it is difficult to keep the distinctives of each straight, such as who founded which religion when, and what each believes. This chapter is to help you in this pursuit.

Concept of God

On the far left side of the spectrum are the monotheistic (one God) religions that say God is the transcendent Creator of the world, and as such he is distinct and separate from his creation.

On the right side of the spectrum are the monistic (God is a oneness) religions that emphasize God's immanence; they believe that God's essence and the world's essence are one and the same.

On the far right side, beyond the monistic religions, are those atheistic (no God) worldviews that deny God's existence. Yet atheism is similar to monism in that both say that ultimate reality is a oneness of substance. With monism, the substance is *spirit*; with atheism, it is *matter* (or energy).

In between the two extremes of the spectrum are the dualistic (two forces) and polytheistic (many gods) religions. There are two kinds of dualistic religions: competing and balancing. The competing dualistic religions have an affinity with the monotheistic religions, and the balancing dualistic religions are similar in some ways to monism.

The gods of the dualistic and polytheistic religions serve as intermediaries to the ultimate reality, or Supreme Being; they are not the ultimate reality itself. The ultimate reality is usually either monotheistic or monistic in nature. As such, the middle of the spectrum has relationships with the two opposing extremes (monotheism and monism/atheism).

Conversely, though, the folk forms of the monotheistic, monistic, and to some extent atheistic religions resemble polytheism. Thus, the two extremes of the spectrum have a relationship with the middle (polytheism).

View of Humanity

Other patterns are also present in the spectrum. To the left, for example, where God is separate from his creation (monotheism), there is more of an appreciation for the unique value of humanity as compared to the rest of creation.

TABLE **9.3.** The spectrum of religions and religious beliefs

	Monotheism	Competing dualism	Polytheism	Balancing dualism	Monism	Atheism
Concept of God	One transcendent God	Two opposing gods	Many gods	Two opposing but interacting and balancing forces	An impersonal oneness	No god
Primary examples	Judaism, Christianity, Islam	Zoroastrianism	So-called tribal religions, Santeria, voodoo, Shinto, and any form of a "folk" religion	Tao-ism—the yin–yang concept	Hinduism, Buddhism, Sikhism, Sufism, the New Age movement	Secular humanism, Marxism, Confucianism
View of humanity	Part of creation, but different in kind from the animals	Made to join in the battle against evil	Can be influenced and even possessed by the spirits	A microcosm of the two interacting forces	Caught in the illusion of separateness, but identical in essence to the oneness	A complex form of matter

	Monotheism	Competing dualism	Polytheism	Balancing dualism	Monism	Atheism
Humanity's primary problem	Breaking God's law (Judaism); rebellion against God (Christianity); failing to seek God's guidance (Islam)	Choosing to do evil	Angering the gods	Living out of alignment with the ways of nature	Ignorance of one's innate divinity	Superstition and irrational thinking
The solution	Living according to God's law (Judaism); being justified by faith based on God's saving work (Christianity); seeking God's guidance (Islam)	Choosing to do right	Appeasing the gods	Living in harmony with the ways of nature	Realizing that our essence is the same as the oneness (enlightenment)	Applying rational thinking to our problems
The afterlife	The person continues in existence in either heaven or hell.	The person continues in existence in either heaven or hell.	Sometimes the person advances to the spirit world.	Usually the person advances to some form of the spirit world.	Either the person is reincarnates or merges into the impersonal oneness.	The person ceases to exist.

To the right (monism/atheism), there is less of a sense that humanity is unique and of special value, as humanity is seen as being different from the rest of nature only in degree, not in kind.

Humanity's Primary Problem

With respect to humanity's primary problem—sin—to the left of the spectrum there is the sense that humanity fails to live up to the moral precepts of a holy God.

To the right, on the other hand, the issue of sin has to do with ignorance, whether of one's true divinity (Hinduism) or of a rational solution to humanity's problems (secular humanism).

The Afterlife

With respect to the afterlife, to the left of the spectrum, the person continues to exist as a conscious individual after death, either in a heaven-like or a hell-like place.

To the right of the spectrum (monism), the goal is for the individual to lose his or her individuality by merging into the impressionable oneness of ultimate reality.

At the extreme right (atheism), because the person consists only of matter, he or she ceases to exist at the point of death as a conscious entity altogether.[70]

Conflicting Worldviews

In *Understanding the Times*, renowned worldview expert David Noebel lists four worldviews that exert the most influence over people in Western society. According to Noebel, the dominant worldviews include humanism, utopianism, New Age, and biblical Christianity. He writes, "The term *worldview* refers to any ideology, philosophy, theology, movement, or religion that provides an overarching approach to understanding God, the world, and man's relations to God and the world."[71]

TABLE **9.4.** Four Western worldview models[71]

	Humanism	Utopianism	New Age	Biblical Christianity
Sources	Humanist Manifestos I and II	Writings of Karl Marx and Vladimir Lenin	Writings of David Spangler, Marilyn Ferguson, and the like	Bible
Theology	Atheism	Atheism	Pantheism	Theism
Philosophy	Naturalism	Dialectical materialism	Nonnaturalism	Supernaturalism
Ethics	Relativism	Proletariat morality	Relativism	Absolutes
Biology	Darwinian evolution	Darwinian/ punctuated evolution	Darwinian/ punctuated evolution	Creation
Psychology	Self-actualization	Behaviorism	Collective consciousness	Mind–body
Sociology	Nontraditional family	Abolition of home, church, and state	Nontraditional home, church, and state	Traditional home, church, and state
Law	Positive law	Positive law	Self-law	Biblical and natural law
Politics	World government (globalism)	New World Order (new civilization)	New Age order	Justice, freedom, and order
Economics	Socialism	Socialism	Universal enlightened production	Stewardship of property
History	Historical evolution	Historical materialism	Evolutionary godhood	Historical resurrection

Noebel contends that every worldview contains distinct perspectives in ten areas: theology, philosophy, ethics, biology, psychology, sociology, law, politics, economics, and history (see table 1.1). All ten disciplines are interrelated, which means that in each case psychology is intertwined with one or more of the other disciplines, including theology.

Ironically enough, prominent humanist Bertrand Russell (1872–1970) inadvertently supported the idea that one cannot separate religion and philosophy.

Every philosophy assumes some view of God, a view we can fit loosely into one of the following categories:

- There is one God (Christianity, Judaism, and Islam).
- There is no God (humanism, utopianism).
- There are many gods (pantheism).
- All is god (New Age).[72]

Humanist Psychology

According to Noebel, humanist psychology adheres to three major assumptions: "Man is good by nature and therefore perfectible; society and its social institutions are responsible for man's evil acts; and mental health can be restored to everyone who gets in touch with his inner 'good' self."[73] This brand of psychology denies the existence of the supernatural and focuses on strictly material entities such as the brain or stimuli and responses to stimuli (that is, behaviorism). Behaviorists believe that human thoughts and personality are determined solely by biological process in the brain.

Utopianism Psychology

Like humanists, utopianists view the mind as material and comprised of merely a series of physical brain activities. Human development is a march toward the perfect social order (which is utopianism) and away from free will. Human beings can be educated and controlled so that they only do good, leading to the perfection of the human race. Proponents of this view take some of the teachings of B. F. Skinner (1904–1990), Ivan P. Pavlov (1849–1936), and John B. Watson (1878–1958), but they modify them as they synthesize behaviorism with free will.

New Age Psychology

The fastest-growing philosophy/religion in the United States is the one known as New Age. The goal of New Age psychology is to achieve higher consciousness, thereby speeding up the work of evolution toward a collective God-consciousness. According to New Age philosophy, you don't need a messiah to die for your sins and give you life; you simply need enlightenment. This view is a Westernized version of Eastern mysticism in which God is impersonal and part of everything. A rock is God, an ant is God, a person is God, and the earth is God. The radical segment of the environmental movement is spurred on by this belief when it regards humans to be of no more value than other entities, such as trees, animals, and the elements of nature. A rock is a tree is a human.

A Biblical Worldview

The American public is inundated with conflicting worldviews in the name of cultural diversity; it is reported daily by the media and is self-evident in our educational, political, and economic systems.

Even in religious circles, the pure beauty of what we possess in Jesus Christ and in the revelation of God's Word escapes many who consider themselves children of God. Commenting on these conflicting worldviews, Noebel puts the biblical perspective in words too profound to omit from this discussion. Thus we quote, with permission, his detailed presentation of the biblical worldview in relationship to the other worldviews:

Many people believe that when Christians confront other worldviews and attempt to speak to such "worldly" disciplines as politics, economics, biology, and law [we add psychology], they are overstepping their bounds. "Mind your own business," we are told. Jesus taught his followers, "You do not belong to the world, but I have chosen you out of the world" (John 15:19).

In the utopianist worldview, there is no acknowledgment of personal responsibility for sin; tragic events in life are due, rather, to society's structures. The cure for humanity's ills is to increase education, remove poverty, and eliminate oppression.

How, then, can the Christian justify his or her claim to a worldview that speaks to every facet of life? Shouldn't a Christian stick to spiritual matters and allow non-Christians to concentrate on the practical matters of running the world?

In short, isn't there a difference between the secular and the sacred? Not according to Dietrich Bonhoeffer, who says we should not distinguish between the two: "There are not two realities, but only one reality, and that is the reality of God, which has become manifest in Christ in the reality of the world."

From the biblical Christian perspective, the ten disciplines addressed in this text reflect various aspects of God and his creative or redemptive order. God created humankind with theological, philosophical, ethical, biological, etc., dimensions. We live and move and have our being (our very essence and existence) within and about these categories.

Why? Because that is the way God created us.

Such being the case, these categories are, from the Christian perspective, sacred and not secular. They are sacred because they are imprinted in the creative order. Both the early record of Genesis and the life of Jesus Christ reflect this truth.

For example, Genesis 1:1, "In the beginning God created the heavens and the earth," is value-laden with theological and philosophical ramifications. Genesis 2:9, "knowledge of good and evil," contains ethical ramifications; Genesis 1:21, "after their kind," biological; Genesis 2:7, "a living soul," psychological; Genesis 1:28, "be fruitful, and multiply, and fill the earth," sociological and ecological; Genesis 3:11, "I commended thee," legal; Genesis 9:6, "whoso sheddeth man's blood," political and legal; Genesis 1:29, "it shall be for food," economic; and Genesis 3:15, "enmity between thee and the woman," historical. All ten disciplines are addressed in just the first few chapters of the Bible because they manifest and accent certain aspects of the creative order.

Further, God manifests himself in the form of Christ in such a way as to underline the significance of each discipline. In theology, for example, Jesus Christ is "the fullness of the Godhead" (Col. 2:9); in philosophy, Christ is the Logos of God (John 1:1); in ethics,

Christ is "the true light" (John 1:9; John 3:19–20); in biology, Christ is "the life" (John 1:4; John 11:25; Col. 1:16); in psychology, Christ is "Savior" (Luke 1:46–47; Titus 2:13); in sociology,

Christ is "Son" (Luke 1:30–31; Isa. 9:6); in law, Christ is lawgiver (Gen. 49:10; Isa. 9:7); in politics, Christ is "King of kings and Lord of lords" (Rev. 19:16; 1 Tim. 6:15; Isa. 9:6; Luke 1:33); in economics, Christ is owner of all things (Ps. 24:1; Ps. 50:10–12; 1 Cor. 10:26); and in history, Christ is the Alpha and Omega (Rev. 1:8). The integration of these various categories into society has come to be known as Western civilization.

The Bible and the life of Jesus Christ provide the Christian with the basis for a complete worldview. Indeed, the Christian gains a perspective so comprehensive that he is commended to "take captive every thought to make it obedient to Christ" (2 Cor. 10:5).[74]

Once we have captured all thoughts and made them obedient to Christ, we are to use these thoughts to "demolish arguments and every pretension that sets itself up against the knowledge of God" (2 Cor. 10:4–5). When nations and people forget God (see Psalm 2), they experience what humankind has experienced in the twentieth century. Nazism and communism, two major movements bereft of the knowledge of God, cost the human race millions of lives. Whittaker Chambers says that communism's problem is not a problem of economics, but of atheism: "Faith is the central problem of this age." Alexander Solzhenitsyn echoes him: "Men have forgotten God."

The apostle Paul insists in Colossians 2 that those who have "received Christ Jesus the Lord" (Col. 2:6) are to be rooted and built up in him, strengthened in the faith as they were taught (Col. 2:7).

While the Christian works to strengthen his faith or worldview, he must see to it that no one takes him "captive through hollow and deceptive philosophy, which depends on human tradition and the basic principles of this world rather than on Christ" (Col. 2:8). From the Christian point of view, humanism, utopianism, and New Age represent "the basic principles of this world." They are based on the wisdom of this world, and not on Christ.[75]

CHAPTER 10

Religious Beliefs

As we have seen, religions are supposed to provide a place where people may gather to see how to beg, adore, and praise God, and ask him for forgiveness. Every single religion adopts a belief so the congregation will be approved before God. As for religions, beliefs are numerous. Every single religion adopts a doctrine, a belief. Human beings have adopted different beliefs, but God himself has established the only way for humankind to be saved: through faith in Jesus Christ. In this chapter we will outline the beliefs of the major world religions.

Religious belief is the belief in the reality of the mythological, supernatural, or spiritual aspects of life. Religious belief is distinct from religious practice or religious behaviors, as some believers do not practice religion and some practitioners do not believe in the religion they practice. Religious beliefs, being derived from ideas that are exclusive to religion, often relate to the existence, characteristics, and worship of a deity or deities; divine intervention in the universe and human life; or the deontological explanations for the values and practices centered on the teachings of a spiritual leader or group. In contrast to other belief systems, religious beliefs are usually codified.[76]

Animism

Definition of Animism

The term *animism* comes from the Latin word *anima*, which means "soul" or "breath." As such, it refers to that which empowers or gives life to something. It follows, then, that animism is the religion that sees the physical world as interpenetrated by spiritual forces—both personal and impersonal—to the extent that objects carry spiritual significance and events have spiritual causes.

Thus, if there is an accident, or if someone is sick, there are spiritual reasons behind such things that must be taken into consideration. Otherwise, the cause behind the accident or the sickness cannot be fully understood or remedied.

The animistic form of a religion is called a folk religion, such as "folk Hinduism" or "folk Islam." The tendency for people to gravitate toward a folk form of their religion explains why many people who come from a country with a Hindu or a Buddhist heritage do not believe the way the "textbook description of their religion says they should believe."[77]

Common Animistic Beliefs and Practices

One God Beyond the Many Spirits

Most animistic religions teach that there is one Supreme Being who exists beyond the intermediate ancestors, spirits, and gods. This god is either by nature monistic (an impersonal oneness) or monotheistic (a personal being). This Supreme Being is either too far removed from his creation or too abstract to be known.

It might be that the Supreme Being uses the intermediate spirits to do his will and to serve as his representatives, but he still cannot be approached or known directly.

The Ultimate–Immediate Division

The animist views the "formal" religions—Christianity, Islam, Hinduism, etc.—as being relevant with respect to the *ultimate* issues, such as who God is, what humanity's problem is, and what happens after death. They see those religions as being irrelevant, however, when it comes to addressing the *immediate* issues of everyday life. This division between the ultimate and the immediate realms is why an animist can be a practicing Catholic but also consult a shaman (an animistic priest who communicates with the spirits) in order to be healed.

The Spiritual Realm

According to animism, the spiritual realm with which we must deal consists of both personal spirit-beings and an impersonal spiritual energy.

The Personal Spirit-Beings

Animists believe there are two different kind of spirit-beings: those that have been embodied (such as deceased ancestors) and those that have not (such as spirits and gods) (Van Rheenen, 259). The spirits are often seen as being mediators between human beings and God, able to intercede on our behalf. But to mediate on our behalf, they must first be given homage (Henry, 8).

Spirit-beings possess specific powers and are localized geographically. Some spirits exert their powers over human endeavors (such as a business venture, a marriage, community relations, or war), while others exert their powers over aspects of nature (such as storms, the seas, or fields).

TABLE 10.1. Differences between the personal spirit-beings of animism and the God of the Bible

The personal spirit-beings of animism	The God of the Bible
Limited to one geographic location	Not limited geographically; God of all the earth and the universe (Acts 17:24)
Have power over various aspects of nature	Has power over all things (Acts 17:24)
Depend on our sacrifices	Doesn't depend on our sacrifices because he has created all things (Acts 17:25) and because he has provided on our behalf the "once and for all" sacrifice (Heb. 9:24–10:14)

An Impersonal Spiritual Force

In addition to teaching about the personal spirit-beings, animistic religions teach that there is an impersonal spiritual energy that infuses special objects, words, and rituals. Such energy gives these objects the power that people need to accomplish their desires.

Animists will often attribute magical powers to an object. For example, the following is a description of a technique for how adherents of folk Islam make a fetish out of the words of the Quran, their sacred scripture:

> One aspect of fetish-making involves writing a verse from the Koran that is relevant to the problem or concern of the person on a piece of paper in water-soluble ink. Before the paper is put inside the fetish, the marabout [a Muslim leader] dips it in water so the ink dissolves. Then the person who will wear the fetish drinks the water, thinking that by doing so the message will be internalized. (Quicksall, 10–11)

TABLE 10.2. Difference between the impersonal spiritual force of animism and the God of the Bible

The impersonal spiritual force of animism	The God of the Bible
The spiritual forces can be manipulated according to the person's will.	God is not moved or manipulated by charms or rituals. That which moves God is a repentant and humble heart before him (Ps. 51:16–17; Prov. 21:3).
The spiritual forces can be used for either good or evil purposes.	God is holy and hates that which is evil (Ps. 5:4). The Bible says, moreover, that the "sacrifice of the wicked is detestable—how much more so when brought with evil intent" (Prov. 21:27)!

The Concept of Sin

Animists are not concerned so much about offending the supreme God; instead, their concern is of a more immediate nature in that they are afraid of offending the local spirits. They realize that an offended spirit will inevitably exact retribution in the form of injury, sickness, failure, or interpersonal strife.

For example, Migene Gonzalez-Wippler, a follower of the animistic religion called Santeria, knew that Eleggua—the name of her god—required his followers to perform a simple offering to him every Monday morning. One Monday, however, Gonzalez-Wippler forgot to perform the ritual offering because she had just returned from a tiring trip and was busy unpacking. As she was walking around her apartment putting things away, she cut her leg on the sharp edge of the handle to the cabinet in which she kept the idol representing her god. "When I pulled back my leg," writes Gonzalez-Wippler, "the door of the cabinet swung open, and there, looking up at me with aggrieved eyes, was Eleggua's image" (Gonzalez-Wippler, 236). Gonzalez Wippler understood the cut to be the price that her god had inflicted on her for having neglected him.

Van Rheenen writes, "Animists live in continual fear of these [spiritual] powers" (Van Rheenen, 20).

Contacting the Spirits

Animists are more inclined than Westerners to attribute spiritual causes to their sickness or bad fortune. Divination, which is "the practice of giving information ... which is not available by natural means" (Henry, 71), is the means by which a person discovers either how he or she has offended some spirit or which person has cast a curse on him or her. Divination is also the means by which one discovers how to resolve the problem—either what the spirit requires or how to throw a counter-curse.

Methods of divination are numerous and varied; they include using tarot cards, palm reading, referring to the I Ching, tea-leaf reading, observing how feathers fall, the throwing of cowry shells, using astrology, using omens, dowsing (see Weldon), performing rituals, engaging in necromancy (contacting the dead), and interpreting dreams and visions. Divination can also be used to discover when it is the most fortuitous time to do such things as ask for someone's hand in marriage, begin constructing a building, sign a contract, or make an investment.

Rev. Silas Kanyabigega, DMin

The Afterlife

There is no universal and consistent doctrine throughout the many animistic religions as to what happens to a person after death. Many see the person's spirit as continuing to exist after death either by being reincarnated into another life on earth or by "graduating" to a higher spiritual level.

The belief is also common that the person who dies becomes an ancestral spirit. The family must then continue to give offerings to that ancestor because it has the power either to protect or to plague the family.[78]

TABLE 10.3. The animistic and Christian worldviews contrasted

	Animism	Christianity
God	God exists, but he is beyond our abilities to know him or communicate with him	God exists, and although he is beyond our comprehension, he is nevertheless knowable; and he has made himself known to us through Jesus Christ and the Bible (Heb. 1:1–2).
Ultimate/ immediate issues	Formal religions are concerned only with the *ultimate* issues of sin and salvation, but animism offers the power to cope with the *immediate* everyday needs.	The God of Christianity is concerned *both with the ultimate and the immediate* issues. God desires to provide not only for our eternal needs but also for our daily needs (1 Peter 5:7).
The spirits	The spirits are seen either as being intermediaries between us and God or as representatives of God.	The spirits are deceptive; they seek to take the place of God in our lives.

	Animism	Christianity
The powers of the spirits	The spirits and the instruments of magic have the power either to do harm to others or to bring benefit to us.	The spirits do have power, but our utilizing such power leads to bondage. God has demonstrated through Jesus Christ that he is greater than the spirits and magic, because "the one who is in you is greater than the one who is in the world" (1 John 4:4; see also Exod. 8:18) and he has "disarmed the powers and authorities" (Col. 2:15). Submitting to God brings freedom (John 8:32–36), not bondage.

Buddhism

Buddhism among the Nations

It is estimated that the number of adherents of Buddhism comprise around 6 percent of the world's population (Barrett, 25), although this figure is difficult to gauge because of Buddhism's ability to assimilate itself into a culture and to influence that culture's underlying beliefs.

Theravada Buddhism (the distinctions between the major forms of Buddhism will be covered later) exists primarily in Myanmar, Cambodia, Laos, Sri Lanka, and Thailand.

Mahayana Buddhism exists primarily in mainland China, Hong Kong, Japan, Taiwan, and Vietnam.

Vajrayana, or Tantric, Buddhism exists primarily in Bhutan, Mongolia, and Tibet.

The Founding of Buddhism

Buddhism was founded by Siddhartha Gautama during the sixth century BC. His life (563–483 BC) coincides with the time when the people of Judah were exiled in Babylon.

Buddha's life can be divided into three periods: enjoyment (563–534 BC),[79] inquiry (534–528 BC), and enlightenment (528–483 BC).[80]

The Spread of and the Splits within Buddhism

For two centuries, Buddhism did not spread beyond the borders of India. Then came King Ashoka, who ruled India from 274 BC to 232 BC. Ashoka was a warrior king who, during one battle, became so revolted by the bloodshed that he resolved to renounce all such fighting. He subsequently converted to Buddhism and devoted himself and his resources to its propagation. Ashoka commissioned Buddhist missionaries to go to other parts of India, as well as to Syria, Egypt, Cyrene, Greece, Sri Lanka, Burma (now Myanmar), and Thailand.[81]

The Beliefs of Buddhism

As we have already seen, there are obviously extreme variations within the religion known as Buddhism. Nevertheless, there are some beliefs that most Buddhists share. These common beliefs are contained in the most basic of Buddhist teachings: the Four Noble Truths.

The First Noble Truth

Life consists of suffering (*dukkha*). This concept of suffering includes the experiences of pain, misery, sorrow, and unfulfillment.

The Second Noble Truth

Everything is impermanent and ever-changing (the doctrine of *anicca*). We suffer because we desire those things that are impermanent.

The Third Noble Truth

The way to liberate oneself from suffering is by eliminating all desire. We must stop craving that which is impermanent.

The Fourth Noble Truth

Desire can be eliminated by following the Eightfold Path, which consists of eight points.

The Eightfold Path

The eight points can be categorized according to three major sections:

Wisdom (Panna)
1. Right understanding
2. Right thought

Ethical Conduct (Sila)
3. Right speech
4. Right action
5. Right livelihood

Mental Discipline (Samadhi)
6. Right effort
7. Right awareness
8. Right meditation

These eight points are not steps that must be done in sequential order. Instead, they are attitudes and actions that are to be developed simultaneously with each other (Rahula, 46).

The first two points, moreover, serve as the foundation from which the other points flow. When one has right understanding, for instance, he or she sees the universe as impermanent and illusory.

As a person attains such a literally selfless perspective, he or she finds the power to speak well of others (right speech), to obey Buddhism's moral commands or abstentions (right action), and to avoid making his or her living through an occupation that breaks the moral precepts of Buddhism (right livelihood).

At the basis of the concept of ethical conduct are the *sila*, or moral precepts. These precepts include the commands to refrain from the following things:

1. The taking of life (all forms, not just human)
2. Stealing
3. Immoral sexual behavior (monks must be celibate)

4. Lying
5. The ingesting of intoxicants.

While the sila address one's actions, the *samadhi* (mental discipline) addresses one's attitudes and state of awareness. *Samadhi* is defined as a deep state of consciousness "in which all sense of personal identity ceases" (Rice, 310). Through right effort, one prevents evil thoughts from entering the mind; through right awareness, one is especially conscious of the events in one's life; and through right meditation, one can attain the bliss of enlightenment.

Buddha's *immediate* goal was to eliminate the cause of suffering. His *ultimate* goal, though, was to become liberated from the cycle of death and rebirth (samsara) by teaching how we can cease craving and thereby eliminate our attachment to and beliefs in the existence of the illusory self.

As one is successful in eliminating such attachment, the effects of karma will have nothing to attach themselves to, which releases the individual from the realm of illusion. At that moment of enlightenment, the person achieves the state of nirvana, the ultimate goal for the Buddhist, and Buddhism's equivalent of salvation.

Nirvana

Buddha described nirvana (Pali, *nibbana*) with the following words:

> There is a sphere which is neither earth, nor water, nor fire, nor air, which is not the sphere of the infinity of space, nor the sphere of the infinity of consciousness, the sphere of nothingness, the sphere of perception, or non-perception, which is neither this world, neither sun nor moon. I deny that it is coming or going, enduring, death, or birth. It is only the end of suffering (Powell, 28).

Achieving nirvana does not mean that the person is annihilated when entering such a state, because, as Buddha reasoned, there never existed any person to be annihilated in the first place.

In regard to the samsara cycle (reincarnation), whereas Hinduism would posit an individual essence that is continuous from lifetime to lifetime, Buddhism does not teach that such a continuous essence exists. According to Buddha, no self exists that is continuous throughout the samsara cycle. Instead, each individual consists of a combination of five "aggregates" called *skandhas*, which include the physical body, emotions, perception, volition, and consciousness (Ch'en, 44). Death causes these aggregates, or parts, to be dismantled. Much like a car, the individual ceases to be a cohesive unit when taken apart piece by piece.

Faith in Buddhism

Faith (Pali: Saddhā; Sanskrit: Śraddhā) is an important constituent element of the teachings of Gautama Buddha—in both the Theravada and Mahayana traditions. The teachings of Buddha were originally recorded in the Pali language; the word *saddhā* is generally translated as "faith."

In the teachings, saddhā is often described as the following:

1. A conviction that something is
2. A determination to accomplish one's goals
3. A sense of joy deriving from the other two.

While faith in Buddhism does not imply blind faith, Buddhist practice nevertheless requires a degree of trust, primarily in the spiritual attainment of Gautama Buddha. Faith in Buddhism centers on the understanding that the Buddha is an awakened being, on an understanding of his superior role as teacher, on the truth of his dharma (spiritual teachings), and on his sangha (community of spiritually developed followers). Faith in Buddhism can be summarized as faith in the Three Jewels: the Buddha, dharma, and the sangha. It is intended to lead to the goal of enlightenment, or bodhi, and nirvana. Volitionally, faith implies a resolute and courageous act of will. It combines the steadfast resolution that one will do something with the self-confidence that one can do it.

As a counter to any form of blind faith, the Buddha's teachings include those that are part of the Kalama Sutra, which exhorts his disciples to investigate any teaching and to live by what is learned and accepted, rather than believing in something simply because it is taught.[82]

TABLE 10.4. Buddhism and Christianity contrasted

	Theravada Buddhism	Mahayana Buddhism	Christianity
God	Nirvana, an abstract void	Nirvana, an abstract void, but also an undifferentiated Buddha essence	A personal God who is self-existent and changeless
Humanity	An impermanent collection of aggregates	An impermanent collection of aggregates. For some, personal existence continues for a while in the Pure Land.	Made in God's image. Personal existence has value. We continue to exist as persons after death.
The problem	We suffer because we desire that which is temporary, which causes us to continue in the illusion of the existence of the individual self.	Same as Theravada	We suffer because of the consequences of our sin, but we also suffer because, being made in God's image, we are fulfilled only when we are in a relationship with our Creator God. Even though we are most fulfilled when in relationship with God, we have rebelled against him and are thus alienated from him.
The solution	To cease all desire in order to realize the nonexistence of the self, thus finding permanence.	To become aware of the Buddha-nature within.	To be forgiven by and reconciled with God. We find permanence in the immutability of God.

	Theravada Buddhism	Mahayana Buddhism	Christianity
The means	Self-reliance. We must follow the Middle Path and accrue karmic merit.	Self-reliance. The means vary, from following the Eightfold Path, to emptying the mind, to accruing merit by performing rituals, to realizing the Buddha-nature within, to depending on the merits of a bodhisattva.	Reliance on God. We must repent of our sins and trust in the saving work of Jesus Christ.
The outcome	To enter nirvana, where the ego is extinguished.	Varies, from returning as a bodhisattva in order to guide others, to entering nirvana, to living in the Pure Land from which one can enter nirvana.	Our existence as individuals survives death. We are fulfilled as we are in eternal fellowship with a loving and personal God.

TABLE 10.5. Buddha and Jesus contrasted

Buddha according to Theravada Buddhism	Jesus
Buddha did not claim to have a special relationship with God. In fact, Buddha did not consider the matter of God's existence to be important, because he did not think it pertained to the issue of how to escape suffering.	Jesus did claim to have a special relationship with God (John 3:16; John 6:44; John 10:30; John 14:6, 9).
Buddha claimed to point to the way by which we could escape suffering and attain enlightenment.	Jesus claimed to be the Way by which we could receive salvation and eternal life (John 14:6; John 5:35).
Buddha taught that the way to eliminate suffering was by eliminating desire.	Jesus taught that the solution to suffering is found not in eliminating desire but in having right desire (Matt. 5:6).

TABLE 10.6. The bodhisattvas and Jesus contrasted

The bodhisattvas according to Mahayana Buddhism	Jesus
There are many bodhisattvas.	There has been only one incarnation of the Son of God.
The bodhisattvas were motivated out of a sense of their own compassion for the world. Their compassion is not a reflection, however, of the void's feelings toward the world.	Jesus is the unique demonstration of God's love for the world (John 3:16; Rom. 5:8; 1 John 4:10).
The bodhisattvas view the physical world as an illusion to be escaped.	The Bible says that Jesus created the universe and that it was declared good (John 1:3; Gen. 1:31).
The bodhisattvas had to overcome their sin (i.e., attachment to the self, ignorance) during the process of going through numerous lifetimes.	Jesus was sinless from the very beginning; it did not take a process to make him sinless (Matt. 27:4; Luke 23:41; 2 Cor. 5:21; Heb. 4:15).

83

Confucianism

Number of Adherents

Confucianism is not a formal religion in the conventional sense. It is a religious belief system that forms the values that are implicit to most Asian people.

This massive group of people includes the Chinese, Japanese, Korean, and Vietnamese. It is estimated that there are 1.3 billion Chinese, 126 million Japanese, 26 million Koreans, and 74 million Vietnamese. If we take about 90 percent of this total who are consciously or unconsciously influenced by this Confucian worldview, the total number would be around 1.5 billion.

East Asia is experiencing a resurgence of interest in Confucianism. Marxism is on the decline in China, and the Chinese people are looking for a spiritual foundation for their values that is both contemporary and Chinese. The rulers of China are not opposed to this resurgence of Confucianism because it emphasizes loyalty.

The Influence of Confucianism

The Confucian work ethic is regarded by many as the basis for the amazingly rapid economic growth in East Asia today. It is safe to say that approximately one-quarter of the world's population lives under such a work ethic.

First, the Confucian work ethic entails a strong commitment to the family. Loyalties in the family are established during the present lifetime and are then continued after death.

Second, it is founded on a strong moral ethic of practicing virtues, giving words of wisdom, doing good works, and having the attitudes of loyalty, trustworthiness, and respect.

Third, it is oriented toward the "eternal," but in a temporal sense. Such an idea sounds contradictory, but the concept of the eternal in Confucianism is not that of the continuation of the person in a transcendent life in heaven. Instead, it is the continuation of the person's ethical influence on the thoughts and values of his or her descendants. As Chan writes, the ancestors' "influence [is] exerted not through their power but through their moral example and inspiration."

The Founding Philosophy of Confucianism

The challenge that ancient Chinese people faced was to unite and harmonize the various tribes that populated the vast plains along the Yellow River. During the Chou dynasty (1122–897 BC), the Duke of Chou solved this problem by establishing the ritual music culture, which was a rationalistic humanistic order that emphasized the need for harmony in human relationships (for further discussion on the ritual music culture, see "The History of Taoism" later in this chapter).

In the ancient scripture called the Book of Rites, it is stated that "music can promote harmony." Yu Tze, one of Confucius's disciples, stated that "the function of rites is harmony." The ritual music culture was a cultural order of harmony that lent itself to the integration of many different tribes coexisting with each other.

The political ideal that was hoped would be established by the ritual music culture was not realized, however, partly because the Duke of Lu failed to follow the prescribed norms.

By the time of Confucius (551–479 BC), this culture had collapsed, taking virtue and social order with it. This collapse gave rise to the problem of how to reconstruct the ideal cultural-political order.

Confucius, which is the Latinized version of the Chinese name K'ung Fu-tzu ("Grand Master K'ung"), was the prime minister of the state of Lu and a well-educated intellectual who was passionately committed to maintaining the ritual music culture. In an effort to restore the cultural-political order of the day, he left his home at the age of fifty-six and traveled extensively throughout China, hoping to persuade the lords and dukes to follow the rites of the ritual music culture. Confucius's hope was "to bring peace and security to the people." His quest to establish a cultural-political order in which there was such peace and security failed, however. So, at the age of sixty-eight, he returned home to teach and to write. (At seventy-three, he died.)

As a result of his failure to change the culture, Confucius asked himself the following questions: Does the failure to reconstruct a harmonious cultural order mean that the concepts of virtue or goodness are not eternal and transcendent? Are good and evil merely relative? If not, what then are the foundations of virtue and goodness? Thus, the problem became a philosophical and metaphysical one: What is the foundation of virtue and goodness in an age of confusion?

While searching for an answer to this problem, Confucius went to a deep level with respect to human nature—the moral level—in order to establish harmony. In other words, Confucius called for each person to reflect seriously on his or her moral decisions and to act responsibly in the face of adversity.

This sense of moral responsibility served as the foundation for the ritual music culture, but that culture collapsed. Confucius was finding, though, that the foundation for such moral responsibility still existed in the moral consciousness of the individual, specifically in the *jen*. Jen, which can be translated simply as "humanity," refers to the ideal goodness, or "good nature," that resides within each individual.

This "good nature" is the source from which all virtues flow. Through jen, each individual has the potential to actualize his or her good nature and thereby realize an ideal state of life.[84]

TABLE 10.7. The three aspects of jen

The goal	Jen is the goal of an ideal humanity that is symbolized in the Analects by the terms "superior person," "gentry intellectual," and a "person of jen." It refers to an ideal whereby the individual has actualized his or her full potential and is manifesting his or her moral perfection.
The process	Jen is the human process that is needed to reach the goal of the ideal person. Included in this process are the practices of self-reflection, self-cultivation, and moral responsibility.
The foundation	Jen is the true nature that resides within each person. According to Confucianism, this true nature is good.

The early Confucianist worldview is summarized in table 10.8.

TABLE 10.8. Early Confucianist worldview

True humanity	Jen ("true humanity") is the basic human quality that is originally good. It provides the source and foundation for all virtues and rites.
The mandate from heaven	Jen is the moral "mandate from heaven. The normal understanding of the phrase *mandate from heaven* would imply an anthropomorphic kind of God who makes moral decrees. Such is not the case in Confucianism, however. Instead, the mandate from heaven refers to the natural law or moral order within things.
The basis for harmony	The harmonious way of living must be based on the person's realization and actualization of jen.

The Confucian Canon

The canon of Confucianism begins with the five classics: the I Ching (the Book of Changes), Shi (the Book of Poetry and Songs), Shu (the Book of Documents), Li (the Book of Rites), and Chun-Chiu (the Book of Spring and Autumn, or the Chronicles of History).

Since the Book of Rites and the Book of Spring and Autumn contain three books of commentary each, the total number of classics is nine. Adding another four books—the Analects, Meng-Zi (the Book of Mencius), Erh-Ya (the Book of Ancient Words), and Hsiao-Ching (the Book of Filial Piety)—makes for the grand total of thirteen classics, or thirteen scriptures. These constitute the canon of Confucian scripture.

The Neoconfucianists of the thirteenth century considered the books Meng-Zi, Chung Yung, and Da Hsueh as the orthodox interpretation of Confucius's thoughts. Chu Hsi, a Neoconfucian teacher, grouped these three books with the Analects (the collections of the sayings of Confucius) and, by doing so, provided a program for learning and self-cultivation. This collection is known as the Four Books. They became the official standard for educators after the fourteenth century AD.

These four books and Chu Hsi's commentaries on them were the basis of the civil service examinations from 1313 to 1905, replacing other classics in importance and influence (Chan, 51).

TABLE 10.9. The contemporary Confucianist worldview

God	Before the time of Confucius, God was spoken of as personal being and was called Ti or Shang-ti. Confucius, however, spoke of ultimate reality as *Tien*, which has the less personal meaning of "heaven" (Chan, 16).
The mandate from heaven	The moral order of things within nature. If there is to be harmony within a culture, then humanity will strive to abide by this moral order.
Central concern	The central concern of Confucianism is to affirm humanity's inherent goodness and to look for a way to actualize it.
Human nature	Human nature is considered to be basically good and potentially perfect. Evil comes only when we are forced to act in an evil way or when we allow our minds to fall toward such an evil inclination.
The way to actualization	The way to actualize this goodness is through education, self-reflection, and self-cultivation, and by behaving in accordance with the established culture.
The world	The world is perceived as a place where one's purpose is to practice goodness, to love one's fellows, and to work hard so as to nourish the earth. A person who actualizes his or her inner goodness will be a coworker of heaven. He or she will also be a person who is creative in bringing goodness to human beings and to other things. Such a person will then realize the harmony that is supposed to exist between humanity and nature.
Heaven	The attaining of heaven in the Christian sense is not a concern in Confucianism. Instead, heaven exists only as the foundation for the creativity that manifests itself in the whole world. Heaven is sometimes perceived as personal, but at other times it is simply a creative moral power and an impersonal principle.

Hinduism

Hinduism among the Nations

It is estimated that adherents of Hinduism make up around 13 percent of the world's population. Such a figure must not be taken as hard-and-fast, however, because the influences of Hinduism's teachings go far beyond those who would actually label themselves as Hindu.

The vast majority of Hindus—some 700 million—live in India, where they account for 82 percent of the population.

Hindus also comprise a significant portion of the population in seven other countries: Bangladesh (11 percent), Bhutan (25 percent), Fiji (41 percent), Mauritius (50 percent), Nepal (89 percent), Sri Lanka (15 percent), Surinam (27 percent), and Trinidad (25 percent) (Johnstone). More than two million Hindus live on the Indonesian island of Bali, although the country of Indonesia as a whole is predominantly Muslim.

Nepal is the only nation where Hinduism is the state religion.

There are more than one million Hindus in North America.

Introducing Hinduism

The origins of Hinduism can be traced back to around 1500 BC in what is now India. It began as a polytheistic and ritualistic religion. The rituals were at first simple enough to be performed by the head of the household. As the centuries passed, however, they became increasingly complex. As a result, it became necessary to create a priestly class and to train those priests to perform the rituals correctly. During this time, the Vedas were written to give the priests instructions as to how to perform the rituals.

As a result of the emphasis on the rituals, the priests became the sole means by which the people could approach and appease the gods. Because of their position as mediators with the gods, the priests gained an increasing amount of power and control over the lives of the people. Finally, around 600 BC, the people revolted. The form of Hinduism that emerged after the revolt emphasized the importance of internal meditation as opposed to the external rituals.

Between 800 BC and 300 BC, the Upanishads were written. The Upanishads, also called the Vedanta ("the end or conclusion of the Vedas"), are the Hindu equivalent of the New Testament. The Upanishads expound the idea that behind the many gods stands one reality, which is called Brahman. Brahman is an impersonal monistic ("all is one") force. The highest form of Brahman is called *nirguna,* which means "without attributes or qualities."

Even after the Upanishads were written, the Hindu concept of God continued to develop. It developed in the direction of God being personal. Nirguna Brahman became *saguna Brahman,* which is "Brahman with attributes." This personified form of Brahman is also called *Ishvara.*

According to Hindu tradition, Ishvara became known to humanity through the *trimurti* (literally, "three manifestations") of Brahman. Those manifestations include Brahma (the Creator), Vishnu (the Preserver), and Siva (the Destroyer). Each of the three deities has at least one *devi,* or divine spouse.

Ishvara became personified even further through the ten mythical incarnations of Vishnu, called avatars. The forms of these incarnations include that of animals (for example, a fish, a tortoise, and a boar) and of persons (for example, Rama, Krishna, and Buddha). Epics such as the Ramayana and the Mahabharata, the latter of which includes the popular Bhagavad Gita, tell the stories of these myths. Beyond the principal deities of the trimurti and the avatars, it is estimated that there are 330 million other gods in Hinduism.

Besides the religion's various concepts of God, Hinduism can also be divided along the lines of whether the physical universe is considered to be real or illusory (maya). The nondualists (*advaita*) see Brahman alone as being real and the world as illusory. The qualified nondualists (*vishishtadvaita*) affirm the reality of both Brahman and the universe in that the universe is extended from the being of Brahman. And the dualists (*dvaita*) see Brahman and the universe as being two distinct realities.

In the course of its history, Hinduism has spawned three other religious movements that have since become world religions: Jainism, Buddhism, and Sikhism.

The Beliefs of Hinduism

Faith in Hinduism evokes the conscious awareness of humanity to realize its sacredness and to know we are all the children of God. Hinduism teaches that it is the one universal breath that unites us all in our aspiring journey in the quest for the eternal truth. The universe is one family that is sustained by the supreme consciousness, which is compassionately seeking the goodwill, harmony, and welfare of all living beings. The true essence and soul of all religions is the love of God and the practice of righteousness in our thoughts, actions, and expressions—which is our primordial heritage. *Ahimsa*, also referred to as nonviolence, is the fundamental tenet of Hinduism. It advocates harmonious and peaceful coexistence, and evolutionary growth in grace and wisdom, for all of humankind unconditionally. Life's true values inspire us to realize that with the pure intent of our energy, we create, and that with the pureness of creation, we are all energized. A faithful Hindu learns of the oneness of evolution and comes to understand that God shines as the soul in different bodies. God makes every form that he or she creates to shine forth resplendently with his or her divine illusion. The indomitable willpower of evolution sacredly resonates. Everything is pure in its essence, and so are all people, which knowledge helps Hindus to identify, discover, recognize, realize, and experience their true nature, their true self, and their divine essence infinitely.

In Hinduism, most of the Vedic prayers begin with the chanting of om. Om is the Sanskrit symbol that resonates the peacefulness ensconced within one's higher self. Om is considered to have a profound effect on the body and mind of the one who chants, and also to create calmness, serenity, healing, and strength for one to prevail within and also in the surrounding environment. When a Hindus chant om, they merge with the pure expression of the energy within themselves, and merge with the consciousness, the infinite self, which is the eternal home of the spirit of life.[85]

The Impersonal Nature of Brahman

Hindus see ultimate reality, Brahman, as being an impersonal oneness that is beyond all distinctions, including personal and moral distinctions. Since Hindus also consider Brahman to be an impersonal force of existence, the universe is seen by most Hindus as being continuous with and extended from the being of Brahman.

The Brahman–Atman Unity

Most adherents of Hinduism believe that they are in their true selves (atman) extended from and one with Brahman. Just as the air inside an open jar is identical to the air surrounding that jar, so the human essence is identical to that of the essence of Brahman. This is expressed through the phrase *Tat tvam asi,* "That thou art."

The Law of Karma

Humanity's primary problem, according to Hinduism, is that we are ignorant of our divine nature. We have forgotten that we are extended from Brahman and that we have mistakenly attached ourselves to the desires of our separate selves, or egos, and thereby to the consequences of our actions.

Because of the ego's attachments to its desires and individualistic existence, we have become subject to the law of karma. The law of karma is the moral equivalent of the natural law of cause and effect. In essence, it says that we reap what we sow. The effects of our actions, moreover, follow us not only in the present lifetime but also from lifetime to lifetime, which is why there is reincarnation.

Samsara (Reincarnation)

Samsara refers to the ever-revolving wheel of life, death, and rebirth (Rice, 310). Hindus believe that people are reaping in this lifetime the consequences of the deeds they committed in previous lifetimes. A person's karma determines the kind of body—whether human, animal, or insect— into which he or she will be reincarnated in the next lifetime.

Moksha (Liberation)

The solution in Hinduism is to be liberated (*moksha*) from the wheel of life, death, and rebirth. Such liberation is attained through realizing that the concept of the individual self is an illusion and that only the undifferentiated oneness of Brahman is real. With such a realization in mind, one must strive to detach oneself from the desires of the ego and thereby attain enlightenment.

Hinduism offers at least three paths by which to attain enlightenment. These are *karma marga* (the way of action and ritual), *jnana marga* (the way of knowledge and meditation), and *bhakti marga* (the way of devotion).

By way of contrast, the direction of the Hindu way to enlightenment is *from humanity to God,* and it is *based on one's own effort.* The direction of the biblical way of salvation, on the other hand, is *from God to humanity* in that it is *based on God's grace* and is a gift to be received through faith (Eph. 2:8–9; 1 John 4:10).

Also, according to the Upanishads, the goal of enlightenment is for the individual self to lose its separate identity in the universal Self. The end result of biblical salvation, on the other hand, is to have an everlasting relationship with God. For the Christian, eternal life means to be in relational *communion* with a personal God, not in an undifferentiated *union* with an impersonal oneness.[86]

Karma and Sin Compared and Contrasted

The Similarities

Both karma and sin involve moral issues. Both affirm the existence of a cause-and-effect relationship between our actions and the results they produce in our present lives (see Prov. 11:18; Prov. 22:8).

TABLE 10.10. The differences between karma and sin

Karma (Hindu concept)	Sin (Christian concept)
Karma does not affect one's relationship with Brahman, which is the essence of existence within all things. Whether one's karma is good or bad makes no difference to the fact that we are unconditionally extended from the oneness of Brahman.	Sin does affect our relationship with God in that we become alienated from him when we sin. One of the attributes of God is absolute moral holiness. Our sin reveals an attitude of rebellion against his moral authority.
The law of karma, which makes morality like a law of nature, does not allow for the possibility of forgiveness. Its consequences are inevitable and inescapable.	Because God is personal, and because persons can forgive, God can forgive us of our sins. Moreover, he has done so through Jesus Christ.

TABLE 10.11. Hinduism and Christianity contrasted[87]

	Hinduism	Christianity
God	Impersonal	Personal
Humanity	Continuous in the sense of being extended from the being of God	Discontinuous in the sense of being separate from the being of God; continuous in the sense of being made in God's image
Humanity's problem	Ignorance	Moral rebellion
The solution	Liberation from illusion and ignorance	Forgiveness of sin and reconciliation with the personal holy God
The means	Striving to detach oneself from the separated ego and seeking to be aware of one's unity with the divine through self-effort	Repenting of sin and trusting in the completed and substitutionary work of Jesus Christ
The outcome	Merge into the oneness; the individual disappears	Eternal fellowship with God; the person is fulfilled in a loving relationship with God

Islam

Islam among the Nations

Muslims (followers of Islam) make up around 20 percent of the world's population. Islam is the second largest religion in the world, trailing only Christianity. Muslims are spread primarily over the areas of North Africa, the Middle East, south central Asia, and Indonesia.

Although Islam began in Saudi Arabia, non-Arab Muslims now outnumber Arab Muslims by a ratio of almost three to one. Also, the four nations with the largest number of Muslims today are all outside the Middle East—Indonesia, with 166 million, 88 percent of the population; Pakistan, with 111 million, 97 percent of the population; Bangladesh, with 97 million,

85 percent of the population; and India, with 93 million, 11 percent of the population.

Roughly one-fifth of the more than 530,000 international students in the United States come from 40 Islamic countries. Most of these countries have a minimal number of Christians in their populations (0%–2%). Moreover, their governments have either closed the countries' borders to missionaries or have made evangelism illegal, or both.

The Founding of Islam

In AD 570, Muhammad was born into an Arabian tribe called the Quraysh. The Quraysh were influential because they controlled the city of Mecca. Mecca was important economically because it served as a convenient resting place for trading caravans. It was important religiously because the Kaaba was located there.

The Kaaba is a cubical structure that, at the time of Muhammad, was said to contain 360 deities. Each Arabian tribe, having handpicked its own deity, came to Mecca each year to pay homage to its god.

It was the custom of those who were spiritually minded to retreat to a place of solitude once a year. Muhammad observed this practice for several years in a cave in Mount Hira. In the year AD 610, Muhammad, at age forty, is said to have received his first revelation from the angel Gabriel. This was the beginning of a series of revelations that were eventually compiled in Islam's sacred scripture, the Quran, which word means "recitations."

Muhammad is said to have doubted initially the origin of these new revelations. He thought that perhaps he had been possessed by jinn, or demons. His wife Khadijah, however, reassured him that his visions were of divine origin and encouraged him to teach that which had been revealed to him.

As Muhammad began to preach publicly, the leaders of his own tribe pressured him to keep quiet about his message of strict monotheism. They viewed such a teaching as a threat to their polytheistic religion and especially to the source of their livelihood, since they benefited economically from the pilgrimages the tribes made to the Kaaba. Muhammad, however, refused to stop preaching. He began to accrue a significant following.

As he continued to preach against polytheism, persecution increased against the followers of this new religion. Eventually, around one hundred Muslim families were forced to flee to a city named Yathrib (now called Medina), which is about two hundred miles north of Mecca. Muhammad followed these families shortly thereafter, fleeing Mecca in the year AD 622. Muslims now look to the year of his flight to Yathrib as the beginning of the Muslim calendar. This event is known as the Hijrah (also spelled *Hegira*), which means "a series of migrations."

After several successful sieges and military victories against Mecca, and after making treaties with the Quraysh tribe, Muhammad and his army took control of Mecca in 630 without a struggle. Upon entering the city, he personally destroyed the idols in the Kaaba. Within a year of Mecca's submission to Muhammad, he was able to unify all the tribes of the Arabian Peninsula under the religion of Islam.

On June 8, 632, Muhammad died.

The Sects of Islam

The two major sects of Islam, Sunnism and Shiism, were divided originally over a dispute as to who should serve as the first caliph, or successor, to Muhammad, who had failed to appoint one before his death. The Sunni Muslims insisted that Muhammad's successor should be elected. The Shiite (or Shia) Muslims thought the successor should come through Muhammad's bloodline, which would have meant that Ali, Muhammad's cousin and son-in-law, would have been his successor. The Sunnis were the ones who got their way.

The Sunnis now comprise 80 percent of the Muslim population. They differ from the Shiites in other ways besides in their dispute over who was to be the original successor. For example, the Sunnis and the Shiites differ with respect to their source of authority. The Sunnis emphasize the authority of the written traditions, which include not only the Quran but also the Sunna ("custom," from which the Sunnis derive their name). The Sunna includes the Hadith, in which the sayings and conduct of Muhammad and his companions are recorded. The Sunna fill in many areas where the Quran is silent. The Sunnis also receive guidance from the principles arrived at by a consensus of the elders, or religious scholars (ulema), who derive their decisions based on the Quran, the Sunna, and subsequent rulings.

The Shiites, on the other hand, are more authority oriented (rather than consensus oriented). When their movement began, they believed that God spoke through an imam, the Muslim equivalent of the Catholic pope. In the ninth century, however, the twelfth imam occulated, or became hidden, and the source of authority was passed on to the ulema, who considered themselves collectively to be the general representatives of the hidden imam. The Shiites await the return of the twelfth imam, called the Mahdi, similar to the way Christians look for the return of Christ. Ayatollah Khomeini of Iran, for example, was a Shiite leader.

Another difference between the two sects is that the Sunnis believe there should be a separation between civil and religious authorities, whereas the Shiites maintain that the religious authorities should exercise both political and religious power.

Sufism is the mystical third wing of Islam. The goal of the Sufi is to renounce worldly attachments, to see only God in all things, and to attain assimilation of the self into the vast being of God.

There are also several minor Muslim sects, including the Wahhabis (primarily in Saudi Arabia), the Druze (primarily in Lebanon, Syria, and northern Israel), the Alawites (primarily in Syria), and the Ahmadiyas (primarily in Pakistan). Beyond the major and minor sects, Islam has also been a contributing factor in two religions: Sikhism and Baha'i.

The Beliefs and Obligations of Islam

The term *Islam* means "submission" to the will of God, and the person who submits is called a Muslim. The religion of Islam can be divided into beliefs (imam) and obligation (*deen*).

God

The central doctrine of Islam is that God is one and that no partner is to be associated with him. To associate a partner with God is to commit the sin of *ishrak* (also spelled *shirk*), for which the Quran offers no forgiveness (Surah 4:48).* Obviously, because of this central doctrine of Islam, the doctrine of the Trinity is offensive to Muslims.

Angels

In the gap between the God of the Quran and humankind exists a hierarchy of angels. The archangel Gabriel is of the highest rank, succeeded by the rest of the angels.

Each person has two angels assigned to him or her, one to record the person's good deeds and the other to record the bad deeds.

At the bottom of the hierarchy are the jinn, from which we get the word *genie*. Muslims believe that the host of jinn were created from fire, are usually bad, and are able to possess people.

The Prophets of God

According to the Quran, God has sent a prophet to every nation to preach the message of there being only one God. In all, 124,000 prophets have been sent, according to tradition. Most are unknown, but many include biblical characters such as Adam, Noah, Abraham, Moses, David, Solomon, Jonah, John the Baptist, and Jesus.

Each prophet was given for a particular age, but Muhammad is the only prophet who is for all time. He is considered to be the "Seal of the Prophets."

The Holy Books

Four of the highest-ranking prophets were given books of divine revelation. Those four are Moses, who was given the Tawrat (Torah); David, who was given the Zabur (psalms); Jesus, who was given the Injil (gospel); and Muhammad, who was given the Quran. Of those four books, Muslims contend that only the Quran has been preserved in an uncorrupted state.

The Day of Judgment

The God of the Quran has decreed that there will be a day when all will stand before him in judgment. On that day, each person's deeds will be weighed in the balance. Those whose good deeds outweigh their bad deeds will be rewarded with paradise; and those whose bad deeds outweigh their good will be sentenced to hell. Whether one's good deeds outweigh one's bad deeds is a subjective matter, though, known only by God. As a result, a Muslim has no assurance that he or she will be accepted by God.

To Recite the Shahadah

The word *shahadah* means "to bear witness." When reciting the shahadah, one says, "I bear witness that there is no God but Allah and that Muhammad is his messenger." Saying the shahadah with sincerity is all it takes to become a Muslim.

To Pray (Salat)

A Muslim is required to say seventeen cycles (*rak'a*) of prayer each day. These cycles are usually spread over five periods of prayer per day—dawn, noon, midafternoon, dusk, and two hours after sunset (Hamada, 162). Muslims may pray either individually or in a group. They must wash themselves in a prescribed manner before praying, which is called ablution, or *wudu'*. When they pray, they must face toward Mecca. The direction of prayer (*qibla*) is marked by the niche, or mihrab, in the mosque (Hinnells, 142). The noon service on Friday is the only time when Muslims are expected to gather together at the mosque.

To Fast (Sawn)

In commemoration of Muhammad's receiving the Quran during the ninth lunar month of Ramadan, Muslims are expected to fast during the daylight hours that month. During the fast, they must abstain from eating, drinking, smoking, and having sexual relations. After sundown, Muslims are allowed to partake in all those things again until sunrise.

To Give Alms (Zakat)

Muslims are commanded to give one-fortieth (2.5 percent) of their income primarily to the poor and needy.

To Make the Pilgrimage (Hajj)

Every Muslim must make the trip to Mecca at least once during his or her lifetime, provided he or she is able to with respect to health and finances. Each pilgrim must wear the white garments called *ihram*, which have the effect of eliminating all class and status distinctions during the hajj. The process of visiting several sacred sites usually takes more than a week. After the pilgrimage, the pilgrim is entitled to be referred to as a hajj.[88]

Faith of Islam

In Islam, faith (iman) is complete submission to the will of God, which includes belief, profession, and the body's performance of deeds consistent with the commission as vicegerent on Earth, all according to God's will.

Iman has two aspects: recognizing and affirming that there is one creator of the universe and that only to this creator is worship due. According to Islamic thought, this comes naturally because faith is an instinct of the human soul. This instinct is then nurtured by parents or guardians, leading a young person to specific religious or spiritual paths. On the other hand, the instinct may not be guided at all.

A Muslim must have a willingness and a commitment to submitting to God and to his prescriptions for living in accordance with vicegerency. In Islam, the Quran is understood to be the dictation of God's prescriptions through the Prophet Muhammad and is believed to have updated and completed the previous revelations that God sent through earlier prophets.

The Quran states in verse 2:62, "Surely, those who believe, those who are Muslims, Jewish, the Christians, and the Sabians; anyone who (1) believes in God, and (2) believes in the Last Day, and (3) leads a righteous life, will receive their recompense from their Lord. They have nothing to fear, nor will they grieve."89

TABLE 10.12. Islam and Christianity contrasted[90]

	Islam	Christianity
God	A singular unity. No partner is to be associated with God.	A compound, or complex, unity—one in essence; three in person.
Humanity	Good by nature	Sinful by nature
Sin	Sin is thought of in terms of rejecting right guidance. It can be forgiven through repentance. No atonement is necessary.	Sin is serious in that it is spoken of as causing spiritual death (Rom. 6:23; Eph. 2:1). It is serious because it reflects an attitude of moral rebellion against the holy God, which causes us to be alienated from him. An atonement is necessary before our relationship with God can be restored.
Salvation	The standard for salvation is having one's good deeds outweigh one's bad deeds. Therefore, salvation is based on human effort.	The standard for salvation is the absolute holiness of God (Matt. 5:48). Therefore, it can only be offered as a gift by God, based on his grace and Jesus's atoning work, and it can be received through faith. Salvation cannot be earned.
Jesus	One of the major prophets. To associate Jesus with God (for instance, to call him the Son of God) is blasphemy. Muslims affirm the virgin birth of Jesus and the miracles that he performed.	The one and only Son of God. John wrote, "Who is the liar? It is the man who denies that Jesus is the Christ. Such a man is the antichrist—he denies the Father and the Son" (1 John 2:22).

	Islam	Christianity
The death of Jesus	According to the Islamic tradition, Jesus did not die on the cross. Instead, he ascended to heaven. Judas died in his place on the cross. Muslims believe that it is disrespectful to believe that God would allow one of his prophets—and especially one of the most honored of the prophets—to be crucified.	Jesus died a physical death and gave his life as the substitutionary atonement for our sins. He then rose from the dead in a physical but immortal body and appeared to hundreds of witnesses (1 Cor. 15). God's specific purpose for sending Jesus into the world was for him to be crucified and to die for our sins (Matt. 20:28; John 3:16; Rom. 8:3; 2 Cor. 5:21; 1 Pet. 1:19–20). Jesus voluntarily gave his life for us (John 6:51; John 10:11–17). The end was not one of dishonor but one of the highest exaltation (Acts 2:29–33; Acts 5:30–31; Phil. 2:8–11).
The Bible	Abrogated by the Quran.	Authentic. Divinely inspired. The final authority in all matters and truth.

Concerning God

Many people assume that the God of the Quran is the same as the God of the Bible. But is that a correct assumption? The following lists compare and contrast the two concepts of God.

The God of the Quran and the God of the Bible

The Similarities

- Both are One.
- Both are transcendent creators of the universe.
- Both are sovereign.
- Both are omnipotent.

- Both have spoken to humanity through messengers or prophets, through angels, and through the written word.
- Both know in intimate detail the thoughts and deeds of human beings.
- Both will judge the wicked.

The Differences

- The God of the Quran is a singular unity, whereas the God of the Bible is a compound unity who is one in essence and three in person (Matt. 28:19; John 10:30; Acts 5:3–4).
- The God of the Quran is not a father and has begotten no sons (Surah 19:88–92; Surah 112:3), whereas the God of the Bible is a triune God who has eternally existed as Father, Son, and Holy Spirit (Matt. 28:19; Luke 3:21–22; John 5:18).
- Through the Quran, God broke into history through a word that is written, whereas through Jesus Christ, God broke into history through the Word, who is a person (John 1:1, 14; Col. 1:15–20; Heb. 1:2–3; John 4:9–10; 1 John 1:1–3).
- The God of the Quran "loves not the prodigals" (Surah 6:142; Surah 7:31, Ali; [Ali has "wasters" instead of "prodigals"]), whereas Jesus tells the story of a father, a metaphor for God the Father, who longs for the return of his prodigal son (Luke 15:11–24).
- "Allah loves not those that do wrong" (Surah 3:140, Ali), and neither does he love "him who is treacherous, sinful" (Surah 4:107, Ali), whereas "God demonstrates his own love for us in this: While we were still sinners, Christ died for us" (Rom. 5:8).
- "Allah desires to afflict them for some of their sins" (Surah 5:49, Ali; also see Surah 4:168–169; Surah 7:179; Surah 9:2; and Surah 40:10), whereas the God of the Bible does not "take any pleasure in the death of the wicked" (Ezek. 18:23) and is "not wanting anymore to perish, but everyone to come to repentance" (2 Pet. 3:9).
- The standard for judgment for the God of the Quran is that our good deeds must outweigh our bad deeds (Surah 7:8–9; Surah 21:47), whereas the standard of the God of the Bible is nothing less

than complete perfection as measured by the holy character of God (Matt. 5:48; Rom. 3:23).

- The God of the Quran provided a messenger, Muhammad, who warned of Allah's impending judgment (Surah 2:119; Surah 5:19; Surah 7:184, 188; Surah 15:89–90) and who declared, "No bearer of a burden can bear the burden of another" (Surah 17:15; Surah 35:18, Ali), whereas the God of the Bible provided a sinless Savior, Jesus, who took our sins upon himself and bore God's wrath in our stead (Matt. 20:28; Matt. 26:28; Luke 22:37; John 3:16; John 10:9–11; 2 Cor. 5:21; Gal. 3:13; 1 Thess. 5:9–10).

Answering the Objections Commonly Raised by Muslims

"The Bible Has Been Corrupted"

Muslims have been taught that the early texts of the Bible were corrupted by the Jews and the Christians. This is known as the doctrine of *tahrif*, or alteration.

As support for this doctrine, Muslims point to the following passages:

- A part of them head the Word of Allah, and perverted [Ali has "altered"] it knowingly after they understood it. (Surah 2:75, Ali)
- And there are among them [the Jews] illiterates, who know not the Book, but (see therein their own) desires, and they do nothing but conjecture. Then woe to those who write the Book with their own hands, and then say: "This is from Allah, to traffic with it for a miserable price!" (Surah 2:78–79, Ali)

These Quranic passages, however, speak of *misinterpreting* scripture and of *passing something off as scripture* that is not scripture, but they *do not speak of altering the actual biblical manuscripts* themselves (Parrinder, 147).

Significantly, the Quran itself considers the previous revelations contained in the Book to be authoritative and authentic revelations from God (Surah 2:136; Surah 4:163). The Quran encourages Jews and Christians to "stand fast by the Law, the Gospel, and all the revelation that has come to you from your Lord" (Surah 5:68). It uses the Torah and the gospel to authenticate Muhammad as the prophet (Surah 7:157), and it encourages those who doubt Muhammad's teachings to "ask those who have been reading the Book from before thee" (Surah 10:94). The Quran also urges people to believe in the previous scriptures (Surah 4:136).

Clearly, it would be inconsistent for the Quran to, on the one hand, advise people to consult the previous scriptures and to believe in them and then, on the other hand, to teach that those scriptures are corrupted and therefore untrustworthy.

With as much as the Quran talks about the previous scriptures as being revealed from God, the Muslim contention that Jews and Christians have altered those scriptures flies in the face of the Quran's own statement that, "None can change His words" (Surah 6:115; also see Surah 6:34 and Surah 10:64). Considering such a statement in the Quran, are Muslims willing to admit that their doctrine of tahrif in fact questions the power of God to protect his revealed word? Would not such questioning be an affront to God?

Consider also the impossibility of corrupting the biblical texts. To accomplish such a feat would mean that the worldwide community of Jews had agreed to the textual changes that the remote and relatively insignificant Jewish community in Medina was suggesting. Then it would have also meant that the Christians of the world, who also possessed the Torah, assented to the changes by the Jews, even though the Christians were not even agreeing among themselves at that time about certain doctrinal issues.

Furthermore, the manuscript evidence does not support the accusation of textual corruption. With respect to the authenticity of the Old Testament, the Dead Sea Scrolls, which date from 100 BC, confirm in an astounding way the accuracy of the Masoretic Manuscripts, which date from AD 900 (Geisler and Nix, 405, 408). The significance of these dates is that they show that the manuscripts that existed *after* the Muslim accusation of tahrif are identical to those that existed long *before* Muhammad even lived.

With respect to the authenticity of the New Testament, biblical scholars have found 3,157 Greek manuscripts that contain either portions or all of the New Testament and that date from the second century on (Geisler and Nix, 466). Of the variants (textual differences) between these manuscripts, 95 percent have to do with trivialities, such as a letter being deleted by mistake. In response to the accusation by Muslims that the variants significantly changed Christian doctrine, it must be stated that no Christian doctrine rests solely on, or is even affected by, a debatable text (Bruce, 20; Geisler and Nix, 474).

The Doctrine of the Trinity

In light of the Muslim sin of ishrak—associating a partner with God—Muslims raise several objections to the doctrine of the Trinity. These, along with responses thereto, are as follows.

Objection no. 1: "Christians worship three gods."

There are several ways to approach this objection. The first way is to affirm your agreement with Islam that there is only one God. Read the biblical passages that assert as much (Deut. 6:4; Mark 12:29–32; 1 Cor. 8:4).

Second, the Bible speaks at times of a compound or complex unity rather than a simple undivided unity. In other words, the word *one* often means there is a plurality in the oneness (Gen. 2:24; Exod. 24:3; Judg. 20:1, 8, 11; Rom. 12:5).

Third, it is not surprising that we, as God's creatures, would not be able to fully understand the nature of our Creator. The difficulty of understanding and explaining the concept of the Trinity is, in fact, evidence *for* its divine origin. It is unlikely that such a concept would be invented by mere humans.

One staff member of International Students Inc. uses an illustration called Flatland to explain this point. Flatland is a two-dimensional realm, and in Flatland reside Mr. and Mrs. Flat. It would be just as difficult for Mr. and Mrs. Flat to comprehend us and our world, in which there are three dimensions, as it is for us to comprehend the nature of God, who exists in several dimensions beyond ours.

Fourth, recall the makeup of the Trinity—that it consists of the Father, the Son, and the Holy Spirit. Because of the following verse, some Muslims believe that the Trinity consists of God, Jesus, *and Mary*: "And when Allah will say: O Jesus, son of Mary, didst thou say to men, Take me and my mother for two gods besides Allah" (Surah 5:116, Ali)?

Fifth, consider the biblical evidence for the triunity of God. In the Bible, the Father is referred to as God (Matt. 11:25; John 6:27; John 8:54; Eph.

4:6), Jesus is recognized as God (Luke 5:17–26; John 1:1; John 20:28), and the Holy Spirit is identified as God (Acts 5:3–4). Even though each is referred to as God, the Bible does not speak of three gods but of the three as being one: "baptizing them in the name [singular] of the Father and of the Son and of the Holy Spirit" (Matt. 28:19).

Plus, the Father, the Son, and the Holy Spirit are all identified as having attributes unique to God. For example, each person of the Trinity existed before anything was created, and each was active in the creation of all things (God: Ps. 146:5–6; Mark 13:19; Acts 4:24; Jesus: John 1:1–3, 14; 1 Cor. 8:6; Col. 1:16–17; Holy Spirit: Gen. 1:1–3).

Moreover, each person possesses the attribute of omnipresence, or being present to all things (God: Jer. 23:24; Acts 17:24–25; Jesus: Matt. 18:20; Matt. 28:20; Eph. 1:23; Holy Spirit: Ps. 139:7–8).

Objection no. 2: "God has no sons."

The second objection that arises from the doctrine of the Trinity has to do with Christians referring to Jesus as the Son of God. When Muslims hear the phrase *Son of God*, they understand it to imply that God had physical relations with a woman in order to have a son. The Quran reads, "Such (was) Jesus the son of Mary: (It is) a statement of truth, about which they (vainly) dispute. It is not befitting to (the majesty of) Allah that He should beget a son" (Surah 19:34–35).

In the Arabic language, there are two words for expressing "son of": *walad* and *ibn*. *Walad* definitely denotes becoming a son through the union of a male with a female. We as Christians would agree that Jesus was not a *waladdu'llah*—"son of God"—in that sense. The Bible says that Jesus was born of the *virgin* Mary (Matt. 1:23; Luke 1:34). Moreover, the Quran itself does not deny the virgin birth of Jesus (Surah 3:47).

Unlike *walad*, however, the word *ibn* can be used in a metaphorical sense. For example, Arabs themselves talk about a traveler as being an *ibnu'ssabil*—"son of the road" (Fellowship, 6). They obviously do not mean by such a phrase that one has had sexual relations with the road. It is in this wider metaphorical sense that Jesus is understood as being the Son of God.

When Jesus referred to God as "my Father" and to himself as "the Son" (Matt. 11:27; John 5:17; John 22–23), he was not talking about his physical birth. Instead, he was claiming to have a special relationship with God that referred to his identity and equality. To be the son of someone is to be of the same order as and to have the same qualities as that person.

The Jews of Jesus's day made it clear that this idea of the sameness of order and quality is how they understood Jesus's statement when they said, "He was even calling God his own Father, *making himself equal with God*" (John 5:18, emphasis added). In another instance, Jesus said, "I and the Father are one" (John 10:30). After Jesus made that statement, the Jews picked up stones to kill him "for blasphemy, because you, a mere man, *claim to be God*" (John 10:33, emphasis added).

One Iranian Christian says that he deals with this controversial issue by specifying that Jesus is "the *spiritual* Son of God." This is not to deny Jesus's humanity, but it is intended to less offensive to Muslims.

Another approach to the "God has no sons" objection is to ask a person who claims such, "Are you not limiting God by saying that he is unable to express himself through human form? Are you not saying that something is then impossible with God? Remember that the angel declared to Mary that 'nothing is impossible with God' (Luke 1:37)."

This subject also includes the issue of the best way God could have communicated to humanity. By way of an illustration, the Vietnam War caused a particular family to be separated. The father was forced to stay in Vietnam, while the wife and two boys were able to travel to the United States. For seventeen years, they communicated with each other only through letters and pictures. The father could see his boys grow up only from a distance. Then finally the governments of Vietnam and the United States made an agreement that allowed the father to travel to the States to see his family. But what if the father said, "I don't really see any need to come see to you in person. Communicating through letters and pictures has been sufficient for seventeen years, so it will continue to be sufficient for me"? What would you think of such a father?

What would you think of a God who, if it were at all possible, would refuse to communicate with his creation in person?

Objection no. 3: "The doctrine of the Trinity contradicts itself."

Muslims often claim that the doctrine of the Trinity contradicts itself. After all, how can something be both three and one?

In response, for a statement to contradict itself it must both affirm and deny the same thing in the same respect. Does the doctrine of the Trinity do that? The answer is no, because the doctrine states that God is *one in essence* (or being, or substance) and *three in person*. Essence and personhood are different. God is three in person in that each person of the Trinity is distinct within the Godhead; God is one in that each person of the Godhead shares the same self-existing essence and other qualities unique to God.

This simultaneous distinction and sameness is seen in John 1:1: "In the beginning was the Word, and the Word was with God, and the Word was God." The word *with* indicates a distinction and a relationship between the persons of the Son (the Word) and the Father (God), while at the same time the phrase "the Word *was* God"—a verb of being—indicates the sameness of essence between the two persons.

Another way to approach the doctrine of the Trinity is to point out how practical it is in that it meets each person's felt needs, such as the following:

Love
God the Father demonstrated his love for us historically by sending his Son to save us (John 3:16; Rom. 5:8; 1 John 4:9–10).

Freedom from guilt and sin
God the Son took our sins upon himself, paid the penalty of death on our behalf, and rose from the dead to give us victory over sin and death (Rom. 5:8; 1 Cor. 5:21; 1 Cor. 15:3–4). Through Jesus we can receive the forgiveness of sins and freedom from guilt (1 John 1:9).

Empathy
Because the Word became flesh and lived among us, we know that God, through Jesus, is able to empathize with our suffering (Phil. 2:6–8; Heb. 4:15).

Hope

Because Jesus physically rose from the dead, we have the hope of personal survival after death. Moreover, because of the life-giving power of the Holy Spirit, we have the assurance of eternal life (Rom. 8:11; see also 2 Cor. 1:22; 5:5; Eph. 1:13–14).

Transformation

God the Holy Spirit indwells us (Rom. 8:9–11; 1 Cor. 3:16), makes our spirit, which was dead, alive (John 3:3–7; 2 Cor. 5:17; Titus 3:5), and gives us the power to submit to God (Rom. 8:5–17).

Communication with God

We can have a personal relationship with God because Jesus has broken the barriers between us and God (Eph. 2:12–18; Col. 1:21–22); because he serves as our Mediator with God (1 Tim. 2:5); and because the Holy Spirit assists us in our communication with God (Rom. 8:26–27).

The Crucifixion

Muslims believe that the God of the Quran would not dishonor his chosen prophet by allowing him to be crucified. One Iranian student asked, "Do we not honor [Jesus] more than you do when we refuse to believe that God would permit Him to suffer death on the cross? Rather, we believe that God took Him to heaven" (Woodberry, 164). Muslims, therefore, deny that Jesus was crucified. They believe instead that he was caught up to heaven and that someone (some say Judas) took his place on the cross.

The following is the primary passage that Muslims use to deny the Crucifixion:

> That they said (in boast), "We killed Christ Jesus the son of Mary, the Messenger of Allah"—but they killed him not, nor crucified him, but so it was made to appear to them, and those who differ therein are full of doubts, with no (certain) knowledge, but only conjecture to follow, for of a

surety they killed him not—nay, Allah raised him up unto himself. (Surah 4:157–158)

A careful reading of the above passage, however, shows that it does not deny that Jesus was crucified; instead, it *denies that the Jews caused Jesus to be crucified*. In point of fact, the Jews did not crucify Jesus, but the Romans did (John 18:31).

Even more important, God was ultimately responsible for Jesus's being crucified (Rom. 8:3–4; 1 Pet. 1:18–20). Even the Quran alludes to that fact in the following verse:

> When Allah said, "O Jesus, I *will cause thee to die and exalt thee in My presence* and clear thee of those who disbelieve and make those who follow thee above those who disbelieve to the day of Resurrection." (Surah 3:54, Ali, emphasis added)

In light of the above passage, it is effective to have a Muslim who disputes the Crucifixion to read Isaiah 53:4–11 in order to see why God caused Jesus to die. Following that, consider together the story of God ordering Abraham to sacrifice his son in Surah 37:101–107 (although the passage is not explicit, Muslims understand the son to be Ishmael):

> So we gave him the good news of a boy ready to suffer and forbear. Then, when (the son) reached (the age of) (serious) work with him, he [Abraham] said: "O my son! I see in vision that I offer thee in sacrifice: Now see what thy view is!" (The son) said: "O my father! Do as thou art commanded: thou will find me, if Allah so wills one practicing patience and constancy!" So when they had both submitted their wills (to Allah) and he had laid him prostrate on his forehead (for sacrifice), We called out to him, "O Abraham! Thou hast already fulfilled the vision!"—thus indeed do We reward those who do right. For this was obviously a trial—and we ransomed him with a momentous sacrifice." (Ali)

There are three questions to ask a Muslim with respect to the above passage:

- If salvation is only a matter of rewarding those who do good, and if God's purpose was only to test Abraham's obedience, why then was there a need for "a momentous sacrifice"? Was it not sufficient that Abraham went as far as he did?
- Who provided the "momentous sacrifice"?
- Is a goat enough to "ransom" humanity on account of our sins?

In light of the above passage from the Quran and the three questions, read what Jesus said concerning his mission: "The Son of Man [Jesus] did not come to be served, but to serve, and to give his life as a ransom for many" (Matt. 20:28). Jesus is the great sacrifice, and God is the one who sent him (John 3:16).

A former Muslim who wrestled with the issue of Jesus's crucifixion said that one thing that really affected him was to see that Jesus "over and over mentioned and predicated his death, and it happened—it really happened." It is helpful, then, to point out the verses in which Jesus predicted His death: Matthew 12:39–40; Matthew 16:4, 21; Matthew 17:22–23; Matthew 20:17–19; Matthew 26:2; Mark 8:31; Mark 9:31; Mark 10:33–34; Luke 9:22, 44; John 10:11; John 17–18; and John 12:32–33.

Rather than seeing the Crucifixion as dishonoring Christ, Muslims should see it not only as resulting in the greatest of honors but also as manifesting the epitome of what it means to be a Muslim. How is that? Consider the following: "And being found in appearance as a man, he humbled himself and *became obedient to death*—even death on a cross! Therefore, *God exalted him to the highest place* and gave him the name that is above every name" (Phil. 2:8–9, emphasis added).

The word *Islam* means "obedience, submission." And it is obedience to God that Jesus demonstrated all the way to the cross! Muslims should honor him for such obedience.

Concerning the issue of God dishonoring one of his chosen prophets, the passage is clear that Christ's obedience led to God's exalting him with the greatest of exaltations (also see Acts 2:29–33 and Acts 5:30–31).

Who, moreover, is being disrespectful, those who say God would deceive by replacing Jesus with someone who looks like him, or those who say God is able to raise his prophet from the dead and thereby conquer sin for all humanity?

Ultimately, the argument concerning the significance of the cross of Christ must not be a theological one but a personal one—what Jesus's death means to you. The Muslim must be shown the difference between the uncertainty of salvation by attempting to live up to the law versus the certainty of salvation by receiving God's grace through faith in Jesus Christ.[91]

Judaism

Introduction

The term *Judaism* is sometimes loosely used to include not only the faith of modern Jews but also the faith of the Old Testament. Sometimes it is used to include the entire Jewish way of life. It is best, however, to use the term *Judaism* to refer to the religion of the rabbis that developed from about 200 BC onward and crystallized following the destruction of the temple in AD 70. In this way Christianity is not described as a daughter religion of Judaism but more correctly as a sister, as both branched out from Old Testament faith.

The Development of Judaism

From around 200 BC onward, new institutions and ways of life developed that distinguished Rabbinic Judaism from the religion of ancient (Old Testament) Israel. New institutions arose such as the synagogue (the house of worship and study), the *yeshivot* (religious academies for the training of rabbis), and the office of the rabbi (a leader holding religious authority).

One of the greatest catalysts in the development of Judaism was the destruction of the temple in AD 70, which resulted in the abolition of sacrifices and the priesthood. Rather than being guided by priests, prophets, or kings, the rabbis became the authorities who established various laws and practices that had normative authority.

Before the eighteenth century, there was basically one kind of Judaism. In contrast, one of the distinguishing features of modern Judaism is the existence of the three main movements, or "branches." These branches are not quite equivalent to what Christians understand by denominations, where one's identity is often tied strongly to a particular denomination and in which one's affiliation is often determined simply by family tradition. The branches of Judaism are more like voluntary associations, with classifications according to cultural and doctrinal formulas (like denominations), but with adherence to a particular branch often governed by personal preference, nearness of a given synagogue, or one's agreement with the rabbi's style and views (like voluntary associations).

Within each branch of Judaism, one will find adherents with varying degrees of observance. Many Jewish people formulate their own informal versions of Judaism and do not fit exactly into any one of these categories. Nevertheless, knowing the distinctions between the branches, and knowing with which branch your Jewish friends align themselves, can be helpful in most witnessing situations.

Orthodox Judaism

There was only one kind of Judaism until the Age of the Enlightenment in the eighteenth century. Only later, to differentiate it from the other branches of Judaism, was this called "Orthodox." Today, Orthodox Judaism is characterized by an emphasis on tradition and strict observance of the law of Moses as interpreted by the rabbis.

Reform Judaism

Reform Judaism began in Germany in the eighteenth century at the time of the Enlightenment, or *Haskalah*. It sought to modernize what were considered outmoded ways of thinking and doing, and to thus prevent the increasing assimilation of German Jewry. Reform Judaism emphasizes ethics and the precepts of the prophets.

Conservative Judaism

This branch developed from nineteenth-century German roots as a middle-ground branch.[92]

TABLE 10.13. The three branches of Judaism[93]

Category	Orthodox	Conservative	Reform
History	Orthodoxy dates back to the days of the Talmud (second to fifth century AD). It was the only form of Jewish practice prior to the eighteenth century and the emergence of Reform Judaism. Orthodoxy today seeks to preserve classical or traditional Judaism.	Conservative Judaism is an American movement with roots in nineteenth-century Germany. It arose as a reaction to what some viewed as the extreme assimilationist tendencies of Reform Judaism. It tried to be a middle ground, attempting to maintain basic traditions while adapting to modern life.	Reform Judaism emerged following the Jewish emancipation from ghetto life in the late eighteenth century. It sought to modernize Judaism and thus stem the tide of assimilation threatening German Jewry. It was thought that Jewish identity could be best maintained by modernization, but others saw this as in fact contributing to assimilation and the loss of Jewish identity.
Other terms	Traditional Torah Judaism	Historical Judaism	Liberal or Progressive Judaism
US membership*	6 percent of all American Jews	35 percent of all American Jews	38 percent of all American Jews
View of scripture	The Torah, meaning essentially the teaching of the Five Books of Moses, is truth. A person must have faith in its essential revealed character. A true Jew believes in revelation and the divine origin of the oral and written Torah. "Oral Torah" refers to various interpretations of the written Torah believed to have been given to Moses along with the	The Bible, both the Torah and the other books, is the Word of God *and* of the word of humankind. It is not inspired in the traditional sense but rather dynamically inspired. Revelation is an ongoing process.	The Bible is a human document preserving the history, culture, legends, and hopes of a people. It is valuable for deriving moral and ethical insights. Revelation is an ongoing process.

Category	Orthodox	Conservative	Reform
	written Torah. The Torah is accorded a higher place than the rest of the Hebrew Bible.		
View of God	God is spirit rather than form. He is a personal God— omnipotent, omniscient, omnipresent, eternal, and compassionate.	The concept of God is nondogmatic and flexible. There is less atheism in Conservative Judaism than in Reform, but most often God is considered impersonal and ineffable.	Reform Judaism allows a varied interpretation of the "God concept" with wide latitude for naturalists, mystics, supernaturalists, or religious humanists. It holds that "the truth is that we do not know the truth."
View of humankind	Humanity is morally neutral, with a good and an evil inclination. A person can overcome his or her evil bent and be perfected by his or her own efforts in observance of the law.	This group tends toward the Reform view, though it is not as likely to espouse humanism. Perfectibility can come through enlightenment. Humanity is "in partnership" with God.	Humanity's nature is basically good. Through education, encouragement, and evolution, a person can actualize the potential already existing within him or her.
View of the tradition of the law	The law is the basis of Judaism. It is authoritative and gives structure and meaning to life. The life of total dedication to the Halakhah (the body of Jewish law) leads to a nearness to God.	Adaptation to contemporary situations is inevitable. The demands of morality are absolute; the specific laws are relative.	The law is an evolving, ever-dynamic religious code that adapts to every age. It is maintained that if religious observances clash with the just demands of civilized society, then they must be dropped.

Category	Orthodox	Conservative	Reform
View of sin	Orthodox Jews do not believe in original sin. Rather, one commits sin by breaking the commandments of the law.	Conservative Jews do not believe in original sin. The individual can sin by way of his moral or social actions.	Reform Jews do not believe in original sin. Sin is interpreted as the ills of society. Humanity is sometimes held to have a "divine spark" within.
View of salvation	Repentance (belief in God's mercy), prayer, and obedience to the law are necessary for a proper relationship with God. "Salvation" is not considered to be a Jewish concept, inasmuch as Jewish people presume a standing with God.	Conservative Jews tend toward the Reform view but include the necessity of maintaining Jewish identity.	"Salvation" is obtained through the betterment of self and society. It is social improvement.
View of the Messiah	The Messiah is a human being who is not divine. He will restore the Jewish kingdom and extend his righteous rule over the earth. He will execute judgment and right all wrongs.	Conservative Jews hold much the same view as Reform Jews.	Instead of believing in the Messiah as a person or divine being, Reform Jews favor the concept of a utopian age toward which humankind is progressing, sometimes called the "Messianic age."
View of life after death	There will be a physical resurrection. The righteous will exist forever with God in the "world to come." The unrighteous will suffer, but disagreement exists over their ultimate destiny.	Conservative Jews tend toward the Reform view but are less influenced by nontraditional ideas such as Eastern mysticism.	Generally, Reform Judaism has no concept of personal life after death. It is said that a person lives on through his or her accomplishments or in the minds of others. Some Reform Jews are influenced by Eastern mystical thought, where souls

Category	Orthodox	Conservative	Reform
			merge into one great impersonal life force.
Distinctives in synagogue worship	The synagogue is a house of prayer as well as a house of study; social aspects are incidental. All prayers are recited in Hebrew. Men and women sit separately. The officiants face the same direction as the congregants.	The synagogue is viewed as the basic institution of Jewish life. Alterations listed under Reform Judaism are found to a lesser degree in Conservative worship.	The synagogue is known as a "temple." The service has been modernized and abbreviated. English, as well as Hebrew, is used. Men and women sit together. Reform temples use choirs and organs in their worship services.
Books to read	Herman Wouk, *This Is My God*, 1961; A. Cohen, *Everyman's Talmud*, 1932	S. Schechter, *Some Aspects of Rabbinic Theology*, 1923; *Emet Ve-emunah: Statement of Principles of Conservative Judaism*, 1988; Marchall Sklare, *Conservative Judaism*, 1972	Eugene B. Borowitz, *Reform Judaism Today*, 1983; *Liberal Judaism*, 1984

* *Source*: 1992 American Jews Yearbook

The Beliefs of Judaism

Above we referred to the fact that Judaism is a religion of deed, not creed. If there is any religious principle (what Christians would call a doctrine) that Judaism explicitly affirms and teaches, it is the unity of God. Deuteronomy 6:4—called the *Sh'ma*—proclaims, "Hear O Israel, the Lord our God, the Lord is one."

Beyond the affirmation of the Sh'ma, there have been attempts at compiling various statements of faith (such as the Thirteen Principles of Maimonides), but they have been few and not widely studied or accepted as binding.

The three branches do have their more or less "official" doctrinal positions on various matters, such as the person of God and the nature of humankind.

These are described in table 10.13. In no way, however, are they binding on any Jewish person.[94]

Jewish Principles of Faith

Faith itself is not a religious concept in Judaism. The only time faith in God is mentioned in the twenty-four books of the Jewish Bible is in Isaiah 43:10. In this verse, the commandment to know God is followed by the commandments to believe and to understand, thus denoting descending importance. However, Judaism does recognize the positive value of *emunah* (generally translated as "faith" or "trust in God") and the negative status of the *apikorus* (heretic), but faith is not as stressed or as central as it is in other religions, especially Christianity and Islam. Faith could be a necessary means for being a practicing religious Jew, but the emphasis is placed on true knowledge, true prophecy, and practice rather than on faith itself. Very rarely does faith relate to any teaching that must be believed.

Judaism does not require one to explicitly identify God (a key tenet of Christian faith called *Avodah Zarah* in Judaism, a minor form of idol worship, is a big sin and strictly forbidden to Jews). Rather, in Judaism, one is to honor a (personal) idea of God, supported by the many principles quoted in the Talmud to define Judaism, mostly by what God is not. Thus there is no established formulation of Jewish principles of faith that are mandatory for all (observant) Jews. In the Jewish scriptures, trust in God—emunah— refers to how God acts toward his people and how they are to respond to him; it is rooted in the everlasting covenant established in the Torah, notably Deuteronomy 7:9: "Know, therefore, that the Lord, your God He is God, the faithful God, Who keeps the covenant and loving kindness with those who love Him and keep His commandments to a thousand generations" (Tanach, Devarim 7:9).

The specific tenets that compose required beliefs and their application to the times have been disputed throughout Jewish history. Today many, but not all, Orthodox Jews have accepted Maimonides' Thirteen Principles of Belief.

A traditional example of emunah as seen in the Jewish annals is found in the person of Abraham. On a number of occasions, Abraham both accepts statements from God that seem impossible and offers obedient actions in response to direction from God to do things that seem implausible (see Gen. 12–15).

The Talmud describes how a thief also believes in God: on the brink of his forced entry, as he is about to risk his life—and the life of his victim—he cries out with all sincerity, "God help me!" The thief has faith that there is a God who hears his cries, yet it escapes him that this God may be able to provide for him without requiring that he abrogate God's will by stealing from others. For emunah to affect him in this way, he needs study and contemplation.

TABLE 10.14. Selected messianic prophecies fulfilled in Jesus[95]

Prophecy	Fulfillment
The Messiah will be from the seed of Abraham (Gen. 18:18); Isaac (21:12); Jacob (Num. 24:17, 19); Judah (Gen. 49:10); Jesse (Isa. 11:1–2, 10); and David (Jer. 23:5–6).	"Jesus ... the son of David, the son of Jesse ... the son of Judah, the son of Jacob, the son of Isaac, the son of Abraham" (Luke 3:31–33).
Born in Bethlehem (Mic. 5:2; also John 7:42).	"So Joseph also went up from the town of Nazareth in Galilee to Judea, to Bethlehem the town of David" (Luke 2:4).
"He was despised and rejected by men" (Isa. 53:3).	"Those who passed by [the cross] hurled insults at him" (Matt. 27:39–44).
"A man of sorrow" (Isa. 53:3).	"Then [Jesus] said to them. 'My soul is overwhelmed with sorrow to the point of death'" (Matt. 26:38).
"Familiar with suffering" (Isa. 53:3).	"He then began to teach them that the Son of Man must suffer many things" (Mark 8:31; also Luke 24:26).

Prophecy	Fulfillment
"Be strong, do not fear; your God will come. ... Then will the eyes of the blind be opened and the ears of the deaf unstopped. Then will the lame leap like a deer, and the mute tongue shout for joy" (Isa. 35:4–6); "The Lord has anointed me to preach good news to the poor" (Isa. 61:1).	"Go back and report to John what you hear and see: The blind receive sight, the lame walk, those who have leprosy are cured, the deaf hear, the dead are raised, and the good news is preached to the poor" (Matt. 11:4–5; also Luke 4:18).
"Surely he took up our infirmities and carried our sorrows" (Isa. 53:4).	"[Jesus] drove out the spirits with a word and healed all the sick" (Matt. 8:16–17).
"The must not ... break any of [the Passover lamb's] bones" (Num. 9:12); "He was pierced" (Isa. 53:5); "They have pierced my hands and feet" (Ps. 22:16; also Zech. 12:10).	"But when they came to Jesus and found that he was already dead, they did not break his legs. Instead, one of the soldiers pierced Jesus's side with a spear" (John 19:33–37).
"But he was pierced *for* our transgressions, he was crushed *for* our iniquities ... the Lord has laid on him the iniquity of us all" (Isa. 53:3–6).	"The Son of Man [came] to give his life as a ransom *for* many" (Matt. 20:28); "God made him who had no sin to be sin *for* us" (2 Cor. 5:21; also John 11:49–51; 1 Cor. 15:3).
"He was oppressed and afflicted, yet he did not open his mouth ... as a sheep before her shearers is silent, so he did not open his mouth" (Isa. 53:7).	"But Jesus remained silent" (Matt. 26:63); "When he was accused by the chief priests and the elders, he gave no answer" (Matt. 27:12).
"They divide my garments among them and cast lots for my clothing" (Ps. 22:18).	"[Jesus's] garment was seamless, woven in one piece. ... 'Let's decide by lot who will get it'" (John 19:23–24).
"He had done no violence, nor was any deceit in his mouth" (Isa. 53:9).	"'I [Judas] have sinned,' he said, 'for I have betrayed innocent blood'" (Matt. 27:4; also Luke 23:41; 2 Cor. 5:21).
He "was numbered with the transgressors" (Isa. 53:12).	"Two robbers were crucified with him" (Matt. 27:38; also Luke 22:37).

Prophecy	Fulfillment
"He was assigned a grave ... with the rich in his death" (Isa. 53:9).	"There came a rich man from Arimathea, named Joseph. ... Joseph took the body ... and placed it in his own new tomb" (Matt. 27:57–60).
"For he made intercession for the transgressors" (Isa. 53:12).	"Father, forgive them, for they do not know what they are doing" (Luke 23:34).
"You will not abandon me to the grave, nor will you let your Holy One see decay" (Ps. 16:10); "Though the Lord makes his life a guilt offering, he will see his offspring and prolong his days" (Isa. 53:10–11).	"Why do you look for the living among the dead? He is not here; he has risen" (Luke 24:5–6; also Acts 2:31–32)!
"The stone the builders rejected has become the capstone" (Ps. 118:22; Isa. 8:14)	"But when the tenants saw the son, they said to each other, 'This is the heir. Come, let's kill him'" (Matt. 21:28–42).

See Rosen, 1976, 58–60, and McDowell, chapter 9.

Marxism

The founder and primary theorist of Marxism, the nineteenth-century German thinker Karl Marx, had a negative attitude toward religion, viewing it primarily as "the opium of the people" and believing that it had been used by the ruling classes to give the working classes false hope for millennia, while at the same time recognizing it as a form of protest by the working classes against their poor economic conditions. In the end, Marx rejected religion.

In the Marxist-Leninist interpretation of Marxist theory, developed primarily by Russian revolutionary Vladimir Lenin, religion is seen as retarding human development. Socialist states that follow a Marxist-Leninist variant are seen as atheistic and explicitly antireligious. Due to this, a number of Marxist-Leninist governments in the twentieth century, such as the Soviet Union and the People's Republic of China, implemented rules introducing state atheism.[96]

However, several religious communist groups exist. Christian communism was important in the early development of communism.[97]

Introduction

Marxist ideology draws its inspiration from the writings of Karl Marx and Friedrich Engels. It stresses the need for a political and economic system that abolishes private property, in which all material goods are held in common by all people. As we shall see, Marxism involves several areas of thought, including not only economics and politics but also ethics, history, human nature, and religion. It is a total worldview.

It is not difficult to understand why Marxist thinking appeals to many people. We live in a world of economic extremes. The disparity between the rich and the poor is wide. Understandably, then, Marxism's promise of economic equality is attractive to many who desire to eliminate such extremes. Marxism also appeals to the idealistic and to those looking for hope and meaning in life but who are disillusioned with other ideologies.

No one knows how many people in the world are committed to Marxism, but there can be no denying that it has had an unsurpassed influence on humankind during the twentieth century. Although it has suffered severe political and economic setbacks in recent years (particularly in the former Soviet Union and Eastern Europe), Marxism remains a viable and appealing ideology for many.

Even in US universities, Marxism wields tremendous influence. An article in *US News and World Report,* January 25, 1982, stated that there were ten thousand Marxist professors on campuses across the United States. An article in the August 29, 1989, issue of the *Denver Post* stated that as many as 90 percent of faculty members at some Midwestern universities were Marxists. The influence of these professors on the thinking of students in US universities should not be underestimated.

History of Marxism

Early Roots

Throughout history there have been people who have proposed ideas similar to those of Karl Marx. In the 300s BC, Plato proposed communal ownership of property by the ruling class in *The Republic.* During medieval times, many religious orders practiced the holding of goods in common. Thomas More in his book *Utopia* (1516) proposed common ownership of property.

Several factors existing in the late 1700s and early 1800s provided the impetus for an increase in this type of thinking. One was the French Revolution, which emphasized the equality of all people. Another was the romantic movement, which fostered a high view of human nature and the perfectibility of people and society. A third was the Industrial Revolution, which thrived on a large unskilled labor force in the factories. Many of these laborers worked and lived under extremely difficult conditions.

In light of the influence of these factors, socialist thinking was found in many writers of the early 1800s. Among these were Henri de Saint-Simon, Charles Fourier, Étienne Cabet, Robert Owen (who founded New Harmony, Indiana), Louis Blanc, Pierre-Joseph Proudhon, Barthélemy Prosper Enfantin, Victor Prosper Considerant, and Auguste Comte.

Karl Marx's Early Years

Karl Marx was born on May 5, 1818, at Trier, Prussia, to Heinrich and Henriette Marx. Heinrich was a lawyer. Both were Jews, having descended from a long line of rabbis. In order to continue his law practice in a "Christian" environment, however, Heinrich converted to Lutheranism in 1816. Karl and his siblings were baptized in 1824.

Marxism after Marx

Though Marx and Engels laid the foundation for the ideology that became known as Marxism, its development was shaped by a number of other writers in the late nineteenth and early twentieth centuries. In 1889, at the meeting of the Second International Workingman's Association in Paris, a conflict arose between Karl Kautsky and Eduard Bernstein. The latter believed that a gradual approach was better than the revolutionary doctrine propounded by Marx. He believed the political and economic system could be changed gradually. Those who followed Bernstein became known as "Revisionists." Modern "Eurocommunism" represented this line of thinking. Kautsky, on the other hand, defended the need for revolution to institute socialism. He became the leading theoretician of orthodox Marxism in the late nineteenth century.

TABLE 10.15. Marxism and Christianity contrasted[98]

	Marxism	Christianity
God	Atheistic—there is no God. Matter is the fundamental reality.	Theistic—there is one Creator God. Reality consists of both matter and spirit.
The nature of humanity	Humanity has evolved from animals. Humanity's nature is determined by economic forces.	Humanity was created by God. Human beings are unique among the rest of creation because we are made in the image of God.
Ethics	There are no transcendent moral absolutes. Whatever advances communism is right.	Moral absolutes are based on God's holy character and commandments.
The problem	Humanity is alienated from the fruit of our labors because of the distinction between the laborer and the owner.	Humanity has rebelled against God, and we reap the results of our sin through personal and social strife.
The solution	Humanity can be "saved" from alienation by eliminating private property and class distinctions. We can each become a "new man" through economic, political, and social means.	Humanity can be saved by trusting in Christ. We can each become a "new man" through the regenerating work of the Holy Spirit (2 Cor. 5:17).
The foundation for hope	Humanity's hope is to be found in political revolution.	Humanity's hope is to be found in the sacrificial death of Jesus Christ, who conquered death for us. Our hope will be fully realized when Jesus returns to rule over all the earth with justice.

The New Age Movement

Introduction

The New Age movement is a Western spiritual movement that developed in the second half of the twentieth century. Its central precepts have been described as "drawing on both Eastern and Western spiritual and metaphysical traditions and infusing them with influences from self-help and motivational psychology." The term *New Age* refers to the coming astrological Age of Aquarius.[99]

The movement aims to create "a spirituality without borders or confining dogmas" that is inclusive and pluralistic. It holds to "a holistic worldview," emphasizing the mind and positing that there is a form of monism and unity throughout the universe. It attempts to create "a worldview that includes both science and spirituality," embracing a number of forms of mainstream science as well as other forms of science that are considered fringe.

The origins of the movement can be found in medieval astrology and alchemy, such as the writings of Paracelsus; in the Renaissance interest in Hermeticism; in eighteenth-century mysticism, such as that of Emanuel Swedenborg, and in beliefs in animal magnetism espoused by Franz Mesmer.

In the nineteenth and early twentieth centuries, authors such as Godfrey Higgins and the esotericists Eliphas Levi, Helena Blavatsky, and George Gurdjieff articulated specific histories, cosmologies, and some of the basic philosophical principles that would influence the movement. It experienced a revival as a result of the work of individuals such as Alice Bailey and organizations such as the Theosophical Society.

The New Age movement gained further momentum in the 1960s, taking influence from metaphysics, perennial philosophy, self-help psychology, and the various Indian gurus who visited the West during that decade. In the 1970s, it developed a social and political component.

The New Age movement includes elements of older spiritual and religious traditions ranging from monotheism to pantheism, pandeism, panentheism, and polytheism, combined with science and Gaia philosophy, particularly archeoastronomy, astronomy, ecology, environmentalism, the Gaia hypothesis, UFO religions, psychology, and physics.

New Age practices and philosophies sometimes draw inspiration from major world religions—Buddhism, Taoism, Chinese folk religion, Christianity, Hinduism, Sufism (Islam), Judaism (especially Kabbalah), and Sikhism—with strong influences from East Asian religions, esotericism, Gnosticism, Hermeticism, idealism, neo-paganism, New Thought, spiritualism, Theosophy, universalism, and Wisdom tradition.[100]

Number of Adherents

The number of adherents of the New Age movement is difficult to ascertain, mostly because the movement is a set of beliefs, not an organization. There are indicators in the culture, however. For example, a poll released by CNN in 1990 estimated that 35 percent of all Americans believed in reincarnation. If accurate, this means that roughly 35 million to 40 million people in the United States believe in one of the central tenets of the New Age. It is also estimated that the percentage of New Age adherents in Europe and South America is slightly higher than in the United States.[101]

Defining the New Age and the Movement

The term *New Age* refers to the coming Aquarian age, which is in the process of replacing the old, or Piscean, age. According to astrologers, every two thousand years constitutes an "age." New Agers predict this Aquarian age will be a time of utopia.

The "movement" is like a smorgasbord for spirituality. It allows the religious consumer to pick and choose from among a wide variety of groups, teachers, and practices. The New Ager is free to choose the "path" or "door" according to whatever suits his or her particular taste in spirituality. A New Age person might be a Hindu, Buddhist, or Wiccan (witch), or an astrologer, channeler, or parapsychologist. His or her cause might be "deep ecology," animal rights, holistic healing, or UFOs. The surface belief, expression, or practice is not that important. What is important is that underneath all the groups and practices, there lies a unifying philosophy that binds the movement together.

The History and Roots of the New Age Movement

The New Age movement has collected and absorbed the beliefs and practices of a wide variety of historical movements. It receives its name—the New Age—from astrology, which predicts a coming age of peace and harmony.

Its basic beliefs come from Hinduism and Buddhism. These religions, passed to the United States directly through Swami Vivekananda, D. T. Suzuki, Paramahansa Yogananda, Yogi Bhajan, Swami Muktananda, Alan Watts, Maharishi Mahesh Yogi, and others, were also passed indirectly through the nineteenth-century transcendentalism of Walt Whitman, Henry David Thoreau, and Ralph Emerson.

The New Age's bent toward channeling—contacting the spirits—came through the Fox sisters, who in 1848 heard rappings that they claimed were coming from a murdered peddler who had been buried beneath their home in Hydesville, New York (Burrows, 21). Such spiritualism also came through the teaching on contacting "ascended masters"—advanced spirit beings—given by Madame Helena Blavatsky (1831–1891), the cofounder (with Henry Olcott) of the Theosophical Society in 1875. It also came through Edgar Cayce, the "Sleeping Prophet" (1877–1945), and through Jane Roberts (1929–1984), who channeled a "spirit entity" named Seth.

The New Age approach to the power of the mind with respect to healing came through Phineas P. Quimby, who helped spawn the mind science groups such as Christian Science (Mary Baker Eddy), the Unity School of Christianity (Charles and Myrtle Fillmore), and the Church of Religious Science (Ernest Holmes). The movement's concern for ecology was received through the Native American religions and through Rachel Carson's *The Silent Spring* (1962).

The New Age movement not only is the result of the teachings, philosophies, and practices of previous movements but also serves as the undergirding influence behind the teachings, practices, and contemporary trends in the following areas:

- Medicine (holistic health, therapeutic touch, Bernie Siegel, Deepak Chopra)
- Education (using guided imagery and meditation in the classroom, "values clarification")

- Politics (globalism, Robert Muller of the United Nations, Planetary Citizens, Global Education Associates)
- Music (Stephen Halpern, Yanni)
- Science (Fritjof Capra's *The Tao of Physics*, the monistic/mystical interpretation of the new physics)
- Psychology (transpersonal psychology, the human potential movement)
- Ecology (the Green movement, "deep ecology")
- Business (transformation technologies, "organizational transformation," Lifespring, Forum, Anthony Robbins)
- Religion (*A Course in Miracles*, Marianne Williamson, Unity School of Christianity) (see Miller, chapters 5–6, and Chandler).

The Core Beliefs of the New Age Movement

The major unifying beliefs of the New Age movement include the following.

The Problem Is That of Perception

Humanity's most fundamental problem has to do with perception. To be more specific, all of humanity is suffering from a severe case of ignorance in that we have forgotten our true nature. We have forgotten that we are unconditionally connected to and emanated from God, which is Universal Mind.

During the "old age" of Pisces, we relied on the dualistic way of thinking that says humankind is unique and separate from the rest of nature. Such a perspective must be changed, however, says the New Age movement. Barbara Marx Hubbard, a leading advocate of the New Age, calls the dualistic worldview the "fatal human flaw [which] is the illusion that we are separated from each other, from nature, and from the creative processes of nature herself" (Hubbard, 239).

The New Age View of God

The goal of the variety of New Age methods and beliefs is to come to the realization of the central truth of the New Age, which is that everything is fundamentally divine because everything flows from the divine oneness that is the existential substance—the essential reality—beneath all things.

When a New Ager speaks of God, he or she is not referring to the Judeo-Christian concept of God as a personal holy being who has existed before all things and is separate from all things. Instead, two keywords describe the New Age movement's concept of God: *monism* and *pantheism.*

Monism is the belief that God is one in the sense of God's being a oneness without duality or differentiation. There is no separation within God. God is "beyond" all such distinctions, including distinctions between persons and between good and evil. The New Age movement characterizes this oneness as a force or an energy. Pantheism is the belief that all is God or all is divine. What this means is that everything is inherently connected to, and is an emanation from, the divine oneness.

The New Age View of Humanity

If God is an underlying life force or a vital energy from which all reality emanates, then it stands to reason that we, as humans, are unconditionally connected to God. If God is the universal self, then we are the particularizations of that universal self. We are like individual streams that flow from the infinite lake. Just as the water in the streams is the same in essence with the water in the lake, so our essence is at one with God.

Christianity teaches that humanity's problem is that we have rebelled against God and have thereby broken our relationship with him. The New Age movement teaches, on the other hand, that there is nothing we can possibly to do sever the connection that exists between us and the divine oneness. Our problem is ignorance, says the New Ager, not rebellion. We have forgotten who we are in our true selves, which is one with the universal self. The goal of yoga, meditation, and other mind-expanding techniques is to experience that oneness. Such an experience will change our lives, because as we experience the oneness—the interconnectedness—with all things, we are transformed to view and to value everything as a manifestation of the Divine.

The Power of the Mind

When the existence of a transcendent God who created all things is denied, as it is in the New Age movement, then the objectivity—the solidness, the otherness—of external reality is diminished. When that happens, the role of the individual in shaping reality increases in importance. That is precisely where the New Age movement is coming from. Moreover, because the basic "stuff" of the universe is mind, as we learn the appropriate techniques, our minds will be able to exert tremendous power over "reality."

The New Age claims about the power of the mind range from the belief that positive thoughts or affirmations manifest themselves in physical health and fulfilled dreams to the idea that, through the act of observation, the consciousness of each individual "actualizes"—brings into reality—one of the many possible, but as yet unrealized, realities.

The Immediate Goal

Some New Agers believe that humanity's goal is the perfection of our ability to love. They believe there are a number of lessons that we need to learn in life before we can go on to the next stage. Reincarnation, which is the idea that our essential selves live from lifetime to lifetime, allows the possibility of learning those lessons. Before entering each lifetime, we choose the situation we are about to enter. For example, we might choose to be born to a family that is part of a racial minority, or choose to be born physically challenged, or choose to have AIDS, or choose to be raped. Each experience provides the opportunity for the person to perfect whatever characteristic he or she needs to develop and to learn whatever lesson he or she needs to learn.

Other New Agers come from a perspective that is closer to the original Hindu concept of reincarnation, which is based on karma. Karma, which simply means "action," is the moral law of cause and effect—"you reap what you sow." According to this view, the actions that are part of one's present life are the direct results of actions committed in earlier lives. If you are murdered, you were probably a murderer in a previous life. If you are poor, you were probably rich in a previous life. And so on.

The Call for Assistance

New Agers encourage people to get in touch with their spirit guides, who are able to assist them along their path of spiritual evolution and transformation. The various kinds of beings that can be contacted include ascended masters, disembodied spirits who lived in physical bodies at one time, UFOs, the spirits of animals, and angels.

The Ultimate Goal

Since ultimate reality, according to the New Age movement, is a oneness that is beyond all separation and differentiation, the *ultimate goal* is for each person to relinquish all attachment and identification with his or her individual ego and to become identified with, or merged into, the universal self. Rather than portraying the dissolution of the individual self as something negative, the New Age movement portrays the eventual merging of all persons into the one in a positive light. It is seen as an expansion of the individual minds into the universal mind.

TABLE 10.16. The New Age movement and Christianity contrasted

	The New Age movement	Christianity
God is ...	Impersonal; without moral distinctions; the life force that underlies nature; the existential substance beneath all things.	Personal; moral; holy; Creator; distinct from his creation.
Humanity is ...	Divine, in that we are ontologically extended (extended in our beings) from God's existential substance. We are unconditionally extended from the oneness, but we are ignorant of our true divine nature.	Made in God's image, but we are ontologically separate (separated in our being) from the transcendent, infinite, and holy God. We are spiritually separated from God because of our sin and rebellion against him.

	The New Age movement	Christianity
Salvation is ...	Gaining a new perspective, in which we see the interconnectedness of all things, including ourselves, with the divine oneness.	Being justified before and reconciled to God through faith in the atoning work of Jesus Christ. Salvation is also being given new life through the transforming power of the Holy Spirit.
Life after death is ...	Spiritual progression for the purpose of attaining enlightenment; expanding one's consciousness into the universal mind.	Spent in either heaven or hell. Either eternal fellowship with the personal God or eternal separation from him.

Secularism

Definition

Secularism is the principle of the separation of government institutions and persons mandated to represent the state from religious institutions and religious dignitaries. One manifestation of secularism is asserting the right to be free from religious rule and teachings or, in a state declared to be neutral on matters of belief, from religion or religious practices imposed on the people by their government. Another manifestation of secularism is the view that public activities and decisions, especially political ones, should be uninfluenced by religious beliefs and/or practices.

Secularism draws its intellectual roots from Greek and Roman philosophers such as Marcus Aurelius and Epicurus; from Enlightenment thinkers such as Denis Diderot, Voltaire, Baruch Spinoza, James Madison, Thomas Jefferson, and Thomas Paine; and from more recent freethinkers and atheists such as Robert Ingersoll and Bertrand Russell.

The purposes and arguments in support of secularism vary widely. In European laicism, it has been argued that secularism is a movement toward modernization and away from traditional religious values (also known as secularization). This type of secularism, on a social or philosophical level, has often occurred while maintaining an official state church or other state support of religion. In the United States, some argue that state secularism has served to a greater extent to protect religion and the religious from governmental interference, while secularism on a social level is less prevalent. Within countries, differing political movements support secularism for varying reasons.[101]

Secularism among the Nations

If one combines the numbers of atheists and nonreligious people, the total number of secularists is around 20 percent of the world's population (Barrett, 25).

In the following countries, atheists or nonreligious individuals make up more than 10 percent of the population (Johnstone): Albania, Australia, China, Cuba, the Czech Republic, France, French Polynesia, Hungary, Italy, Japan, North Korea, Macao, Mongolia, Netherlands, New Zealand, Poland, Romania, Singapore, Sweden, the former USSR, the United Kingdom, Uruguay, Vietnam, and the former Yugoslavia.

The Beliefs of Secularism

The Denial of God

The most fundamental tenet of secularism is the denial of the existence of the supernatural. Matter is all that exists.

According to secularism, belief in God is nothing more than a projection of humankind's own thoughts and desires. God did not make humankind in his image; instead, humankind made God in its image.

The Denial of Miracles

After God's existence is denied, it is logical then to conclude that miracles— the result of God's intervention—are not possible. The miracles recorded in the Bible, secularists surmise, must have been the embellishments of the authors who were promoting their particular religious' agenda (Geisler and Brooks, chapter 5; Geisler, 1992).

The Fact of Evolution

Secularists assert that the existence and complexity of the universe can be sufficiently explained through naturalistic principles as set forth in the theory of evolution. Personality and mind are also the products of the evolutionary process and are sufficiently explained through the interaction of chemical and biological elements. Thus, there is no "ghost in the machine."

The Potential of Humanity

Secularists see religion as being restrictive and escapist. Religion does nothing more than assuage the fears of an ignorant people. If humanity is to survive, secularists say, humankind must face problems squarely and find the answers within themselves, reason, and science. Secularism begins and ends with humanity. Humanity will be able to face the issues squarely only when freed from the shackles of religion.

The Centrality of Science

Secularists are confident that the scientific method of inquiry is the only reliable avenue by which to discover truth and knowledge. According to the secularistic point of view, there is an irreconcilable antagonism between reason and faith; science and religion; and empirical observation and revealed authority. The two avenues to truth and knowledge are mutually exclusive.

The Stress on Relativity

Secularists deny that there is an absolute moral reference point beyond humanity, such as a holy God. They contend that humankind does not need an absolute moral standard beyond itself in order to have a sufficient foundation and motivation for moral behavior. Humanity is by nature good, and all that is needed to realize that innate goodness is education, not religious transformation.

The Finality of Death

Secularists believe that at death, the individual ceases to exist in any cohesive or conscious form. As the signatories of the Humanist Manifesto II wrote, "There is no credible evidence that life survives the death of the body" (Lamont, 293).

TABLE 10.17. Secularism and Christianity contrasted

	Secularism	Christianity
God	Matter, in one form or another, is all that has existed from eternity and all that will ever exist.	God alone is infinite and eternal. The material universe is finite and has not always existed. God created it out of nothing.
Humanity	Humanity is by nature monistic (a oneness) in that the person consists of only one substance: matter. Humanity represents the highest point of the gradual and random processes of evolution.	Humanity is by nature dualistic in that the person consists of two substances: body and spirit. Humanity, being made in the image of God, represents the highest point of God's creation.
Humanity's problem	Humanity depends on the escapist promises of religion, rather than facing problems squarely and believing that humankind has the potential to create a world in which peace and justice will prevail.	Humanity has rebelled against a personal and holy God. As a result, we live for ourselves and place our hope in false gods, such as success, money, nature, science, and education.
The solution	Extending the scientific method of rational inquiry into all aspects of life, while at the same time maintaining a sense	Humanity's being restored to right relationship with a holy God through faith in Jesus Christ. While Christianity encourages the rational inquiry

	Secularism	Christianity
	of compassion for the individual.	of science, it opposes scientism, which goes beyond the limits of science in that it claims that the scientific method is a sufficient avenue to all truth.
Jesus Christ	At most, Jesus was a good moral teacher. Because the biblical authors embellished the details of Jesus's life, though, we can be certain of very little concerning the historical details of his life.	Jesus was the very embodiment of God on earth. The Bible meets the qualifications for being authentic history. It records that Jesus lived, died for our sins, and rose from the dead.
After death	There is no survival of the person's consciousness after death.	There is personal survival after death, either eternal life with God or eternal separation from him.

Shinto

Definition

Shinto, also known as kami-no-michi, is the indigenous religion of Japan. It is defined as an action-centered religion focused on ritual practices to be carried out diligently so as to establish a connection between present-day Japan and its ancient past. Founded in 660 BC according to Japanese mythology, Shinto practices were first recorded and codified in the written historical records of the Kojiki and Nihon Shoki in the eighth century. Still, these earliest Japanese writings do not refer to a unified Shinto religion, but rather to a collection of native beliefs and mythology. *Shinto* today is a term that applies to the religion of public shrines devoted to the worship of a multitude of gods (*kami*) and suited to various purposes such as war memorials and the harvest festival, It also applies to various sectarian organizations. Practitioners express their diverse beliefs through a standard language and practice, adopting a similar style of dress and ritual, dating from around the time of the Nara and Heian periods.

The word *Shinto* ("way of the gods") was adopted, originally as *Shindo*, from the written Chinese *Shendao* (神道; pinyin: shén dào), combining two kanji: "shin" (神), meaning "spirit" or "kami", and "tō" (道), meaning a philosophical path or study (from the Chinese word *dào*).

The oldest recorded usage of the word *Shindo* is from the second half of the sixth century. Kami are defined in English as "spirits," "essences," or "gods," referring to the energy generating the phenomena. Since Japanese language doesn't distinguish between singular and plural, *kami* refers to the divinity, or sacred essence, that manifests in multiple forms. Rocks, trees, rivers, animals, places, and even people can be said to possess the nature of kami. Kami and people are not separate; they exist within the same world and share its interrelated complexity.

Shinto is the largest religion in Japan, practiced by nearly 80 percent of the population, yet only a small percentage of these identify themselves as Shintoists in surveys. This is due to the fact that *Shinto* has different meanings in Japan: most of the Japanese attend Shinto shrines and beseech kami without belonging to an institutional Shinto religion, and since there are no formal rituals to become a member of folk Shinto, Shinto membership is often estimated by counting those who join organized Shinto sects. Shinto has one hundred thousand shrines and twenty thousand priests in the country.

According to Inoue (2003)

In modern scholarship, the term *Shinto* is often used with reference to kami worship and related theologies, rituals, and practices. In these contexts, *Shinto* takes on the meaning of "Japan's traditional religion," as opposed to foreign religions such as Christianity, Buddhism, Islam, and so forth.[102]

Historical Roots

To Westerners, Japan remains an enigma. This is nowhere more true than in its religions. Japan's traditional faith, Shinto (or kami-no-michi—"the way of the gods") is rooted in Japan's national history and is intricately intertwined with its culture.

165

Rev. Silas Kanyabigega, DMin

Early Formative Period (Prehistory–AD 790)

The phrase *early Shinto* (before AD 538–552) describes the religious life that flourished in Japan before Buddhism arrived there in the sixth century after Christ. The main written sources describing early Shinto are documents called Kojiki and Nihongi (chronicles of early myths recorded after 712 by members of the imperial court) and the Engishiki (descriptions of early prayers and rituals).

Early Interaction with Buddhism (552–710)

Between 538 and 552, new religions came to Japan from China and Korea. The arrival of Buddhism, Confucianism, and Taoism initiated new dynamics of religious interaction. In early Shinto, each community probably worshipped its local deity according to provincial custom. But under the influence of other faiths, the adherents of Shinto gradually organized their deities into a pantheon and coordinated a system of shrines.

Period of Development (AD 790–1600)

Heian Period (794–1185)

As the Japanese moved their capital from Nara to Kyoto (784–794), the culture was moving toward feudalism. The imperial court was developing a highly stylized aesthetic cultural life.

The Japanese consider the period after the move to Kyoto as the epitome of classical Japanese culture. The upper classes valued and aspired to *miyabi*, an elusive sense of courtly elegance and refined aesthetic taste.

Period of Consolidation and Renewal (1600–present)

Tokugawa Period (1600–1867)

Increasing political conflict and chaos after the Kamakura period gradually ended when a group of very determined feudal lords set out to unify and

166

stabilize the country. The most revered of these is Tokugawa Ieyasu (1542–1616). While his predecessors had made considerable progress, it was Tokugawa who finally established a new shogunate with the seat of power in the new city of Edo (now Tokyo). These men not only conquered their rival feudal lords but also took control of the important Buddhist headquarters at Nara and of the imperial line itself.

For two and a half centuries, the Tokugawa government brought relative peace to Japan. The government became very protective of its own power, intrusive in the lives of the people, and resistant to international influence. As part of this policy, the Tokugawa shoguns banned Christianity but made Buddhism a branch of the state. The Tokugawa governors also revived Confucianism, an active faith of moral obligation or duty.

TABLE 10.18. The nature of the Shinto gods (kami) contrasted with God

Shinto	Christianity
There are many gods (kami).	There is one triune God.
The kami are procreated by other gods.	God created all things and persons.
The kami indwell material objects and the natural world.	God transcends the world in his being.
The kami may be either helpful or hurtful.	God is loving and absolutely good.
The kami are the gods of Japan.	God is the Creator and Lord of all peoples.

TABLE 10.19. The human relationship to the gods (kami) or to God

Shinto	Christianity
The kami are offended by ritual or ceremonial pollution related to blood or death.	God is alienated by the moral rebellion expressed by the self-centeredness or disobedience of his creatures.
The kami might commune with those who are ritually purified and who wait for their presence.	God promises to be present to anyone who calls upon him for forgiveness.

Shinto	Christianity
Shinto believers can fulfill their duty while following their own life agenda.	Christians follow God when they fulfill God's agenda and will.
Shinto believers gain the good graces of the kami by following the principles of purification.	Christians enjoy a relationship with God through trustful reliance on (faith in) God.
Enjoying the good graces of the kami depends on human efforts.	A relationship with God is a gift (grace) that no one can earn.

Taoism

Definition

Taoism, or Daoism, is a philosophical, ethical, and religious tradition of Chinese origin that emphasizes living in harmony with the Tao (also romanized as Dao). The term *Tao* means "way," "path," or "principle," and can also be found in Chinese philosophies and religions other than Taoism. In Taoism, however, Tao denotes something that is both the source and the driving force behind everything that exists. It is ultimately ineffable: "The Tao that can be told is not the eternal Tao."

While Taoism drew its cosmological notions from the tenets of the School of Yin-Yang, the Tao Te Ching, a compact and ambiguous book containing teachings attributed to Laozi (Chinese: 老子; pinyin: Lǎozǐ; Wade–Giles: Lao Tzu), is widely considered its keystone work. Together with the writings of Zhuangzi, the Tao Te Ching forms the philosophical foundation of Taoism. This philosophical Taoism, individualistic by nature, in its institutionalized forms, however, evolved over time in the shape of a number of different schools. Taoist schools traditionally feature reverence for Laozi and immortals, or ancestors, along with a variety of divination and exorcism rituals, and practices for achieving ecstasy, longevity, or immortality.

Taoist propriety and ethics may vary depending on the particular school, but in general Taoism tends to emphasize wu-wei (action through nonaction), naturalness, simplicity, spontaneity, and the Three Treasures: compassion, moderation, and humility.

Taoism has had profound influence on Chinese culture in the course of the centuries, and clerics of institutionalized Taoism (Chinese: 道士; pinyin: dàoshi) usually take care to note distinction between their ritual tradition and the customs and practices found in Chinese folk religion, as these distinctions sometimes appear blurred. Chinese alchemy (especially *neidan*), Chinese astrology, Chan (Zen) Buddhism, several martial arts, traditional Chinese medicine, feng shui, and many styles of qigong have been intertwined with Taoism throughout history. Beyond China, Taoism also had influence on surrounding societies in Asia.

After Laozi and Zhuangzi, the literature of Taoism grew steadily and was compiled in the form of a canon—the Daozang—which was published at the behest of the emperor. Throughout Chinese history, Taoism was several times nominated as a state religion. After the seventeenth century, however, it fell from favor.

Like other religious activity, Taoism was suppressed in the first decades of the People's Republic of China (and even persecuted during the cultural revolution), but people continued to practice it in Taiwan. Today, it is one of five religions recognized in the PRC, and although it does not travel readily from its Asian roots, it claims adherents in a number of societies.[103]

Introduction

It is important to understand the concepts of Taoism, because they lie at the heart of the Asian cultures—China, Korea, Japan, and Vietnam. One Chinese scholar wrote the following:

> No one can hope to understand Chinese philosophy, religion, government, art, medicine—or even cooking—without a real appreciation of the profound philosophy taught in [the Tao Te Ching]. ... No other Chinese classic of such small size has exercised so much influence. (Chan, 136, 137)

But what is Taoism all about? What are the principles that lie behind this religion/philosophy that was founded over twenty-five hundred years ago and that has had such a grip on the thinking of the Asian world and now, increasingly, on the West?[216]

The History of Taoism

The Ritual Music Culture

Harmony characterized the Chinese society during the first four centuries of the Chou dynasty (1111–249 BC; Chan, xv). The basis for the harmony was a set of principles called the ritual music culture (see also the section on Confucianism).

The ritual music culture was based on the idea that there are certain "ways" of doing things as mandated by heaven (the Tao). These ways were termed "rituals," or *li*, but the idea of rituals went beyond our limited understanding of that term. *Rituals* referred to the proper way of doing things, especially with regard to how to relate to people of higher or lower classes and to those within the family. It was the responsibility of the emperor to rule according to the li, and as he did so, it was presumed he would promote the welfare of the people.

The term *music* in the ritual music culture refers to the sense in which the customs of society were to be like music in that they were to be "conducted with style like an artistic performance" (Graham, 11). The idea, then, behind the ritual music culture was that social harmony would result when the rulers promoted a sense of civility, appropriateness, and virtue among the people.

The principles of the ritual music culture succeeded in producing harmony in China for four centuries. That harmony began to falter, however, when the feudal states within China started to fight against one another for land and power.

In an effort to restore the harmony, a number of itinerant scholars and political theorists traveled throughout the country attempting to influence the rulers with their theories and worldviews (Mair, 1994, xvii). Confucius (551–479 BC) was the most influential of those scholars and political theorists. He pushed for a return to the precepts of the ritual music culture. The innovation that Confucius brought to the situation was that *all the people*, not just the emperor, were to live according to the mandated pattern of heaven, or the Tao (Lau, 28).

In spite of Confucius's efforts, however, the social conditions in China continued to deteriorate. What was especially shocking to the Chinese was that the fighting was without restraint. Conflicts had arisen even during the Chou dynasty, but they were fought in accordance with established rules. The present wars were being fought without regard for the proper ways of doing battle. For example, the victorious rulers would sometimes boil the bodies of the defeated and then drink the soup (Welch, 19).

Lao Tzu

Lao Tzu (pronounced "Lau-tz"), a contemporary of Confucius, considered Confucius and his ritual music culture to be responsible for China's state of chaos. He wrote in the Tao Te Ching, the scripture of Taoism, "When righteousness is lost, only then does the doctrine of propriety arise. Now, propriety is a superficial expression of loyalty and faithfulness, and the beginning of disorder" (chap. 38; Chan, 158). Lao Tzu was saying that the imposing of external laws reflects the breakdown of internal laws and that harmony will not result when laws are imposed on the people.

Legend has it that Confucius met with Lao Tzu in order to ask about the rituals. Lao Tzu responded to Confucius by saying, "Give up, sir, your proud airs, your many wishes, mannerisms, and extravagant claims. They won't do you any good, sir! That's all I have to tell you" (Blakney, 27). Lao Tzu was telling Confucius that he was going about creating harmony in the wrong way. He was accusing Confucius, rightly or wrongly, of imposing a morality on the people. He considered it a natural reaction of the people to rebel against the imposition of such a moral authoritarianist.

Lao Tzu saw that the answer to the social chaos was to be found in the Tao (pronounced "dow") and in the principle of *wu-wei*, which is the principle of purposeful "inaction."

To realize harmony again, Lao Tzu taught, our only "action" should be to align ourselves with the natural flow of the Tao and to let it work its natural course through us. The less the government is involved in this process, the better."

Chuang Tzu

Chuang Tzu, who lived sometime between 399BC and 295 BC, took the ideas in the Tao Te Ching as his starting point, developed them further, and emphasized the mystical nature of the Tao. Chuang Tzu's work is called the Chuang Tzu.

Chuang Tzu places more emphasis than does Lao Tzu on the ability of the individual to transform himself or herself through the realization of the *Te* (pronounced as "duh"), which is the universal Tao manifested in the individual.

The Search for Immortality

The teachings of Lao Tzu, Chuang Tzu, and Lieh Tzu—another teacher, who came after Chuang Tzu—comprise the foundations for *philosophical* Taoism. In the centuries that followed, however, Taoism left its philosophical and metaphysical roots and turned to what has been called *religious* Taoism. This religious Taoism would more appropriately be called "magical" Taoism, as it concerned itself with the development of techniques to utilize the forces of the Tao in order to attain magical powers and immortality.

The change from philosophical Taoism to religious Taoism took place when the developers of religious Taoism interpreted passages from the three foundational teachers in a literal way. Such passages, however, were probably intended to be interpreted figuratively—as goals to be aimed for only in a spiritual sense (Welch, 92).

Out of this literalistic movement flowed several streams of thought and practice (Welch, 92–97):

- Hygiene
  This stream of thought was not the idea that "cleanliness is next to godliness," but that one can use the chi—the breath, or vital energy within—to purify oneself and thereby attain immortality.

- Alchemy
  This stream in Taoism sought to change natural elements into an elixir of life that would make one immortal.

- P'eng-lai
  This name refers to a mythical island (or islands) that was actually being searched for at the time. The belief was that immortal beings and a drug that prevents death would be found on this island.

After a while, these three streams of thought and practice in Taoism merged together and were joined by other magical techniques for attaining immortality. Plus, religious Taoism incorporated a movement that created a host of gods. Around the third century AD, however, philosophical Taoism made a resurgence through a movement called "Pure Conversation." In Pure Conversation, scholars again studied the primary scriptures of Taoism—the Tao Te Ching and the Chuang Tzu. This resurgence of philosophical Taoism has continued to this day.

The Beliefs of Taoism

The Tao

The Tao Te Ching, in most translations, begins with the following two lines: "The Tao (Way) that can be told of is not the eternal Tao; The name that can be named is not the eternal name" (chap. 1; Chan, 139). As these words imply, the Tao is a mysterious thing; it's beyond knowing, beyond description, and beyond identification. If we think we understand the Tao, it's because we have oversimplified it. Nevertheless, even though the Tao is unknowable and indescribable, the Tao Te Ching does attempt to describe it, as in the following passage:

> There was something undifferentiated and yet complete,
> Which existed before heaven and earth.
> Soundless and formless,
> it depends on nothing and does not change.
> It operates everywhere and is free from danger.
> It may be considered the mother of the universe.
> I do not know its name; I call it Tao.

The Te

Te is that pattern within each object that makes it what it is; it is our individuality, our uniqueness. Te, moreover, is each individual's inner connection to the universal Tao. Therefore, as we are true to who we are in our own unique nature, we will work in harmony with the natural flow of the universe.

Taoism says that we need to accept the Te—the unique pattern—for what it is, both in ourselves and in other things. We should resist, therefore, making everything conform to our limited idea of what is right. When such conformity is imposed on an object or a person, it, or he or she, will resist, and that resistance is the result of our having not taken into consideration the unique pattern within that person or object. For example, while we as humans would be uncomfortable sleeping in a damp place, a frog would feel right at home (chap. 2; Fung. 11). But which way of sleeping is right? Both, depending on whether we're talking about a frog or a person. It would go against the Te, though, to impose either way of sleeping on the other.

The resistance that is elicited when one's Te, or unique pattern, is violated is why we should act toward others with a certain "inaction," as discussed in the next section.

The Principle of Inaction (Wu-Wei)

In observing the fighting that was going on between the feudal states, Lao Tzu noticed that force was inevitably responded to with force. He also noticed that the initial force eventually brought about its own defeat (Welch, 20). Lao Tzu wrote, "Violent and fierce people do not die a natural death" (chap. 42; Chan, 161). He saw that this principle was true not only in the cases involving physical violence but also in the cases of one person imposing his or her will on someone else. It was because when someone imposed his or her will on an object or a person, the pattern—Te—within that object or person resisted.

The way, then, to achieve one's purpose, says Lao Tzu, is to work with the pattern—the Te—within things rather than to impose one's will on them. This is, in essence, the principle of wu-wei, or "inaction." *Wu-wei* is a purposeful "taking no unnatural action" (Chan, 791); it's a deliberate removing of one's hands from something and letting nature, or the Tao, take its course.

Te–Yang Duality

The Tao Te Ching says that "the One produced the two." The "two" are the yin and the yang—the opposing but, at the same time, balancing and interacting forces within nature. Table 10.20 provides some examples.

TABLE 10.20. Yin and yang contrasted

Yin	Yang
Female	Male
Cold	Hot
Passive	Active
Negative	Positive
Dark	Light
Death	Life
Good	Evil
Right	Left
Weak	Strong
Responsive	Aggressive
Contraction	Expansion

Even though the two forces are opposites of each other, they also interact with each other, and by doing so life and nature are produced.

As we look at nature, we are to view it as a whole, as manifesting both the yin and the yang, for they are mutually dependent—we cannot know the one apart from the contrast of the other. For example, we cannot know the good without the evil to give us perspective. The symbol for yin and yang—a circle with black and white halves curling into each other—denotes this interactive and interdependent relationship.

The yin and the yang were also used in the Taoist—in fact, in the Chinese—practice of divination. In Chinese religious life, the summer and winter solstices were the most important times of the year when the forces of yin and yang reached their peaks and gave way to each other. The Spring Festival (also called Chinese New Year) is one of these times. To a people who believed that their lives were centered in the flow of the natural world, this was an important time for divining the future. Fortune-tellers and mediums were sought for help in making big decisions, such as for weddings, funerals, and large investments, and their advice was followed to the letter.

Even today and in the most modern of Chinese cities, spiritual advisors are regularly consulted for big decisions. What we in the West would call "superstition," the Chinese would call "going with the flow." and would, at all costs, avoid getting out of touch with the natural flow of nature. With respect to the yin–yang duality, one does not try to avoid one or the other; rather, it is important to live in harmony between them both, never having too much of either.[104]

Satanology (the Study of Satan)

Introduction

A study of theology is not complete without an examination of the origin of evil (before the Fall in the garden), the force behind evil, and the personification of evil in the person of Satan.

The primary source of correct information about Satan is scripture, which is perhaps the only reliable source. Since secrecy is one of the characteristics of Satan, it is understandable that so many Christians are deceived concerning his nature and work. Satan has blinded them about it. He is most effective when he keeps himself hidden from public sight.

Therefore, from an apologetic standpoint, to deny the existence of Satan is to suggest that Jesus Christ is not divine (even though he repeatedly claimed divinity), and that his ministry was comparable to the mission of a lunatic. Yet scripture is indeed the inerrant Word of God, and the testimony of Jesus Christ is fully authoritative as to the person of Satan.[105]

The Personality of Satan

The Devil is a real person. Originally, he was created in time as one of God's angels, possessing all the attributes of angels. He was an incorporeal being with the power of personality. Even after his rebellion and fall, Satan remained a person. He is identified in scripture by personal pronouns, and he is involved in various activities belonging only to persons. Those who deny the existence of a Devil with personality have no biblical basis for their conclusions.

God does not deny the personality of Satan. When Satan appeared with the angels, "The Lord said unto Satan, Hast thou considered my servant Job" (Job 1:8)? Later in the story, the Bible notes, "Satan came also among them to present himself before the Lord" (Job 2:1). In Zechariah's vision of the high priest's meeting with Satan, "The Lord said unto Satan, The Lord rebuke thee, O Satan; even the Lord that hath chosen Jerusalem rebuke thee" (Zech. 3:2). When tempted by Satan, Jesus six times used personal pronouns in his conversation with Satan (Matt. 4:7, 10).

Satan demonstrated intellectual ability, emotions, and an active will. His intelligence is reflected in his ability to memorize scripture. When he tempted Jesus (Matt. 4:6), he cited an obscure verse out of context (Ps. 91:11–12) to give authority to his temptation. His superior intellect is further demonstrated by his ability to organize in excess of a hundred million angels under him. The Bible also portrays the Devil's temptations with terms like *wiles* (Eph. 6:11), *depths* (Rev. 2:24), and *devices* (2 Cor. 2:11).

Jesus warned Peter of the volitional side of Satan when he told him, "Satan hath desired to have you that he may sift you as wheat" (Luke 22:31). James identified fear as part of the emotional experience of all fallen angels (James. 2:19). They also have the sensation of pain, because they will someday "be tormented day and night for ever and ever" (Rev. 20:10).

It is the will of Satan that best characterizes him. Isaiah cited the fall of Satan coming as a result of his attempt to take the place of God in heaven. Satan revealed his selfish nature in the exclamation "I will" five times (Isa. 14:12–15). The apostle Paul also identified pride as the sin of Satan (1 Tim. 3:6).

Satan is also identified as performing acts normally ascribed to persons. He exercised the power of word selection as he tempted both Eve (Gen. 3:1–6) and Jesus (Matt. 4:1–11). He is currently accusing the brethren "before our God day and night" (Rev. 12:10). On at least two occasions, Satan engages in battle (Rev. 12:17; Rev. 20:8–9). When Moses appeared before Pharaoh, Satan demonstrated limited power to perform miracles when he turned the Egyptian magicians' rods into serpents (Exod. 7:12).

Satan has great power, but he is not omnipotent. Satan has great wisdom (much of it accumulated by experience), but he is not omniscient. Satan has his emissaries seemingly at every place, and his world system is ubiquitous, but he is not omnipresent.

Satan's driving motivation apparently focuses upon a total abrogation or a major hindering of the plan of God. On four separate occasions scripture explores Satan's motivation. In Isaiah 14, Genesis 3, Luke 4, and 2 Thessalonians 2, a vivid picture unmasks Satan as he seeks to take by force an unlawful throne. Try as he might, Satan's most cunning plans will always fall short of their ultimate objective, because the creature is never able to excel beyond the Creator. As Christ is Lord of Lords and King of Kings, Satan must recognize and acknowledge that his existence is dependent upon the deity of Jesus Christ.

The Origin of Satan

As one begins to study Satanology, the obvious question eventually emerges: where did Satan come from? If God is indeed a benevolent God and is able to exercise complete authority and power, where did Satan's evil objectives come from, and furthermore, why did God allow Satan to go as far as he did without attempting to stop him?

God could not have created anything evil. Originally, humankind was created in the image and likeness of God, but humanity fell into sin when Adam exercised his will in rebellion against God. Satan was also originally created as a being with power of personality and the freedom of choice. He was an angel with apparent honor and leadership in heaven. But when Satan's pride blinded him and led him to exercise his will in rebellion against God, he was cast out of heaven (Isa. 14:12–15; cf. 2 Pet. 2:4 and Jude 6).

Three prominent factors were present within Satan's mind as he sought to unlawfully ascend to the highest throne in the heavens. According to 1 Timothy 3:6, the first is pride: "Lest being lifted up with pride he falls into the condemnation of the devil."[106] Satan's ambitious pride in his God-given splendor convinced him that he was worthy of God's throne and glory.

Secondly, unbelief was also in the mind of Satan. As a result, he failed to believe that God would really punish him if he committed a sin. As a small child will wonder if his parents will really punish him, Satan, deluded by his pride, did not seriously purposely test his parent's prohibitions in order to find out if God would punish him.

Thirdly, Satan undoubtedly entertained thoughts of self-deception. He deceived himself into believing that he could actually wrestle the throne of God away from the Almighty. With blinded confidence, Satan and his host moved upon the throne, only to be met with a barrage of divine judgments.[107]

> Concerning the problem of the first sin of the first angel, it may be observed that, under existing conditions, almost every avenue along which sin advances was wanting. Self-assertion against God was the only direction in which such a being could sin. On this patent truth Hooker has written: "It seemeth therefore that there was no other way for angels to sin, but by reflex of their understanding upon themselves, when being held with admiration of their own sublimity and honor, the memory of their subordination unto God and their dependency on Him was drowned in this conceit; whereupon their adoration, love and imitation of God could not choose but be also interrupted" (Eccl. Pol., Book I, ch. iv. 2 cited by Gerhart, ibid. 672). This conceit which assumed self-direction where the Creator proposed to be the authority and guide, is alluded to by the Apostle when he wrote of a "novice" in matters of church order: "lest being lifted up with pride he fall into the condemnation [crime] of the devil" (1 Tim. 3:6; cf. Isa. 14:12; Ezek. 28:17 NIV).[107]

Commenting on the motive behind Satan's rebellion, Lewis Sperry Chafer writes, "The essential evil character of sin here, as everywhere, is an unwillingness on the part of the creature to abide in the precise position in which he has been placed by the Creator."[108]

Driven by an inner sense of false authority, Satan and his evil host embarked upon a fivefold series of "I will"s, or objectives.

Satan's Five Objectives

To Ascend into Heaven

The ultimate desire of Satan was to take God's place. Lucifer's first attempt involved his ascent into the abode of God. The Bible identifies three heavens. The first heaven is the sky surrounding our planet, the atmosphere. The second heaven is the stellar heaven, which is apparently the abode of angels. The third heaven is the dwelling place of God (2 Cor. 12:1–4). When Lucifer determined to ascend into heaven, he sought to move into the third heaven, the dwelling place of God. Satan wanted to ascend above the position and place where he was created and assume the place of his Creator.

That His Throne Be Exalted

Satan sought authority over the other angels and wanted to be exalted above the stars. The term *star* is often used in the Bible to identify angels (Rev. 1:20; Rev. 12:4). Some commentators believe Satan ruled the angels as an archangel along with Michael and Gabriel. If this were the case, Satan then sought to expand his sphere of authority over Michael and Gabriel and those angels they ruled. If Satan could have accomplished this, he would be the ultimate authority in heaven, perhaps taking the place of God over the angels. If this trinity of archangels existed before the Fall, it may suggest why a third of the angels fell with Satan (Rev. 12:4). Since scripture is silent on the nature of Gabriel's position, a second view, as espoused by some theologians, suggests the following:

> As there is one archangel among angels that are holy, so there is one archangel among angels that are unholy.[109] In regard to Satan's apparent successfulness in soliciting the loyalty of many thousands of angels, Ezekiel offers us some very helpful insight by the repeated usage of the word *merchandise* (28:5, 16, 18). It is also translated "traffick," which means "to go about," suggesting as [the theologian G. H.] Pember does, that Satan slandered God in an effort to attract others to join in his rebellion against God.[110]

To Govern Heaven

Satan desired to "sit also upon the mount of the congregation, in the sides of the north" (Isa. 14:13). The phrase *mount of the congregation* is an expression relating to ruling in the kingdom of God (Isa. 2:1–4). Lucifer seemed to be saying, "I want a share in the kingdom." The problem was that he wanted God's share. The "north side" is a term relating to God's presence in scripture (Ps. 75:6–7). During the millennial reign of Christ, Christ will rule this earth from the north (Ps. 48:2).

To Ascend Above the Heights

There can be no question that Satan was prepared to attempt a coup in heaven. His desire was not simply to get closer to God, but to surpass God. "I will ascend above the heights of the clouds" (Isa. 14:14). Clouds are often used to refer to the glory of God. In fact, 100 of the 150 uses of the word *cloud* in the King James Version have to do with divine glory.

As illustrated in these passages, Jehovah appeared in the cloud (Exod. 16:10); the cloud was termed "the cloud of Jehovah" (Exod. 40:38); when Jehovah was present, the cloud filled the house (1 Kings 8:10); Jehovah rides upon a swift cloud (Ps. 104:3; Isa. 19:1); Christ is to come, as he went upon the clouds of heaven (Matt. 24:30; Acts 1:9; Rev. 1:7); so the ransomed people appear (Israel: Isa. 60:8; and the church, 1 Thess. 4:17). Chafer, 49.

Satan sought a glory for himself that surpassed the glory of God. Paul revealed the ultimate desire of Satan when he wrote, "Who opposeth and exalteth himself above all that is called God, or that is worshipped; so that he as God sitteth in the temple of God, shewing himself that he is God" (2 Thess. 2:4).

To Be Like the Most High

When Abraham paid his tithes to Melchizedek, this priest "blessed him and said, Blessed be Abram of the most high God, possessor of heaven and earth" (Gen. 14:19).

"The Most High" (El Elyon) means "the possessor of heaven and earth," one who exercises divine authority in both spheres. When Jesus appeared to his disciples in Galilee after his death, he said, "All power is given unto me in heaven and in earth" (Matt. 28:18). Satan sought the authority of God for himself. By becoming most high, Satan would be the possessor of heaven and earth. By ascending into heaven, he would rule angels and ultimately enjoy a messianic rule.

Since his fall, Satan has become a zealot for propagating evil and immorality among the human race. This thought leads one to seriously question the sanity of those who seek to exalt and worship a fallen and judged angel who for all intents and purposes literally hates their existence.[111]

The Origin of Evil

Many theologians discuss the origin of evil in relation to Adam and Eve while in the Garden of Eden. However, the actual origin of evil was not initiated on an earthly scene, but within the glories of heaven. Humankind was tempted by an external force. Although this does not make humankind any less guilty, it does suggest to us that evil was present in the universe prior to Genesis.

On the other hand, Satan's sin arose within his own heart, leading many to believe that this is why no salvation is possible for angels, whereas it is available to humankind.

As put forth earlier, why did Satan choose to forfeit the glories of heaven for a chance to seize the throne of God? To answer this question by citing Lucifer's selfish ambitious pride is correct. Yet the heart of the matter is much deeper and asks two additional questions: "How could an uninfluenced, unfallen angel sin?" and "How could a holy God permit any creature to fall?" The nature of these questions goes beyond the origin of Satan, though not inherently separated from his actions, and seeks to intelligently understand how evil came into existence. The complexity of the situation is referred to by F. C. Jennings when he writes the following:[112]

> Some will perhaps ask, if he did not come from God, as the Devil, since God cannot produce evil, where did he come from, or how was he produced in that evil character? I have neither wish nor ability to go into matters too high, or too deep for plain people like myself, yet may we perhaps, even in a simple way, get some light on this problem.

We have seen him presented to us in Scripture as the highest expression of creature perfection. Then let me ask, "Which is highest in the scale of creation, a tree or a stone?" You at once answer "a tree." "Why?" Because it has more freedom in life and growth." "True. Which is highest, a tree or an ox?" "An ox." "Why?" "Because it has will and freedom of motion according to that will, which the tree lacks." "True again. Once more: Which is higher, an ox or a man?" "The man." "Why?" "Again because he is not controlled—narrowed—limited by the laws that shut in the brute creation. By his spirit he is capable of recognizing his Creator, he becomes therefore a creature with a moral responsibility; but this predicates a greater freedom of will, and its powers of going in any direction."

Then do you not see how the highest of all creatures must, by that very fact, be launched from his Maker's hand, with no external clog of heavy flesh—a gross material body that forbids the free and full exercise of his desires—with no internal law compelling him ever to continue on certain prescribed moral lines whether good or bad; but with liberty and power of going in any direction. Indeed in such perfect equipoise as to leave him truly free.[113]

The Time of Satan's Fall

Since scripture never clearly mentions a precise time of Satan's fall, it is necessary to use deductive reasoning to pinpoint this time without contradicting the revealed truth we process.

The Fall in Eternity Past

Some would argue that Satan's creation and fall must have occurred in eternity past, usually before creation. People who think this cite as their proof the text of Job 38:4–7, which suggests that angels were present and sang together as the world was being created. A second proof text used is Ezekiel 28:13–19, which seems to suggest that sufficient time was needed for Satan to be created, to secretly plan his attempt to overthrow God, to rally the support of an angelic host, and to move upon the throne of God. The first verse in the Bible is a summary statement of all creation and is not necessarily the first chronological step of creation. Therefore, the statement "In the beginning God created the heaven(s)" allows the creation of angels long before the first day of earth's creation.

The Fall Occurring in the Gap between Genesis 1:1 and Genesis 1:2

Many believe that Satan was created in the same creative experience that is described with, "In the beginning God created the heaven and the earth" (Gen. 1:1). The word *heaven* is plural in the Hebrew, implying that the three heavens were created in the original creative act. Actually, creation involves the whole of heaven and its innumerable parts.

When God created the heaven, it probably included the creation of his throne (only God is eternal in his nature, not his throne) and those beings (angels) who worship him. Obviously, when the angels were created, Satan was included in that act. Between the act of creation and God's pronouncement, "The earth was without form and void" (Gen. 1:2), there was destruction upon the original creation, including Satan for his insurrection against God. Hence they deduce that Satan, who was beautiful and desirable in Ezekiel 28, but who became subtle and dangerous in Genesis 3, must have fallen during the catastrophic judgment upon the original creation.

The Fall After Creation

The creation of Satan occurred during the six days of creation, thus necessitating that Satan's fall occurred shortly after his creation. Supporters of this view would quote Exodus 20:11, "For in six days the Lord made heaven and earth, the sea, and all that in them is, and rested the seventh day: wherefore, the Lord blessed the sabbath day, and hallowed it." Some support can be rallied for this third view, which does not really demand a short period of time between Satan's creation and fall. According to Genesis 1:31, God clearly announced that everything that he made was very good (this could not be true if sin was already present in the universe). In between the end of the sixth day and the appearance of Satan (in his fallen state) in Genesis 3, we cannot be dogmatic about the exact amount of time, but it should be sufficient time for Satan to incite his rebellion against God. Writing on this subject, J. O. Buswell states the following:[114]

> The Scripture does not indicate precisely at what time, with reference to the creation of the world and man, the angels were created. Satan, the leader of the angels who fell, makes his appearance as a creature already fallen, while man is still in the Garden of Eden. If the phrase, "everything which he had made," in Genesis 1:31 means everything without exception, then we must infer that the angels had been created before the end of the sixth day, but that the fall of Satan and the evil angels took place after God's pronouncement that "everything he had made" was "all very good" (Gen. 1:31). So far as the teaching of the Scripture is concerned, the creation of the angels may have taken place at any time prior to the end of the sixth day. The fall of Satan must have taken place between the end of the sixth day and the temptation of man in the Garden of Eden.[115]

The Character of Satan

The Bible describes the character of Satan in three ways. First, certain names or titles are ascribed to him that reflect his true nature. Second, his subtle character describes his behavior. In the third place, Satan is described through his nature and his kingdom.

Names of Satan

Just as God uses his own names to reveal who he is and what his nature is, so God has revealed the nature of Satan through his name. Over thirty different names or titles are given to this sinful fallen angel. Unlike Western practices of randomly selecting a name for a person, those in the Eastern lands place great stress upon the name, as it depicts specific characteristics of that person.

TABLE 10.21. The names and titles of Satan

1. Satan – Job 1:6	16. Wicked One – 1 John 3:12
2. Devil – Rev. 12:7	17. Prince of the power of the air – Eph. 2:2
3. Apollyon – Rev. 9:11	18. Prince of this world – John 14:30
4. Beelzebub – Matt. 12:27	19. God of this age – 2 Cor. 4:4
5. Belial – 2 Cor. 6:15	20. Dragon – Rev. 12:9
6. Old Serpent – Rev. 20:2	21. Beast out of the bottomless pit – Rev. 11:7
7. Adversary – 1 Pet. 5:8	22. Accuser of the brethren – Rev. 12:10
8. Anointed cherub – Ezek. 28	23. Angel of the bottomless pit – Rev. 9:11
9. Deceiver of the whole world – Rev. 12:9	24. Angel of light – 2 Cor. 11:14
10. Evil One – John 17:15	25. Enemy – Matt. 13:39
11. Leviathan – Isa. 27:1	26. Father of Lies – John 8:44
12. Lucifer – Isa. 14:12	27. Liar – John 8:44
13. Murderer – John 8:44	28. Prince of demons – Matt. 9:34
14. Roaring lion – 1 Pet. 5:8	29. Man of sin – 2 Thess. 2:3
15. Son of the morning – Isa. 14:12	30. Thief – John 10:10

Satan's Subtle Character

The Bible makes no effort to hide the craftiness of Satan. When false teachers and false apostles appeared in the church at Corinth, Paul wrote, "And no marvel; for Satan himself is transformed into an angel of light" (2 Cor. 11:14). The apostle acknowledged that one of his purposes in writing the Second Epistle to the Corinthians was "lest Satan should get an advantage of us; for we are not ignorant of his devices" (2 Cor. 2:11). He further recognized the cunning and subtle character of Satan when he advised the Ephesians to "put on the whole armor of God, that ye may be able to stand against the wiles of the devil" (Eph. 6:11).

In stark contrast to Satan's original lofty and majestic position as protector of God's throne, he has now become the embodiment of evil. By employing for evil all the cunning and shrewd wisdom with which he was endowed, Satan is truly a formidable enemy to those who acknowledge Jesus Christ as their Lord.

Evil Nature of Satan

It is the nature of a human being that causes him or her to act as he or she does. The same principle exists as we try to better understand Satan. John identified the Devil as the originator and chief practitioner of sin (1 John 3:8). He further described Satan as "that wicked one" (1 John 5:18). Jesus called Satan a liar (John 8:44) and a thief (John 10:10). The evil acts of Satan are a natural expression of his evil nature. "The thief cometh not, but for to steal, and to kill, and to destroy" (John 10:10). The apostle Paul recognized the destructive nature of Satan when he wrote, "The god of this world hath blinded the minds of them which believe not, lest the light of the glorious gospel of Christ, who is the image of God, should shine unto them" (2 Cor. 4:4).

Nature of Satan's Kingdom

In order to constitute a kingdom, certain factors must be present. There must be a king (government structure), subjects to rule over, a designated geographical area to rule over, and a common, unifying goal that stimulates the existence of the foregoing three things. In Satan's kingdom, it is blatantly obvious that Satan rules with an iron fist, demanding strict obedience from his demonic followers, lest his kingdom suffer internal divisions (Luke 11:18). The subjects of Satan's kingdom are twofold: those angels who fell during his rebellion, and the hearts of unregenerate human beings (Luke 8:44).

The domain of Satan's kingdom is not just the physical earth, but the world system that denies the supernatural and exalts the natural. The common and unifying goal of Satan's kingdom focuses upon hindering the plan of God and manipulating as many souls as possible to eternal separation from God.[116]

Judgment of Satan and His Kingdom

TABLE **10.22.** Chronology of Satan's judgment

A	Record of Satan's fall (second heaven)	Isa. 14:12–17; Ezek. 28; Luke 10:18
B	Indictment recorded	Gen. 3:16
C	Judgment penalty displayed	Col. 2:14; Heb. 2:14–15; John 12:13; John 16:11
D	Confinement to earth (first heaven)	Rev. 12:12–17
E	Confinement during the millennium	Isa. 24; Rev. 20
F	Execution of judgment	Rev. 20:10

Record of Satan's Fall

In Isaiah 14, Ezekiel 28, and Luke 10:18 are separate testimonies of Satan's sin and removal from the presence of God's throne. Although these testimonies emphasize different aspects of Satan's fall (Ezekiel deals with Satan's position prior to the fall; Isaiah focuses on his militant attempt to grasp the throne of God; and Christ describes the sudden and swift expulsion from heaven), they are internally consistent.

Some have argued that Luke 10:18 refers not to a past judgment, but to a futuristic judgment (Rev. 12). The context is not explicit as to which event Christ was referring. However, the more probable interpretation is a reference to Satan's fall in Genesis. Support for this conclusion is found in the immediate context: the excited apostles, while reporting to Jesus their successful confrontations with the demon world, cause him to reflect back to the time when Satan was cast down from the third heaven, allowing him to see how Satan is even now being defeated by his apostles.

Indictment Recorded

When a person commits a crime and reasonable suspicion attributes the crime to him, he is indicted with a particular charge. In Genesis 3, humankind and Satan are clearly charged by God with committing sin. As a result, God issues the various curses upon the guilty parties. With humankind, the indictment can possibly be rescinded. However, with Satan, no parole is possible.

Judgment Penalty Displayed

Through the death of Christ, Satan was judged and his work destroyed. Hebrews 2:14–15 reads, "Forasmuch then as the children are partakers of flesh and blood, he also himself likewise took part of the same; that through death he might destroy him that had the power of death, that is, the devil; and deliver them who through fear of death were all their lifetime subject to bondage." Even through Satan has been judged and openly humiliated, he has not yet actually received his punishment.

In 1 Peter 5:8, Satan is still actively destroying the receptivity of the souls of human beings to the gospel, but in Revelation 20:10 his judgment will be completed.[117]

Confinement to the Earth

During the great tribulation, as John the Beloved describes in Revelation 12, Satan will be cast down from heaven by Michael. Some erroneously believe that John is simply describing Satan's original fall from heaven in Genesis or possibly the casting down related to the death of Christ. Yet a careful reading of Revelation 12:5–12 reveals a chronology of events, some of which have already transpired and some which are still future, even to our time. In verse 5 John tells us of the birth of Christ and his ascension to glory before Pentecost. From verse 5 to verse 6, a large span of history is quickly passed over as John introduces us to the great tribulation, in which the woman (Israel) is forced to flee for her life into the wilderness for 1,260 days. After Israel's flight, the battle rages in the second heaven, resulting in the expulsion of Satan and his demons to the first heaven, or the immediate earth. It is the future expulsion that so enrages Satan that he empowers the Beast (Rev. 13) to further vent his wrath upon God's chosen people.

Confinement during the Millennium

At the end of the great tribulation, while the blood is still flowing from the Battle of Armageddon, Satan will be bound and cast into the bottomless pit for a thousand years. According to Revelation 20:1–3, the earth will again enjoy the blessings of God, humankind will enjoy longevity of life, and there will be no satanic temptations.

Execution of Judgment

Near the end of the millennial period, Satan is loosed and allowed to deceive many, forming a final rebellion against Christ, who rules in Jerusalem.

In Revelation 20:9–10, God intercedes, totally annihilates all opposition, and casts the Devil permanently into the lake of fire, never again to tempt humankind to do evil.

The Work of Satan

All of Satan's work is against God. At times he actively opposes the work or plan of God. On other occasions, he simply imitates God so as to draw people away from the simple plan of God. But in the final analysis, Satan is bound by his corrupted nature to destroy all that he can. These three points comprise the outline of this section.

TABLE 10.23. The threefold work of Satan

1. Opposition to the will and work of God
2. Imitation of the work of God
3. Destruction of all that is good

Opposition to God

Jesus portrayed the Devil in one of his parables as the Enemy of God (Matt. 13:39). As such, the Devil is constantly opposing God and all God does. Satan first appeared in the Garden of Eden to oppose the plan and work of God that he established in paradise.

That opposition betrayed itself continually in this attempt to destroy the messianic line. Then Satan sought to destroy the race God sought to redeem. When God chose a people of his own, the nation of Israel, Satan unreservedly sought their destruction. Throughout the life of Christ, Satan sought to distract the Savior from his mission. God works through the church today, so Satan is opposed to the work of God there. According to Chafer, Satan is actively opposing the program of God in no less than twenty-four different areas. As the last days draw nearer we can expect an increase in Satan's work (2 Tim. 3:1–9).

1. Satan repudiated God in the beginning (Isa. 14:12–14).
2. He drew a third of the stars of heaven after him (Rev. 12:4).
3. He sinned from the beginning (1 John 3:8).
4. He is a liar from the beginning (1 John 8:44).
5. In the Garden of Eden he belittled God and advised the first parents to repudiate God (Gen. 3:1–5).
6. He insinuated to Jehovah that Job loved and served him only as he was hired to do so (Job 1:9). No greater insult could be addressed to Jehovah than to claim that he is not really to be loved on the ground of his own worthiness, but that people like Job to *pretend* to love him because Satan, being rich, has hired them to do so.
7. When permitted to act his own part, Satan brought five terrible calamities upon Job (Job 1:13–2:7).
8. He stood up against Israel (1 Chron. 21:2; Ps. 109:6; Zech. 3:1–2).
9. He weakened the nations (Isa. 14:2).
10. He made the earth to tremble (Isa. 14:16).
11. He did shake kingdoms (Isa. 14:16).
12. He makes the world a wilderness (Isa. 14:17).
13. He destroys the cities of the world (Isa. 14:17).
14. He opened not the house of his prisoners (Isa. 14:17).
15. He causes war on earth with all its horrors; for when bound, war ceases, and when loosed, war is resumed (Rev. 20:2; Rev. 7–8).
16. He tempted the Son of God forty days and then left him but for a season. He proposed to Christ that he forsake his mission, that he distrust his Father's goodness, and that he worship the Devil (Luke 4:1–13).

17. He bound a daughter of Abraham for eighteen years (Luke 13:16; cf. Acts 10:38).
18. He entered Judas and prompted him to betray the Son of God (John 13:2).
19. He blinds the minds of those who are lost (2 Cor. 4:3–4).
20. He takes the Word out of the hearts of the unsaved, lest they should believe and be saved (Luke 8:12).
21. He deals with saints with wiles and snares (Eph. 6:11; 2 Tim. 2:26).
22. He has exercised and abused the power of death (Heb. 2:14; cf. Rev. 1:18).
23. He, an adversary, as a roaring lion goeth about seeking whom he may devour (1 Pet. 5:8).
24. He is opposed to God, is the persecutor of saints, and is the Father of Lies through his idolatry. Chafer, 73–74.

a. In relation to the messianic line

As soon as God in his righteousness judged the first sin in the Garden of Eden, he also in his mercy promised a Redeemer. He said to Satan, "And I will put enmity between thee and the women, and between thy seed and her seed: it shall bruise thy head, and thou shalt bruise his heel" (Gen. 3:15). With the accuracy of his foreknowledge, God predicted Satan's opposition to the coming Redeemer. It did not take long to materialize. With the birth of Abel, the Devil began his opposition. Satan worked in Cain to kill his brother Abel. With Abel dead, the line would be broken and the Messiah could never be born. But God replaced Abel with Seth (Gen. 4:25). Every attempt to destroy the godly line by extinction or by sexual contamination was an attempt by Satan to destroy the coming Messiah. Even in a small way, the danger to David, the shepherd boy, was an attempt to carry out Satan's plot. David twice tangled with wild beasts (1 Sam. 17:35). Satan may have felt David's great sin with Bathsheba would prevent God from using him in the line of Messiah, but in contrast, it was that very relationship God chose to use (Matt. 1:6).

At one point in Israel's history, the royal lineage was nearly destroyed when Athaliah sought to kill every person of royal birth. However, the protective action of Jehosheba preserved the life of Joash until he was able to assume the throne with the help of Jehoiada the high priest (2 Kings 11:1–5).

b. In relation to the human race

God created humankind in his image and likeness to have fellowship with God and dominion over the earth. When Satan approached Eve in the garden, he promised Eve not only that she would not die (Gen. 3:4) but also that eating the fruit would lead her to experience life on a higher plane (Gen. 3:5). With the entrance of sin into the human race, Satan knew God would have to judge them as he had judged him. Satan sought to contaminate the human race by leading them into grievous sins (Gen. 6:5). God did judge most of them for their sin, but eight—Noah and his family—were kept safe in the ark (Gen. 7:13). In the parable of the sower (Matt. 13:4–19), Satan is seen actively removing the message of the gospel from the hearts of unbelievers. Satan doesn't necessarily have to steal the message of salvation from human beings' hearts. He is equally effective in diluting the message with erroneous teaching, replacing it with a more appealing desire, or simply dismissing it as being a fanatical and old-fashioned perspective. Very few realize that Satan's temptations are both negative and positive; he takes away the seed sown and he sows tares.

c. In relation to Israel

From the time of the call of Abraham, the Devil has been the enemy of the Jew. God told Abraham, "Look now toward heaven, and tell [count] the stars, if thou be able to number them: and he said unto him, so shall thy seed be" (Gen. 15:5). After the nation of Israel went to Egypt and began to grow as God has promised, Satan moved Pharaoh to command the destruction of all male children (Exod. 1:16). Later, Satan used the personal animosity of Haman toward Mordecai to plan the first systematic genocide of the Jews. The book of Esther records this attempt and Haman's ultimate defeat (Esther 3:6; Esther 7:9–10). Satan has continued to raise up anti-Semitic leaders who have unsuccessfully attempted to exterminate the Jews.

d. In relation to Christ

At the birth of Christ, Satan used Herod to plan the murder of all male children Jesus's age in Bethlehem (Matt. 2:16). After Jesus spent forty days in the wilderness, Satan himself tempted Jesus, trying to destroy the ministry of Christ before he could redeem the world (Matt. 4:1–11). On other occasions, Satan used Peter (Matt. 16:23) and Judas (John 13:27) to attempt to thwart Christ from his purpose.

Even in the final hours before Jesus's death, Satan attempted to convince him to bypass the cross. After Christ died and was buried, Satan inspired the Jewish leaders to appoint guards and seal the tomb in a feeble effort to prevent the resurrection.

e. In relation to the church

Jesus said, "I will build my church; and the gates of hell shall not prevail against it" (Matt. 16:18). From the first mention of the church in scripture, Jesus taught that it would be in opposition to Satan. The picture of gates is not that of a church struggling to hold out against the incredible opposition of the near overwhelming forces of hell, but rather that of an aggressive church smashing down the strongholds of the Devil as he feebly attempts to keep the dynamic church from winning people to Christ.

As we read the book of Acts, we see this principle at work. Opposition toward the church stimulated the church to engage in more aggressive outreach. Throughout history, Satan has actively opposed the work of God by torturing and killing saints. But the martyrs have been the seed of the church. Under the most severe opposition, God has worked to glorify himself. His church has not only survived the opposition of the Devil; it has survived it victoriously.

f. In relation to scripture

History is replete with examples of evil people seeking to undermine humankind's confidence in the Bible. The Roman emperor Diocletian ratified an edict that would secure the death of all those possessing a copy of the New Testament scriptures. The Spanish Inquisition saw the destruction of many Bibles. The rise of modern science introduced a new method of examining traditional values and absolutes, which gave birth to German rationalization. The Catholic Church sought to keep the scriptures from the masses, suggesting that only the church had the authority to interpret the scriptures. Voltaire publicly boasted that the Bible would be obsolete within several decades and his work would replace it. More recently, attempts have been made to exclude "meaningless or less profitable passages" from scripture, or to neutralize the scripture in order to rid it of its prejudices. Although the motive behind these alterations may or may not be overtly evil, they nonetheless fail to honor the warning in Revelation 22:18–19, which strongly advises against removing from or adding to the scripture.

g. In relation to accomplishing God's will

In spite of themselves and their opposition to God, Satan and his demons execute God's plans of punishing the ungodly or chastening the good. In relation to the ungodly, Psalm 78:49 states, "He cast upon them the fierceness of his anger, wrath, and indignation and trouble, by sending evil angels among them." This verse suggests that God employs Satan and his demon host to keep the evil acts of the ungodly in check. Initially, the idea of God using Satan to control in part the world's evil sounds paradoxical. However, one must understand that every human being is the object of Satan's hatred, and as long as human beings (even the most ungodly) are allowed to breathe, there exists the possibility that they might accept Christ as their Lord and Savior.

Satan is also used by God to chasten the good. In the Corinthian church, an immoral problem developed and the leadership failed to actively deal with it. When Paul learned of it, his counsel was firm yet gracious: "Deliver such an one unto Satan for the destruction of the flesh, that the spirit may be saved in the day of the Lord Jesus" (1 Cor. 5:5). Eventually the fallen brother was restored to fellowship, yet this likely would not have occurred if he had not been excommunicated from the church and subjected to sifting by Satan. A similar situation occurred with Hymenaeus and Alexander, about which Paul in 1 Timothy 1:20 states, "Hymenaeus and Alexander, whom I delivered unto Satan, that they may learn not to blaspheme." Through excommunication, Paul had hoped to alter their conduct; however, the greater fear experienced by these men was not the alienation of fellowship but the subjection to Satan's authority.

Finally, Satan is used by God to develop specific circumstances to carry out the will of God. When Satan moved upon the mind of Herod to slaughter the male children in Bethlehem, it was in fulfillment of God's prophecy. The working of Satan in the heart of Ananias and Sapphira and their ultimate death became the catalyst for a sudden surge in church growth.

In the future, Satan will be used of God to draw the nations together for the Battle of Armageddon, the outcome of which is already recorded. Nonetheless, blinded by self-deception and the rejection of God's Word, Satan will be instrumental in producing the proper setting for Christ's return to the earth.

TABLE 10.24. The counterfeits of Satan

Jesus is the Son of God – Ps. 2:1	Satan is the god of this world – Eph. 2:2
Trinity – Matt. 28:20	Triunity – Rev. 20:10
Mystery of godliness –1 Tim. 3:16	Mystery of iniquity – 2 Thess. 2:7
Children of God – John 1:12	Children of Satan – John 8:44
God's mark on his servants – Rev. 7:3	Satan's mark of the Beast – Rev. 13:16
Miracles of Christ – Matt. 4:23	Miracles of Satan – 2 Thess. 2:9
Christ the true Light – John 1:7	Angel of Light – 2 Cor. 11:14
Christ appoints apostles – Matt. 10:1	Satan's counterfeit apostles – 2 Cor. 11:13

Imitation

One of Satan's desires is to be like the Most High (Isa. 14:14), if not to be God. But Satan is not God, nor is his nature anything like God's. To accomplish his desire, Satan imitates God and carries out much of his work by counterfeit righteousness rather than a manifestation of his wicked nature. Table 10.24 contrasts the works of God and the Devil's attempts to reproduce them.

From the very beginning, it has been Satan's desire to be like God (Isa. 14:14). In his present work, Satan is attempting to duplicate the works of God. Almost everything God has established, Satan has duplicated. There even exists today a satanic "bible" and a church of Satan. When Moses stood before the Egyptian pharaoh, delivered his message, and validated it with the miracles that God gave to him, undoubtedly Pharaoh was not impressed, as he had seen his own priests on occasions perform similar feats. Satan's inability to create or be original offers us some insight into the mental capacity of Satan.

During the tribulation, Satan's agents, the Antichrist and the False Prophet, along with Satan himself, will substitute triunity for the triune Godhead. The Antichrist will perform miracles to prove his credibility as a substitute Christ. The Antichrist will actually be killed and raised again from the dead, or will have an apparent death wound that will give the illusion that he has been raised from the dead. In either case, the attempt is to substitute as messiah and take the place of Christ.

Today, Satan is attempting to substitute an apostate church for the true church. His ministers (2 Cor. 11:15), are those who are humanitarian and outwardly commendable, yet inwardly they are enemies of the true gospel. Satan's work of imitation is similar to his attempts to infiltrate the church.

Infiltration

"Satan transforms himself into an angel of light" (2 Cor. 11:14) so he can infiltrate among the people of Christ and affect the work of God. Jesus claimed that some who call themselves Christians would not be permitted entrance into heaven because they do not truly know him (Matt. 7:23). By the end of the first century, Satan was clearly trying to control the church of Jesus Christ from both the outside (Rev. 2:13) and the inside (Jude 4). The apostle Paul warned the Ephesian pastors that Satan would attempt to destroy the church by sending into the church evil men who would attempt to corrupt good men (Acts 20:29–30).

The destructiveness of infiltration was apparent during the fourth century when the Roman emperor Constantine amalgamated the church and state. Prior to the union, the church surged in growth, despite the flame of persecution that snuffed out hundreds of Christian lives. With his appointment as the new leader in AD 312, Constantine eventually made Christianity simply one of the official religions of the empire. Many might have thought that with the absence of persecution, the true church would greatly increase and eventually usher in the millennium. Yet, as history records, this was not the case. The true church mingled with the false church. The fervor it once possessed began to mellow into lofty cathedrals and cold orthodoxy.[118]

Destruction

A third aspect of the work of Satan is to corrupt all that God has created. The nature of Satan is opposite to the nature of God. When Satan cannot imitate God's work and he is unable to infiltrate, he will do all he possibly can to destroy God's work. "The thief cometh not, but for to steal, and to kill, and to destroy: I am come that they might have life, and that they might have it more abundantly" (John 10:10). Satan's destruction is carried out in several ways.

a. Deceiving the nations

Some of Satan's destructive energies are directed against the nations of this world. When Jesus returns, Satan will be sealed in a pit, "that he should deceive the nations no more" (Rev. 20:3). This will happen during the millennial rule of Christ. Currently, though, Satan has freedom to perform his deceptive work among the nations. The extent of Satan's domain among the nations is hinted at by Daniel (10:12–14). In response to Daniel's prayer, God sent a heavenly messenger to deliver his message to Daniel. However, the angel was hindered in his journey for twenty-one days by the prince of the Kingdom of Persia. This message of scripture suggests that a powerful angel is assigned to a specific geographical location to hinder in every possible respect the work of God. The strength of the evil angel excelled for a time.

b. Deceiving the unsaved

Satan is aggressively keeping the unsaved from understanding the gospel. Paul explained to the Corinthians, "The god of this world hath blinded the minds of them which believe not, lest the light of the glorious gospel of Christ, who is the image of God, should shine unto them" (2 Cor. 4:4). Not content with blinding the unsaved so they cannot understand the gospel, Satan has another strategy. "Then cometh the devil, and taketh away the word out of their hearts, lest they should believe and be saved" (Luke 8:12). The book of Acts records one account after another where the Devil used human beings to oppose the progress of the gospel. Satan's strategy is simple: if he can prevent people from hearing the gospel and understanding what Christ offers them, then they will be content to go their own way.

In regard to salvation, it has been stated that it is hard for an individual to go to hell, simply because God places so many roadblocks in the pathway that points to salvation. Yet this statement overlooks in part the blinded condition of the unsaved who stumble over God's invitations to salvation. This does not suggest that Satan is more powerful than God in human affairs (1 John 4:4). It does describe the extreme similarities between God and Satan, in their respective positive and negative external influence upon the human mind. Although God, unlike Satan, can examine and know a person's inner motivation, Satan and his demonic host nonetheless can examine a person's actions and conversation to receive a fairly clear grasp of each individual's inner purpose. This means Satan cannot read the thoughts of human beings, but he can predict their thoughts and actions based on his knowledge of their sinful nature. With this information, Satan is able to strike at a person's weakest point and destroy him or her. In relation to the unsaved, Satan employs at least five separate methods to hinder the reception of God's Word and the internalizing of the truth, as outlined by Sanders:

> He snatches the good seed of the Word. "When anyone hears the word of the kingdom, and does not understand it, the evil one comes and snatches away what has been sown in his heart" (Matt. 13:4, 19, italics added). The picture is, of course, of birds swooping down and picking up the grain fallen from the sower's hand on the hard-beaten path. Even so, the devil snatches away good seed of the word before it can sink into the understanding and be received by faith. This is the activity of the devil whenever the Word is preached. It underlines the fact we should pray after the preaching as well as before, for this subtle stratagem is all too often successful. How frequently the solemn impression of a powerful sermon is dissipated by idle chatter after service. The good seed is snatched away.
>
> He lulls the unbeliever into a false sense of peace. "When a strong man fully armed guards his own homestead, his possessions are undisturbed" (Luke 11:21). The context makes it clear Satan is the strong man who drugs the senses

of his victims, assures them there is nothing in God to fear, and no judgment to anticipate. He deflects the shafts of conviction which the Holy Spirit directs at their hearts, and says, "Peace, peace, when there is no peace."

He lays snares for the unwary. "If perhaps God may grant them repentance leading to the knowledge of the truth, and they may come to their senses and escape from the snare of the devil, having been held captive by him to do his will" (2 Tim. 2:25–26). The devil is a master of subtlety, and adept at concealing his snares. He is too wise a hunter to lay snares in the sight of his victims.

He gains advantage over men by concealing his true and sinister purpose, by masquerading as an angel of light. "For such men are false apostles, deceitful workers, disguising themselves as apostles of Christ. And no wonder, for even Satan disguises himself as an angel of light" (2 Cor. 11:13–14). He is much more likely to succeed when he tempts certain people by appearing in the guise of a benefactor than as a foul fiend or a roaring lion.

He deceives those whose minds are not subject to the Word of truth. "The serpent of old who is called the Devil and Satan, who deceives the whole world" (Rev. 12:9). He was successful in deceiving Eve. "The woman being quite deceived, fell into transgression" (1 Tim. 2:14), because she entertained doubts the devil injected into her mind concerning the truth of God's Word, instead of immediately rejecting the disloyal suggestion. He is still active unceasingly in deceiving men about the integrity and authority of God's Word. This is the focal point of the great theological controversies of our day.

He mixes truth with error. "While men were sleeping, his enemy came and sowed tares among the wheat ... and he [the landowner] said to them, an enemy has done this!" Mat 13:15, 28). His strategy is to include enough truth in his teaching to make error appear both credible and palatable—the great appeal and hidden danger of many cults in vogue today. So much seems good and true that injection of error is not obvious.

To achieve his end, Satan will quote or misquote Scripture as best suits his purpose. He is ingenious.

He employs orthodox language, while giving the old words used a new and heterodox content. This is especially true in theological circles, where theological double talk confuses the issues and conceals the error.[119]

c. Defeating the saved

To merely defeat a Christian temporarily must be the most frustrating aspect of Satan's work. He cannot destroy the child of God. He will use the lust of the flesh, the lust of the eyes, and the pride of life to attack Christians (1 John 2:15–16). Satan will attack them directly or indirectly. If Satan cannot get a Christian to fall into the pollution of sin, he will push the believer beyond the will of God into legalism or fanaticism. On occasion a Christian may stumble, but the Bible teaches, "A just man falleth seven times, and riseth up again" (Prov. 24:16). The Christian is not able to defeat the Devil in herself, but she is victorious as she allows the power of Christ to live in her. "Ye are of God, little children, and have overcome them: because greater is he that is in you, than he that is in the world" (1 John 4:4). But remember, the fact that Satan cannot ultimately destroy us does not mean he will not tempt us.

Satan has successfully tempted Christians to lie to God in the past (Acts 5:3). He is called the "accuser of the brethren" (Rev. 12:10). He seeks to hinder Christians in their work for God (1 Thess. 2:18) and to defeat them in their Christian walk (Eph. 6:12). Satan tempted one Christian to engage in immorality in Corinth (1 Cor. 5:1). He attempted to destroy the Corinthian church by sowing tares of dissension (Matt. 13:38–39) among the believers (1 Cor. 3:1–7). Also, Satan will attempt to destroy the church by sending in unsaved members and leaders (2 Cor. 11:5; 2 Cor. 13–15). If internal opposition falls, Satan will attack the church through external persecution (Rev. 2:10). However, none of Satan's attempts to destroy the Christian need be successful, as we have been promised victory over Satan (2 Cor. 2:14).[120]

How to Overcome Satan

It should be more natural for us to defeat Satan than to be defeated by him. God has revealed certain principles in his Word that can protect the Christian against defeat. But more than insulating against evil, these principles should make the Christian victorious. The Bible clearly states, "There hath no temptation taken you but such as is common to man: but God is faithful, who will not suffer you to be tempted above that ye are able; but will with the temptation also make a way to escape, that ye may be able to bear it" (1 Cor. 10:13). This way to escape is found by applying biblical principles to each temptation.

The Principle of Respect

Too often Christians rely on fleshly strength for victory. Though Jesus is greater than the Devil (1 John 4:4), we must still have a healthy respect for our Enemy. A good football team, if they become overconfident, may lose to a lesser team. Overconfidence will cause a team to play carelessly, allowing the opposition to do things they could not otherwise accomplish. So if a Christian does not realize that Satan possesses the ability to defeat him, he will allow Satan to gain victories where he could not otherwise do so. Even Michael the archangel was not prepared to confront Satan except in the name of the Lord (Jude 9).

The Principles of Removal

It has often been said that one bad apple will spoil the whole barrel. The leaven principle means that evil will spread surely and purposefully through the good dough. A wise Christian should evaluate his life and avoid those areas where he or she is more likely to be tempted. Paul reminds us to "abstain from all appearance of evil" (1 Thess. 5:22).

When Joseph found himself tempted by Potiphar's wife, "he left his garment in her hand, and fled, and got him out" (Gen. 39:12). Paul also applied this principle, but in reverse, to false teachers, meaning that we should not only remove ourselves from evil but also remove its influence from our lives. "A man that is an heretick after the first and second admonition reject"

(Titus 3:10). By separating ourselves from the source of the temptation both morally and geographically, we can gain a temporary victory over the Devil. The word *temporary* is used because no one is ever immune to temptation, not until death.

The Principle of Resistance

The principle of resistance possesses both a positive and negative aspect. It is positive in the sense of submitting to God. Marvin R. Vincent defines *submit* as "to place or arrange under." Christians should place themselves under the biblical principles and the divine protection of Almighty God.[121] To live the Christian life apart from submission to God's authority and protection is tantamount to a haughty spirit of self-reliance, which is folly.

The negative aspect of resistance demands resistance to the Devil. "Submit yourselves therefore to God. Resist the devil, and he will flee from you" (James 4:7). Vincent defines *resist* as "to withstand," noting that "the verb means rather *to be firm against onset,* than *to strive* against it."[122]

All of the above compels us to believe that we are to actively engage in the spiritual battle with our spiritual instruments, with the purpose of not only stopping Satan's temptation but also advancing upon his kingdom. It is possible for the Christian to send the Devil running in defeat by taking definite action. The apostle Peter advised the believer that he or she should not give in to Satan, but "resist steadfast in the faith" (1 Pet. 5:9). We would not be defeated if we would speak the name of Jesus Christ and refuse to listen to Satan's temptation. When Jesus was tempted, he gained the victory by using the scripture to resist the Devil (Matt. 4:1–11).

The Principle of Readiness

"Be prepared" is the watchword of the tempted Christian. "Watch ye and pray, lest ye enter into temptation" (Mark 14:38). Paul advised the Ephesians, "Put on the whole armor of God, that ye may be able to stand against the wiles of the devil" (Eph. 6:11).

The prepared Christian will recognize his or her weak areas and strengthen them. David assured us that memorizing scripture will help keep us from sin (Ps. 119:1, 11).

One who is serious about gaining victory over some besetting sin should concentrate on memorizing several verses of scripture that deal with that particular area of weakness in a human being's life. Also, such a person should be certain he or she is fully equipped to meet the Devil in battle.

TABLE 10.25. Things that protect against the Devil

1. Girdle (belt) of truth
2. Breastplate of righteousness
3. Shoes of the preparation of the gospel
4. Shield of faith
5. Helmet of salvation
6. Sword of the Spirit
7. All prayer
(Eph. 6:13–17)

a. The belt of truth

In ancient warfare, prior to any exchange with the enemy, the belt was the first piece of armor to be secured, simply because the breastplate and sword were attached to it. The belt was normally a thick leather strap that surrounded the waist of the warrior. In addition to holding up the other instruments of war, the belt was used by the warrior to bind up the lower portion of his garments, which were tucked under the belt, in order to free himself from tangling his feet while in pursuit, thus providing greater mobility. The significance of "of truth" indicates the unifying and strengthening factor in the life and experience of the Christian soldier. Since the Garden of Eden, Satan has sought to disqualify or dilute the nature of absolute truth with hypocrisy and half-truths. The Christian soldier who wishes to seriously confront his or her Enemy must steadfastly bind up his mind in the great truths of God's holiness, love, power, and unfailing faithfulness.

b. The breastplate

The function of the breastplate, which covered the body of from neck to thigh, was to protect the soldier's vital organs. Righteousness here is not understood as an abstract quality of righteousness developed from moral achievements. It is the righteousness of Jesus Christ imputed to us. More specifically, it is his righteousness worked in us by the Holy Spirit. Sanctification or integrity of character gives us freedom over condemnation from our own hearts, and allows us to take great strides into the raging battle without having to relive a struggle with past or current failures.

c. The shoes

Military officials place great emphasis on the footwear of their soldiers because improper shoes can hamper mobility and readiness. Josephus records that the sandals of the Roman soldiers were thickly studded with nails to equip the men for long, swift marches. The figure here, then, is readiness, the antithesis being lethargy and apathy. Willingness to capitalize on a witnessing opportunity should characterize the mental prowess of every equipped and prepared Christian.

d. The shield

The typical Roman shield measured four feet in length and two and one-half feet in width. Each shield was made of brass, which was covered with several layers of leather. Prior to the battle, the shields would be dipped in water until the leather was completely saturated. The purpose of this exercise was to douse the fiery arrows that the enemy used. Arrows in ancient times were often dipped in pitch and set afire before they were shot. The oblong shield afforded the necessary protection to blunt the arrows and extinguish the fire. Just so, an unshakable trust in our God effectively stays the arrows and extinguishes their possible devastation. Believers who do not possess confidence in their Lord vacillate. James tells us that such a one is unstable and destined for failure (James 1:18).

e. The helmet

The helmet, normally constructed of leather and brass, has special reference to protecting the mind. An unguarded, undisciplined mind opens the believer to a barrage of attacks, ranging from thoughts of lust to doubting the existence of God.

It has been stated that the idle mind is the Devil's workshop; hence the greater need to bring into captivity "every thought to the obedience of Christ" (2 Cor. 10:5). An examination of salvation produces a three-dimensional spectrum: namely, the past, present, and future. In the past we have been saved from the guilt and condemnation of our sins—justification. In the present we are being saved from the influences of sin—sanctification. In the future we will be saved from the presence of sin and its effect upon us—glorification. In light of these observations, the helmet represents a valuable defensive implement in time of war.

f. The sword

So far, the implements of war described were primarily defensive, but still they were necessary for offensive attacks. With the sword, the emphasis is on the offensive attack. Furthermore, apart from putting on the different pieces of defensive armor, very little human involvement was necessary, but with the sword a greater demand is made upon human participation. The Roman sword was short, strong, and sharp, and required close hand-to-hand confrontation with the enemy for use. The sword represents the skillful and practical application of scriptural truths and principles to our daily experiences. We are not to walk in our own efforts, but rather to seek the help of the Spirit of the living God (divine involvement), together with living a lifestyle in submission to the biblical principles (human involvement).

g. All prayer

The last piece of armor we must appropriate is the lethal weapon of all prayer. Unlike the other implements, which have a specific location on the body, the weapon of all-prayer should permeate all of these locations and give all body parts a strong sense of unity and invulnerability. The admonition of Paul is to "pray without ceasing," (1 Thess. 5:17). The implication of this piece of armor is the vital role assumed by the Holy Spirit in taking our poor and inadequately expressed words and ushering them into the presence of God with "groanings which cannot be uttered" (Rom. 8:26–27).[123]

[This armour] is not like those antiquated suits we are accustomed to look at with curiosity in the Tower of London, or elsewhere; it is for present use, and has never been improved upon. Modern weapons are out of date in a few years—this armour, never. God does not tell us to look at it, to admire it, but to put in on; for armour is not one atom of use until it is put on. Jennings, 152–153.

Conclusion

The Bible teaches the existence of a personal Devil, the author of sin, who tries to destroy the work of God. When Christians see evidence of sin, all they need to think is soberly of their enemy, recognizing the existence of a person seeking their destruction. Peter warns us even today, "Be sober, be vigilant; because your adversary the devil, as a roaring lion, walketh about, seeking whom he may devour" (1 Pet. 5:8). Apart from total dependence upon God, we cannot win the victory over the Devil.

Rwandan Traditional Belief (Before Christianity)

Introduction

Rwandan territory, quadrilateral in shape, is in Central Africa. Rwanda is situated between the following coordinates:

- Latitude 1°04'5" S and 2°05'1" S
- Longitude 28°53'E and 30°53' East

In the theoretical time zone that goes from South Africa to Finland, Rwanda has a climate tempered by altitude. The country is situated between 1,000 m and 4,500 m of altitude, which separates Central Africa and East Africa. The Rwandan neighbor to the south is Burundi. Tanzania is to the east, Uganda is to the north, and the Democratic Republic of Congo is to the west. Rwanda is one of the smallest territories of the African continent with an area of 26,338 km.[125]

Rwandan People and Their Traditional Faith

Imana

Among Rwandans, God is known as "Imana." For them, Imana is a supreme being responsible for all, and is governor of all. Given this point of view, we can say that people of Rwanda are monotheistic. Imana is omnipotent, omniscient, and omnipresent.

However, the attributes of Imana are found in the theophoric names, such as Habyalimana (It is God who gives birth), Hakizimana (It is God who saves), Harelimana (It is God who educates), and Ilihose (God is everywhere). Furthermore, God is spiritual and immaterial. Despite much anthropomorphism in the language, Imana remains in the providence of humankind. He is transcendent in his interventions in the affairs of human beings, and is immanent because his providence or welfare suggests that he does not behave like human beings.

The Worship of Ancestors

The Munyarwada was convinced of the existence of survival. The spirits of the dead (*Abazimu*) live in the underworld and are governed by Nyamuzinda. They celebrate the ancestral worship to calm some Bazimu. They offer sacrifices so that they do not harm the living.

Based on these convictions, traditional Rwandan people had heroes; the best known was Ryangombe (who was an old man). After death, the insiders will inhabit Ryangombe's paradise called Kalisimbi.

Ryangombe is the servant of God (Imana) and acts as an intermediary between God and human beings (mostly insiders: the Imandwa). The disciples' lives are protected by the deceased Imandwa.

However, note that the role of Ryangombe was mostly soteriological. By joining the Imandwa sect, the Munyarwanda seeks that which he lacks in traditional religion.[124]

The Baha'i Faith

The Baha'i faith is a monotheistic religion emphasizing the spiritual unity of all humankind. Three core principles establish a basis for Baha'i teachings and doctrine: the unity of God (there is only one God who is the source of all creation); the unity of religion (all major religions have the same spiritual source and come from the same God); and the unity of humanity (all humans have been created equal, and that diversity of race and culture is seen as worthy of appreciation and acceptance). According to the Baha'i faith's teachings, the human purpose is to learn to know and love God through such methods as prayer, reflection, and being of service to humanity.

The Baha'i faith was founded by Baha'u'llah in nineteenth-century Persia. Baha'u'llah was exiled from Persia to the Ottoman Empire for his teachings, and he died while officially still a prisoner. After Baha'u'llah's death, the religion, under the leadership of his son, Abdu'l-Bahá, spread from its Persian and Ottoman roots and gained a footing in Europe and the United States. It was consolidated in Iran, where it suffers intense persecution.

After the death of Abdu'l-Bahá, the leadership of the Baha'i community entered a new phase, evolving from a single individual to an administrative order with both elected bodies and appointed individuals. There are probably more than five million Baha'is around the world in more than two hundred countries and territories.

In the Baha'i faith, religious history is seen to have unfolded through a series of divine messengers, each of whom established a religion that was suited to the needs of the time and to the capacity of the people. These messengers include Abrahamic figures, such as Moses, Jesus, and Muhammad, as well as Dharmic ones, such as Krishna and Buddha. For Baha'is, the most recent messengers are the Báb and Baha'u'llah. In Baha'i belief, each consecutive messenger prophesied of messengers to follow, and Baha'u'llah's life and teachings fulfilled the end-time promises of previous scriptures. Humanity is understood to be in a process of collective evolution, and the need of the present time is for the gradual establishment of peace, justice, and unity on a global scale.[125]

Beliefs

Three core principles establish a basis for Baha'i teachings and doctrine: the unity of God, the unity of religion, and the unity of humanity. From these postulates stems the belief that God periodically reveals his will through divine messengers whose purpose is to transform the character of humankind and to develop, within those who respond, moral and spiritual qualities. Religion is thus seen as orderly, unified, and progressive from age to age.

God

The Baha'i writings describe a single, personal, inaccessible, omniscient, omnipresent, imperishable, and almighty God who is the creator of all things in the universe. The existence of God and the universe is thought to be eternal, without a beginning or end. Though inaccessible directly, God is nevertheless seen as conscious of creation, with a will and purpose that is expressed through messengers termed "manifestations of God."

Baha'i teachings state that God is too great for humans to fully comprehend, or to create a complete and accurate image of, by themselves. Therefore, human understanding of God is achieved through his revelations via his manifestations. In the Baha'i religion, God is often referred to by titles and attributes (for example, the All-Powerful, or the All-Loving), and there is a substantial emphasis on monotheism. Such doctrines as the Trinity are seen as compromising, if not contradicting, the Baha'i view that God is single and has no equal. The Baha'i teachings state that the attributes applied to God are used to translate godliness into human terms and also to help individuals concentrate on their own attributes in worshipping God to develop their potentialities on their spiritual path. According to the Baha'i teachings, the human purpose is to learn to know and love God through such methods as prayer, reflection, and being of service to others.

Baha'i Faith and the Unity of Religion

Baha'i notions of progressive religious revelation result in their accepting the validity of the well-known religions of the world, whose founders and central

210

figures are seen as manifestations of God. Religious history is interpreted as a series of dispensations, where each manifestation brings a somewhat broader and more advanced revelation, one suited for the time and place in which it was expressed.

Specific religious social teachings (for example, the direction of prayer, or dietary restrictions) may be revoked by a subsequent manifestation so that a more appropriate requirement for the time and place may be established.

Conversely, certain general principles (for example, neighborliness, or charity) are seen to be universal and consistent. In Baha'i belief, this process of progressive revelation will not end; however, it is believed to be cyclical. Baha'is do not expect a new manifestation of God to appear within one thousand years of Baha'u'llah's revelation.

Baha'i beliefs are sometimes described as syncretic combinations of earlier religious beliefs. Adherents to the Baha'i religion, however, assert that their religion is a distinct tradition with its own scriptures, teachings, laws, and history. While the religion was initially seen as a sect of Islam, most religious specialists now see it as an independent religion, with its religious background in Shia Islam being seen as analogous to the Jewish context in which Christianity was established. Muslim institutions and clergy, both Sunni and Shia, consider Baha'is to be deserters or apostates from Islam, which has led to Baha'is being persecuted. Baha'is themselves describe their faith as an independent world religion differing from the other traditions in its relative age and in the appropriateness of Baha'u'llah's teachings to the modern context. Baha'u'llah is believed to have fulfilled the messianic expectations of these precursor faiths.

Human Beings

The ringstone symbol represents humanity's connection to God. The Baha'i writings state that human beings have a rational soul, and that this provides the species with a unique capacity to recognize God's station and humanity's relationship with its creator. Every human is seen to have a duty to recognize God through his messengers and to conform to their teachings. Through recognition and obedience, service to humanity, and regular prayer and spiritual practice, the soul, according to the Baha'i writings, becomes closer to God, the spiritual ideal in Baha'i belief. When a human dies, the soul passes into the next world, where its spiritual development in the physical world becomes a basis for judgment and advancement in the spiritual world. Heaven and hell are taught to be spiritual states of nearness to or distance from God that describe relationships in this world and the next, and not physical places of reward and punishment achieved after death. The Baha'i writings emphasize the essential equality of human beings and the abolition of prejudice. Humanity is seen as essentially one, though highly varied; its diversity of race and culture is seen as worthy of appreciation and acceptance. Doctrines of racism, nationalism, caste, social class, and gender-based hierarchy are seen as artificial impediments to unity. The Baha'i teachings state that the unification of humanity is the paramount issue amid the religious and political conditions of the present world.[126]

Branhamism

A man called William Marrion Branham, who was born on April 6, 1909, and died on December 24, 1965, was a servant of God and an American Christian generally recognized as the person responsible for opening the revival after World War II.

Someone thought that Branham was an unlikely leader and that his preaching was hesitant and simply beyond belief. But William Branham became a prophet at one period of time. He was not giant. He was gentle and middle-aged, with piercing eyes.

Branham mobilized his audiences with similar stories about God and the angels. Night after night, in front of thousands of believers, he identified diseases of and pronounced words of healing to some participants.

His supposed "revelation" was his most controversial claim to be called the prophet of the end of the times, like Elijah of the Laodicean church age. His theology seemed weird and complicated. Many people admired him personally. During Branham's last days, his followers of Branham placed him at the center of a cult Pentecostal in nature. Branham has disappeared into obscurity, although some people continue to follow him and believe in him as their prophet.

CHAPTER 11

Heaven

Question: How to get to heaven? What are the ideas from the different religions?

Answer: There appear to be five major categories regarding how to get to heaven in the world's religions.[128]

Most believe that hard work and wisdom will lead to ultimate fulfillment, whether that is unity with god (Hinduism, Buddhism, and Baha'i) or freedom and independence (Scientology, Jainism). Other religions, like Unitarianism and Wicca, teach that the afterlife is whatever you want it to be—and salvation is a nonissue because the sinful nature doesn't exist. A few religions espouse that either the afterlife doesn't exist or it is too unknowable to consider.[129] Those who worship the Judeo-Christian God generally hold that faith in God and/or Jesus and the accomplishment of various deeds, including baptism or door-to-door evangelism, will ensure that the worshipper will go to heaven. Only Christianity teaches that salvation is a free gift of God through faith in Christ (Eph. 2:8–9) and that no amount of work or effort is necessary or possible to get to heaven.

Atheism and Heaven

Most atheists believe there is no heaven—no afterlife at all. Upon death, people simply cease to exist. Other atheists attempt to define the afterlife using quantum mechanics and other scientific methods.

Baha'i and Heaven

Like many other religions, Baha'i doesn't teach that humankind was born with a sinful nature or that humanity needs saving from evil. Human beings simply need saving from their erroneous beliefs of how the world works and how they are to interact with the world. According to Baha'i, God sent messengers to explain to people how to come to this knowledge: Abraham, Krishna, Zoroaster, Moses, Buddha, Jesus, Muhammad, and Baha'u'llah. These prophets progressively revealed the nature of God to the world.

Upon death, Baha'i teaches, a person's soul continues its spiritual journey, perhaps through the states known as heaven and hell, until it comes to its final resting point and is united with god.

Buddhism and Heaven

Buddhism also believes that reaching heaven, or nirvana, means to be rejoined in spirit with God. Reaching nirvana, a transcendental, blissful, spiritual state, requires following the Eightfold Path. This includes understanding the universe, and acting, speaking, and living in the right manner and with the right intentions. Mastering these and the other of the eight paths will return a worshipper's spirit to God.

Chinese Religion and Heaven

Chinese religion is not an organized church but an amalgamation of different religions and beliefs including Taoism and Buddhism. Upon death, worshippers are judged. The good are sent either to a Buddhist paradise or a Tao dwelling place. The bad are sent to hell for a period of time and are then reincarnated.

Christianity and Heaven

Christianity is the only religion that teaches that human beings can do nothing to earn or pay their way into heaven. A human being, slave to the sinful nature he or she was born with, must completely rely on the grace of God in applying Jesus Christ's sacrifice to his or her sins. Upon death, the spirits of Christians go to a temporary paradise, while the spirits of unbelievers go to another temporary holding place.

At the final judgment, Christians are given a new body and thereafter spend eternity with God in paradise, while unbelievers are separated from God for eternity in hell.

Confucianism and Heaven

Confucianism concentrates on appropriate behavior in life, not on a future heaven. The afterlife is unknowable, so all effort should be made to make this life the best it can be, to honor ancestors, and to respect elders.

Eastern Orthodoxy and Heaven

Eastern Orthodoxy is a Judeo-Christian derivative that reinterprets key scripture verses in such a way that works become essential if one is to reach heaven.

Orthodoxy teaches that faith in Jesus is necessary for salvation, but where Christianity teaches that becoming more Christlike is the result of Christ's influence in a believer's life, Orthodoxy teaches that it is a part of the salvation process. If that process (called *theosis*) is not performed appropriately, a worshipper can lose his or her salvation.

After death, the devout live in an intermediate state where this theosis can be completed. Those who have belief but did not accomplish sufficient progress in theosis are sent to a temporary "direful condition," and will go to hell unless the living devout pray and complete acts of mercy on their behalf. After final judgment, the devout are sent to heaven and the others to hell. Heaven and hell are not locations, but reactions to being in the presence of God, as there is nowhere he is not present. For followers of Christ, God's presence is paradise, but for the unsaved, being with God is eternal torment.

Hinduism and Heaven

Hinduism is similar to Buddhism in some ways. Salvation (*ormoksha*) is reached when the worshipper is freed from the cycle of reincarnation and his or her spirit becomes one with god. One becomes free by ridding oneself of bad karma—the effect of evil action or evil intent. This can be done in three different ways: through selfless devotion to and service of a particular god, through understanding the nature of the universe, or by mastering the actions needed to fully appease the gods. In Hinduism, with over a million different gods, there are differences of opinion regarding the nature of salvation. The Advaita school teaches that salvation occurs when one is able to strip away the false self and make his or her soul indistinguishable from that of god. The dualist insists that one's soul always retains its own identity even as it is joined with god.

Islam and Heaven

Islam is a takeoff on Judaism and Christianity. Muslims believe salvation comes to those who obey Allah sufficiently so that their good deeds outweigh their bad deeds.

Muslims hope that repeating what Muhammad did and said will be enough to get them into heaven, but they also recite extra prayers, fast, go on pilgrimages, and perform good works in hope of tipping the scales. Martyrdom in service to Allah is the only work guaranteed to send a worshipper to paradise.

Jainism and Heaven

Jainism came to be in India about the same time as Hinduism. The two are very similar. In Jainism, a person must hold the right belief, have the right knowledge, and act in the right manner. Only then can his or her soul be cleansed of karma. But in Jainism, there is no creator. There is no higher god to reach or lend aid. Salvation occurs when a human being becomes master of his or her own destiny, liberated and perfect, filled with infinite perception, knowledge, bliss, and power.

Jehovah's Witnesses and Heaven

The teachings of the Watchtower Society lead us to categorize the Jehovah's Witnesses as a cult of Christianity that misinterprets the book of Revelation. Similar to Mormons, Jehovah's Witnesses teach different levels of heaven. The anointed are 144,000 who receive salvation by the blood of Christ and will rule with him in paradise. They are the bride of Christ. For all others, Jesus's sacrifice only frees them from Adam's curse of original sin, and having faith is merely the opportunity to earn their way to heaven. They must learn about kingdom history, keep the laws of Jehovah, and be loyal to "God's government"—the 144,000 leaders, 9,000 of whom are currently on the earth. They must also spread the news about the kingdom, including door-to-door proselytizing. Upon death, they will be resurrected to live in the millennial kingdom, where they must continue a devout life. Only afterward are they given the opportunity to formally accept Christ and live for eternity under the rule of the 144,000.

Judaism and Heaven

Jews believe that they can, as individuals and as a nation, be reconciled to God. Through sin (individual or collective), they can lose their salvation, but they can also earn it back through repentance, good deeds, and a life of devotion.

Mormonism and Heaven

Mormons believe their religion to be a derivative of Judeo-Christianity, but their reliance on extra-grace works belies this. They also have a different view of heaven. To reach the second heaven under "general salvation," one must accept Christ (either in this life or the next) and be baptized, or be baptized by proxy through a living relative. To reach the highest heaven, one must believe in God and Jesus, repent of sins, be baptized in the church, be a member of the Church of Latter-Day Saints, receive the Holy Ghost by the laying on of hands, obey the Mormon Word of Wisdom and all God's commandments, and complete certain temple rituals including marriage. This "individual salvation" leads to the worshipper and his or her spouse becoming gods and giving birth to spirit children who return to earth as the souls of the living.

Roman Catholicism and Heaven

Roman Catholics originally believed that only those in the Roman Catholic Church could be saved. Joining the church was a long process consisting of classes, rituals, and baptism. People who had already been baptized but were not members of the Roman Catholic Church had different requirements and may have even already been considered Christians.

Baptism is "normatively" required for salvation, but this can include "baptism of blood" (i.e., martyrdom) or "baptism of desire" (wanting to be baptized really badly). From the catechism: "Those who die for the faith, those who are catechumens, and all those who, without knowing of the Church but acting under the inspiration of grace, seek God sincerely and strive to fulfill his will, are saved even if they have not been baptized." Despite the changes through the years, baptism (or the desire for baptism) is still required for salvation.

According to Catholicism, upon death, the souls of those who rejected Christ are sent to hell. The souls of those who accepted Christ and performed sufficient acts to be purified of sin go to heaven. Those who died in faith but did not complete the steps to be purified are sent to purgatory, where they undergo temporary painful punishment until their souls are cleansed. Purification by torment may be lessened by suffering during life and the offerings and prayers of others on the sinner's behalf. Once purification is complete, the soul may go to heaven.

Scientology and Heaven

Scientology is similar to Eastern religions in that salvation is achieved through knowledge of self and the universe. The "thetan" (Scientology's answer to the soul) travels through several different lifetimes in an attempt to expel painful and traumatic images that cause a person to act fearfully and irrationally. Once a Scientologist is "cleared" of these harmful images and becomes an "operating thetan," he or she is able to control thought, life, matter, energy, space, and time.

Shinto and Heaven

The afterlife in Shinto was originally a dire Hades-like realm. Matters of the afterlife have now been transferred to Buddhism. This salvation is dependent on penance and avoiding impurity or pollution of the soul. Then one's soul can join those of its ancestors.

Sikhism and Heaven

Sikhism was created in reaction to the conflict between Hinduism and Islam, and carries on many of Hinduism's influences—although Sikhs are monotheistic. According to the Shinto religion, evil is merely human selfishness. Salvation is attained by living an honest life and meditating on God. If good works are performed sufficiently, the worshipper is released from the cycle of reincarnation and becomes one with God.

Taoism and Heaven

Like several other Eastern religions (e.g., Shinto, Chinese folk religions, and Sikhism), Taoism adopted many of its afterlife principles from Buddhism. Initially, Taoists didn't concern themselves with worries of the afterlife and, instead, concentrated on creating a utopian society. Salvation was reached by aligning with the cosmos and receiving aid from supernatural immortals who resided on mountains, islands, and other places on earth. The result was immortality. Eventually, Taoists abandoned the quest for immortality and took on the afterlife teachings of Buddhism.

Unitarian Universalism and Heaven

Unitarians are allowed to and encouraged to believe anything they like about the afterlife and how to get there. In general, however, they believe that people should seek enlightenment in this life and not worry too much about the afterlife.

Wicca and Heaven

Wiccans believe many different things about the afterlife, but most seem to agree that there is no need for salvation. People either live in harmony with the Goddess by caring for her physical manifestation—the earth—or they don't, in which case their bad karma is returned to them threefold. Some believe souls are reincarnated until they learn all their life lessons and become one with the Goddess. Some are so committed to following their individual path that they believe individuals determine what will happen when they die; if worshippers think they're going to be reincarnated or sent to hell or joined with the Goddess, they will be. Others refuse to contemplate the afterlife at all. Either way, they don't believe in sin or anything they need saving from.

Zoroastrianism and Heaven

Zoroastrianism may be the first religion that stated that the afterlife is dependent upon one's actions in life. There is no reincarnation, just a simple judgment that takes place four days after death. After a sufficient amount of time in hell, however, even the condemned can go to heaven. To be judged righteous, a Zoroastrianist can use knowledge or devotion, but the most effective way is through action.[129]

Heaven, the Eternal Home of the Saved

Most people in this world, even those who deny the existence of hell, talk about the existence of some form of paradise after death.[130] A song written over a hundred years ago proclaimed, "Everybody talkin' 'bout heaven ain't goin' there."

> One of the first references to heaven noted Abraham "looked for a city." Just as a family moving into a new home will want to know every detail about the house, the neighborhood, area churches, schools, bus lines, and shopping centers, so those going there should want to know every detail about their future Home. Jesus said, "I go to prepare a place for you" (John 14:2). Of all areas of theological study, this is perhaps the one most interesting to many Christians.[131]

As Lewis Sperry Chafer correctly notes, "Probably no Bible theme is more agreeable to the mind of man than that of heaven. This is especially true of those who through advancing years of physical limitations are drawing near to the end of the realities of earth."[131]

220

The Location of Heaven

The Bible seems to teach that there are four heavens. The fact that "Jesus passed through the heavens" (Heb. 4:14) indicates there is more than one heaven. Also, Jesus "ascended up far above all heavens" (Eph. 4:10), which indicates that one heaven is above another. Paul taught there were at least three heavens when he testified of being "caught up to the third heaven" (2 Cor. 12:1–4). Apparently, these heavens (three) shall pass away and be replaced with a fourth heaven, described as "a new heaven" (2 Pet. 3:10; Rev. 21:1). The first heaven is the atmosphere. This term is used in scripture to refer to the air and atmosphere that surrounds human beings and all other created life on earth (Matt. 6:26; James 5:8). The second heaven is the stellar spaces, or outer space (Matt. 24–29; Gen. 15:5). The third heaven is described as the dwelling place of God. While much is unknown about this heaven, it is the place where God is located (Rev. 3:12; Rev. 20:9).

While it is popular in some circles to limit one's definition of heaven to "a state of bliss," it is difficult to harmonize this with the biblical teaching and inference of a localized place called heaven. Augustus H. Strong argues that heaven is a place, because the body of Christ must be located.[132]

> Is heaven a place, as well as a state? We answer that this is probable, for the reason that the presence of Christ's human body is essential to heaven, and that this body must be confined to a place. Since deity and humanity are indissolubly united in Christ's single person, we cannot regard Christ's human soul as limited to a place without vacating his person of its divinity. But we cannot conceive of his human body as thus omnipresent. As the new bodies of the saints are confined to place, so, it would seem, must be the body of their Lord. But, though heaven be the place where Christ manifests his glory through the human body which he assumed in the incarnation, our ruling conception of heaven must be something higher even this, namely, that of a state of holy communication with God.[133]

The Biblical Description of Heaven

The splendor and beauty of heaven far outshines anything the human mind can comprehend. It will be impossible to completely comprehend heaven until we arrive on location, but the scriptures do reveal heaven as a huge and colorful city. Beyond that, the biblical description of heaven reads like a list of superlatives. The following is according to Chafer:

> In attempting to portray to the mind of man the glories of the celestial sphere, language has been strained to its limits; yet we may believe that no considerable portion of that wondrous glory has ever been revealed. Who can comprehend the blessedness that will be experienced by the redeemed in Heaven, or that has already come to human hearts in anticipation of that wonderful place! It is characterized as a place of abundant life (1 Tim. 4:8), of rest (Rev. 14:13), of knowledge (1 Cor. 13:8–10), of holiness (Rev. 21:27), of service (Rev. 22:3), of worship (Rev. 19:1), of fellowship with God (Rev. 21:3), of fellowship with other believers (1 Thess. 4:8), and of glory (2 Cor. 4:17).[134]

The most complete description of heaven is that of the bride city in the final two chapters of Revelation. Some would argue that it is wrong to describe heaven in specific terms, claiming that these are only heavenly symbols to represent the idea that the presence of God is beautiful.

The bride city described by John will be the largest city ever built (Rev. 21:16). This description of heaven suggests that it will be a gigantic cube or pyramid (foursquare). According to our present measurements, 12,000 furlongs would be equivalent to 1,500 miles or 2,400 kilometers. If placed in the United States, this city would reach from New York City to Denver, Colorado, and from the Canadian border to Florida. If the New Jerusalem takes the form of a sphere, it will be slightly larger than the moon that presently circles our globe.

Despite its immense size, the city consists of fine details, as described by Thiessen:

We read that its foundations are garnished with "all manner of precious stone" (Rev. 21:10, 20). Twelve of these are named. It has twelve gates, bearing the names of the twelve tribes of Israel (Rev. 21:12, 13); and the twelve foundations bear the names of the twelve apostles (Rev. 21:14; cf. Eph. 2:20). The wall is of jasper and the city is of pure gold (Rev. 21:18). Every gate is a pearl (Rev. 21:21). We are told that the gates are never closed (Rev. 21:25); but that twelve angels stand before them (Rev. 21:12). Its street is of pure gold (Rev. 21:21). There is in it the river of life and the tree of life (Rev. 22:1, 2). It has no need of sun or moon; "for the glory of God did lighten it, and the lamp thereof is the Lamb" (Rev. 21:23). All these things indicate that this is a literal city.[135]

Heaven will be the most beautiful city ever built. The city wall will stand some 216 feet high (Rev. 21:17) and will be built of jasper. It will be as beautiful as a crystal-clear diamond, as bright as a transparent icicle in the sunshine (Rev. 21:18).

In addition to adding to the beauty of the eternal state, the walls, according to John Ritchie, emphasize the security of the city.

The "wall great and high" (verse 12) speaks of security, but though secure from all human or Satanic molestation, the city is not like Jericho of old—"straitly shut up," for its gates (twelve in number) tell of ingress and egress. These gates will not be shut by day (verse 25), and as there is "no night there," they will be open perpetually.

A great city like London never has its gates shut, for through them come from every quarter of the land, and at all hours, the supplies she needs. The gates of the Bride-city are open always, not for supplies to come in, but for supplies to go out to the earth.[136]

TABLE 11.1. What is missing from heaven

Tears	Rev. 12:1	Defilement	Rev. 21:27
Death	Rev. 21:4	Abomination	Rev. 21:27
Sorrow	Rev. 21:4	Curse	Rev. 22:3
Crying	Rev. 21:4	Liars	Rev. 21:27
Pain	Rev. 21:4	Sun	Rev. 21:23
Night	Rev. 21:25	Moon	Rev. 21:23

137

Heaven is also a place of memory. The question is often asked, "Will we know one another in heaven?" The answer is yes! David said that he would know his son (2 Sam. 12:22–23). Moses and Elijah, who had died long ago, were recognized by Peter, James, and John (Mark 9:4–5). Also, it appears we will recognize Abraham, Isaac, and Jacob (Matt. 8:11). Paul talked of a time when he would be known and know others also (1 Cor. 13:12).

The Inhabitants of Heaven

Heaven is more than the eternal home of the saved. Many others will forever live with us there. These inhabitants include God, his angels, and his special creations. Both saved Jews and Gentiles will live in perfect harmony. Citizens of every linguistic group and race will live in heaven for eternity. It will be the ultimate international community. The following will inhabit heaven:

Angels

John "heard the voice of many angels about the throne in heaven" (Rev. 5:11). These include several kinds of angels. The seraphim, a special kind of angel who deals with God's altar, will be present in heaven (Isa. 6:1–7). Another special angelic group who deals with God's throne, the cherubim, will also be there (Ps. 99:1). And of course, Gabriel and Michael will be there too.

Elders

The Bible identifies twenty-four elders around the throne of God in heaven (Rev. 4:4). Much has been speculated concerning the identity of this group. One suggestion is that these men are twelve tribal leaders of Israel and the twelve apostles of Jesus. Another is that they represent the saved, both Jews and Gentiles.

Saved Israel

Hebrews 11 lists a number of individuals and groups who practiced faith in the Old Testament. Concerning them, it is said "they desire a better county" (Heb. 11:6). These who have experienced saving faith have an eternal place in heaven.

Church

One of the first events after the rapture will be the marriage supper of the Lamb. This is when the church, the bride of Christ, will be presented to her groom, the Lord Jesus Christ. The New Jerusalem has been described as "the wedding ring of the church."

Nations

Many Bible scholars believe Christians in heaven will retain some of their ethnic distinctions and perhaps even be organized as nations. Twice the scriptures use the plural term *peoples* describing the citizens of heaven (Zeph. 3:20; Rev. 2:13).

Also, John recognized the ethnic distinctions of some of the redeemed in heaven (Rev. 7:9). However, in heaven, there will be perfect acceptance by all of everyone there. The unity of heaven's inhabitants, not their diversity, will be the dominant characteristic.

The Triune God

Heaven is, of course, the eternal home of each member of the Trinity of God. The Father sits upon the throne in heaven (Rev. 4:2-3). John saw Jesus standing in heaven (Rev. 5:6). Though not as prominent, the Holy Spirit also lives in heaven and is thrice quoted in John's account of his experience there (Rev. 3:13; Rev. 14:13; Rev. 22:17).

As people grow older, their attitude toward heaven often changes. They no longer think so much of the geography of that land, as of individuals known and loved who have died and gone on before. When preaching on heaven, D. L. Moody often related the following story:

> When I was a boy, I thought of heaven as a great, shining city, with vast walls and domes and spires, and with nobody in it except white-robed angels, who were strangers to me. By and by my little brother died; and I thought of a great city with walls and domes and spires, and a flock of cold, unknown angels, and one little fellow that I was acquainted with. He was the only one I knew at the time. Then another brother died; and there were two that I knew. Then my acquaintances began to die; and the flock continually grew. But it was not until I had sent one of my little children to his Heavenly Parent—God—that I began to think I had a little in there myself. A second went, a third went; a fourth went; and by this time I had so many acquaintances in heaven, that I did not see any more walls and domes and spires.
>
> I began to think of the residents of the celestial city as my friends. And now so many of my acquaintances have gone there, that it sometimes seems to me that I know more people in heaven than I do on earth.[138]

The Activities of Heaven

Heaven is often thought of in terms of angels sittings on clouds with harps and singing in choirs. At best, this imbalanced view represents a small part of heaven. Though described as the eternal rest of the believer, heaven will be a very active place.

TABLE 11.2. What to do in heaven

Learn	1 Cor. 13:9–10
Sing	Rev. 15:3
Worship	Rev. 5:9
Serve	Rev. 22:3
Lead	2 Tim. 2:12; Rev. 22:5
Fellowship with others	Matt. 16:3
Eat	Rev. 2:17

[139]

A Life of Fellowship

In heaven, we will enjoy communion with the Lord Jesus Christ for all eternity. "They shall see his face" (Rev. 22:4). Christ predicts our future unity with his: "I will come again, and receive you unto myself; that where I am, there ye may be also" (John 14:3). When a human being is in perfect fellowship with God, his or her relationship with society is affected. Richard W. DeHaan has correctly observed as follows:

> In the new heavens and new earth man will realize a perfect society of righteousness and harmony, something he has never been able to achieve. The problems of individual freedom and social responsibility have not yet been solved, either by capitalism with its emphasis upon the individual, or communion with its stress upon the right of the community. In our eternal home the perfect society will become a reality, for individual identity on one hand, and harmonious variety on the other, will finally be achieved.[140]

A Life of Rest

One of the results of original sin was the curse of toil and sweat in a life of work. When we arrive in heaven, we will continue to work, but the agony of labor will be gone. "Blessed are the dead which die in the Lord from henceforth: Yes, saith the Spirit that they may rest from their labors" (Rev. 14:13).

A Life of Service

We will work in heaven, but rather than dread the thought of labor and suffer the physical pain from grueling drudgery, we will enjoy our work. The curse will be gone. "And his servants shall serve him" (Rev. 22:3). As Moody states,

> There is not such a great difference between grace and glory after all. Grace is the bud, and glory the blossom. Grace is glory begun, and glory is grace perfected.
>
> It will not come hard to people who are serving God down here to do it when they go up yonder. They will change places, but they will not change employments.[141]

A Life of Growth

We will not instantaneously know everything when we arrive in heaven. Instead, we will spend a lifetime growing in knowledge and maturity. Christians will learn facts about God and his plan. We will grow in love. Also, we will learn how to serve him and grow in our ability to serve him. "The leaves of the trees were for the healing of the nations" (Rev. 22:2). The word *healing* also means growth, implying the advancement of heaven's inhabitants.

A Life of Worship

Jesus said at the beginning of his ministry, "The Father seeketh such to worship him" (John 4:23). Since the Father wanted people to worship him while they were on earth, this will not change when they get to heaven. "And after these things I heard a great voice of much people in heaven saying, Alleluia; Salvation, and glory, and honor, and power, unto the Lord our God" (Rev. 19:1).

CHAPTER 12

Hell

Hell is a place of eternal punishment for the wicked. In the New Revised Standard Version (NRSV), the word *hell* is only used in the New Testament, where it translates from the Greek *gehenna*. It is thus distinct from Sheol and Hades, names for the realm of the dead that the NRSV simply transliterates from Hebrew and Greek respectively. Some English translations, including the King James Version, use *hell* to translate Sheol and Hades, as well as gehenna.

The Greek word *gehenna* is derived from the Hebrew word *gehinnom*, meaning "valley of Hinnom," also known as the "valley of the son of Hinnom" (2 Chron. 28:3; 2 Chron. 33:6; Neh. 11:30; Jer. 7:31–32; Jer. 19:2, 6; Jer. 32:35). Located west and south of Jerusalem and running into the Kidron Valley at a point opposite the modern village of Silwan, the Valley of Hinnom once formed part of the boundary between the tribes of Judah and Benjamin (Josh. 15:8; Josh. 18:16; Neh. 11:30).[142]

Some scholars countered that Christ descended into hell triumphantly after his death in order to show himself as the defeater and conqueror of death, Satan, and hell. The New Testament does not reflect any passion or activity of Jesus between death and resurrection.

Most interpreters agree that Ephesians 4:8 first concerns Christ's descent (v. 9), and then his triumphant ascent after his death and resurrection: from heaven to earth (Incarnation) or from earth to grave (Sheol). Others contend that the descent occurred after Jesus's ascension and say that it depicts the return to the earth of the exalted Christ as the Spirit and Pentecost.[143]

Hell, the Eternal Abode of the Unsaved

No one really wants to talk about hell, but it exists as a definite part of the eternal plan of God. Hell is not the Devil's playground, nor is it someone's punishment on earth. God created hell, a real place where real people will suffer real punishment for a real eternity. One of the primary dangers of false religions is their denial of this place.

Biblical Teaching Concerning the Character of Hell

The biblical doctrine of hell is revealed by the use of many words and figures in both the Old and New Testaments. Each of these contributes something to the complete revelation concerning hell. Even with these many descriptions, our knowledge of such a place necessarily remains limited. The Creator of humankind understands there is a psychological limit to humankind's ability to comprehend horror.

Still, as Strong observes, the final state of the wicked is described as being thrown into eternal fire (Matt. 25:41); the pit of the abyss (Rev. 9:2, 11); outer darkness (Matt. 8:12); torment (Rev. 14:10, 11); eternal punishment (Matt. 25:46); the wrath of God (Rom. 2:5); a second death (Rev. 21:8); eternal destruction away from the face of the Lord (2 Thess. 1:9); and eternal sin (Mark 3:29).[144]

Terms used to in scripture to describe hell include the following:

- Sheol (Ps. 139:8; Deut. 32:22; Job 26:6)
- Hades (Luke 16:19–31)
- Tartaros (2 Pet. 2:4)
- Gehenna (2 Chron. 33:6; Jer. 7:31, Rev. 19:20; Rev. 20:10, 14, 15; see also Matt. 5:22, 29, 30; Matt. 10:28; Matt. 18:9; Matt. 23:15, 33; Mark 9:43, 45, 47; and Luke 12:5)[145]
- Retribution (Prov. 14:12; Prov. 16:25; Matt. 7:13; Rom. 5:12)
- Prison (1 Pet. 3:19; Rev. 20:7; see also 1 Pet. 3:19; 2 Pet. 2:4–9)[146]
- Chains (2 Pet. 2:4; Jude 6; Rev. 20:1)
- Stripes (Luke 12:48)

- Weeping and gnashing of teeth (Matt. 8:12; Matt. 13:42, 50; Matt. 22:13; Matt. 24:51; Matt. 25:30; Luke 13:28)
- Pit of the abyss or bottomless pit (John 9:1–2:11; John 11:7; John 17:8; John 20:1, 3)
- Outer darkness (Matt. 8:12)

The uses of darkness in the Bible are many and various. Darkness is used as a symbol of (a) moral depravity and its punishment (the wicked walk and work in darkness [Ps. 82:5; Prov. 2:13; John 3:19; Rom. 13:12], and their reward is to "sit in darkness" [Ps. 107:10] or to be "cast forth into the outer darkness" [Matt. 8:12]; (b) things mysterious or inexplicable (1 Kings 8:12; Ps 97:2); (c) trouble and affliction (2 Sam. 22:9; Job 5:14; Prov. 20:20; Isa. 9:2; cf. Gen. 15:12); (d) punishment (Lam. 3:2; Ezek. 32:8; Zeph. 1:15); (e) death (1 Sam. 2:9; Job 10:21; Eccl. 11:8); (f) nothingness (Job 3:4–6); (g) and human ignorance (Job 19:8; 1 John 2:11).[147]

Hell is a place of destruction (2 Thess. 1:9; Rev. 9:11; 1 Thess. 1:8) and torment (Luke 16:23, 28). Of the various words for "suffering" in the New Testament, *torment* may be the most severe. The word *torment* means "pain, anguish" (Matt. 4:24), particularly the pain inflicted by the ancients in order to induce people to confess of their crimes. These torments or tortures were the keenest that could be inflicted, such as the rack, or scourging, or burning. The use of the word in Matthew 4:24 denotes that the suffering of the wicked can be represented only by the extremist forms of human suffering.[148]

The rich man described Hades as "a place of torments" (Luke 16:28). That torment is the result of several aspects of the suffering endured in that place. The first torment a person encounters in hell is the torment of burning. The rich man acknowledged, "I am tormented in this flame" (Luke 16:24). While it is wrong to say that all the torture in hell comes from the flame, it would be also wrong to explain away the literal flames of hell. A second aspect of the torment of hell is sight. Jesus suggested that people in hell could see the blessed state of the righteous (Luke 16:23). The scriptures never mention people in heaven viewing the suffering of the lost, because there is pain even in viewing the suffering of others. Those in hell suffer, however, more severely from the constant sight of what might have been, and what is.

231

The Valley of Hinnom

The Valley of Hinnom had been desecrated by the sacrifice of the children to Moloch so that it, as an accursed place, was used for the city garbage where worms gnawed and fires burned. It is thus a vivid picture of eternal punishment.

Fire

Probably the best-known popular image of hell is that of fire. The rich man is described as tormented by the flame (Luke 16:24), and people are salted with fire (Mark 9:49), cast into the lake of fire (Rev. 20:15), and cast into a furnace of fire (Matt. 13:42). Further, fire and brimstone (Rev. 21:8) and the unquenchable flame (Mark 9:43, 45–46, 48) are used to describe hell. The use of fire to describe hell not only is descriptive but also emphasizes the continuous suffering of the lost. See also Genesis 19:24.

> Second death. (James 2:26, Rev. 19:20; 20:10) Chafer, Major Bible Themes, 296.

> Wrath of God (Rom. 1:18) See also 1 Pet. 1:17; Heb. 10:29. William Evans, "Wrath"[150]

Eternity

The above adjectives applied to hell ascribe to it a degree of suffering that is beyond the realm of human comprehension. Once we add the word *eternity* to all the words that describe suffering, hell is compounded far beyond human understanding. It is one thing to be the object of God's wrath; it is an entirely different thing to be the object of that wrath for eternity. It is one thing to be in torment; it is something else to be eternally tormented. If hell were in any sense tolerable for its inhabitants, the concept of eternity makes it completely intolerable.[149]

CHAPTER 13

Christianity

Jesus

"Jesus is the central figure of Christianity and a major prophet of Islam. Jesus (name), as given name and surname, derived from the Latin name Iesus and the Greek Ἰησοῦς (Iesous)."[150]

If you read the pages of the Sacred Book (the Bible) with faith and the illumination of Holy Spirit, you don't need another demonstration to meet or to find Jesus Christ there as the living God.

The scripture exclaims, "One thing I know, that I was blind, and now I see" (John 9:25).

"My ears had heard of you; but now [that I have read the Bible] my eye sees you" Job 42:5.

- The Son is Lord (John 1:14; John 17:5).
- The Son is supreme (Col. 1:18 [as to his position and not time]; Mark 2:5–7; Matt. 14:33; Luke 24:52; John 5:26–29; Phil. 2:10; Heb. 1:8).
- The Son can do anything (i.e., he is omnipotent) (John 1:3; Col. 1:16; Heb. 1:10; Mark 4:39; Mark 5:41; Rom. 1:4).
- The Son knows everything (i.e., he is omniscient) (John 16:30–21:17; Matt. 9:4; John 1:48; John 6:64; John 13:3).
- The Son can be everywhere at once (i.e., he is omnipresent) (Eph. 1:20; Matt. 28:10–20).
- The Son is revealed (John 2:11; John 8:12; Heb. 1:3).
- The Son is always the same (Heb. 13:8).
- The Son is just (2 Tim. 4:8; Heb. 1:9).

- The Son is holy (Acts 4:30).
- The Son is full of grace (2 Cor. 8:9; Matt. 9:36; Jude 21).

The Work of Christ Before His Incarnation

His Power in Creating the Universe

Among the three persons of the Trinity is Jesus Christ, who has the power to create in his attributions (John 1:3). In him is life (John 1:4). Through the Son, God created the world (Heb. 1:1). The Son sustains the world by his powerful Word (Heb. 1:3). In him all things hold together (Col. 1:17).

Jesus of Nazareth is God. When Jesus had a human body, he was truly God and truly Man. He came as incarnate Man when he was miraculously conceived by the Virgin Mary by the power of the Holy Spirit.

Jesus came into the world to save us. He suffered, he was crucified, he died, and he was buried for us.

Jesus Christ overcame death when he was resurrected from the dead. He is resurrected with a body of incomparable beauty. He ascended into heaven, and now sits at the right-hand side of the Father as a King, interceding for us. He is the only Mediator between God and humankind. He will return and will judge all human beings.

Jesus Christ lived without sin. He agreed to be our propitiation for our sin. When he died on the cross, he took on the punishment that was meant for us, thereafter offering salvation to whoever believes in him.

Jesus's Revelation of God (John 1:18)

No one has ever seen God the Father. Only the Son knows him (John 1:18). By this verse, we learn that the apparitions of God of the Old Testament were the appearances of the Son. Sometimes that was in human form, sometimes an angel, sometimes as fire. God appeared to Abraham (Gen. 12:7); Isaac (Gen. 26:2); Jacob (Gen. 35:9); Moses (Exod. 3:2); Ishmael (Lev. 9:23); Joshua (Josh. 5:13–15); Gideon (Judg. 6:12); Manoah, (Judg. 13:11); Samuel (1 Sam. 3:21); David (2 Chron. 3:1); Solomon (1 Kings 9:2); Isaiah (Isa. 6:1); and Ezekiel (Ezek. 1:28).

What is wonderful is that God is revealed to us through his Son. How glorious is our God!

Jesus of Nazareth

Jesus (/'dʒiːzəs/; *Greek: Ἰησοῦς [Iesous]*), who lived on earth from about 6–4 BC to 30–33 AD), and who is also referred to as Jesus of Nazareth, is the central figure of Christianity. The teachings of most Christian denominations hold him to be the Son of God. Christianity regards Jesus as the awaited Messiah of the Old Testament and refers to him as Jesus Christ, a name that is also used in non-Christian contexts.[151]

Virtually all modern scholars of antiquity agree that Jesus existed historically, although the quest for the historical Jesus has produced little agreement on the historical reliability of the gospels and on how closely the biblical Jesus reflects the historical Jesus. Most scholars agree that Jesus was a Jewish rabbi from Galilee who preached his message orally, was baptized by John the Baptist, and was crucified in Jerusalem on the orders of the Roman prefect Pontius Pilate. Scholars have constructed various portraits of the historical Jesus, which often depict him as having one or more of the following roles: the leader of an apocalyptic movement, Messiah, a charismatic healer, a sage and philosopher, or an egalitarian social reformer. Scholars have correlated the New Testament accounts with non-Christian historical records to arrive at an estimated chronology of Jesus's life. The most widely used calendar era in the world (abbreviated as "AD," alternatively referred to as "CE") counts from a medieval estimate of the birth year of Jesus.

Christians believe that Jesus has a "unique significance" in the world. Christian doctrines include the beliefs that Jesus was conceived by the Holy Spirit, was born of a virgin, performed miracles, founded the church, died by crucifixion as a sacrifice to achieve atonement, rose from the dead, and ascended into heaven, from whence he will return. The great majority of Christians worship Jesus as the incarnation of God the Son, the second of three persons of a Divine Trinity. A few Christian groups reject Trinitarianism, wholly or partly, as nonscriptural.

In Islam, Jesus (commonly transliterated as "Isa") is considered one of God's important prophets and the Messiah. To Muslims, Jesus is a bringer of scripture and was born of a virgin, but he was neither the Son of God nor the victim of crucifixion. According to the Quran, Jesus was not crucified but was physically raised into the heavens by God. Judaism rejects the Christian and Islamic belief that Jesus was the awaited Messiah, arguing that he did not fulfill the messianic prophecies in the Tanakh.[152]

Christ

Christ (/kraɪst/) (ancient Greek: Χριστός, Christós, meaning "anointed") is a translation of the Hebrew מָשִׁיחַ (Māšîaḥ) and the Syriac ܡܫܝܚܐ (M'shiha), "the Messiah," and is used as a title for Jesus in the New Testament. In common usage, "Christ" is generally treated as being synonymous with Jesus of Nazareth.[153]

The followers of Jesus became known as Christians (as in Acts 11:26) because they believed Jesus to be the Messiah (Christós) prophesied in the Hebrew Bible, for example in the confession of Peter.[155]

Jesus came to be called "Jesus Christ," meaning "Jesus the Christós" (i.e., "Jesus the Anointed," or "Jesus the Messiah"), by his followers after his death and believed resurrection. Before, Jesus was usually referred to as "Jesus of Nazareth" or "Jesus son of Joseph." In the epistles of Paul the apostle, the earliest texts of the New Testament, Paul most often refers to Jesus as "Christ Jesus" or "Christ." Christ was originally a title, yet later it became part of the name Jesus Christ, though it is still also used as a title in the reciprocal use Christ Jesus, meaning "the Messiah Jesus."

Jesus was not, and is not, accepted by most Jews as their Messiah. Religious Jewish people still await the Messiah's first coming, whereas Christians await the Second Coming of Christ, which is when, they believe, he will fulfill the rest of messianic prophecy. Muslims accept Jesus as the Messiah (known as Isa al-Masih) but not as the Son of God. The area of Christian theology called Christology is primarily concerned with the nature and person of Jesus Christ as recorded in the canonical gospels and the letters of the New Testament.

Christ and Salvation in Christianity

> She will bear a son, and you shall call his name Jesus, for he
> will save his people from their sins.

In Matthew 1:21, the name Jesus was selected by divine direction. In Colossians 1:15–16, the apostle Paul views the Nativity of Jesus as an event of cosmic significance that changed the nature of the world by paving the way for salvation.[156] Christian teachings present the love of Christ as a basis for his sacrificial act that brought forth salvation.

In John 14:31 Jesus explains that his sacrifice was performed so "that the world may know that I love the Father, and as the Father gave me commandment, even so I do." Ephesians 5:25 then states, "Christ also loved the church, and gave himself up for it."

In the second century, Irenaeus expressed his views of salvation in terms of the imitation of Christ and his theory of recapitulation. For Irenaeus, the imitation of Christ is based on God's plan of salvation, which involves Christ as the "last Adam." He viewed the Incarnation as the way by which Christ repaired the damage done by Adam's disobedience.[154]

For Irenaeus, salvation was achieved by Christ's restoring humanity to the image of God. He saw the Christian imitation of Christ as a key component of the path to salvation.

For Irenaeus, Christ succeeded on every point on which Adam failed. Irenaeus drew a number of parallels. For example, just as the fall of Adam resulted from the fruit of a tree, Irenaeus saw redemption and salvation as the fruit of another tree: the cross of crucifixion.

Following in the Pauline tradition, in the fifth century Augustine of Hippo viewed Christ as the Mediator of the new covenant between God and humanity and as the conqueror over sin. He viewed Christ as the cause and reason for the reconciliation of humankind with God after the fall of Adam, and he saw in Christ as being the path to Christian salvation.[155]

The Deity of Jesus Christ

Jesus Christ, the second person of the Trinity, is equal with the Father in nature, yet the Father sent him to die for the sins of the world, which indicates that Christ is submissive to the Father in duties.

Jesus of Nazareth possessed all the divine attributes of the Father and was one with the Father, yet he was separate in person.

Christ effected redemption for humankind because in him was united both the human and divine natures. In humanity, Christ was totally human; in deity, Jesus was unalterably God.

Yet in Jesus Christ was a single undivided personality in which these two natures were vitally and undividedly united, so that Jesus Christ is not God and man, but the God-man. For all these reasons and more, Christ is God. The following reasons help classify and demonstrate his deity.[156]

The nature of the claims of Jesus Christ attest to his deity simply because Jesus Christ claims to be God.

There are eight aspects to Jesus's claim to deity. In the Gospel of John, Jesus uses the Jehovahistic I AM, which identifies him with deity ("I am the way"; "I am the resurrection"; "I am the door"; and so forth). Also, the Jehovahistic I AM is used without the figures of speech (in John 8:25, 56–59 and John 18:6, 8, the pronoun *he* is not in the Greek). Augustine believed that salvation is available to those who are worthy of it, through faith in Christ.[157]

Jesus identifies himself with God in the baptismal formula (Matt. 28:19). He claims to be one with the Father (John 10:30) and says that the person who saw him was seeing the Father (John 14:9). When Jesus claimed to forgive sins (Mark 2:5–7), he was assuming a prerogative that belonged to God. When he allowed people to worship him, he was asserting himself as Deity, for he was approving an act that belonged to the Deity (Matt. 14:33; 28:9; John 20:28, 29).

Jesus claimed to possessive the comparative attributes of omnipresence, omniscience, and omnipotence. He claimed to be in heaven (John 3:13). He claimed that the dead would respond to his authority (Luke 7:14) and that nature would obey his word (Mark 4:39).

Finally, Jesus claimed to have a special relationship to the heavenly Father by addressing him as "my Father" (John 5:18). This is a common expression today, as many Christians say "my Father" when speaking of God, but when Jesus said "my Father," the Jewish leaders recognized that he claimed deity for himself and they responded accordingly. "Therefore, the Jews sought the more to kill him [Jesus], because he not only had broken the sabbath, but said also that God was his Father, making himself equal with God" (John 5:18).

On a visit to Jerusalem, Jesus was asked for a clear statement concerning his claim. He responded, "I and my Father are one" (John 10:30). The Jews understood him to be saying, "I am the son of God" (John 10:36). On several occasions, they attempted to kill Jesus for claiming to be God. When the religious leaders finally brought Jesus to Pilate for crucifixion, it was because of his claims. They accused him of blasphemy. "The Jews answered him, we have a law, and by our law he ought to die, because he made himself the Son of God" (John 19:7). Conservative theologians have always noted and emphasized the fact that Christ claimed to be God. Ibid. Theology for Today, p. 156

TABLE 13.1. Jesus is Jehovah

Of Jehovah	Mutual title or act	Of Jesus
Isa. 40:28	Creator	John 1:3
Isa. 45:22; Isa. 43:11	Savior	John 4:42
1 Sam. 2:6	Raise the dead	John 5:21, 25
Joel 3:12	Judge	John 5:27; cf. Matt. 25:31
Isa. 60:19–20	Light	John 8:12
Exod. 3:14	I Am	John 8:58, cf. John 18:5–6
Ps. 23:1	Shepherd	John 10:11
Isa. 42:8; cf. Isa. 48:11	Glory of God	John 17:1, 5
Isa. 41:4; Isa. 44:6	First and Last	Rev. 1:17; Rev. 2:8.
Hosea 13:14	Redeemer	Rev. 5:9
Isa. 62:5; Hosea 2:16	Bridegroom	Rev. 21:2. cf. Matt. 25:1–13
Ps. 18:2	Rock	1 Cor. 10:4
Jer. 31:34	Forgiver of sins	Mark 2:7, 10

Of Jehovah	Mutual title or act	Of Jesus
Ps. 148:2	Worshipped by angels	Heb. 1:6
Through the Old Testament	Addressed in prayer	Acts 7:59
Ps. 148:5	Creator of angels Col. 1:16)	Col. 1:16
Isa. 45:23	Confessed as Lord	Phil. 2:11

The preexistence and eternality of Jesus Christ both attest to his deity. The Bible teaches that Jesus Christ is the second person of the Trinity. As such, he is equal with God the Father in attributes and nature. Since God is eternal, any proof that demonstrates that Jesus Christ lived before his birth points to his deity. The term *preexistence* means that Christ existed in the Old Testament. To this, Jesus Christ testified, "Before Abraham was, I am" (John 8:58). The Jews understood he was claiming deity, so they took stones to kill him for blasphemy (John 8:59). Paul adds to the proofs of his preexistence: "He is before all things" (Col. 1:17). The proof that Christ appeared to people in the Old Testament in Christophanies also lays the foundation for his deity (see section III).

The term *eternality* means that Jesus Christ is not limited by time, that he has no beginning or end. To this testifies the writer to the Hebrews, "Jesus Christ the same yesterday, and today, and forever" (Heb. 13:8). The same writer also states of Christ, "They [the heavens and earth] shall perish; but thou remains" (Heb. 1:11). To make the eternality of Christ emphatic, he adds, "Thy years shall not fail" (Heb. 1:12).

The Triune Nature of God

God is one God in three persons: Father, Son, and Holy Spirit. Each member of the Trinity is completely God. As part of the Trinity, Jesus Christ, who is God the Son, is Deity.

The deity of the Trinity has been recognized from the beginning; "from the time that it was, there am I: and now the Lord God, and his Spirit, hath sent me" (Isa. 48:16). When Christians are baptized, they are baptized "in the name of the Father, and of the Son, and of the Holy Ghost" (Matt. 28:19). Everything that is true about God is true of every member of the Trinity of

God. Since God has existed from eternity past (Ps. 90:2), every member of the Trinity has existed equally as long (see Chapter 4: The Trinity). Ibid., Theology for Today, p. 158

The New Testament authors ascribe the work of creation to Christ. Another proof for the deity of Jesus Christ is the description of his works. John sets him forth as Creator: "All things were made by him and without him was not anything made that was made" (John 1:3). Paul noted, "For by him were all things created, that are in heaven, and that are in earth, visible and invisible, whether they be thrones, or dominions, or principalities, or powers: all things were created by him, and for him" (Col. 1:16).

The fact that worship was given to and accepted by Jesus demonstrates his deity. Only God is worthy of and can rightly be worshipped. The fact that Jesus allowed people to worship him shows that he conceived of himself as Deity (Matt. 14:33; 28:9; John 20:28–29). But others also taught that Jesus Christ should be worshipped, implying they ascribed deity to him (Acts 7:59–60; 1 Cor. 1:2; 2 Cor. 13:14; Phil. 2:9–10; Heb. 1:6; Rev. 1:5–6; Rev. 5:12–13).

TABLE 13.2. The names or titles of Christ in John 1

Word	Life	Flesh
God	Light	Only begotten of the Father
Light of humankind	True Light	Jesus Christ
Only begotten Son	Lord	Jesus
Lamb of God	Son of God	Rabbi
Master	Messiah	Christ
Jesus of Nazareth	The son of Joseph	King of Israel
Son of Man	Him	He

Jehovah

Perhaps the most honored of all names of God in scripture is that of Jehovah. Yet as was illustrated earlier in this chapter, Jesus is equated with Jehovah throughout the scriptures. The name is derived from the Hebrew verb *to be* and is the name God used most often when relating to humankind, especially in covenant. Scotchmen suggests, "The identification of our Lord Jesus Christ with the Lord of the Old Testament results in an explicit doctrine of his deity."[159] Particularly in the Gospel of John, Jesus reveals himself as the "I Am" of the Old Testament.

TABLE 13.3. The great I Am's

1	"I am the bread of life."	John 6:35
2	"I am the light of the world."	John 8:12
3	"I am the door."	John 10:9
4	"I am the good shepherd."	John 10:11
5	"I am the resurrection and the life."	John 11:25
6	"I am the way, the truth, and the life."	John 14:6
7	"I am the vine."	John 15:5
1	"I am … I am" (Exod. 3:14).	John 4:26; John 8:58; John 18:5, 6, 8

Son of God

Another name of Jesus Christ in the New Testament is "Son of God," which is used by Christ in referring to his deity. In the Old Testament the reference to the sonship of Christ is, "I will declare the decree: The Lord hath said unto me, Thou art my Son; this day have I begotten thee" (Ps. 2:7). This verse reveals a conversation between God the Father and God the Son. The Father calls the second person of the Trinity by the name "Son" and says, "I have begotten thee." Again the Bible teaches, "A son is given" (Isa. 9:6).

When the expression *Son of God* is used by and of Christ, it is obviously a reference to his divine relationship to God the Father. Christians are the "sons of God" (not capitalized), and they call God their Father. Jesus identifies a special relationship to his Father.

The key to understanding when Jesus became the Son of God is in understanding the meaning of the word *day* in Psalm 2:7. The word *day* does not refer to a twenty-four-hour period in time. God lives beyond time. This word means an eternal day. Technically, the sonship of Jesus Christ is called "eternal generation." Jesus did not become the Son of God at a point of time. He has eternally been in the process of being generated as the Son in God's eternal day. The conclusion is that there never was a time that Christ was not the Son of God.

Son of Man (Jesus's Favorite Term to Describe Himself)[160]

Jesus used the term *Son of Man* when discussing his earthly ministry (Matt. 8:20; Matt. 9:6; Matt. 11:19; Matt. 16:13; Luke 19:10; Luke 22:48), when foretelling his passion (Matt. 12:40; Matt. 17:9, 22; Matt. 20:18), and in teaching regarding his return in power and great glory (Matt. 13:41; Matt. 24:27, 30; Matt. 25:31; Luke 18:8; Luke 21:36). The Jew who heard this title would immediately think, *Messiah*. Montefiore argues, "If Jesus said these words we can hardly think that he distinguished between himself, the Son of Man, and the Messiah. The Son of Man must be the Messiah, and both must be himself."[161]

Karl Kreyssler and Henry Scheffrahn wrote, "Jesus clearly believed Himself to be the fulfillment of the Old Testament prophecies of the Messiah. In referring to Himself, He continually used the title 'The Son of man' from David's vision."[162]

Concerning this name of Christ, Stevenson notes the following:

> This was the designation which our Lord habitually used concerning himself. It is not found in the New Testament on any other lips than his own—except when his questioners quoted his words (John 12:34), and in the one instance of Stephen's ecstatic exclamation in the moment of his martyrdom, "Behold, I see the heavens opened, and the Son of man standing on the right hand of God" (Acts 7:56). It was clearly a Messianic title, as the Jews recognized (John 12:34).[163]

Word

One of the most important titles of Christ is "the Word." Pink suggested that "a word is (1) a medium of manifestation," (2) "a means of communication," (3) "and a method of revelation."[164]

In his commentary on the Fourth Gospel, Tenney suggests the following:

> The term LOGOS, which occurs four times, includes more than its English translation, "word." A word is an idea expressed through a combination of sounds or of letters. Without the idea or concept behind it, the medium would be meaningless. KXBZ might represent a radio station; but as a combination of letters and or sounds, if it could be pronounced, it has no meaning whatsoever because no concept is attached to it. Just so the term LOGOS implies the intelligence behind the idea, the idea itself, and the transmissible expression of it. The term was used technically in the Greek philosophy of this period, particularly by the Stoics, to devote the controlling Reason of the universe, the all-pervasive Mind which ruled and gave meaning to all things. Logos was one of the purest and most general concepts of that ultimate intelligence, Reason, or Will that is called God.

> Scholars debate whether John borrowed the term *word* from the Greeks or the Jews. If the term is Greek, there may be numerous philosophical implications. If the term is Hebrew, he may be making reference to wisdom in Proverbs 5–8. Probably Jesus is called the Word of God because this phrase is used over twelve hundred times in the Old Testament to refer to the revelation or message of God, as in the phrase "the Word of God came to" a certain prophet. Jesus Christ was also the message, meaning, or communication from God to men. Jesus was everything the written and spoken Word of the Lord was in the Old Testament. Jesus is therefore the expression, revelation and

communication of the Lord. He is both the incarnate and inspired Word.[165]

TABLE **13.4.** Ten conclusions about the Word in John 1:1–18

1	The phrase *in the beginning* is not a reference to a point in time but a reference to eternity past.
2	The personality of the Word is evident in that it is capable of individualizing Jesus.
3	The Word has active and personal communication with God.
4	There are two centers of consciousness in that the Word was God yet also was "face-to-face" with God.
5	The Word has the essence of deity.
6	The Father and the Word are one.
7	The Word is the avenue by which God expresses or reveals himself.
8	The incarnate Word is the continuity of the preincarnate Word.
9	As God lived in a tent, spoke in a tent, and revealed himself in the Old Testament tabernacle, so the Word is tabernacled among us.
10	The Incarnation of the Word is the unique revelation of God.

Additional Names of Christ.

There are many additional names of Christ that reveal truth concerning the second person of the Trinity.

The following list was compiled by T. C. Horton and Charles E. Hurlburt.[166]

Names of Christ in Scripture

The seed of the woman
The stone of Israel
Wall of fire
The branch
The messenger of the covenant
The Son of Righteousness

Son of Abraham
A governor
Friend of sinners
A sower
My [God's] beloved Son
The Bridegroom
Good Master
One Son, His [God's] well beloved
The Son of the Highest
The Highest
The Babe
The salvation of God
A sign
Lord of Sabaoth
A certain Samaritan
A light to lighten the Gentiles
A certain nobleman
The Word
The only begotten of the Father
A prophet mighty in deed and word
Rabbi
The gift of God
The true bread from heaven
The Living Bread
The Resurrection
Master
The Life
Our keeper
My Lord and my God
The Holy One and just
A Prince and a Savior
Lord of all
Jesus of Nazareth
His [God's] own Son
The Man whom he [God] hath ordained
The firstborn among many brethren

Minister of the circumcision
Righteousness
The last Adam
My strong Rock
A strong tower
Rain upon mown grass
The headstone of the corner
Ointment poured forth
Excellent
A rose of Sharon
The chiefest among ten thousand
Jehovah of Hosts
A great light
The mighty God
The Light of Israel
The root of Jesse
A nail fastened in a sure place
A shadow from the heat
A crown of glory
A sure foundation
A hiding place from the wind
My Maker
A commander
Our Potter
The Hope of Israel
Resting place
A plant of renown
Stronghold
A ruler
The Prince of Princes
King over all the earth
The King
The light of the city
Purifier
The Son of David
Emmanuel

Rev. Silas Kanyabigega, DMin

A Nazarene
My beloved
Jesus the Christ, Master
Our brother
Jehovah, my God
Refiner
Jesus Christ
Jesus
The young child
The servant of Jehovah
The Christ
The prophet of Nazareth
The carpenter
Thou Son of the Most High God
Christ, the Son of the Blessed
God my Savior
The dayspring from on high
The consolation of Israel
The child Jesus
A great prophet
The master of the house
The chosen of God
The Light of humankind
The Lamb of God
The King of Israel
Messiah
The Bread of God
His [God's] only begotten Son
The Bread of Life
I Am
One shepherd
A grain of wheat
The Truth
The Way
The Vine
The Overcomer

248

The Man
The head of every human being
The Lord from heaven
The wisdom of God
Lord both of the dead and the living
Our Passover
That spiritual rock
A quickening spirit
The head
Head over all things
Shiloh (peacemaker)
A scepter
The son of Mary
A ransom
Son of Man
The King of the Jews
Horn of salvation
Christ, the Lord
The Lord's Christ
The glory of the people of Israel
The Holy One of God
Physician
The Christ of God
A guest
The True Light
The Son of God
The Light of the World
The Good Shepherd
The Christ, the Savior of the World
The door of the sheep
The Christ, the Son of God
The sent of the Father
A man approved of God
The Prince of Life
The Just One
Judge of the quick and the dead

Jesus Christ our Lord
God blessed forever
The Deliverer
The power of God
Sanctification
The foundation
Thine [God's] Holy One
The holy child Jesus
Lord Jesus
Redemption
Lord over all
The Lord of glory
The unspeakable gift
He that filleth all in all
Christ
Our peace
The first fruits of them that sleep
One Lord
A sacrifice to God
The Lord Jesus Christ
The firstborn of every creation
The Beginning
Christ our life
Lord of Peace
The Mediator
Blessed and only potentate
The great God
Brightness of his glory
The upholder of all things
The captain of our salvation
The builder
King of Righteousness
The minister of the sanctuary
Mediator of a better covenant
Mediator of the new covenant
The great shepherd of the sheep

A lamb without blemish or spot
The bishop of souls
The daystar
That eternal life
The propitiation
The true God
Jesus Christ
The Savior of the World
The prince of the kings of the earth
The First and the Last
The hidden manna
The beginning of the creation of God
The Lamb slain
The Lamb in the midst of the throne
A sweet-smelling Savior
His [God's] dear Son
Creator of all things
The firstborn from the dead
All in all
Our hope
The Man Christ Jesus
The judge of the quick and the dead
God our Savior
God
The apostle
The Great High Priest
The forerunner
The surety
Author of eternal salvation
Higher than the heavens
He that shall come
The author of faith
A priest forever
My Helper
That worthy name
A living stone

A stone of stumbling
A rock of offense
A chief cornerstone
Lord and Savior Jesus Christ
The Advocate
Jesus Christ the Righteous
The Son of the Father
The faithful witness
The first begotten of the dead
He that liveth
The lion of the tribe of Judah
King of Saints
Lord God omnipotent
Faithful and true
The bright and morning star
An offering
The image of the invisible God
The head of the body
Hope of glory
The Lord Christ
Christ Jesus
God manifest in the flesh
The righteous judge
Heir of all things
The sin purger
The express image of his person
The seed of Abraham
The High Priest
King of Peace
Our intercessor
Separate from sinners
The testator
A rewarder
The finisher of faith
Jesus Christ the same
The Word of Life

The just
An elect stone
A precious stone
The chief shepherd
The Son
Eternal life
The Almighty
The morning star
The Alpha and Omega
The amen
The faithful and true witness
Lord of Lords
King of Kings
The testifier
The temple
The offspring of David
Word of God

The Christophanies

The preexistence of Christ is further substantiated by the many recorded Christophanies in the Bible. A Christophany is the manifestation of God in visible and bodily form before the Incarnation. Some call them theophanies, but *Christophanies* is a better term to describe an appearance of Christ. Often the Bible identifies these appearances as "the angel of the Lord."

A closer look at the references of these events will demonstrate that this angel was more than just another angel—he was God. At other times, these Christophanies were an appearance of Jesus in physical form, but he was not identified as the angel of the Lord.

The term *Christophany* is used by many contemporary writers to identify certain appearances of Christ. In his work on the subject, James Borland explains, "The term Christophany in this work will denote those unsought, intermittent and temporary, visible and audible manifestations of God the Son in human form, by which God communicated something to certain conscious human beings on earth prior to the birth of Jesus Christ."

The Angel of the Lord

By far the most common appearance of Jesus Christ in the Old Testament is as the angel of the Lord. There can be no question that he is God. When he appeared, it was usually to an individual who was commissioned to do a special work for God. The angel of the Lord took the time personally to enlist that individual in his service.[167]

TABLE 13.5. The angel of the Lord[167]

Reference	Occasion	Called of God
Gen. 16:7–13	To Hagar	Gen. 16:13
Exod. 3:2–4:17	Burning bush	Exod. 3:10
Judg. 6:11–24	To Gideon	Judg. 6:22
Judg. 13:2–23	To Samson's mother	Judg. 13:18, 22

The term *angel of the Lord* is used generally to identify any angel or messenger of God, but it is also used to identify a specific angel of the Lord. On several occasions, the angel of Jehovah is distinguished from Jehovah (Zech. 1:12–13; Gen. 24:7; Exod. 23:20; Exod. 32:34; Isa. 63:9; Judg. 2:1–5).

That he is the second person of the Trinity is based on the four reasons listed in table 13.6.

TABLE 13.6. Why the angel of the Lord is Christ

1	Both the angel of Jehovah and Christ are visible.
2	The angel of Jehovah never appears after the Incarnation.
3	Both the angel of Jehovah and Christ are sent by the Father.
4	Both the angel of Jehovah and Christ execute judgment for God.

A Man (Gen. 18:1–33; Gen. 32:24–32; Dan. 3:23–29)

On at least three occasions, Jesus appeared in a Christophany as a human before the Incarnation. On these occasions, he appeared among human beings as a man. Three men appeared to Abraham and Sarah to confirm

God's provision of a son and to inform Abraham of the coming destruction of Sodom and Gomorrah. One of these men is identified as "the Lord" (Gen. 18:1, 13, 17, 20, 26–27, 30–33) and is also called "the Judge of all the earth" (Gen. 18:15). This person must have been Jesus Christ, because the scripture reads, "No man hath seen God at any time; the only begotten Son, which is in the bosom of the Father, he hath declared him" (John 1:18). Since Christ is the only one of three persons of the Trinity to be seen, we are left to believe that this man on this occasion, and the angel of the Lord who is called God, was in fact the second person of the Trinity, Jesus Christ. Jesus is the only member of the Trinity to have taken on a physical body at any time (besides the Holy Spirit's brief coming in the form of a dove).

At a later time, Christ appeared to Jacob and wrestled with him during the night. Jacob recognized the next morning that he had met with God. "And Jacob named the place Peniel; for I have seen God face to face, and my life is preserved" (Gen. 32:30). On a third occasion, Jesus joined the three young Hebrews in Nebuchadnezzar's furnace. Though Nebuchadnezzar was assured that he had thrown only three men into the furnace, "He ... said, Lo I see four men loose, walking in the midst of the fire, and they have no hurt; and the form of the fourth is like the Son of God" (Dan. 3:25).[167]

Messianic Prophecies

Before the Incarnation of Christ, a great deal concerning Jesus's life and ministry had been recorded prophetically. These prophecies were all fulfilled literally in Christ's first advent, which assures us those prophecies relating to his Second Advent will also be literally fulfilled. Some of these are recorded in obscure or figurative language (cf. Gen. 49:10; Isa. 11:1). Even though predicative in nature, these prophecies were normally written in the past tense. Because prophecies are horizontal and not vertical in nature, often they may include aspects of Christ's first advent and Second Advent (cf. Isa. 61:1–2).

When interpreting messianic prophecies, two principles should be remembered. The first is that of time element. One prediction may be fulfilled at two intervals. When Christ read from Isaiah 61:1–2, he stopped in the middle of verse 2, because the next part referred to his Second Advent.

The second principle is that of double fulfillment, that a prophecy may be fulfilled more than once in some cases (cf. Joel 2:28–32; Acts 2:16). Though not comprehensive, table 1 3.7summarizes some of the major prophecies concerning Christ.[168]

TABLE 13.7.

Prophecy	Testament	New Testament
Born of the seed of woman	Genesis 3:15	Galatians 4:4
Born of a virgin	Isaiah 7:14	Matthew 1:23
Son of God	Psalm 2:7	Matthew 3:17
Seed of Abraham	Genesis 32:18	Galatians 3:16
Son of Isaac	Genesis 21:12	Luke 3:23, 34
Son of Jacob	Numbers 24:17	Luke 3:23, 34
Tribe of Judah	Genesis 49:10	Hebrews 7:14
Family line of Jesse	Isaiah 11:1	Matthew 1:6
Through David 2	Samuel 7:12	Matthew 1:1
Born at Bethlehem	Micah 5:2	Matthew 2:1
Time of his birth	Daniel 9:25	Galatians 4:4
Presented with gifts	Psalm 72:10	Matthew 2:11
Herod kills the firstborn male children	Jeremiah 31:15	Matthew 2:16
His preexistence	Micah 5:2	Colossians 1:17
Descent to Egypt	Hosea 11:1	Matthew 2:14–15
He shall be called Lord	Psalm 110:1	Luke 2:11
Shall be Immanuel	Isaiah 7:14	Matthew 1:23
Shall be a Prophet	Deut. 18:18	Matthew 21:11
Priest	1 Sam. 2:35	Hebrews 3:1
King	Numbers 24:17	Matthew 27:37
Judge	Isaiah 33:22	John 5:30
Special anointing of Holy Spirit	Isaiah 61:1–2	Luke 4:15–21
Preceded by a messenger	Isaiah 40:3,5	John 1:23
Called a Nazarene	Isaiah 11:1	Matthew 2:23
Zealous for God	Psalm 69:9	John 2:15–17
Ministry to begin in Galilee	Isaiah 9:1	Matthew 4:12, 13, 17
Ministry of miracles	Isaiah 35:5–6	Matthew 9:35
Teacher of parables	Psalm 78:2	Matthew 13:34
He was to enter the temple	Malachi 3:1	Matthew 21:12
He was to enter Jerusalem on a donkey	Zechariah 9:9	Matthew 21:6–11

Prophecy	Testament	New Testament
Stone of stumbling to the Jews	Psalm 118:22	1 Peter 2:7
Light to the Gentiles	Isaiah 60:3	Acts 13:47–48
Resurrection	Psalm 61:10	Acts 2:31
Ascension	Psalm 68:18	Acts 1:9
Seated at right hand of God	Psalm 110:1	Hebrews 1:3
Betrayed by a friend	Psalm 41:9	Matthew 10:4
Sold for thirty pieces of silver	Zechariah 11:12	Matthew 26:15
Money thrown in God's house	Zechariah 11:13	Matthew 27:5
Price given for potter's field	Zechariah 11:13	Matthew 27:7
Forsaken by disciples	Zechariah 13:7	Mark 14:50
Accused by false witnesses	Psalm 35:11	Matthew 20:59–61
Wounded and bruised	Isaiah 53:5	Matthew 27:26
Dumb before his accusers	Isaiah 53:7	Matthew 27:12–19
Smitten	Isaiah 50:6	Matthew 26:67
Mocked	Psalm 27:7–8	Matthew 27:31
Fell under the cross	Psalm 109:24–25	Matthew 27:31, 32
Hands and feet pierced	Psalm 22:16	Luke 23:33
Crucified with thieves	Isaiah 53:12	Matthew 27:38
Prayed for his persecutors	Isaiah 53:12	Luke 23:34
Rejected by his own people	Isaiah 53:3	John 7:5, 48
Hated without cause	Psalm 69:4	John 15:25
Friends stood far off	Psalm 38:11	Luke 23:49
People shook their heads	Psalm 109:25	Matthew 27:39
Stared upon	Psalm 22:17	Luke 23:35
Garments parted and lots cast	Psalm 22:18	John 19:23, 24
Suffered thirst	Psalm 69:21	John 19:28
Gall and vinegar offered him	Psalm 69:21	John 19:28–29
Forsaken by God	Psalm 21:1	Matthew 27:46
Committed himself to God	Psalm 31:5	Luke 23:46
Bones not broken	Psalm 34:20	John 19:33
Heartbroken	Psalm 22:14	John 19:34
Side pierced	Zechariah 12:10	John 19:34
Darkness over land	Amos 8:9	Matthew 27:45
Buried in rich man's tomb	Isaiah 53:9	Matthew 27:57–60
Voluntary death	Psalm 40:6–8	
Vicarious suffering	Isaiah 53:4–6	

Prophecy	Testament	New Testament
Ridiculed	Psalm 22:6, 7	
Spat upon	Isaiah 50:6	Matthew 27:67

The Types of Jesus Christ

The religion of the Jews was in part to point them to Christ, who is the fulfillment of the law. It is only natural, then, to expect the various feasts of the Jewish calendar to be typical of Christ.

TABLE **13.8.**

The feast (Lev. 23)	The fulfillment in Christ
Passover (April)	Death of Christ (1 Cor. 5:7)
Unleavened bread (April)	Holy walk for Christ (1 Cor. 5:8)
First fruits (April)	Resurrection of Christ (1 Cor. 15:23)
Pentecost (June)	Outpouring of the Spirit of Christ (Acts 1:5, Acts 2:4)
Trumpets (September)	Israel's regathering by Christ (Matt. 24:31)
Atonement (September)	Cleansing by Christ (Rom. 11:26)
Tabernacles (September)	Rest and reunion with Christ (Zech. 14:16–18)

Table 13.8 illustrates how Jesus fulfilled the major feasts in the Jewish years as recorded in Leviticus 23.[168]

The study of types should be governed by several guiding principles. First, it should be recognized that every type had a historical reality. To argue that an event has a typical significance is not to deny its historicity or to remove any meaning from that context. The primary purpose of a type is not to be a type, but to accomplish the historic purpose. In accomplishing that aim, the type forms an analogy.

Not only does a type speak of a historic reality, but also it identifies a spiritual reality. It is a likeness that was ordained by God. That which exists in the Old Testament is similar to some other truth in the New Testament. Although it appears that most types are in the Pentateuch, they are scattered throughout the scriptures.[169]

The Kingship of Christ

God appeared reluctant to give Israel a king like the Gentile nations had because he was their king. But when God finally allowed Israel to have a king, the earthly sovereign was made responsible to represent him. The king was the leader of the nation and filled the third "anointed" office. In this matter, Christ so fills the anointed office of King.

Jesus Is King

The kingship of Christ is seen in his deity. Because he is God, he is also King. Paul gave praise "Unto the King eternal, immortal, invisible, the only wise God, be honor and glory forever and ever" (1 Tim. 1:17). In heaven, "they sing the song of Moses the servant of God, and the song of the Lamb, saying, Great and marvelous are thy works, Lord God Almighty; just and true are thy ways, thou King of saints" (Rev. 15:3). The Romans considered their Caesar to be a god. Christians, on the other hand, recognized Jesus alone to be their King. The idea of calling Jesus "King" implied a claim to his deity.

Jesus Has a Kingdom

Every king has a domain over which he rules. Jesus is no exception. Jesus said, "My kingdom is not of this world" (John 18:36), but he never denied he had a kingdom. It was the custom of the Romans to identify the crime of a condemned man on the cross upon which he died. Jesus was executed as "the King of the Jews" (John 19:19). When Christ returns to this earth, he will do so to establish his kingdom. Revelation 20 describes his future kingdom as a thousand-year reign of peace on the earth. Theologians call this the millennial kingdom, and it is discussed more fully later in *True Faith*.

Jesus Has Subjects

Christ is now a ruler to those who submit their lives to him. Someday, the following will happen: "At the name of Jesus every knee shall bow, of things in heaven, and things in earth, and things under the earth; and ... every tongue should confess that Jesus Christ is Lord" (Phil. 2:10–11). Today, those who receive Christ as Lord and Savior recognize the kingship of Christ in their life. Jesus told a parable equating the Christian with a servant. He concluded, "So likewise ye, when ye shall have done all those things which are commanded you, say, we are unprofitable servant: we have done that which was our duty to do" (Luke 17:10). One of the unique differences between the Christians of the New Testament and those of today is their attitude toward their relationship with Christ. Christians of the New Testament saw him as a supreme ruler and themselves as slaves in comparison. Perhaps if we had a similar biblical conviction today, we would see similar biblical results.

The Virgin Birth of Christ

At the beginning of this century, liberal theologians were greatly influenced by the humanistic attitude toward Christianity that manifested itself in an anti-supernatural approach to doctrine. Fundamental doctrines were denied, such as the verbal inspiration of scriptures, the substitutionary atonement, the physical resurrection, and the bodily return of Jesus Christ at the end of this age. Of the fundamentals, the Virgin Birth was usually the first to be denied. Liberal theologians tried to maintain that belief in the Virgin Birth was not necessary; hence, it could be denied.

The virgin birth of Christ is not an independent doctrine that we can receive or reject without affecting our Christianity. It is one of the foundation stones of Christianity. Our faith will crumble if this doctrine is removed, as it is tied to inerrancy, Christ's sinless character, the atonement, and other key doctrines of the Bible. If Jesus was not born of a virgin, then he would be unable to save himself, because he would not be a sinless Savior. If we cannot accept the virgin birth of Christ, very little credibility remains in the Bible. Therefore, we must understand the Virgin Birth if we are going to understand our faith.

The Virgin Birth in Prophecy

As many as seven biblical authors believed and wrote of the virgin birth of Christ. Together, these people wrote twenty-nine or thirty books of the Bible. If we chose to deny this doctrine, we would raise the issue of the credibility of some of the most prominent and prolific Bible writers. This is true of both the Old Testament and the New Testament. Three of these seven authors spoke prophetically of the Virgin Birth. The others wrote after the fact.

Moses

When Moses quoted the words of God in Genesis 3:15, he became the first biblical writer to imply the Virgin Birth. After Adam and Eve sinned in the Garden of Eden, God had to immediately judge their sin. Even in judgment, however, God demonstrated himself as a merciful God. He told the Serpent, "I will put enmity between thee and the woman, and between thy seed and her seed, it shall bruise thy head, and thou shalt bruise his heel" (Gen. 3:15).

When God introduces a theological subject in scripture, usually he speaks embryonically (called the law of first reference). This means that the doctrine is there in "seed" form. When God introduced the prospect of salvation to Adam and Eve and the whole human race, the implication of the Virgin Birth was present. This first mention of salvation in scripture alludes to the Virgin Birth when it speaks or "her seed."

Isaiah

Probably the best-known Old Testament verse teaching of the Virgin Birth is found in Isaiah. God had instructed Isaiah to allow King Ahaz to ask God to perform a miracle. Ahaz, apparently apathetic to God and the divine message, refused to ask God for a sign. The Lord chose to give a sign to the king, who rejected it: "Therefore the Lord himself shall give you a sign; Behold, a virgin shall conceive, and bear a son, and shall call his name Immanuel" (Isa. 7:14).

Jeremiah

The third Old Testament writer to speak prophetically of the Virgin Birth was also a major prophet. "How long wilt thou go about, O thou backsliding daughter? For the Lord hath created a new thing in the earth, A women shall compass a man" (Jer. 31:22). Most of the early fundamentalist writers pointed to this verse to show that even the Weeping Prophet believed in and taught the Virgin Birth. Though women have given birth to men since the birth of Eve's first son, the emphasis here is on God's performing a new thing. This requires a unique event, different from just the birth of another baby boy. Jeremiah's use of the word *create* in this verse implies the Lord will use his divine power to accomplish the task. Older commentaries agree that the word *man* could be a reference to the God-man (Isa. 9:6).

The Virgin Birth in History

As three Old Testament writers wrote prophetically of the Virgin Birth, four New Testament writers wrote historically of the Virgin Birth.

Matthew

Just as the Virgin Birth was implied at the beginning of the Old Testament, so it is fully revealed at the beginning of the New Testament. Matthew clearly believed Mary was a virgin until the birth of Christ. He cites Isaiah 7:14, identifying the birth of Christ as the fulfillment of Isaiah's prophecy (Matt. 1:22–23). On two occasions, Matthew identifies the Holy Spirit as the source of Mary's son (Matt. 1:18, 20). In listing the genealogical data concerning Christ, Joseph is listed as the husband of Mary but not as the father of Jesus. Even though this is an argument from silence, its omission is not accidental. Matthew records that Joseph married Mary knowing her condition. Then he clearly states, "And knew her not till she had brought forth her firstborn son; and called his name Jesus" (Matt. 1:25). Even in announcing the birth of Jesus, it was the birth of "her son" (vs. 25), not "his son" or even "their son."

In Matthew's account of the birth of Christ, there are at least seven direct or indirect statements suggesting Jesus was born of a virgin. Since Matthew was one of the original twelve apostles, it is reasonable to assume that the doctrine of the virgin birth of Christ was one of the original parts of the apostles' doctrine taught to the members of the Jerusalem church (Acts 2:42).

Luke

Matthew's Gospel was written by a Jew and primarily to a Jewish audience. The only other Gospel writer to emphasize the virgin birth of Christ was a Gentile writing primarily to a Gentile audience. It is particularly significant that Luke, a medical doctor, should be among the men whom the Holy Spirit chose to comment on the doctrine of the Virgin Birth. Luke twice calls Mary a virgin. He tells of an angel sent by God "to a virgin espoused to a man whose name was Joseph, of the house of David; and the virgin's name was Mary" (Luke 1:27). When she learned she was to become a mother, "Then said Mary unto the angel, how shall this be, seeing I know not a man" (Luke 1:34)? Later, Luke listed the family tree of Mary, not Joseph. Here he identified Jesus as "being (as was supposed) the son of Joseph" (Luke 3:23).

Luke also teaches the Virgin Birth by his careful phrases. He calls Jesus "the Son of the Highest" (Luke 1:32) and "the Son of God" (Luke 1:35), but he never clearly identifies Jesus as the son of Joseph. Luke was both a medical doctor and historian concerned with accuracy "to write unto thee in order ... that thou mightest know the certainty of those things, wherein thou hast been instructed" (Luke 1:3–4). The Virgin Birth was not simply a rumor; rather, it was an event that was investigated by a historian who was also a physician. Because a woman trusted her doctor, Mary probably told Dr. Luke more of the details of the Virgin Birth than she would tell others. Luke then wrote under the inspiration of the Holy Spirit the events of which he was sure.

John

John records the events of Jesus's arguing his divine origin with the Jewish leaders. Jesus told them he came from the heavenly Father (John 8:38). The Jews answered Jesus by saying that their father was Abraham (v. 39). Then in retaliation, the Jews cast a "veiled accusation" at Jesus. They said, "We be not born of fornication" (John 8:41). In this they imply that Jesus was born out of wedlock. From this, we gather that news of Mary's pregnancy before the wedding to Joseph was public knowledge. This gives added historical credibility to the Virgin Birth.

Paul

The fourth New Testament writer to teach the Virgin Birth is the apostle Paul. Writing to the churches in the province of Galatia, he said, "But when the fullness of the time was come, God sent forth His Son, made of a woman, made under the law" (Gal. 4:4). The readers of Galatians were concerned with Old Testament law, so they would have been careful to list the genealogies from father to son. But Paul recognized the uniqueness of this birth. Jesus was "made of a woman." This means more than a simple acknowledgement that Jesus had a mother. It suggests that Jesus had only a mother.

TABLE **13.9.** Four statements of Christ's sinlessness

Scripture	Truth
2 Cor. 5:2	Christ knew no sin.
Heb. 4:15	Christ was without sin.
1 Pet. 2:22	Christ did not sin.
1 John 3:5	In Christ is no sin.

This is a reasonable assumption when we realize that both Paul and Luke were closely related in the ministry, and both accepted the Virgin Birth.

The Virgin Birth in Theology

At stake in the controversy surrounding the doctrine of the virgin birth of Christ are a number of other doctrines. If Jesus had a human father, he would have inherited a sinful nature. In that case, he would be unable to save himself, let alone be the sinless substitute for the sins of the world. With human parents, it would have been impossible for him to be the Son of God.

Sinless Character of Christ

If Jesus had a human father, he would have inherited the sinful nature of Adam, the head of the human race. "Wherefore as by one man sin entered into the world, and death by sin, so death passed upon all men, for all have sinned" (Rom. 5:12). It would only have taken one sin to make Jesus a sinner. The only way Jesus could be a man without a sinful nature was to have parents without a sinful nature. Jesus is the only begotten Son of the heavenly Father and was born of a virgin, being conceived by the Holy Spirit. Hence he became flesh.

Word of Salvation

When Paul implied the virgin birth of Christ, he also identified a purpose in Christ's coming, "to redeem them that were under the law, that we might receive the adoption of sons" (Gal. 4:5). God required a lamb "without blemish or spot" as a sacrifice for sin (Exod. 12:5). Jesus was unblemished in that he did not have a sinful nature, and unspotted in that he lived a sinless life. Because of this, Paul can say, "For he [God] hath made him [Christ] to be sin for us, who knew no sin" (2 Cor. 5:21).

Son of God

A man can only be the son of his father. This universal principle also applies to the Son of God. Jesus is called "the Son of the Highest" (Luke 1:32) and the "Son of God" (Luke 1:35). This could only be true if Mary was a virgin when she conceived and gave birth to her son.

Inerrancy

A key battle among theologians today is over the question of inerrancy. If the doctrine of the Virgin Birth is false, then we can have no confidence in the accuracy of anything else in scripture. Table 13.10 illustrates what books of the Bible we would be forced question if we denied the Virgin Birth.

TABLE 13.10. The Virgin Birth and inerrancy

	Virgin Birth taught	Author	Writings
1	Gen 3:15	Moses	Genesis, Exodus, Leviticus, Numbers, Deuteronomy
2	Isa. 7:14	Isaiah	Isaiah
3	Jer. 31:22	Jeremiah	Jeremiah, Lamentations
4	Matt. 1	Matthew	Matthew
5	Luke 1:3	Luke	Luke, Acts (Hebrews?)
6	John 1:13	John	1 John, 2 John, 3 John, Revelation
7	Gal. 4:4	Paul	Romans, 1 Corinthians, 2 Corinthians, Galatians, Ephesians, Philippians, Colossians, 1 Thessalonians, 2 Thessalonians, 1 Timothy, 2 Timothy, Titus, Philemon, (Hebrews?)

If the Virgin Birth is an unreliable fact, then twenty-four or twenty-five of the sixty-six books of the Bible are also unreliable.

Supernatural Power of God

When Mary was confronted with the announcement that she would give birth to the Son of God, she asked, "How shall this be, seeing I know not a man" (Luke 1:34)? She learned the answer to her question when the angel observed, "For with God nothing shall be impossible" (Luke 1:37). If the truth were known, the real reason some theologians deny the virgin birth of Christ is their unwillingness to recognize a supernatural God.[170]

The Hypostatic Union

Understanding the Perfection of Christ

A most difficult doctrine to understand concerning Christ is the relationship between his divine and human nature. The Bible affirms that Jesus is both God and man. But does this mean he is half God and half man, or does it maintain he is God sometimes and man at other times? The answer seems to imply a contradiction, as Christ is completely God at all times and completely man at the same time. Is it possible for two different capacities and natures to occupy the same space and identical existence at the same time? Would such a union make Christ less than God or more than a man? Would such a union of the divine and human result in a hybrid being whose nature was a mixture of Deity and humanity? Christianity has generally affirmed that Jesus is the God-man.

The term is hyphenated to reflect that Jesus is totally God and totally human at the same time. Both sides of the second person of the Trinity are seen in the titles that describe him. In the Gospel of John, Jesus is often called the Son of God, which implies his deity, while in Luke he is often called the Son of Man, which implies his humanity.

He is at all times 100 percent God in his nature, words, and actions. Yet at the same time he is not diminished in his humanity. He is 100 percent man. He left footprints in the sand as he walked on the shore of the Sea of Galilee. He needed rest when he was tired and nourishment when he hungered; but the winds and waves obeyed him because he was God. He was at all times and in every way the God-man, totally God and totally man. This union of divine and human is one of the most difficult doctrines to understand, yet it is foundational to understanding the person of Christ. And if Christ is not properly perceived, then Christianity is not properly understood.

The difficulties become less severe when the central issues are clarified. The doctrine involves questions concerning the union of two natures and not the union of two persons.

Before analyzing the hypostatic union, it is necessary to define the term. First, a clear distinction must be made between the person of Christ and the natures of Christ. The confusion or misunderstanding of these two terms easily results in heresy.

Nature is defined in the *Merriam-Webster Dictionary* as "the inherent character or basic constitution of a person or thing."

The Incarnation

The most familial thing that people usually remember about Jesus is his birth, celebrated at Christmas. Many who have a basic acquaintance with the events surrounding that birth fail to understand that it represents the merging of God and man into one human body. John summarizes this miracle in one statement. "And the Word was made flesh, and dwelt among us" (John 1:14). When we use the term *Incarnation*, we are speaking of the miracle of God becoming human yet remaining God.

The Eternal Word

The title *Word*, used only by the apostle John, implies the deity of Jesus Christ. The usual meaning of the term *word* is "a medium of communication." When John called Jesus the Word, he was implying that God communicated himself to humankind through Jesus Christ. Marvin R. Vincent observes as follows:

> The Logos of John is the real, personal God (i 1), the Word, who *was* originally before the creation with God, and *was* God, one in essence and nature, yet personally distinct (i. 1, 18); the revealer and interpreter of the hidden being of God; the reflection and visible image of God, and the organ of all His manifestations to the world.[171]

The Word was the embodiment of a person—showing to people what God was and what God revealed to them.

Jesus is the perfect, ultimate revelation of God. The first eighteen verses of the Gospel of John provide our fullest description of the Word. "In the beginning was the Word" (John 1:1) refers to the eternal origin of Christ. He did not begin at a specific point in time. Secondly, we are told through the use of *became* that at a point in time he became incarnate or assumed humanity. "The Word became flesh and dwelt among us" (John 1:14). Thirdly, the Word was engaged in active personal communion with God. This is seen where "The Word was with God" (John 1:1). The term *with* means Jesus was face-to-face with God. The fact that the Word and God are identified separately suggests the plurality of the Godhead, with both considered to be the Deity. Also, the deity of Christ is clearly asserted in the statement "the Word was God" (John 1:1). Yet this verse cannot be translated "God was the Word," or "the Word was a God," as some religious cults suggest. To do so would ignore the rules of Greek grammar.[172]

Groups like the Jehovah's Witnesses are unable to find a single reputable Greek scholar to acknowledge the possibility of translating the verse "the Word was a God" or "God was the Word," because that would be a violation of grammatical rules and would also deny the distinction between the person of God the Father and the person of Christ.

"Sometimes with a noun which the context proves to be definite the article is not used. This places stress upon the qualitative aspect of the noun rather than its mere identity." In other words, John 1:1 declares that the Word is of the same nature as God, that he is Deity; also see A. T. Robertson and W. Davis, *A New Short Grammar of the Greek Testament* (New York: Harper and Brothers, 1933), 279.

"As a rule when the article is used with the one and not with the other means that the particular noun is the subject ... in John 1:1 the meaning has to be 'the Logos was God,' not 'God was the Logos.'"

Even though Christ and the Father are separate, note the fourth observation: this passage concerns the unity of the Father and Son. They are one together—two consciousnesses, yet one essence. "There is nothing which is said to be true of God which is not said to be true of Christ and to the same degree of infinite perfection."[173]

John also points out that the Word was the avenue by which God expressed or revealed himself. "No man hath seen God at any time; the only begotten Son, who is in the bosom of the Father, he had declared him" (John 1:18). The incarnate Word, which is the continuation of the preincarnate Word, is the avenue whereby God showed people what he was like.

A final and crucial observation concerning the Word may be made in this passage: "The Word was made flesh and dwelt among us" (John 1:14). The word *dwell* means "to reside in the tabernacle." In the Old Testament, God's glory dwelt in the tabernacle. As the Israelites set up their tents in the wilderness around the tabernacle, the Shekinah (glory of God) descended on the holy of holies. This meant God's presence dwelt with Israel.

In the New Testament, God comes to live with humankind in the human form. God does not choose a tent to live with humankind in the human form, but he dwells in a human body, a human tent. Just as God dwelt with Israel by his glory cloud in the Old Testament, so God dwells in a human tabernacle with his people in the New Testament. The body of Jesus Christ is likened to a tent that is called glorious. The idea of God dwelling among his people is prominent throughout scripture. "What had been hinted at and even realized in a dim, imperfect fashion earlier was perfectly fulfilled in the Word made flesh."[174]

The Union of Christ's Two Natures

When we think of the dual nature of Christ, we must somehow not divide him into two parts as if he had a schizophrenic personality or was two persons in one body. Rather we must think of him in unity; he is the God-man. This union has been described in a number of ways.

The Union of Two Natures in One Person

This union of the two natures of Christ into one person means that the two merged into the person of Christ. Common humankind is material and nonmaterial, body and soul. A person's personality exists in his or her immaterial nature, or intrinsic being. Jesus possessed both a divine nature and a human nature, but the result was one person. He had one intellect, one set of emotions, and one volitional ability to make decisions. He did not vacillate between his previous experience as God and his human experience learned on earth. Christ had one coherent personality. He was one person.

The Union of Two Natures Was Complete

Jesus did not act as God on some occasions and as a man at other times. We do not say that he performed miracles as God and suffered on the cross as a man. What Jesus did, he did as a unity. He was at all times and in all ways the God-man.

The Union of Two Natures Was Constant

Some have tried to understand the God-man by recognizing his work as God at times and his work as a man at other times. The hypostatic union guarantees the constant presence of both the divine and human natures of Christ at all times.

The Union of His Two Natures Is Eternal

When Christ took on human flesh in the Incarnation, he did not give it up when he ascended back into heaven. Today we worship a person who is both God and man. The physical body that was born in Bethlehem is now seated at the right hand of God. The Hebrews were told of Jesus, "But this man, because he continueth ever, hath an unchangeable priesthood" (Heb. 7:24). Jesus is the Man seated in glory. Paul reminded Timothy, "There is one God, and one mediator between God and man, the man, Christ Jesus" (1 Tim. 2:5). He reminded the Romans that their salvation was dependent upon the work of a man who had overcome the failing of the first man (Rom. 5:12–21). Augustus H. Strong agrees: "The union of humanity with deity in the person of Christ is indissoluble and eternal."[175]

Factors Related to the Hypostatic Union

In the following sections, three outlines are used. These come from Dr. John F. Walvoord's book *Jesus Christ Our Lord*. These outlines are being used because they provide the most complete and comprehensive overview of several factors related to the hypostatic union. These outlines also present concisely many of the most profound truths regarding this vital doctrine.

TABLE 13.11. The relation of the two natures of Christ[175]

1	The two natures are inseparably united in such a way that there is no mixture or loss of their separate identity.
2	The two natures of Christ cannot lose or transfer a single attribute.
3	The two natures of Christ are not only united without affecting the respective attributes of the two natures but are also combined in one person.
4	The attributes of both natures are properly attributed to his person.

Expounding on Table 13.11

The first point is that two natures were inseparably united in such a way that there was no mixture or loss of their separate identity.[176] In the union of Christ's two natures, both natures remained distinct. The human and divine natures did not mingle or merge together into a third nature with a different expression. The idea that Christ's two natures merged into a third nature would implies the loss of each's separate identity. This is called the Monophysite heresy of the Eutychians. Eutychus was condemned in AD 451 by the Council of Chalcedon.

The second point is that the two natures of Christ cannot lose or transfer a single attribute.[177] The deity of Christ demands that his divine nature remain unchanged. The loss of any attribute would change his nature. Since attributes are the manifestation of the nature, it would be impossible for any nature to manifest attributes it does not possess. In the person of Christ, the attributes of both his natures may be found, but never does the human nature reflect divine attributes, nor does the divine nature reflect human attributes. Each attribute finds its source in its respective nature within Christ's person. "It is emphatically said that the one nature does not change into the other. Each nature retains its properties and the properties of the one can never become the properties of the other."[178]

The third point is that the two natures of Christ are not only united without affecting the respective attributes of the two natures but also are combined in one person.[179] Jesus Christ was not two persons in one body; rather, he was one person with two natures. His personality was never divided. He was not God and a man living together in one body. He was the unique person, the God-man.

The fourth point is that the attributes of both natures are properly attributed to Christ's person.[180] Although the attributes of both the divine and human natures remain intrinsic to their respective natures, they are all intrinsic to the person of Christ. Since the person of Christ includes two distinct natures, whatever attributes are characteristic of either nature will be characteristic of Christ's person. It must be reemphasized at this point that sin is not an essential element of human nature. It became a parasite attached to human nature at the time of Adam's fall.

TABLE 13.12. A sevenfold classification of the person of Christ[181]

| 1 | Some attributes are true of his whole person. |
| 2 | Some attributes are true only of deity, but the whole person is the subject. |

3	Some attributes are true only of humanity, but the whole person is the subject.
4	The person may be described according to divine nature, but description is predicated on the human nature.
5	The person may be described according to human nature, but the description is predicated on the divine nature.
6	The person may be described according to the divine nature, but the description is predicated on both natures.
7	The person may be described according to human nature, but the description is predicated on both natures.

Expounding on Table 13.12

Regarding the first point, that some attributes are true of his whole person, there is only one person. As such, Christ possessed characteristics that would be true of his whole person. Christ must be God and he must be man. This is essential. In order for Christ to be the Mediator (1 Tim. 2:5) between God and humankind, he has to possess human and divine attributes. But the point must be reemphasized: these attributes belong to the incarnate Christ.

In light of the second point, that some attributes are true only of deity but the whole person is the subject, Christ possesses characteristics true only of his deity, but his whole person is subject to the Deity. When Christ spoke in John 8:58, "Before Abraham was, I am," he spoke as a united person, but what he said was true only of his divine nature. The same type of statement is found in John 17:5, where Christ declares his existence with the Father before the Incarnation. The whole person of Christ is speaking, but only his divine nature is preexistent.

Regarding the third point, that some attributes are true only of Christ's humanity but his whole person is the subject, Christ has characteristics of humanity, but his whole person is subject to humanity. In John 4:6, Jesus is said to have been "wearied" (tired). Matthew 4:2 speaks of Jesus as being hungry. These verses show that the person of Christ experienced conditions characteristic only of humanity (i.e., not of God). God does not become fatigued or hungry, but human beings need food and rest. In these particular circumstances, the God-man was subjected to his human nature.

Regarding the fourth point, that Christ's person may be described according to divine nature but the description is predicated by the human nature—for the purpose of this discussion, *predicate* should be understood as "to take from or add to." In Matthew 9:1–8, Christ is questioned because he exhibited his divine prerogative by telling a palsy-stricken man, "Thy sins be forgiven thee." The verbal attack from the scribes came because they failed to recognize the deity of Christ as presupposed in his declaration that he could forgive sins. Then Christ healed the palsy victim to reveal his divine nature, which the scribes had not recognized. Even after the miracle, the multitude did not view Christ according to his divine nature, but according to his human nature. Verse 8 says they "glorified God, which had given such power unto men."

In light of the fifth point, that the person may be described according to human nature but the description is predicated on the divine nature, we note that in John 8:40, Jesus calls himself a man whom the unbelieving Jews sought to kill. The context of this declaration of his humanity also includes a declaration of his deity (in verse 58). In verse 42, Christ states that his rejection by these Jews is due to the fact that he proceeded from God the Father, whereas these men were not children of God. These verses describe Christ as a man but also show he is God.

The sixth point tells us that the person of Christ may be described according to the divine nature, but the description is predicated on both natures. John 18:4 says that when Judas and the soldiers went to the garden at Gethsemane to take Jesus captive, "Jesus therefore, knowing all things that should come upon him, went forth, and said unto them, 'Whom seek ye?'" Christ is shown to possess divine knowledge of the forthcoming events, yet the subsequent verses tell of his voluntary submission to his captors.

In verse 11, he rebukes Peter's attempt to free him and rhetorically asks, "The cup which my Father hath given me, shall I not drink it?" These verses describe Christ's divine nature, yet they also show him voluntarily submitting to the torture and death that his human body must undergo to provide redemption for humankind.

The seventh point is that the person may be described according to human nature, but the description is predicated on both natures. John 19:30 relates the closing scenes of Christ's crucifixion, "When Jesus therefore had received the vinegar, he said, it is finished: and he bowed his head, and gave up the ghost."

Again the human nature of Christ is portrayed as experiencing thirst, but more importantly, the person of Christ is viewed as having died. The euphemistic phrase *gave up the ghost* tells us of Christ's death. Death is an experience that is almost always associated with only the human nature of Christ.

However, when Christ died on the cross, his divine nature, as well as his human nature, died. Death is not cessation of life but is equivalent to separation. The Father was separated from the sin that was on his Son. Although God, being omnipresent, could not be separated, in a sense their fellowship was broken. There was not a real breach in the Trinity, as God is immutable. If you sin and your fellowship with God is broken, you, in a sense, are forsaken by God—that is, his fellowship is taken from you. This does not mean that God is not there. God of necessity is everywhere. God is in hell, even, because he is omnipresent. Christ's divine nature, in a sense, died in that he was separated from God.

There is a serious problem here that has never been resolved. How could there be a breach in the Trinity? Luther asked, "How could God, be forsaken being God?" The most important results of the hypostatic union have been summarized well by Walvoord and appear in the following chart.

TABLE 13.13. Important results of the union of the two natures in Christ[182]

1	The union of the two natures in Christ is related vitally to his acts as an incarnate person.
2	The eternal priesthood of Christ is also based on the hypostatic union.
3	The prophetic office of Christ is related to the act of incarnation.
4	The kingly office of Christ is dependent upon both the divine and human natures, which would have been impossible apart from the Incarnation.
5	The incarnate person of Christ is worshipped as the sovereign God.
6	In the ascension of the incarnate Christ to heaven, not only was the divine nature restored to its previous place of infinite glory, but also the human nature was exalted.
7	The union of the two natures in Christ, while not affecting any essential attribute of either nature, did necessarily require certain unique features to be manifested, such as the absence of the sin nature, freedom from any act of sin, and lack of a human father.

Rev. Silas Kanyabigega, DMin

Is Jesus the Only Way to God?

Introduction

The best place to begin is with scripture. We need to understand biblically why Christians consider Christ to be the only way to salvation. One of the most important reasons for such exclusivity has to do with what the Bible says is the problem that lies at the core of the human condition and the unique solution that such a problem requires.

Humanity's Problem and the Bible's Solution

What does the Bible say is wrong with humanity? The Bible teaches that although we are created in God's image and are of unique and special value to him, we are nevertheless deeply and permanently stained by sin. Sin is, at its root, an attitude of rebellion against, and independence from, God. The Bible says, moreover, that all have sinned (Rom. 3:23).

The most severe consequence of our sin is that it separates us from God. The prophet Isaiah wrote, "But your iniquities have separated you from your God; your sins have hidden his face from you" (Isa. 59:2; see also Hab. 1:13).

Another consequence of our sin is that it causes our spiritual death. Just as physical death occurs when the spirit is separated from the body, so spiritual death results when we separate ourselves from God. Paul wrote, "You were dead in your transgressions and sins" (Eph. 2:1). No other religion portrays humanity as being as bad off spiritually as does Christianity, for a person cannot be any worse off than being dead.

The Bible uses several terms to describe what the solution to humanity's problem is, and each term implies that there is only one way to resolve that problem.

Forgiveness

The Bible says we have offended a holy God and that we need to be forgiven of that offense before we can be in fellowship with him. There are not many ways to receive such forgiveness; only the One who has been offended can

276

forgive us of our offense (Mark 2:5–7). Jesus alone paid the penalty for our sin through his death on the cross (2 Cor. 5:21). He thereby cleared the way for God both to remain true to his holy character and to extend the offer of forgiveness to us. Thus, John could write, "If we confess our sins, [God] *is faithful and just and will forgive* us our sins" (1 John 1:9, emphasis added; see also Rom. 3:22–26).

Reconciliation

The Bible says we have separated ourselves from God relationally because of our rebellion and sin: "We all, like sheep, have gone astray, each of us has turned to his own way" (Isa. 53:6). The solution to our being separated from God is that our relationship with God be restored. Our need for such reconciliation indicates, again, that there is only one way to resolve the problem of our having separated ourselves from God.

How many ways are there, after all, for me to restore a relationship that I am entirely responsible for having broken? Only one! It is done through the confession of my guilt and the subsequent hope that the offended one will be gracious enough to forgive me.

Humanity is in the same kind of situation with God. If we are ever to have any hope of being in a relationship with God, we need to take steps to restore our relationship, which means to confess our guilt before God.

Regeneration

The Bible says we are spiritually dead. Such a concept, again, implies exclusiveness with respect to the solution to humanity's problem. That is because dead people cannot help themselves, and because the only one who has the power to give life is God. Our need is to be made spiritually alive, or regenerated. "To be made spiritually alive" is the meaning of such biblical phrases as to be "born again" (John 3:3–6) and to be "born of God" (John 1:12). God provided Jesus Christ as the One through whom that life would come: "God, who is rich in mercy, made us alive with Christ even when we were dead in transgressions" (Eph. 2:4–5). Jesus said, "I am the resurrection and the life. He who believes in me will live, even though he dies" (John

11:25). He demonstrated the truth of those words by rising from the dead. No other founder of a religion can make such an astounding claim.

Christianity and the Other Religions

There is no indication in scripture that any other religious message besides the Gospel of Jesus Christ is capable of restoring us to a relationship with God. Jesus himself said, "I am the way and the truth and the life. No one comes to the Father except through me" (John 14:6; see also Peter's words in Acts 4:12).

The Bible teaches that there is a spiritual dimension in the origin of religions, and that the intention of the spirits is to deceive humanity and to deflect us from the truth (see John 8:44; 2 Cor. 11:13–14). Paul wrote that people will "follow deceiving spirits and things taught by demons" (1 Tim. 4:1). From the beginning, Satan has distorted the truths of God (Gen. 3:1–5), and his purpose all along has been to "blind the minds of the unbelieving" (2 Cor. 4:4).

One of Satan's lies, and one of the ways in which he blinds people to the truth, is through religions that deflect us from recognizing the full extent of our sinful condition and from accepting God's provision of grace through Jesus Christ. For example, the non-Christian religions have either denied, diminished, or disregarded the absolute holiness of God (see Chapter 9: World Religions Overview). As God's holiness is distorted, we become vulnerable to being deceived into thinking that perhaps the goal of salvation is achievable through our own human effort, thus blinding us to our need for a Savior.[183]

In table 13.12, Walvoord uses the definite article *the* before the word *predicate*. However, the seven points aforementioned are explained by the author from his perspective.

CHAPTER 14

The Heart of the Cross

Everything is purified with blood, and without the shedding
of blood there is no forgiveness of sins. —Hebrews 9:22

The Problem of Forgiveness

According to the Gospel, the cross of Christ is the only ground on which
God forgives sins. The problem of forgiveness is constituted by the inevitable
collision between divine perfection and human rebellion, between God as
he is and us as we are. The obstacle to forgive is neither our sin alone nor our
guilt alone, but the divine reaction in love and wrath toward guilty sinners.
Although indeed "God is love," we have to remember that his love is *holy
love*, love that yearns over sinners while at the same time refusing to condone
their sin. How, then, could God express his holy love—his love in forgiving
sinners—without compromising his holiness, and his holiness in judging
sinners without frustrating his love?

Confronted by human evil, how could God be true to himself as holy
love? In Isaiah's words, how could he be simultaneously "a righteous God
and a Savior" (Isa. 45:21)? For despite the truth that God demonstrated his
righteousness by taking action to save his people, the words *righteousness* and
salvation cannot be regarded as simple synonyms. Rather, his saving initiative
is compatible with, and expressive of, his righteousness. At the cross in holy
love, God through Christ paid the full penalty of our disobedience himself.
He bore the judgment we deserve in order to bring us the forgiveness we do
not deserve. On the cross, divine mercy and justice were equally expressed
and eternally reconciled. God's holy love was "satisfied."[184]

The Gravity of Sin

The very word *sin* has in recent years dropped from most people's vocabulary. It belongs to traditional religious phraseology, which, at least in the increasingly secularized West, is now declared by many to be meaningless. Moreover, if and when sin is mentioned, it is most likely to be misunderstood. What is it, then?

The New Testament uses five main Greek words for sin, which together portray its various aspects, both passive and active. The most common is *hamartia*, which depicts sin as a missing of the target, the failure to attain a goal. *Adikia* is "unrighteousness" or "iniquity," and *poneria* is "evil of a vicious or degenerate kind." Both these terms seem to speak of an inward corruption or perversion of character. The more active words are *parabasis* (with which we may associate the similar *paraptoma*), a "trespass" or "transgression," the stepping over a known boundary, and *anomia*, "lawlessness," the disregard or violation of a known law. In each case an objective criterion is implied, either a standard we fail to reach or a line we deliberately cross.

The emphasis of scripture is on the godless self-centeredness of sin. Every sin is a breach of what Jesus called "the first and great commandment," not just by failing to love God with all our being but also by actively refusing to acknowledge and obey him as our Creator and Lord.[185]

We have rejected the position of dependence that our createdness inevitably involves and have made a bid for independence. Worse still, we have dared to proclaim our self-dependence, our autonomy, which is to claim the position occupied by God alone. Sin is not a regrettable lapse from conventional standards; its essence is hostility to God (Rom. 8:7), issuing in active rebellion against him.

Once we have seen that every sin we commit is an expression (in differing degrees of self-consciousness) of this spirit of revolt against God, we are able to accept David's confession: "Against you, you only, have I sinned and done what is evil in your sight" (Ps. 51:4). In committing adultery with Bathsheba, and in arranging to have her husband, Uriah, killed in battle, David had committed extremely serious offenses against the couple and against the nation. Yet it was God's laws that he had broken and thereby ultimately God whom he had chiefly offended.[186]

Human Moral Responsibility

The Bible takes sin seriously because it takes *humanity* seriously. As we have seen, Christians do not deny the fact—in some circumstances—of diminished responsibility, but we affirm that diminished responsibility always entails diminished humanity. To say that somebody "is not responsible for his [or her] actions" is to demean that person as a human being. It is part of the glory of being human that we are held responsible for our actions. Then, when we also acknowledge our sin and guilt, we receive God's forgiveness, enter into the joy of his salvation, and therefore become yet more completely human and healthy. What is unhealthy is every wallowing in guilt that does not lead to confession, repentance, faith in Jesus Christ, and therefore forgiveness.

God's Holiness and Wrath

We have considered the seriousness of sin as rebellion against God, the continuing responsibility of men and women for their actions, and their consequent guilt in God's sight and liability to punishment. But can we think of God as "punishing" or "judging" evil? Yes, we can—and we must.[187]

Indeed, the essential background to the cross is not only the sin, responsibility, and guilt of human beings but also the just reaction of God to these things—in other words, his holiness and wrath.

That God is holy is foundational to biblical religion. So is the corollary that sin is incompatible with his holiness. His eyes are "too pure to look on evil," and he "cannot tolerate wrong." Therefore, our sins effectively separate us from him, so that his face is hidden from us and he refuses to listen to our prayers (Hab. 1:13; Isa. 59:1). As a consequence, it was clearly understood by the biblical authors that no human being could ever set eyes on God and survive the experience. People might perhaps be permitted to see his "back," but not his "face"; the sunshine, but not the sun (e.g., Exod. 33:20–23; Judg. 13:22). And all those who were granted even a glimpse of his glory were unable to endure the sight.

Moses "hid his face, because he was afraid to look at God." When Isaiah had his vision of Yahweh enthroned and exalted, he was overwhelmed by the sense of his uncleanness. When God revealed himself personally to Job, Job's reaction was to "despise" himself and to "repent in dust and ashes." Ezekiel saw only "the appearance of the likeness of the glory of the Lord," in burning fire and brilliant light, but it was enough to make him fall prostrate to the ground. At a similar vision, Daniel also collapsed and fainted with his face to the ground. As for those who were confronted by the Lord Jesus Christ, even during his earthly life when his glory was veiled, they felt a profound discomfort. For example, he provoked in Peter a sense of his sinfulness and of his unfitness to be in his presence. And when John saw his ascended magnificence, he "fell at his feet as though dead."[188]

Closely related to God's holiness is his wrath, which is in fact his holy reaction to evil. We certainly cannot dismiss it by saying that the God of wrath belongs to the Old Testament whereas the God of the New Testament is love.

What is common to the biblical concepts of the holiness and the wrath of God is the truth that they cannot coexist with sin. God's holiness exposes sin; his wrath opposes it. So sin cannot approach God, and God cannot tolerate sin. Several vivid metaphors are used in scripture to illustrate this stubborn fact.[189]

The first is *height*. Frequently in the Bible, the God of creation and covenant is called "the Most High God" and is personally addressed in several psalms as "Yahweh Most High."[189] His lofty exaltation expresses his sovereignty over the nations, the earth, and "all gods" (e.g., Ps. 97:9; Ps. 99:2), and also his inaccessibility to sinners.

The second picture is that of *distance*. God is not only "high above" us but also "far away" from us. We dare not approach too close. Indeed, many are the biblical injunctions to keep our distance. "Do not come any closer," God said to Moses out of the burning bush. So it was that the arrangements for Israel's worship expressed the complementary truths of his nearness to them because of his covenant and his separation from them because of his holiness. Even as he came down to them at Mount Sinai to reveal himself to them, he told Moses to put limits for the people around the base of the mountain and to urge them not to come near.

The third and fourth pictures of the holy God's unapproachability to sinners are those of *light* and *fire*. "God is light," and "our God a consuming fire." Both discourage, indeed inhibit, too close an approach. Bright light is blinding—our eyes cannot endure its brilliance—and in the heat of the fire, everything shrivels up and is destroyed. So God "lives in unapproachable light." "No one has seen or can see" him. And those who deliberately reject the truth have "only a fearful expectation of judgment and of raging fire that will consume the enemies of God. ... It is a dreadful thing to fall into the hands of the living God."[190]

The fifth metaphor is the most dramatic of all. It indicates that the holy God's rejection of evil is as decisive as the human body's rejection of poison by *vomiting*. Vomiting is probably the body's most violent of all reactions. The immoral and idolatrous practices of the Canaanites were so disgusting, it is written, that "the land vomited out its inhabitants," and the Israelites were warned that if they committed the same offenses, the land would vomit them out as well.

Moreover, what is said to be the land's repudiation of evil was in reality the Lord's. For in the same context, he is represented as declaring that he "abhorred" the Canaanites because of their evil doings. The identical Hebrew word is used of him in relation to the stubborn disobedience of Israel in the wilderness. "For forty years I was angry with [literally, "loathed"] that generation." Here too the verb probably alludes to nauseating food, as it does in the statement, "We detest this miserable food!" Our delicate upbringing may find this earthy metaphor distinctly embarrassing. Yet it continues in the New Testament. When Jesus threatens to "spit" the lukewarm Laodicean church people out of his mouth, the Greek verb literally means "to vomit" (*emeo*). The picture may be shocking, but its meaning is clear. God cannot tolerate or "digest" sin and hypocrisy. They cause him not merely distaste, but also disgust. They are so repulsive to him that he must rid himself of them. He must spit or vomit them out.[191]

All five metaphors illustrate the utter incompatibility of divine holiness and human sin. Height, distance, light, fire, and vomiting all say that God cannot be in the presence of sin and that if it approaches him too closely it is repudiated or consumed.

We must, therefore, hold fast to the biblical revelation of the living God who hates evil, is disgusted and angered by it, and refuses ever to come to terms with it. In consequence, we may be sure that when he searched in his mercy for some way to forgive, cleanse, and accept evildoers, it was not along the road of moral compromise.[192]

It had to be a way that was equally expressive of his love and of his wrath.

As Emil Brunner put it, "Where the idea of the wrath of God is ignored, there also will there be no understanding of the central conception of the Gospel: the uniqueness of the revelation in the Mediator."[193] Similarly, "Only he who knows the greatness of wrath will be mastered by the greatness of mercy."[194]

The essential background to the cross, therefore, is a balanced understanding of the gravity of sin and the majesty of God. If we diminish either, we thereby diminish the cross. If we reinterpret sin as a lapse instead of a rebellion, and God as indulgent instead of indignant, then naturally the cross appears superfluous. But to dethrone God and enthrone ourselves not only dispenses with the cross but also degrades both God and humans. A biblical view of God and ourselves, however—that is, of our sin and of God's wrath—honors both. It honors human beings by affirming them as responsible for their own actions, and it honors God by affirming him as having moral character.

Satisfaction of Sin

No two words in the theological vocabulary of the cross arouse more criticism than *satisfaction* and *substitution*. Yet it is in defense of these words that this chapter and the next are written. In combination ("satisfaction through substitution"), they may even seem intolerable. How, people ask, can we possibly believe that God needed some kind of "satisfaction" before he was prepared to forgive, and that Jesus Christ provided it by enduring as our "substitute" the punishment we sinners deserved? Are not such notions unworthy of the God of the biblical revelation, a hangover from primitive superstitions, indeed frankly immoral?

Satisfying the Devil through the Victory of Christ

The notion that it was the Devil who made the cross necessary was widespread in the early church.[195] To be sure, Jesus and his apostles did speak of the cross as the means of the Devil's overthrow. But some of the early fathers were extremely injudicious in the ways in which they represented both the Devil's power and how the cross deprived him of it. They all recognized that since the Fall, and on account of it, humankind has been in captivity not only to sin and guilt but also to the Devil. They thought of him as the lord of sin and death, and as the major tyrant from whom Jesus came to liberate us.[195]

Satisfying the Law

Another way of explaining the moral necessity of the divine "satisfaction" at the cross has been to exalt the law. Sin is "lawlessness" (1 John 3:4), a disregard for God's law and a disobedience of it. But the law cannot be broken with impunity. Sinners therefore incur the penalty of their lawbreaking. They cannot simply be let off. The law must be upheld, its dignity defended, and its just penalties paid. The law is thereby "satisfied."

A popular illustration of this truth is the story of King Darius in the book of Daniel (Dan. 6). He appointed 120 satraps to rule Babylonia and set three administrators over them, of whom Daniel was one. Further, Daniel's exceptional qualities and distinguished service were such that the king planned to promote him over all his colleagues. This aroused their jealousy, and they immediately began to plot his downfall. Watching him like hawks, they tried to find some inconsistency or inefficiency in his conduct of public affairs so that they could lodge charges against him. But they failed, "because he was trustworthy and neither corrupt nor negligent" (Dan 6:4). So they turned their scrutiny on his private life; their only hope, they reckoned, was to find him guilty of some technical fault in connection with his regular religious devotion. They managed to persuade the king to "issue an edict and enforce the decree that anyone who prays to any god or man during the next thirty days, "except to be king himself, would be thrown into the lions' den" (Dan 6:7). With incredible naïveté, the king fell into their trap. By putting the decree into writing, he even made it unalterable, "in accordance with the laws of the Medes and Persians, which cannot be repealed" (Dan. 6:8–9).

The publication of the decree reached Daniel's ears but did not lead him to change his routine. On the contrary, he continued three times a day to pray to his God. His practice was to do so kneeling in his upstairs room, the windows of which opened toward Jerusalem. There he was visible to passers-by, and there his enemies duly saw him. The latter went back to the king immediately and reported Daniel's flagrant breach of the royal decree. "When the king heard this, he was greatly distressed; he was determined to rescue Daniel and made every effort until sundown to save him" (Dan 6:14). But he could find no solution to the legal problem he had created for himself. His administrators and satraps reminded him that "according to the law of the Medes and Persians no decree or edict that the king issues can be changed" (Dan 6:15). So Darius reluctantly bowed to the inevitable and gave the order for Daniel to be thrown into the lions' den. The law had triumphed.

Many are the preachers (I among them) who have used this story to highlight the divine dilemma. Darius respected Daniel and labored long to find some way of saving him, but the law must take its course and not be tampered with.

So God loves us sinners and longs to save us, but he cannot do so by violating the law that has justly condemned us. Hence the cross, in which the penalty of the law was paid and its sanctity vindicated.

Again, "God cannot abolish that moral constitution of things which he has established." It is true that Dean Wace went on to qualify these statements by reminding us that the moral world is not "a kind of moral machine in which laws operate as they do in physical nature," and that "we have to do not simply with an established order but with a living personality, with a living God." Nevertheless, he refers again to "the penalty necessarily involved in the violation of the Divine law."[196]

The Holy Love of God

What does this have to do with the atonement? Just that the way God chooses to forgive sinners and reconcile them to himself must, first and foremost, be fully consistent with his own character. It is not only that he must overthrow and disarm the Devil in order to rescue his captives. It is not even only that he must satisfy his law, his honor, his justice, or the moral order. It is that he must satisfy himself. Those other formulations rightly insist that at least one expression of himself must be satisfied, either his law or honor or justice or moral order; the merit of this further formulation is that it insists on the satisfaction of God himself in every aspect of his being, including both his justice and his love.

So then, the cross of Christ "is the event in which God makes known his holiness and his love simultaneously, in one event, in an absolute manner." "The cross is the only place where the loving, forgiving, merciful God is revealed in such a way that we perceive that his holiness and his love are equally infinite." In fact, "the objective aspect of the atonement ... may be summed up thus: it consists in the combination of inflexible righteousness, with its penalties, and transcendent love."[197]

286

At the same time, we must never think of this duality within God's being as irreconcilable. For God is not at odds with himself, however much it may appear to us that he is. He is "the God of peace," of inner tranquility, not turmoil. True, we find it difficult to hold in our minds simultaneously the images of God as the Judge who must punish evildoers and of the Lover who must find a way to forgive them. Yet he is both, and at the same time. In the words of G. C. Berkouwer, "In the cross of Christ God's justice and love are *simultaneously* revealed,"[198] while Calvin, echoing Augustine, was even bolder. He wrote of God that "in a marvellous and divine way he loved us even when he hated us."[199] Indeed, the two are more than simultaneous; they are identical, or at least alternative, expressions of the same reality. For "the wrath of God is the love of God," Brunner wrote in a daring sentence, "in the form in which the man who has turned away from God and turned against God experiences it."[200]

Again, if we spoke less about God's love and more about his holiness, more about his judgment, then we should say much more when we did speak of his love.[201]

Yet again, without a holy God, there would be no problem of atonement. It is the holiness of God's love that necessitates the atoning cross.[202]

This vision of God's holy love will deliver us from caricatures of him. We must picture him neither as an indulgent God who compromises his holiness in order to spare and spoil us nor as a harsh, vindictive God who suppresses his love in order to crush and destroy us. How then can God express his holiness without consuming us, and express his love without condoning our sins? How can God satisfy his holy love? How can he save *us* and satisfy *himself* simultaneously? We reply at this point only that, in order to satisfy himself, he sacrificed—indeed substituted—himself for us. What that means will be our concern in the next chapter to understand.

> Beneath the cross of Jesus
> I fain would take my stand—
> The shadow of a mighty rock
> Within a weary land ...
> O safe and happy shelter!
> O refuge tried and sweet!
> O trysting-place, where heaven's love
> And heaven's justice meet!

CHAPTER 15

The Self-Substitution of God

We have located the problem of forgiveness in the gravity of sin and the majesty of God, that is, in the realities of who we are and who he is. How can the holy love of God come to terms with the unholy lovelessness of humankind? What would happen if they were to come into collision with each other? The problem is not outside God; it is within his own being. Because God never contradicts himself, he must be himself and "satisfy" himself, acting in absolute consistency with the perfection of his character. "It is the recognition of this divine necessity, or the failure to recognize it," wrote James Denney, "which ultimately divides interpreters of Christianity into evangelical and non-evangelical, those who are true to the New Testament and those who cannot digest it."[203]

Moreover, as we have seen, this inward necessity does not mean that God must be true to only a part of himself (whether his law, or honor, or justice), or that he must express one of his attributes (whether love or holiness) at the expense of another, but rather that he must be completely and invariably himself in the fullness of his moral being. T. J. Crawford stressed this point: "It is altogether an error ... to suppose that God acts at one time according to one of his attributes, and at another time according to another. He acts in conformity with all of them at all times."

> As for the divine justice and the divine mercy in particular, the end of his [that is, Christ's] work was not to bring them into harmony, as if they had been at variance with one another, but jointly to manifest, and glorify them in the redemption of sinners. It is a case of *combined action*, and

not of *counteraction*, on the part of these attributes, that is exhibited on the cross.[204]

How then could God express simultaneously his holiness in judgment and his love in pardon? Only by providing a divine substitute for the sinner so that the substitute would receive the judgment and the sinner the pardon. We sinners still of course have to suffer some of the personal, psychological, and social consequences of our sins, but the penal consequence, the deserved penalty of alienation from God, has been borne by another in our place, so that we may be spared it.

The vital questions that must now occupy us are these: Who is this "substitute"? And how are we to understand and justify the notion of his substituting himself for us?

The best way to approach these questions is to consider the Old Testament sacrifices, since these were the God-intended preparation for the sacrifice of Christ.

Sacrifice in the Old Testament

"The interpretation of Christ's death as a sacrifice is imbedded in every important type of the New Testament teaching."[205] Sacrificial vocabulary and idiom are widespread. Sometimes the reference is unambiguous, as when Paul says Christ "gave himself up for us as a fragrant offering [*prosphora*] and sacrifice [*thysia*] to God" (Eph. 5:2).

At other times the allusion is less direct, simply that Christ "gave himself" (e.g., Gal. 1:4) or "offered himself" (e.g., Heb. 9:14) for us, but the background of thought is still the Old Testament sacrificial system. In particular, the statement that he died "for sin" or "for sins" (e.g., Rom. 8:3 RSV and 1 Pet. 3:18 respectively) self-consciously borrows the Greek translation of the "sin offering" (*peri hamartias*).

Indeed, the letter to the Hebrews portrays the sacrifice of Jesus Christ as having perfectly fulfilled the Old Testament "shadows." For he sacrificed himself (not animals), once and for all (not repeatedly), and thus secured for us not only ceremonial cleansing and restoration to favor in the covenant community but also the purification of our consciences and restoration to fellowship with the living God.

Sacrifices were offered in a wide variety of circumstances in the Old Testament. The first express the sense human beings have of belonging to God by right, and the second their sense of alienation from God because of their sin and guilt. Characteristics of the first were the "peace" or "fellowship" offering, which was often associated with thanksgiving (Lev. 7:12), the burnt offering (in which everything was consumed), and the ritual of the three annual harvest festivals (Exod. 23:14–17). Characteristics of the second were the sin offering and the guilt offering, in which the need for atonement was clearly acknowledged. It would be better to distinguish them, as B. B. Warfield did, by seeing in the former "man conceived merely as creature" and in the latter "the needs of man as sinner." Or, to elaborate the same distinction, in the first the human being is "a creature claiming protection," and in the second "a sinner craving pardon. ... Then God is revealed in the sacrifices on the one hand as the Creator on whom humanity depends for its physical life, and on the other as simultaneously the Judge who demands and the Savior who provides atonement for sin."[206]

In contrast to God's revealed will, either he put worship before atonement or he distorted his presentation of the fruits of the soil from recognition of the Creator's gifts into an offering of his own. The notion of substitution is that one person takes the place of another, especially in order to bear that person's pain and so save him or her from it.[207]

The clearest statement that the blood sacrifices of the Old Testament ritual had a substitutionary significance, however, and that this was why the shedding and sprinkling of blood was indispensable to atonement, is to be found in this statement by God explaining why the eating of blood was prohibited: "For the life of a creature is in the blood, and I have given it to you to make atonement for yourselves on the altar; it is the blood that makes atonement for one's life" (Lev 17:11).

Three important affirmations about blood are made in this text. First, blood is the symbol of life. This understanding that "blood is life" seems to be very ancient. It goes back at least to Noah, whom God forbade to eat meat that had its "lifeblood" still in it (Gen. 9:4), and was later repeated in the formula "the blood is the life" (Deut. 12:23). The emphasis, however, is not on blood flowing in the veins, the symbol of life being lived, but on bloodshed, the symbol of life ended, usually by violent means.

Second, blood makes atonement, and the reason for its atoning significance is given in the repetition of the word *life*. It is only because "the life of a creature is in the blood" that "it is the blood that makes atonement for one's life." One life is forfeit; another life is sacrificed instead. What makes atonement "on the altar" is the shedding of substitutionary lifeblood. T. J. Crawford expressed it well: "The text, then, according to its plan and obvious import, teaches the *vicarious* nature of the rite of sacrifice. *Life was given for life,* the life of the victim for the life of the offerer," indeed "the life of the innocent victim for the life of the sinful offerer."[208]

Third, blood was given by God for this atoning purpose. "I have given it to you," he says, "to make atonement for yourselves on the altar." So we are to think of the sacrificial system as God-given, not of human origin, and of the individual sacrifices not as a human device to placate God but as a means of atonement provided by God himself.

This Old Testament background helps us to understand two crucial texts in the Letter to the Hebrews. The first is that "without the shedding of blood there is no forgiveness" (Heb. 9:22), and the second is that "it is impossible for the blood of bulls and goats to take away sins" (Heb. 10:4).

No forgiveness without blood meant no atonement without substitution. There had to be life for life or blood for blood. But the Old Testament blood sacrifices were only shadows; the substance was Christ. For a substitute to be effective, it must be an appropriate equivalent. Animal sacrifices could not atone for human beings, because a human being is "much more valuable ... than a sheep," as Jesus himself said (Matt. 12:12). Only "the precious blood of Christ" was valuable enough (1 Pet. 1:19).

Jesus Christ's Death

In light of the evidence about the sin-bearing nature of Jesus's death, we now know how to interpret the simple assertion that "he died for us." The proposition *for* can translate either as "hyper" ("on behalf of") or "anti" ("instead of"). Most of the references have *hyper-*. For example, "While we were still sinners, Christ died for us" (Rom. 5:8), and again, "One died for all" (2 Cor. 5:14).

Anti comes only in the ransom verses, namely in Mark 10:45 (literally "to give his life as a ransom instead of many") and in 1 Timothy 2:6 ("who gave himself as a ransom for all men," where *for* is again "hyper" but the preposition "anti" is in the noun, *antilytron*).

The two prepositions do not always adhere to their dictionary definitions, however. Even the broader word *hyper* ("on behalf of") is many times shown by its context to be used in the sense of *anti* ("instead of"), as, for example, when we are said to be "ambassadors for Christ" (2 Cor. 5:20), or when Paul wanted to keep Onesimus in Rome to serve him "on behalf of" his master Philemon, that is, in his place (Philem. 13). The same is clear in the two most outspoken statements of the meaning of Christ's death in Paul's letters. One is that "God made him who had no sin to be sin for us" (2 Cor. 5:21), and the other is that Christ has "redeemed us from the curse of the law by becoming a curse for us" (Gal. 3:13). Some commentators have found these assertions difficult to accept.

Karl Barth called the first "almost unbearably severe,"[209] and A. W. F. Blunt described the language of the second as "almost shocking."[210] In both cases, what happened to Christ on the cross ("made sin," "becoming a curse") is said by Paul to have been intended "for us," on our behalf or for our benefit. But what exactly did happen? The sinless one was "made sin for us," which must mean that he bore the penalty of our sin in our stead, and he redeemed us from the law's curse by "becoming a curse for us," which must mean that the curse of the law lying upon us for our disobedience was transformed to him, so that he bore it in our stead.

Both verses go beyond these negative truths (that he bore our sin and curse to redeem us from them) to a positive counterpart. On the one hand, he bore the curse in order that we might inherit the blessing promised to Abraham (Gal. 3:14), and on the other, God made the sinless Christ to be sin for us, in order that "in him we might become the righteousness of God" (2 Cor. 5:21). Both verses thus indicate that when we are united to Christ, a mysterious exchange takes place: he takes our curse so that we may receive his blessing; he becomes sin with our sin so that we may become righteous with his righteousness.

Elsewhere Paul writes of this transfer in terms of "imputation." On the one hand, God declined to "impute" our sins to us, or "count" them against us (2 Cor. 5:19), with the implication that he imputed them to Christ instead. On the other, God has imputed Christ's righteousness to us (Rom. 4:6; 1 Cor. 1:30; Phil. 3:9). Many are offended by this concept, considering it both artificial and unjust on God's part to arrange such a transfer. Yet the objection is due to a misunderstanding, which Thomas Crawford clears up for us. "Imputation," he writes, "does not at all imply the transference of one person's moral qualities to another." Such a thing would be impossible. He goes on to quote John Owen to the effect that "we ourselves have done nothing of what is imputed to us, nor Christ anything of what is imputed to him."

"It would be absurd and unbelievable to imagine," Crawford continues, "that the moral turpitude of our sins was transferred to Christ, so as to make him personally sinful and ill-deserving; and that the moral excellence of his righteousness is transferred to us, so as to make us personally upright and commendable." No, what was transferred to Christ was not moral qualities but legal consequences:

he voluntarily accepted liability for our sins. That is what the expressions "made sin" and "made a curse" mean. Similarly, "the righteousness of God," which we become when we are "in Christ," is not here righteousness of character and conduct (although that grows within us by the working of the Holy Spirit), but rather a righteousness standing before God.[211]

When we review all this Old Testament material (the shedding and sprinkling of blood, the sin offering, the Passover, the meaning of "sin-bearing," the scapegoat, and Isaiah 53), and consider its New Testament application to the death of Christ, we are obliged to conclude that the cross was a substitutionary sacrifice. Christ died for us. Christ died instead of us. Indeed, as Jeremias put it, this use of sacrificial imagery "has the intention of expressing the fact that Jesus died without sin in substitution for our sins."[212]

Who Is the Substitute?

The key question we now have to address is this: exactly who was our substitute? Who took our place, bore our sin, became our curse, endured our penalty, died our death? To be sure, "while we were still sinners, Christ died for us" (Rom. 5:8). That would be the simple, surface answer. But who was this Christ? How are we to think of him?

Was Christ just a man? If so, how could one human being possibly—or justly—stand in for other human beings? Was he then simply God, seeming to be a man, but not actually being the man he seemed? If so, how could he represent humankind? Besides this, how could he have died? In that case, are we to think of Christ neither as man alone nor as God alone, but rather as the one only God-man who, because of his uniquely constituted person, was uniquely qualified to mediate between God and humankind? Whether the concept of substitutionary atonement is rational, moral, plausible, acceptable, or above all biblical depends on our answers to these questions. The possibility of substitution rests on the identity of the substitute. We need therefore to examine in greater depth the three explanations that I have sketched above.

The first proposal is that the substitute was the *man* Christ Jesus, viewed as a human being and conceived as an individual separate from both God and us, an independent third party. Those who begin with this a priori lay themselves open to gravely distorted understandings of the atonement and so bring the truth of substitution into disrepute. They tend to present the cross in one or the other of two ways, according to whether the initiative was Christ's or God's. In the one case, Christ is pictured as intervening in order to pacify an angry God and wrest from him a grudging salvation. In the other, the intervention is ascribed to God, who proceeds to punish the innocent Jesus in place of us, the guilty sinners who deserve the punishment.

In both cases, God and Christ are sundered from one another: either Christ persuades God or God punishes Christ. What is characteristic of both presentations is that they denigrate the Father. Reluctant to suffer himself, he victimizes Christ instead. Reluctant to forgive, he is prevailed on by Christ to do so. He is seen as a pitiless ogre whose wrath has to be assuaged, whose disinclination to act has to be overcome, by the loving self-sacrifice of Jesus.

Jesus Christ is said to be the "propitiation" for our sins and our "advocate" with the Father (1 John 2:2 AV), which at first sight suggests that he died to placate God's anger and is now pleading with him in order to persuade him to forgive us. But other parts of scripture forbid us to interpret the language of propitiation and advocacy in that way.

The whole notion of a compassionate Christ inducing a reluctant God to take action on our behalf founders on the fact of God's love.

There was no *umstimmung* in God, no change of mind or heart secured by Christ. On the contrary, the saving initiative originated in him. It was "because of the tender mercy of our God" (Luke 1:78) that Christ came, "because of his great love for us" (Eph. 2:4; cf. John 3:16; 1 John 4:9–10), because of "the grace of God that brings salvation" (Titus 2:11).

As for the other formulation (that God punished Jesus for our sins), it is true that the sins of Israel were transferred to the scapegoat, that "the Lord laid on him," his suffering servant, all our iniquity (Isa. 53:6), that "it was the Lord's will to crush him" (Isa. 53:10), and that Jesus applied to himself Zechariah's prophecy that God would "strike the shepherd" (Zech. 13:7; Mark 14:27). It is also true that in the New Testament God is said to have "sent" his Son to atone for our sins (1 John 4:9–10), "delivered him up" for us (Acts 2:23; Rom. 8:32), "presented him as a sacrifice of atonement" (Rom. 3:25), "condemned sin" in his flesh (Rom. 8:3), and "made him ... to be sin for us" (2 Cor. 5:21). These are striking statements.

But we have no liberty to interpret them in such a way as to imply either that God compelled Jesus to do what he was unwilling to do himself or that Jesus was an unwilling victim of God's harsh justice. Jesus Christ did indeed bear the penalty of our sins, but God was active in and through Christ doing it, and Christ was freely playing his part (e.g., Heb. 10:5–10).

We must not, then, speak of God punishing Jesus or of Jesus persuading God, for to do so is to set them over against each other as if they acted independently of each other or were even in conflict with each other. We must never make Christ the object of God's punishment or God the object of Christ's persuasion, because both God and Christ are subjects, not objects, taking the initiative together to save sinners. Whatever happened on the cross in terms of "God-forsakenness" was voluntarily accepted by both in the same holy love that made atonement necessary. It was "God in our nature forsaken of God."[213]

If the Father "gave" the Son, the Son "gave" himself. If the Gethsemane "cup" symbolized the wrath of God, it was nevertheless "given" by the Father (John 18:11) and voluntarily "taken" by the Son.

If the Father "sent" the Son, the Son "came" himself. The Father did not lay on the Son an ordeal he was reluctant to bear, nor did the Son extract from the Father a salvation he was reluctant to bestow. There is no suspicion anywhere in the New Testament of discord between the Father and the Son, "whether by the Son wresting forgiveness from an unwilling Father or by the Father demanding a sacrifice from an unwilling Son"[214] There was no unwillingness in either. On the contrary, their wills coincided in the perfect self-sacrifice of love.

God's Anger

God's anger is as fire spoken of as "burning," "quenching," and "consuming." It is true that human beings are also said to "burn with anger."[215] But this vocabulary is much more frequently applied in the Old Testament to Yahweh, who "burns with anger" whenever he sees his people disobeying his law and breaking his covenant.[216] In fact, it is precisely when he is "provoked" to anger that he is said to "burn" with it,[217] or his anger is said to "break out and burn like fire."[218] In consequence, we read of "the fire of his anger" or "the fire of his jealousy"; indeed, God himself unites them by referring to "the fire of my jealous anger."[219]

As with the provocation of Yahweh to anger, so with the fire of his anger certain inevitability is implied. In the dry heat of a Palestinian summer, fires were easily kindled. It was the same with Yahweh's anger—never from caprice, however, but always only in response to evil. Nor was his anger ever uncontrolled. On the contrary, in the early years of Israel's national life, "Time after time he restrained his anger and did not stir up his full wrath."[220] But when he "could no longer endure" his people's stubborn rebellion against him, he said, "The time has come for me to act. I will not hold back; I will not have pity, nor will I relent. You will be judged according to your conduct and your actions" (Ezek. 24.4)[221]

If a fire was easy to kindle during the Palestinian dry season, it was equally difficult to put out. So with God's anger. Once righteously aroused, he "did not turn away from the heat of his fierce anger, which burned against Judah." Once kindled, it was not readily "quenched."[222] Instead, when Yahweh's anger "burned" against people, it "consumed" them. That is to say, as fire leads to destruction, so Yahweh's anger leads to judgment, because Yahweh is "a consuming fire."[223] The fire of his anger was "quenched," and so "subsided" or "ceased," only when the judgment was complete,[224] or when a radical regeneration had taken place, issuing in social justice.[225]

So through Ezekiel, Yahweh warns Judah that he is about to "accomplish" (AV), "satisfy" (RSV), or "spend" his anger "upon" or "against them."[226] They have refused to listen to him and have persisted in their idolatry. So now at last, "The time has come, the day is near. ... I am about to pour out my wrath on you and spend my anger against you" (Ezek. 7:7, 8). It is significant that the "pouring out" and the "spending" go together, as what is poured out cannot be gathered again, and what is spent is finished. The same two images are coupled in Lamentations 4:11: "The Lord has given full vent [*kalah*] to his wrath; he has poured out his fierce anger." Indeed, only when Yahweh's wrath is "spent" does it "cease." The same concept of inner necessity is implied by these verbs. What exists within Yahweh must be expressed; and what is expressed must be completely "spent" or "satisfied."

For the Sake of God's Name

Jeremiah 14 expresses with emphatic thoroughness the recognition that Yahweh is and always will be true to his name, that is, to himself. The situation was one of devastating drought: the cisterns were empty, the ground was cracked, the farmers were dismayed, and the animals were disorientated (Jer. 14:1–6).

In their extremity, the Israelites cried to God, "Although our sins testify against us, O Lord, do something for the sake of your Name" (Jer. 14:7). In other words, "although we cannot appeal to you to act on the ground of who *we* are, we can and do on the ground of who *you* are." The Israelites, remembering that they were God's chosen people, begged him to act in a way that would be consistent with his gracious covenant and steadfast character; recall that they added, "We bear your name" (Jer. 14:8–9). In contrast to the pseudoprophets, who were preaching a lopsided message of peace without judgment (Jer. 14:13–16), Jeremiah prophesied "sword, famine and plague" (Jer. 14:12). But he also looked beyond judgment to restoration. Convinced that Yahweh would act, he said to him, "For the sake of your name" (Jer. 14:21).

The same theme was further developed in Ezekiel 36. There Yahweh promised his people restoration after judgment, but he was disconcertingly candid about his reasons. "It is not for your sake, O house of Israel, that I am going to do these things, but for the sake of my holy name" (Ezek. 36:22). The Israelites had profaned God's name, causing it to be despised and even blasphemed by the nations. But Yahweh would take pity on his great name and once more demonstrate its holiness, its uniqueness, before the world. For then the nations would know that he was the Lord, the Living One (Ezek. 36:21, 23). When God thus acts "for the sake of his name," he is not just protecting it from misrepresentation; he is determining to be true to it. His concern is less for his reputation than for his consistency.

In the light of all this biblical material about the divine self-consistency, we can understand why it is impossible for *God* to do what Christ commanded *us* to do. He told us to "deny ourselves," but "God cannot deny himself" (Mark 8:34; 2 Tim. 2:13 RSV). Why is that? Why is it that God will not do, indeed cannot do, what he tells us to do? It is because God is God and not human, let alone fallen humankind. We have to deny or disown everything within us that is false to our true humanity. But there is nothing in God that is incompatible with his true deity and therefore nothing to deny. It is in order to be our true selves that we have to deny ourselves; it is because God is never other than his true self that he cannot and will not deny himself. He can empty himself of his rightful glory and humble himself to serve. Indeed, it is precisely this that he has done in Christ (Phil. 2:7–8). But he cannot repudiate any part of himself, because he is perfect. He cannot contradict himself. This is his integrity. As for us, we are constantly aware of our human inconsistencies; they usually arouse a comment. "It's so uncharacteristic of him," we say, or "You are not yourself today," or "I've come to expect something better from you." But can you imagine saying such things to or about God? He is always himself and never inconsistent. If he were ever to behave "uncharacteristically," in a way that is out of character with himself, he would cease to be God and the world would be thrown into moral confusion. No, God is God; he never deviates one iota, not even one tiny hair's breadth, from being entirely himself.[227]

God in Christ

Our substitute, then, who took our place and died our death on the cross was neither Christ alone (since that would make him a third party thrust in between God and us) nor God alone (since that would undermine the historical Incarnation), but *God in Christ,* who was truly and fully both God and man and who on that account was uniquely qualified to represent both God and humankind and to mediate between them. If we speak only of Christ suffering and dying, we overlook the initiative of the Father. If we speak only of God suffering and dying, we overlook the mediation of the Son. The New Testament authors never attribute the atonement either to Christ, in such a way as to disassociate him from the Father, or to God, in such a way as to dispense with Christ, but rather to God and Christ, or to God acting in and through Christ with the latter's wholehearted concurrence.

The New Testament evidence for this is plain. In surveying it, it seems logical to begin with the announcement of the Messiah's birth. The names he was given were Jesus ("divine Savior" or "God saves") and Emmanuel ("God with us"). For in and through his birth God himself had come to the rescue of his people, to save them from their sins (Matt. 1:21–23). Similarly, according to Luke, the Savior who had been born was not just, in the familial expression, the Christ of the Lord, the Lord's anointed, but actually "Christ the Lord," himself both Messiah and Lord (Luke 2:11).

When Jesus's public ministry began, his personal self-consciousness confirmed that God was at work in and through him. For though he did speak of "pleasing" the Father (John 8:29) and "obeying" him (John 15:10), of doing his will and finishing his work (e.g., John 4:34; John 6:38–39; John 17:4; John 19:30), this surrender was entirely voluntary, so that his will and the Father's were always in perfect harmony.[228] More than that, according to John he spoke of a mutual "indwelling," he in the Father and the Father in him, even of a "union" between them (e.g., John 14:11; John 17:21–23; John 10:30).

This conviction that Father and Son cannot be separated, especially when we are thinking about the atonement, since the Father was taking action through the Son, comes to its fullest expression in some of Paul's great statements about reconciliation. For example, "All this is from God" (referring to the work of the new creation, 2 Cor. 5:17–18), who "reconciled us to himself through Christ" and "was reconciling the world to himself in Christ" (2 Cor. 5:18–19). It does not seem to matter much where, in translating the Greek, we place the expressions "through Christ" and "in Christ." What matters is that God and Christ were together active in the work of reconciliation, indeed that it was in and through Christ that God was effecting the reconciliation. The nail that pierces the hand of Jesus goes through to the hand of God. The spear thrust into the side of Jesus goes through into God's.[229]

We began by showing that God must "satisfy himself," responding to the realities of human rebellion in a way that is perfectly consonant with his character. This internal necessity is our fixed starting point. In consequence, it would be impossible for us sinners to remain eternally the sole objects of his holy love, since he cannot both punish and pardon us at the same time. Hence the second necessity, namely, substitution. The only way for God's holy love to be satisfied is for his holiness to be directed in judgment upon his appointed substitute in order that his love may be directed toward us in forgiveness. The substitute bears the penalty so that we sinners may receive the pardon. Who, then, is the substitute? Certainly not Christ, if he is seen as a third party. Any notion of penal substitution in which three independent actors play a role—the guilty party, the punitive judge, and the innocent victim—is to be repudiated with the utmost vehemence. It would not only be unjust in itself but also would reflect a defective Christology. Christ is not an independent third person, but the eternal Son of Father, who is one with the Father in his essential being.

What we see, then, in the drama of the cross is not three actors but two, ourselves on the one hand and God on the other. Not God as he is in himself (the Father), but God nevertheless, God-made-man-in-Christ (the Son). Hence the importance of those New Testament passages that speak of the death of Christ as the death of God's Son, for example, "God so loved the world that he gave his one and only Son" (John 3:16); "he ... did not spare his own Son" (Rom. 8:32); and "we were reconciled to God through the death of his Son" (Rom. 5:10). For in giving his Son, he was giving himself. This being so, it is the Judge himself who in holy love assumed the role of the innocent victim, as in and through the person of his Son, he himself bore the penalty that he himself inflicted. As Dale put it, "The mysterious unity of the Father and the Son rendered it possible for God at once to endure and to inflict penal suffering."[230] There is neither harsh injustice nor unprincipled love nor Christological heresy in that; there is only unfathomable mercy. For in order to save us in such a way as to satisfy himself, God through Christ substituted himself for us. Divine love triumphed over divine wrath by divine self-sacrifice.

The cross was an act simultaneously of punishment and amnesty, severity and grace, justice and mercy. Seen thus, the objections to a substitutionary atonement evaporate. There is nothing even remotely immoral here, since the substitute for the lawbreakers is none other than the divine Lawmaker himself. There is no mechanical transaction either, since the self-sacrifice of love is the most personal of all actions. And what is achieved through the cross is not merely an external change of legal status, since those who see God's love there and are united to Christ by his Spirit become radically transformed in outlook and character.

We strongly reject, therefore, every explanation of the death of Christ that does not have at its center the principle of "satisfaction through substitution," indeed divine self-satisfaction through divine self-substitution. The cross was not a commercial bargain with the Devil, let alone one that tricked and trapped him; nor was it an exact equivalent, a quid pro quo to satisfy a code of honor or technical point of law; nor was it a compulsory submission by God to some moral authority above him from which he could not otherwise escape; nor was it a punishment of a meek Christ by a harsh and punitive Father; nor was it a procurement of salvation by a loving Christ from a mean and reluctant Father; nor was it an action of the Father that bypassed Christ as Mediator. Instead, the righteous, loving Father humbled himself to become in and through his only Son flesh, sin, and a curse for us, in order to redeem us without compromising his own character.

The theological words *satisfaction* and *substitution* need to be carefully defined and safeguarded, but they cannot in any circumstances be given up. The biblical gospel of atonement is of God satisfying himself by substituting himself for us.

The concept of substitution may be said, then, to lie at the heart of both sin and salvation. For the essence of sin is human beings substituting themselves for God, while the essence of salvation is God substituting himself for humankind. Humankind asserts itself against God and puts itself where only God deserves to be; God sacrifices himself for humankind and puts himself where only humankind deserves to be. Humankind claim prerogatives that belong to God alone; God accepts penalties that belong to humankind alone.

If the essence of the atonement is substitution, at least two important inferences follow, the first theological and the second personal. The theological inference is that it is impossible to hold the historic doctrine of the cross without holding the historic doctrine of Jesus Christ as the one and only God-man and Mediator. As we have seen, neither Christ alone as man nor the Father alone as God could be our substitute. Only God in Christ, God the Father's own and only Son-made-man, could take our place. At the root of every caricature of the cross there lies a distorted Christology. The person and work of Christ belong together. If he was not who the apostles say he was, then he could not have done what they say he did. The Incarnation is indispensable to the atonement. In particular, it is essential to affirm that the love, the holiness, and the will of the Father are identical with the love, the holiness, and the will of the Son. God was in Christ reconciling the world to himself.

CHAPTER 16

The Achievement of the Cross

The Salvation of Sinners

Moved by the perfection of his holy love, God in Christ substituted himself for us sinners. That is the heart of the cross of Christ. It leads us to turn now from the event to its consequences, from what happened on the cross to what was achieved by it.

Why did God take our place and bear our sin? What did he accomplish by his self-sacrifice, his self-substitution? The New Testament gives three main answers to these questions, which may be summed up in the words *salvation, revelation,* and *conquest.* What God in Christ has done through the cross is to rescue us, disclose himself, and overcome evil. In this chapter we shall focus on salvation through the cross.

It would be hard to exaggerate the magnitude of the changes that have taken place as a result of the cross, both in God and in us, especially in God's dealings with us and in our relations with him. Truly, when Christ died and was raised from death, a new day dawned, a new age began.

This new day is "the day of salvation" (2 Cor. 6:2), and the blessings of "such a great salvation" (Heb. 2:3) are so richly diverse that they cannot be neatly defined. Several pictures are needed to portray them. Just as the church of Christ is presented in scripture as his bride and his body, the sheep of God's flock and the branches of his vine, his new humanity, his household or family, the temple of the Holy Spirit, and the pillar and buttress of the truth, so the salvation of Christ is illustrated by the vivid imagery of terms like *propitiation, redemption, justification, and reconciliation,* which are to form the theme of this chapter. Moreover, although the images of the church are visually incompatible (one cannot envisage the body and the bride of Christ simultaneously), underlying them all is the truth that God is calling out a people for himself, so the images of salvation are incompatible (justification and redemption conjure up respectively the divergent worlds of law and commerce), yet underlying them all is the truth that God in Christ has borne our sin and died our death to set us free from sin and death.

Such images are indispensable aids to human understanding of doctrine. And what they convey, being God-given, is true. Yet we must not deduce from this that to have understood the images is to have exhausted the meaning of the doctrine. For beyond the images of the atonement lies the mystery of the atonement, the deep wonders of which, I guess, we shall be exploring throughout eternity.

Images of salvation (or of the atonement) is a better term than *theories*. This is because theories are usually abstract and speculative concepts, whereas the biblical images of the atoning achievement of Christ are concrete pictures and belong to the data of revelation. They are not alternative explanations of the cross, providing us with a range to choose from, but are complementary to one another, each contributing a vital part to the whole. As for the imagery, *propitiation* introduces us to rituals at a shrine, *redemption* to transactions in a marketplace, *justification* to proceedings in a court of law, and *reconciliation* to experiences in a home or family. My contention is that "substitution" is not a further "theory" or "image" to be set alongside the others, but rather the foundation of them all, without which each lacks cogency. If God in Christ did not die in our place, there could be neither propitiation, nor redemption, nor justification, nor reconciliation. In addition, all the images begin their life in the Old Testament but are elaborated and enriched in the New Testament, particularly by being directly related to Christ and his cross.[231]

Propitiation

Propitiation properly signifies the turning away of wrath by an offering. In the New Testament, this idea is conveyed by the use of *hilaskomai* (Heb. 2:17), *hilasterion* (Rom. 3:25), and *hilasmos* (1 John 2:2; 4:10)." The biblical terms for propitiation denote the fact that satisfaction was made for the sins of the world by Christ's death. The justice of God had been offended by the sin of humankind. The sin could not be retracted and the nature of God could not forgive the sinner without a payment of satisfaction. The price of satisfaction was the blood of Jesus Christ, and the act of satisfaction is propitiation. The Bible teaches that Jesus is the propitiation for the world. "He is the propitiation for our sin, and not for ours only but also for the sins of the whole world" (1 John 2:2; cf. 1 John 4:10; Heb. 9:5; Luke 18:13; Rom. 3:25).

The concept of propitiation involves the satisfying of God's just wrath against sin—by the holiness of Jesus Christ's death. Romans 3:25–26 declares the mercy, forbearance, and righteous justice of God in his setting forth of Christ to be our propitiation. God gave his Son for our sin. Christ did more than die for us; he turned around and gave himself up for God's wrath. This is the ultimate in love in that Christ, being God, went against his nature for us.

The necessity of propitiation is found in the holiness of God and the sinfulness of humankind. A holy God cannot look on sin. Neither can sin stand in the presence of God. "Our God is a consuming fire" (Heb. 12:29). The death of Jesus Christ satisfies the justice of God that must be poured upon sin. The coordinate reason for propitiation is the love of God as proclaimed in 1 John 4:10. A holy God could justly consign all sinful people to hopeless condemnation, but because of his love he provided a propitiation.

Hebrews 9:2–5 describes briefly the Old Testament tabernacle and its furnishings. Verse 5 speaks of the "mercy seat," which was a lid on the Ark of the Covenant. The terms *mercy seat* (*hilasterion*) and *propitiation* are synonymous. (Other verses that amplify this doctrine are Romans 3:25; 1 John 2:2; and 1 John 4:10.) In Luke 18:13 the praying publican realized that the law could never satisfy the demands of a holy God. Therefore, he prayed, "God, be merciful to me a sinner." The term *merciful* is *hilastheti*, and the verse may properly be translated as, "God be propitious (satisfied) to me a sinner." Today we would pray the publican's prayer: "Lord, look upon me as you would look upon the mercy seat of Christ's death, and be satisfied."

The demands of the law are satisfied. God's moral nature was offended when humankind broke God's law and partook of the fruit of the garden. Everyone sinned in Adam, the head of the human race, and was guilty before God.

The law condemned not only Adam but also every person who sinned, and it would continue condemning because of the demands of the law.

The law could not be abrogated because it was a reflection of God's holy character. The law demanded a penalty for every transgression. The law was a unit, and to break one law was to break all of the laws (James 2:10). Hence, the demand of all of the law was upon every person who broke any of it.

One aspect of the "good news" is that Jesus has satisfied all the demands of the law against all persons. He even satisfied the demands of the law against those who reject him.

Jesus nailed the demands of the law to the cross and made an end of the law (Col. 2:14–15; Eph. 2:15–16).

The law is no longer in effect as a moral judge to condemn humankind. Christ lifted the law from all (including the unsaved). This does not mean all will go to heaven. A person is no longer condemned for breaking the law; he or she is condemned for rejecting Jesus Christ.

Matthew 5:17 is one of the strongest New Testament statements attesting that Christ has satisfied all the demands of the law. In this verse, Jesus states, "Think not that I am come to destroy the law or the prophets: I am not come to destroy but to fulfill." The Greek word translated as "to fulfill" is an aorist infinitive of *pleroo* and denotes the idea of "carrying out" and "completion."

The goal of the mission of Jesus is fulfilment (Matt. 5:17b); according to Matthew 5:17a, this is primarily fulfillment of the law and the prophets, that is, of the whole of the Old Testament (IV, 1058, 15). He has come in order that God's Word may be completely fulfilled, in order that the full measure appointed by God himself may be reached in him.

His work is an act of obedience also and specifically in the fact that he fulfills God's promise (cf. Matt. 3:15). He actualizes the divine will stated in the Old Testament from the standpoint of both promise and demand.[232]

The demands of the law include total obedience and absolute righteousness (James 2:10; 1 Pet. 1:15–16; Lev. 11:44). Romans 10:4 declares, "For Christ is the end of the law for righteousness to everyone that believeth." In regard to this verse, F. F. Bruce notes the following:

> The word *end* (*telos*) has a double sense; it may mean "goal" or "termination." On the other band, Christ is the goal at which the law aimed in that he is the embodiment of perfect righteousness, having "magnified the law and made it honorable" (cf. Isa. 42:21). On the other hand (and

this is the primary force of Paul's words), Christ is the termination of the law in the sense that with him the old order, of which the law formed part, has been done away, to be replaced by the new order of the Spirit. In this new order, life and righteousness are available through faith in Christ; therefore, no one need attempt any more to win these blessings by means of the law.[233]

It should be noted that in satisfying the demands of the law, Christ did not "destroy" (Matt. 5:17) or abolish the law. The law has a use today. Galatians 3:19–25 says that the law serves as a schoolmaster to show us we are sinners. First Timothy 1:8–10 also speaks of the law as good in that it shows sinners their sin.

Two abuses of the law are (1) its use as a means of salvation and (2) its use as a means of achieving spiritually. The law was never intended to give salvation, only to show the need for God's grace. And people who think they are going to become spiritual by keeping the law are Pharisees. Spirituality is of the Holy Spirit and one cannot become spiritual apart from the Holy Spirit.[234]

Christians of Early Generation's Concept

Western Christians of earlier generations were quite familiar with the language of propitiation in relation to the death of Christ. This is because the Authorized (King James) Version of the Bible, on which they were brought up, contained three explicit affirmations of it by Paul and John:

- Paul: "Christ Jesus, whom God hath set forth to be a propitiation through faith in his blood" (Rom. 3:24–25).[235]
- John: "We have an advocate with the Father, Jesus Christ the righteous: and he is the propitiation for our sins" (1 John 2:1–2).
- John: "Herein is love, not that we loved God, but that he loved us, and sent his Son to be the propitiation for our sins" (1 John 4:10).

Although this language was well-known to our forebears, they were not necessarily comfortable in using it. To "propitiate" somebody means to appease or pacify his or her anger. Does God then get angry? If so, can offerings or rituals assuage his anger? Does he accept bribes? Such concepts sound more pagan than Christian. It is understandable that primitive animists should consider it essential to placate the wrath of gods, spirits or ancestors, but are notions like these worthy of the Christian God? Should we not have grown out of them? In particular, are we really to believe that Jesus by his death propitiated the Father's anger, inducing him to turn from it and to look upon us with favor instead?

Crude concepts of anger, sacrifice, and propitiation are indeed to be rejected. They do not belong to the religion of the Old Testament, let alone to the religion of the New Testament. This does not mean, however, that there is no biblical concept of these things at all.

What is revealed to us in scripture is a pure doctrine (from which all pagan vulgarities have been expunged) of God's holy wrath, his loving self-sacrifice in Christ, and his initiative to avert his own anger. It is obvious that wrath and propitiation (the latter being the placating of wrath) go together. It is when the wrath is purged of unworthy ideas that the propitiation is thereby purged. The opposite is also true. It is those who cannot come to terms with any concept of the wrath of God who repudiate any concept of propitiation. Here, for example, is Professor A. T. Hanson's view: "If you think of the wrath as an attitude of God, you cannot avoid some theory of propitiation. But the wrath in the New Testament is never spoken of as being propitiated, because it is not conceived of as being an attitude of God."[236]

It is this discomfort with the doctrines of wrath and propitiation that has led some theologians to examine the biblical vocabulary. They have concentrated on a particular word group that the Authorized Version translates in "propitiatory" terms, namely the noun *hilasmos* (1 John 2:2; 1 John 4:10), the adjective *hilasterios* (Rom. 3:25, where it may be used as a noun), and the verb *hilaskomai* (Heb. 2:17; also Luke 18:13 in the passive, which should perhaps be rendered "be propitiated—or propitious—to me, a sinner"). The crucial question is whether the object of the atoning action is God or humans. If the former, then the right word is *propitiation* (appeasing God); if the latter, the right word is *expiation* (dealing with sin and guilt).

If we are to develop a truly biblical doctrine of propitiation, it will be necessary to distinguish it from pagan ideas at three crucial points, relating to why propitiation is necessary, who made it, and what it was.

First, the reason why propitiation is necessary is that sin arouses the wrath of God. This does not mean (as animists fear) that he is likely to fly off the handle at the most trivial provocation, still less that he loses his temper for no apparent reason at all. For there is nothing capricious or arbitrary about the holy God. Nor is he ever irascible, malicious, spiteful, or vindictive. His anger is neither mysterious nor irrational. It is never unpredictable, but always predicable, because it is provoked by evil, and evil alone. The wrath of God is his steady, unrelenting, unremitting, uncompromising antagonism to evil in all its forms and manifestations. In short, God's anger is poles apart from ours. What provokes our anger (injured vanity) never provokes his; what provokes his anger (evil) seldom provokes ours.

Second, who makes the propitiation? In a pagan context it is always human beings who seek to avert the divine anger either by the meticulous performance of rituals, or by the recitation of magic formulae, or by the offering of sacrifices (vegetable, animal, or even human). Such practices are thought to placate the offended deity. But the gospel begins with the outspoken assertion that nothing we can do, say, offer, or even contribute can compensate for our sins or turn away God's anger. There is no possibility of persuading, cajoling, or bribing God to forgive us, because we deserve nothing at his hands but judgment. Nor, as we have seen, has Christ by his sacrifice prevailed on God to pardon us. No, the initiative has been taken by God himself in his sheer mercy and grace.

This was already clear in the Old Testament, in which the sacrifices were recognized not as human works but as divine gifts. They did not make God gracious; they were provided by a gracious God in order that he might act graciously toward his sinful people. "I have given it to you," God said of the sacrificial blood, "to make atonement for yourselves on the altar" (Lev 17:11). And this truth is yet more plainly recognized in the New Testament, not least in the main texts about propitiation. God himself "presented" or "put forward" (RSV) Jesus Christ as a propitiatory sacrifice (Rom. 3:25). It is not that we loved God but that he loved us and sent his Son as a propitiation for our sins (1 John 4:10). It cannot be emphasized too strongly that God's love is the source, not the consequence, of the atonement. As P. T. Forsyth expressed it, "The atonement did not procure grace, it flowed from grace."[237]

God does not love us because Christ died for us; Christ died for us because God loved us. If it is God's wrath that needed to be propitiated, it is God's love that did the propitiating. If it may be said that the propitiation "changed" God, or that by it he changed himself, let us be clear: he did not change from wrath to love, or from enmity to grace, since his character is unchanging. What the propitiation changed was his dealings with us. "The distinction I ask you to observe," wrote P.T. Forsyth, "is between a change of feeling and a change of treatment. ... God's feeling toward us never needed to be changed. But God's treatment of us, God's practical relation to us— that had to change."[238] He forgave us and welcomed us home.

Third, what was the propitiatory sacrifice? It was neither an animal, nor a vegetable, nor a mineral. It was not a thing at all, but a person. And the person God offered was not somebody else, whether a human person, or an angel, or even his Son considered as somebody distinct from or external to himself. No, he offered himself. In giving his Son, he was giving himself.

As Karl Barth wrote repeatedly, "It was the Son of God, i.e., God himself." For example, "The fact that it was God's Son, that it was God himself, who took our place on Golgotha and thereby freed us from the divine anger and judgment, reveals first the full implication of the wrath of God, of his condemning and punishing justice." Barth also argued as follows:

> Because it was the Son of God, i.e., God himself, who took our place on Good Friday, the substitution could be effectual and procure our reconciliation with the righteous God. ... Only God, our Lord and Creator, could stand surety for us, could take our place, could suffer eternal death in our stead as the consequence of our sin in such a way that it was finally suffered and overcome.[239]

And all this, Barth makes clear, was an expression not only of God's holiness and justice but also of "the perfections of the divine loving," indeed of God's "holy love."

So then, God himself is at the heart of our answer to all three questions about the divine propitiation. It is God himself who in holy wrath needs to be propitiated, God himself who in holy love undertook to do the propitiating, and God himself who in the person of his Son died for the propitiation of our sins. Thus God took his own loving initiative to appease his own righteous anger by bearing it his own self in his own Son when he took our place and died for us. There is no crudity here to evoke our ridicule, only the profundity of holy love to evoke our worship.

In seeking thus to defend and reinstate the biblical doctrine of propitiation, we have no intention of denying the biblical doctrine of expiation. Although we must resist every attempt to replace propitiation by expiation, we welcome every attempt to see them as belonging together in salvation. Thus F. Buchsel wrote that "*hilasmos* ... is the action in which God is propitiated and sin expiated."[240] Dr. David Wells has elaborated this succinctly:

> In Pauline thought, humankind is alienated from God by sin and God is alienated from humanity by wrath. It is in the substitutionary death of Christ that sin is overcome and wrath averted, so that God can look on humankind without displeasure and humankind can look on God without fear. Sin is expiated and God is propitiated.[241]

Redemption

We now move on from propitiation to redemption. In seeking to understand the achievement of the cross, the imagery changes from temple court to marketplace, from the ceremonial realm to the commercial, from religious rituals to business transactions. At its most basic, to redeem is to buy or buy back, whether as a purchase or a ransom. Inevitably, then, the emphasis of the redemption image is on our sorry state—indeed our captivity—in sin, which made an act of divine rescue necessary. Propitiation focuses on the wrath of God that was placated by the cross, on redemption on the plight of sinners from which they were ransomed by the cross.

And *ransom* is the correct word to use. The Greek words *lytroo* (usually translated "redeem") and *apolytrosis* ("redemption") are derived from *lytron* ("a ransom" or "price of release"), which was almost a technical term in the ancient world for the purchase or manumission of a slave. In view of "the unwavering usage of profane authors," namely that this word group refers to "a process involving release by payment of a ransom price,"[242] often very costly, wrote Dr. Leon Morris, we have no liberty to dilute its meaning into a vague and even cheap deliverance. We have been "ransomed" by Christ, not merely "redeemed" or "delivered" by him. B. B. Warfield was right to point out that we are "assisting at the death bed of a word. It is said to witness the death of any worthy thing—even of a worthy word. And worthy words do die, like any other worthy thing—if we do not take good care of them."[243]

Sadder still is "the dying out of the hearts of men of the things for which the words stand."[244] Here Warfield was referring to his generation's loss of a sense of gratitude to him who paid our ransom. In the Old Testament, property, animals, persons, and the nation were all "redeemed" by the payment of a price.

The right (even the duty) to play the role of kinsman redeemer and buy back a property that had been alienated, in order to keep it in the family or tribe, was illustrated in the case of both Boaz and Jeremiah.[245]

When we enter the New Testament and consider its teaching about redemption, two changes immediately strike us. Although it is still inherent in the concept both that those needing redemption are in a bad plight and that they can be redeemed only by the payment of a price, now the plight is moral rather than material, and the price is the atoning death of God's Son. This much is already evident in Jesus's famous "ransom saying," which is foundational to the New Testament doctrine of redemption: "The Son of Man did not come to be served, but to serve, and to give his life as a ransom for many" (Mark 10:45). The imagery implies that we are held in captivity from which only the payment of a ransom can set us free, and that the ransom is nothing less than the Messiah's own life. Our lives are forfeit; his life will be sacrificed instead.[246]

Justification

The two pictures we have so far considered have led us into the temple precincts (propitiation) and the marketplace (redemption). The third image (justification) will take us into the court of law. Justification is the opposite of condemnation (e.g., Rom. 5:18; Rom. 8:34), and both are verdicts of a judge who pronounces the accused either guilty or not guilty. There is logic in the order in which we are reviewing these great words that describe the achievement of the cross. Propitiation inevitably comes first, because until the wrath of God is appeased (that is, until his love has found a way to avert his anger), there can be no salvation for human beings at all. Next, when we are ready to understand the meaning of salvation, we begin negatively with redemption, meaning our rescue at the high price of Christ's blood from the grim captivity of sin and guilt. Justification is its positive counterpart.

The vocabulary of justification and condemnation occurs regularly in the Old Testament. Moses gave instructions to the Israelite judges that they were to decide cases referred to them, "acquitting [i.e., justifying] the innocent and condemning the guilty" (Deut. 25:1). Everybody knew that Yahweh would never "acquit [justify] the guilty" (Exod. 23:7), and that "acquitting the guilty and condemning the innocent—the Lord detests them both" (Prov. 17). The prophet Isaiah pronounced a fierce woe against magistrates who "acquit the guilty for a bribe, but deny justice to the innocent" (Isa. 5:23). To condemn the righteous and justify the unrighteous would be to turn the administration of justice on its head. It is against this background of accepted judicial practice that Paul must have shocked his Roman readers when he wrote, "God ... justifies the wicked" (Rom. 4:5).

How could God conceivably do such a thing? It was outrageous that the divine Judge should practice what—in the very same Greek words—he had forbidden human judges to do. Besides, how could the Righteous One declare the unrighteous righteous? The very thought was preposterous.

In order to summarize Paul's defense of the divine justification of sinners, I will select four of his key phrases relating successively to justification's source, ground, means, and effects.

First, the *source* of our justification is indicated in the expression *justified by his grace* (Rom. 3:24), that is, by his utterly undeserved favor.

Since it is certain that "there is no one righteous, not even one" (Rom. 3:10), it is equally certain that no one can declare herself to be righteous in God's sight.[247] Self-justification is a sheer impossibility (Rom. 3:20). Therefore, "it is God who justifies" (Rom. 8:33); only he can. And he does it "freely" (Rom. 3:24—*dorean*, "as a free gift, gratis"), not because of any works of ours, but because of his own grace. In Tom Wright's neat epigram, "No sin, no need for justification: no grace, no possibility of it."[248]

Grace is one thing; however, justice is another. And justification has to do with justice. To say that we are "justified by his grace" tells us the source of our justification but says nothing about a righteous basis of it, without which God would contradict his own justice. So another key expression of Paul's, one that introduces us to the *ground* of our justification, is *justified by his blood* (Rom. 5:9). *Justification* is not a synonym for *amnesty*, which strictly is pardon without principle, a forgiveness that overlooks—even forgets (*amnestia* is "forgetfulness")—wrongdoing and declines to bring it to justice. No, justification is an act of justice, of gracious justice. Its synonym is "the righteousness of God" (Rom. 1:17; Rom. 3:21), which might for the moment be explained as his "righteous way of righteousing the unrighteous." Dr. J. I. Packer defines it as "God's gracious work of bestowing upon guilty sinners a justified justification, acquitting them in the court of heaven without prejudice to his justice as their Judge."[249]

When God justifies sinners, he is not declaring bad people to be good or saying that they are not sinners after all; he is pronouncing them legally righteous, free from any liability to the broken law, because he himself in his Son has borne the penalty of their lawbreaking. That's why Paul is able to bring together in a single sentence the concepts of justification, redemption, and propitiation (Rom. 3:24–25). The reasons why we are "justified freely by God's grace" are that Christ Jesus paid the ransom price and that God presented him as a propitiatory sacrifice. In other words, we are "justified by his blood." There could be no justification without atonement.

Third, the *means* of our justification is indicated in Paul's favorite expression, *justified by faith*.[250] Grace and faith belong indissolubly to one another, since faith's only function is to receive what grace freely offers. We are not, therefore, justified by our faith, as we are justified by God's grace and by Christ's blood. God's grace is the source and Christ's blood the ground of our justification; faith is only the means by which we are united to Christ. As Richard Hooker put it with his usual precision, "God doth justify the believing man, yet not for the worthiness of his belief, but for his worthiness who is believed."[251]

Reconciliation

The word *reconciliation* is not found in the Hebrew text of the Old Testament, but it is found in the English text in such places as, "Poured the blood at the bottom of the altar, and sanctified it, to make reconciliation upon it" (Lev. 8:15), and "Seventy weeks are determined upon thy people ... to make reconciliation for iniquity" (Dan. 9:24). The word *kaphar* is used in these Old Testament references, translated as the word *atonement*. Here, the translators are substituting the word *reconciliation* for a specific aspect of the atonement.[252] Brown, Driver, and Briggs correctly define *kaphar* to mean "to cover, to wash away, to pacify, to obliterate."[253]

In the New Testament, Paul's use of the word for reconciliation, *katallage*, has the concept of God taking people up again into fellowship with him.[254] Paul notes this meaning: "You, that were sometime alienated and enemies in your mind by wicked works, yet now hath he reconciled" (Col. 1:21). Therefore in the act of reconciliation, humankind is reunited with God. The implication is that humankind, once in favor with God (in the garden), is now reunited to fellowship with God in the death of Jesus Christ. Again Paul says, "That he might reconcile both unto God in one body" (Eph. 2:16). Whereas the rebellious sinner was previously disapproved and dispatched from a positive relationship with God, he or she is now rendered "no longer disapproved." Now humankind is in a favorable position with God because of reconciliation.

This does not imply humankind is saved. Humankind is placed in a savable position, but human beings must choose to be saved. One must guard against assuming that those after the cross are in a better position than those who preceded the cross. God is able to look at the Old Testament saint in anticipation of Christ's death as easily as he sees the New Testament saint in the shadow of the cross.

In the act of salvation, God looks at the blood of his Son (redemption); God's wrath is satisfied (proposition); the broken law no longer accuses the offender; and therefore, God no longer views humankind as an alien and rebel. The result of this is the act of reconciliation. Human beings are now savable because they are in a savable position to God. However, the act of reconciliation does not make a human being a child of God, which implies regeneration, because that would be universalism (i.e., all are saved because of the death of Christ), but all can now come to the Father through Jesus Christ (John 14:6) by accepting Jesus Christ (John 1:12).

The Bible never teaches that God is reconciled. In the famous hymn "And Can It Be," Charles Wesley uses the phrase, "My God is reconciled," when in reality humankind is reconciled when God is propitiated. John Murray in his book *Redemption Accomplished and Applied* has aptly stated the following:

> Reconciliation presupposes disrupted relations between God and humanity. It implies enmity and alienation. This alienation is twofold, our alienation from God and God's alienation from us. The cause of the alienation is, of cause, our sin, but the alienation consists not only in our unholy enmity against God but also God's holy alienation from us.[255]

With the death of Christ, God's holy enmity toward humankind was terminated. Humankind was positionally reconciled to God. However, actual reconciliation occurs when the sinner applies the atoning blood of Christ to his or her life. The doctrine of reconciliation is not an experiential doctrine that works out into person's lifestyle. Instead, reconciliation is a change in relationship that is enacted in heaven.

The object of reconciliation is the world, as Paul writes, "That God was in Christ, reconciling the world unto himself" (2 Cor. 5:19). There is a double transference associated with the act of reconciliation. First, our sins were imputed to Jesus Christ, "for he hath made him to be sin for us" (2 Cor. 5:21). The second act of imputation is, "that we might be made the righteousness of God in him" (2 Cor. 5:21).

In the act of salvation, the righteousness of Jesus Christ was placed on the account of the sinner, and in reverse, the sins of sinners were assumed by Jesus Christ when he died for the sins of the world.

It is noteworthy to realize that the tense of the verb *reconciled* suggests that this work is specifically a work of God and is completed. Therefore, unregenerate humankind today is not guilty of sin under the Old Testament law. Rather, humankind's guilt and punishment stems from a rejection of Christ as personal Savior and Lord.

A sinner may feel that God does not love him or that God is not close to him. However, the sinner cannot determine God's perspective on him solely by his feeling. He is as close to God as Jesus Christ. When Adam sinned in the garden, human beings turned their backs on God and God tuned his back on humankind. However, in the death of Jesus Christ, God turned around (propitiation) and now no longer has anger toward humankind. Reconciliation means God has favor and mercy toward humankind and that humankind is in a position to be saved. However, human beings must call upon the Lord and be converted.

Judgment of the Sinful Nature

The judgment of the sinful nature is a positional result where Jesus Christ in his death paid the penalty for sin and dealt judicially with the believer's old nature.

Every person is a sinner on three accounts: First, every person is guilty of personal sin (1 John 1:10). Personal sin is an act of rebellion against God in thought and deed. It includes sins of omission or commission. Individuals are fully responsible for these sins. The penalty for personal sins is separation from God. The consequences of personal sin include both earthly results and eternal punishment. The remedy for personal sin is the substitutionary death of Jesus. By faith in Christ, people are forgiven and thus redeemed.

Second, a person is a sinner because of imputed sin. This has to do with the individual's standing in heaven. Adam sinned, and therefore death came (Rom. 5:12). The penalty for imputed sin is physical death. There are two ways that imputed sin is transmitted, either the federal headship or the seminal headship. The federal headship view states that the transmission of imputed sin is from Adam directly to me. The seminal headship view states that the transmission of imputed sin was from Adam, to my successive ancestors, and through them to me. The remedy for imputed sin is Jesus's righteousness imputed to us.

Third, a person is a sinner because of his or her sinful nature. Every individual is born with a sinful nature inherited from his or her parents (1 John 1:8; Ps. 51:5). This sinful nature is the tendency to do evil. The penalty for the sinful nature is spiritual and physical death. The sinful nature is transmitted through the father to the child. The remedy for the sinful nature is that it was judged at the cross. The key verse is Romans 6:6, in which it is evident that the sinful nature already has been judged. "Knowing this, that our old man [the sinful nature] is crucified with him, that the body of sin might be destroyed, that henceforth we should not serve sin" (Rom. 6:6).

Although the desire and ability to sin will remain in the Christian as long as he or she dwells here on earth in a mortal body, Christ's death effected the legal pronouncement that the old (sinful) nature is dead. Romans 6:1–16 describes the death of the sinful nature and also prescribes the course of action for each Christian to take when faced with his or her own sinful nature: the judgment of the sinful nature is a judicial view by which God enables believers to accomplish practical holiness in their lives (1 Pet. 1:14–15) by realizing that their old (sinful) nature was "crucified with Christ" (Rom. 6:6; Gal. 2:20; 2 Cor. 5:17; Rom. 8:1).

Basis for Daily Cleansing

When Christ died for the sin of the world, he dealt with the legal and judicial obligation to God. This was not a limited act; instead, Christ dealt with all sin of all humankind of all ages. When the believer accepts Jesus Christ as his or her Savior, the moral implications of the transaction are applied to his or her account. The person is justified (nonexperiential) and given a new nature (experiential). But what about the sins that are committed by the Christian after he or she becomes saved?

TABLE 16.1.

Romans 6:1–6
Know – verse 9
Reckon – verse 11
Yield – verse 13
Obey – verse 16

There is a difference between judicial and personal guilt. Judicial guilt is the nonexperiential condition of the sinner who stands guilty before God. This person was born in sin, has a sinful nature, and personally commits sin. At Calvary, this individual's relationship to God has changed, and she no longer is guilty. However, personal guilt is experiential in nature and becomes a means by which a sinner is convicted of her sins. When the Christian consciously sins, she will experience personal guilt (if she has not hardened her conscience) but will not have judicial guilt again.

The Basis of Forgiving Sins Committed Before Christ Died on the Cross

Many Christians have wrongly thought that the blood of lambs sacrificed in the Old Testament was the basis for forgiving sin. Some are just as wrong in thinking that when a Jew attempted to keep the law, it was the basis of his or her sanctification. In every dispensation, a person was saved by faith through grace. A person kept the law as an expression of his or her obedience to and fellowship with God, and on the same basis he or she offered the blood sacrifice to God. It is not possible that "the blood of bulls and goats could take away sins" (Heb. 10:4).

The blood sacrifice of lamb was a type that pictured the coming "lamb of God that taketh away the sin of the world" (John 1:20). As a prefigure, it portrayed the coming sacrifice that atoned for the sin of the world. In one aspect, the sin was covered (the Old Testament meaning for *atonement* is "to cover," *kaphar*) until Christ "took away sin" (John 1:29).

Paul reminds us, "Whom God hath set forth to be a propitiation through faith in his blood, to declare his righteousness for the remission of sins that are past" (Rom. 3:25). In this sense, Christ dealt with the sin that was committed before Calvary.

The etymological aspect of *kaphar* has been aptly stated by Lewis Sperry Chafer. He wrote as follows:

> The Hebrew word *kaphar* express with divine accuracy precisely what took place on the Godward side of the transaction. The sin was covered, but not "taken away," pending the foreseen death of Christ.
>
> To translate *kaphar* by "atonement," which etymologically may mean at-one-ment, could truthfully convey no more than that the offender was at one with God by a transaction which rested only on a symbolism. On the human side, the offender was pardoned; but on the divine side the transaction was lacking the one and only act which could make it conform to the requirements of infinite holiness.[256]

A famous evangelist tells the story of taking a light tan suit on an ocean cruise. He planned to wear the suit when preaching each evening, but he spilled food on the suit the first night and the spot wouldn't come out. His wife used her talcum powder to cover the spot so he could wear the suit, but the powder came out. Each night he had to re-cover the spot with talcum powder. In the same way, the blood atonement covered the Old Testament sin, and, since the sacrifice was not permanent, the saint had to continually bring a blood sacrifice. But Christ "was once offered to bear the sins of many: and unto them that look for him shall he appear the second time without sin unto salvation" (Heb. 9:28).

The fourth image of salvation, which illustrates the achievement of the cross, is reconciliation. It is probably the most popular of the four because it is the most personal. We have left behind us the temple precincts, the slave market, and the courts of law; we are now in our own home with our family and friends. True, there is a quarrel, even enmity, but to reconcile means to restore a relationship, to renew a friendship. So an original relationship is presupposed, which, having been broken, has been recovered by Christ

The first thing that has to be said about the biblical gospel of reconciliation, however, is that it begins with reconciliation to God and continues with a reconciled community in Christ. *Reconciliation* is not a term the Bible uses to describe "coming to terms with oneself," although it does insist that it is only through losing ourselves in love for God and neighbor that we truly find ourselves.

Reconciliation with God, then, is the beginning. This is the meaning of atonement. It alludes to the event through which God and human beings, previously alienated from one another, are made "at one" again. The word occurs only once in the New Testament's Authorized (King James) Version, namely in the statement that through Christ "we have now received the atonement" (Rom. 5:11), that is to say, "the reconciliation." It is significant that in Romans 5:9–11, which is one of the four great passages on reconciliation in the New Testament, to be reconciled and to be justified are parallels. "Since we have now been justified by his blood" is balanced by "if, when we were God's enemies, we were reconciled to him through the death of his Son." The two states, although both are affected by the cross, are not identical, however.

Justification is our legal standing before our judge in the court; reconciliation is our personal relationship with our Father in the home. Indeed, the latter is the sequel and fruit of the former. It is only when we have been justified by faith that we have peace with God (Rom. 5:1), which is reconciliation.[257]

Two other New Testament terms confirm this emphasis that reconciliation means peace with God, namely *adoption* and *access*. With regard to the former, it was Jesus himself who always addressed God intimately as "Abba, Father," who gave us permission to do the same, approaching him as "our Father in heaven." The apostles enlarged on the concept. John, who attributes our being children of God to our being born of God, expresses his sense of wonder that the Father should have loved us enough to call us, and indeed make us, his children (John 1:12–13; 1 John 3:1–10). Paul, on the other hand, traces our status as God's children to our adoption rather than to our new birth, and emphasizes the privileges we have in being sons and daughters instead of slaves, and therefore God's heirs as well (e.g., Rom. 8:14–17; Gal. 3:26–29; Gal. 4:1–7).

Access (*prosagoge*) to God is another blessing of reconciliation. It seems to denote the active communion with God, especially in prayer, that his reconciled children enjoy. Twice, Paul brackets "access to God" and "peace with God," the first time attributing them to our justification rather than to our reconciliation (Rom. 5:1–2), and the second time explaining "access" as a Trinitarian experience in that we have access to the Father through the Son by the Spirit (Eph. 2:17–18) and "we may approach God with freedom and confidence" (Eph. 3:12). Peter uses the cognate verb, declaring that it was in order to "bring" us to God (*prosago*) that Christ died for us once for all, the righteous instead of the unrighteous (1 Pet. 3:18). And the writer to the Hebrews borrows from the Day of Atonement ritual in order to convey the nearness to God that Christ by his sacrifice and priesthood has made possible. "Since we have confidence to enter the Most Holy Place by the blood of Jesus," he (or perhaps she) writes, "let us draw near to God with a sincere heart in full assurance of faith" (Heb. 10:19–22).

Thus, reconciliation, peace with God, adoption into his family, and access into his presence all bear witness to the same new relationship into which God has brought us.

But reconciliation has a horizontal as well as a vertical plane. God has reconciled us to one another in his new community, as well as to himself. A second great New Testament passage (Eph. 2:11–22) focuses on this, and in particular on the healing of the breach between Jews and Gentiles, so that sometimes it is not clear which reconciliation Paul is referring to. He reminds his Gentile Christian readers that formerly they were on the one hand "excluded from citizenship in Israel and foreigners to the covenants of promise" and on the other "separate from Christ ... and without God in the world" (Eph. 2:12). So they were "far away" from both God and Israel, doubly alienated; "but now in Christ Jesus," he goes on, "you who once were far away have been brought near through the blood of Christ"—near to God and near to Israel (Eph. 2:13). In fact, Christ, who "himself is our peace," has broken down the barrier between these two halves of the human race and has "made the two one" (Eph. 2:14). He has both "abolished" the law's regulations, which kept them apart, and "created" in himself "one new man out of the two, thus making peace" (Eph. 2:15). Knowing the mutual bitterness and contempt that Jews and Gentiles felt for each other, this reconciliation was a miracle of God's grace and power. It has resulted in the emergence of a single, new, unified humanity whose members through the cross have been reconciled both to God and to one another. Formerly enemies, they have had their reciprocal hostility put to death. They are now fellow citizens in God's kingdom, brothers and sisters in God's family (Eph. 2:19), fellow members of Christ's body, sharing together in the messianic promise (Eph. 3:16). This complete equality of Jew and Gentile in the new community is the "mystery" that for centuries had been kept secret but that now God has revealed to the apostles, especially to Paul, the apostle to the Gentiles (Eph. 3:4–6).

There are four principal New Testament images of salvation, taken from the shrine, the market, the court of law, and the home. Their pictorial nature makes it impossible to integrate them neatly with one another. Temple sacrifices, legal verdicts, the slave in the market, and the child in the home all clearly belong to different worlds. Nevertheless, certain themes emerge from all four images.

First, each highlights a different aspect of our human need. Propitiation underscores the wrath of God upon us; redemption, our captivity to sin; justification, our guilt; and reconciliation, our enmity against God and alienation from him. These metaphors do not flatter us. They expose the magnitude of our need.

Second, all four images emphasize that the saving initiative was taken by God in his love. It is he who has propitiated his own wrath, redeemed us from our miserable bondage, declared us righteous in his sight, and reconciled us to himself. Relevant texts leave us in no doubt about this: "God ... loved us, and sent his Son to be the propitiation for our sins" (1 John 4:10 AV); "God ... has come and has redeemed his people" (Luke 1:68); "It is God who justifies" (Rom. 8:33); "God ... reconciled us to himself through Christ" (2 Cor. 5:18).

Third, all four images plainly teach that God's saving work was achieved through the bloodshedding, that is, the substitutionary sacrifice of Christ. With regard to the blood of Christ, the texts are again unequivocal. "God presented him as a propitiatory sacrifice, through faith in his blood" (Rom. 3:25); "In him we have redemption through his blood" (Eph. 1:7); "We have now been justified by his blood" (Rom. 5:9); "You who once were far away have been brought near [i.e., reconciled] through the blood of Christ" (Eph. 2:13; cf. Col. 1:20). Since Christ's blood is a symbol of his life laid down in violent death, it is also plain in each of the four images that he died in our place as our substitute. The death of Jesus was the atoning sacrifice because of which God averted his wrath from us, the ransom price by which we have been redeemed, the condemnation of the innocent that the guilty might be justified, and the sinless One being made sin for us.

So substitution is not a "theory of the atonement," nor is it even an additional image to take its place as an option alongside the others. It is rather the essence of each image and the heart of the atonement itself. None of the four images could stand without it. I am not of course saying that it is necessary to understand, let alone articulate, a substitutionary atonement before one can be saved. Yet the responsibility of Christian teachers, preachers, and other witnesses is to seek grace to expound it with clarity and conviction. The better people understand the glory of the divine substitution, the easier it will be for them to trust in the Substitute.[258]

CHAPTER 17

The Savior of the World

The New Testament's contribution to the understanding of salvation lies in its witness to Jesus, the Christ (Messiah), the Savior of the World (John 4:42; Luke 2:11). Jesus (which name means "to save") was born to save his people from their sin (Matt. 1:21). It is Jesus, and Jesus alone, who is the agent of God's salvation (Acts 4:12).[259]

The Nature of God

The nature of God is of perfect and complete holiness. This is not an optional or arbitrary matter; it is the way God is by nature. Being contrary to God's nature, sin is repulsive to him. He is allergic to sin, so to speak. He cannot look upon it.

Status of the Law

The second major factor to be considered as we construct our theory of the atonement is the status of God's moral and spiritual law. The law should not be thought of as something impersonal and foreign to God, but as the expression of God's person and will. He does not command love and forbid murder simply because he decides to do so. His very nature issues in his enjoining certain actions and prohibiting others. God pronounces love good because he himself is love. On the contrary, lying is wrong because God himself cannot lie. This means that, in effect, the law is something of a transcript of the nature of God.

The Human Condition

Another crucial factor in our understanding of the atonement is the nature and condition of humanity. We noted earlier (pp. 643–48) the fact of total depravity, by which we meant not that humans are as wicked as they can possibly be, but rather that they are utterly unable to do anything to save themselves or to extricate themselves from their condition of sinfulness. Since this is true, it follows that the atonement, to accomplish for humanity what needed to be done, had to be made by someone else on humankind's behalf.

Christ

Our understanding of Christ's nature is crucial here. Earlier we stated that Christ is both God and human (chapter 13). He is the eternal preexistent second person of the Trinity. He is God in the same sense and to the same degree as is the Father, a sense in which no other human has ever been or will ever be divine. To his deity he added humanity. He did not give up his deity in any respect; he only gave up the independent exercise of his divine attributes.

In our understanding, Jesus's humanity means that his atoning death is applicable to human beings. Because Jesus was really one of us, he was able to redeem us. He was not an outsider attempting to do something for us. He was a genuine human being representing the rest of us. This is implied in what Paul says in Galatians 4:4–5: "God sent forth his Son … born under law, to redeem those under law."

Not only is Jesus human, but also he is *completely* human. He took not merely the physical nature of a human being but also the full psychological makeup of humanity. He felt the full gamut of normal human emotions. Thus he was able to redeem all of human nature, because he assumed all of what it means to be truly human.

In addition, Jesus's death is of sufficient value to atone for the entire human race. The death of an ordinary human could scarcely have sufficient value to cover that individual's own sins, let alone those of the whole race. But Jesus's death is of infinite worth. As God, Jesus did not have to die. In dying, he did something God would never have to do. Because he was sinless, he did not have to die in payment for his own sins. Thus his death can atone for the sins of all of humankind.

The Pauline Writings

When we turn to Paul's writings, we find a rich collection of teaching on the atonement, teaching that conforms with what the Gospels say on the subject. Paul also identifies and equates Jesus's love and working with that of the Father. Numerous texts can be cited: "God was reconciling the world to himself in Christ" (2 Cor. 5:19); "But God demonstrates his own love for us in this: While we were still sinners, Christ died for us" (Rom. 5:8); "For what the law was powerless to do in that it was weakened by the sinful nature, God did by sending his own Son in the likeness of sinful man to be a sin offering. And so he condemned sin in sinful man" (Rom. 8:3); "He who did not spare his own Son, but gave him up for us all—how will he not also, along with him, graciously give us all things" (Rom. 8:32)?

Paul frequently thought of and referred to the death of Christ as a sacrifice. In Ephesians 5:2, he describes it as "a fragrant offering and sacrifice to God." In 1 Corinthians 5:7, he writes, "For Christ, our Passover lamb, has been sacrificed." His numerous references to Christ's blood also suggest a sacrifice: there was "a sacrifice of atonement, through faith in his blood" (Rom. 3:25). "We have now been justified by his blood" (Rom. 5:9); "In him we have redemption through his blood" (Eph. 1:7); we "have been brought near through the blood of Christ" (Eph. 2:13); he has reconciled to himself all things, "making peace through his blood, shed on the cross" (Col. 1:20).[260] Ladd has pointed out, however, that there was very little actual shedding of Christ's blood as such.[261]

While there was a loss of blood when the crown of thorns was put on Jesus's head and when the nails were driven into his flesh, it was not until after he had died that blood (mixed with water) gushed forth (John 19:34). So the references to Christ's blood are not to his actual physical blood per se, but to his death as a sacrificial provision for our sins.

Finally, Paul regards Christ's death as propitiatory; that is, Christ died to appease God's wrath against sin.

Reconciliation

The death of Christ also brings to an end the enmity and estrangement that exist between God and humankind. Our hostility toward God is removed.

The emphasis in scripture is usually that we are reconciled to God, that is, he plays the active role; he reconciles us to himself.

Penal Substitution

By Jesus Christ's offering himself as a sacrifice, by his substituting himself for us, actually bearing the punishment that should have been ours, he appeased the Father and effected a reconciliation between God and humanity.

The Atonement as a Demonstration of God's Love

It is true that the death of Christ is a powerful demonstration of the love of God and therefore a strong motivating incentive for us to love God and be reconciled to him. But once again, the valid insight of the theory is dependent on the fact that he died *for us.*

According to the moral-influence theory, Christ's death was not necessary in an objective sense—that is to say, God could have forgiven us our sins without the death of Jesus. There was no inherent obstacle to his simply forgiving us or, more correctly, simply accepting us back into fellowship with him. There was no need for retribution. But in that case, would we look upon Christ's death as a demonstration of love or an act of foolishness? The death of Christ is a beautiful demonstration of God's love and thus a powerful incentive to us to abandon our hostility toward God and respond in repentance and faith to the offer of grace.

The Implications of Substitutionary Atonement

The substitutionary theory of the atoning death of Christ, when grasped in all its complexity, is a rich and meaningful truth. It carries several major implications for our understanding of salvation:

- The penal-substitution theory confirms the biblical teaching of the total depravity of all humans. God would not have gone so far as to put his precious Son to death had it not been absolutely necessary. Humans are totally unable to meet their own need.

- God's nature is not one-sided, nor is there any tension between its different aspects. He is not merely righteous and demanding, nor merely loving and giving. He is righteous, so much so that sacrifice for sin had to be provided. He is loving, so much so that he provided that sacrifice himself.
- There is no other way of salvation but by grace, and especially the death of Christ. It has an infinite value and thus covers the sins of all humankind for all time. A finite sacrifice, by contrast, cannot even fully cover the sins of the individual offering it.
- There is security for the believer in his or her relationship to God. This is because the basis of the relationship, Christ's sacrificial death, is complete and permanent. Although our feelings might change, the ground of our relationship to God remains unshaken.

We must never take lightly the salvation we have. Although it is free, it is also costly, because it cost God the ultimate sacrifice. We must therefore always be grateful for what he has done; we must love him in return and emulate his giving character. "This is love: not that we loved God, but that he loved us and sent his Son as an atoning sacrifice for our sins" (1 John 4:10).

Christ died for all persons, but his atoning death becomes effective only when accepted by the individual.

The Logical Order of Salvation

The logical order of the initial aspects of salvation is a special calling, leading to conversion and ultimately regeneration.

Conversion

The image of turning from sin is found in both the Old and New Testaments. In the Book of Ezekiel, we read the word of the Lord to the people of Israel:

> Therefore, O house of Israel, I will judge you, each one according to his ways, declares the Sovereign Lord. Repent! Turn away from all your offenses; then sin will not be your downfall. Rid yourselves of all the offenses you have

> committed, and get a new heart and a new spirit. Why will
> you die, O house of Israel? For I take no pleasure in the
> death of anyone, declares the Sovereign Lord. Repent and
> live! (Ezek. 18:30–32)

Later Ezekiel is told to warn the wicked to turn from their ways (Ezek. 33:7–11). In Ephesians 5:14, Paul uses different imagery, but the basic thrust is the same: "Wake up, O sleeper, rise from the dead, and Christ will shine on you." In Acts, we find Peter advocating a change in direction of life: "Repent, then, and turn to God, so that your sins may be wiped out, that times of refreshing may come from the Lord" (Acts 3:19). While contemporary evangelists frequently plead, "Be converted," it is noteworthy that in the passages we have cited, the command is in the active: "Convert!"

Conversion is a single entity that has two distinguishable but inseparable aspects: repentance and faith. Repentance is the unbeliever's turning away from sin, and faith is his or her turning toward Christ. They are, respectively, the negative and positive aspect of the same occurrence. In a sense, each is incomplete without the other and each is motivated by the other. As we become aware of sin and turn from it, we see the necessity of turning to Christ for the provision of his righteousness. Conversely, believing in Christ makes us aware of our sin and thus leads to repentance.[262]

Repentance

The negative aspect of conversion is the abandonment or repudiation of sin. This is what we mean by repentance. It is based on a feeling of godly sorrow for our sin. In examining repentance and faith, we should remember that they cannot really be separated from one another. We deal with repentance first, because it logically precedes faith.

Faith

As repentance is the negative aspect of conversion, turning from one's sin, so faith is the positive aspect, laying hold of the promises and the work of Christ. Faith is at the very heart of the gospel, as it is the vehicle by which we are enabled to receive the grace of God.

So Great Salvation[263]

The following list has been taken from Lewis Sperry Chafer and H. L. Willmington and has also been expanded to suggest aspects of this "so great salvation" (Heb. 2:3).

1. Foreknown (Rom. 8:29; 1 Pet. 1:2)
2. Elect (1 Thess. 1:4; Rom. 8:33; Col. 3:12)
3. Predestinated (Eph. 1:11; Rom. 8:29–30; Eph. 1:5)
4. Chosen (Matt. 22:14; 1 Pet. 2:4)
5. Called (1 Thess. 5:24)
6. Foreordained (1 Pet. 1:20)
7. Reconciled by God (2 Cor. 5:18–19; Col. 1:20)
8. Reconciled to God (Rom. 5:10; 2 Cor. 5:20)
9. Made near (Eph. 2:13)
10. Given the ministry of reconciliation (2 Cor. 5:18)
11. Made an ambassador (2 Cor. 5:20)
12. Accepted by God (Eph. 1:6)
13. Given access to God (Rom. 5:2)
14. Redeemed by God (Col. 1:14; 1 Pet. 1:18; Rom. 3:24)
15. Passed from death to life (John 5:24)
16. Removed from a place of condemnation (Rom. 8:1; 1 Cor. 11:32; John 3:18)
17. Given liberty (Gal. 5:1)
18. Delivered from Satan (Col. 1:13)
19. Delivered from self (Rom. 6)
20. Delivered from law (Rom. 6:14; Gal. 3:25; 2 Cor. 3:11)
21. Dead to the law (Rom. 7:4)
22. Application of the propitiation (1 John 2:2; Rom. 3:25–26)
23. Application of the atonement (covering of sins) (Gen. 22:8)
24. Conscience purged (Heb. 9:14)
25. Application of Christ our sin-bearer (1 Pet. 2:24; Rom. 4:25)
26. Acceptance of Christ as our Substitute (Rom. 4:3–25)
27. Application of a ransom (Matt. 20:28)
28. Made a living stone (1 Pet. 2:5)
29. Become part of the bride of Christ (Eph. 5:25–27)

30. Engrafted into the Vine (John 15:1–8, 16)
31. Engrafted into the olive tree (Rom. 11:17)
32. Crucified with Christ (Gal. 2:20)
33. Dead with Christ (Rom. 6:4)
34. Planted together with Christ (Rom. 6:5)
35. Quickened together with Christ (Rom. 6:4; Col. 2:13)
36. Raised together with Christ (Rom. 6:4; Col. 3:1)
37. Set together with Christ (Eph. 2:6)
38. Worker together with Christ (1 Thess. 5:10)
39. Live together with Christ (1 Thess. 5:10)
40. Glorified together (Rom. 8:17, 30)
41. Dead to sin (1 Pet. 2:24)
42. Born again (John 1:12; John 3:7)
43. Become actual sons and daughters of God (1 John 3:3)
44. Become adopted sons and daughters of God (Rom. 8:25)
45. Made a new creation (2 Cor. 5:17)
46. Regenerated (Titus 3:5)
47. Made servants (Rev. 22:2)
48. Made vessels of honor (2 Tim. 2:21)
49. Made vessels of mercy (Rom. 9:23)
50. Made a child of the resurrection (Luke 20:36)
51. Made a child of the day (1 Thess. 5:5)
52. Made a child of Abraham (Gal. 3:7, 29)
53. Made a child of light (1 Thess. 5:5)
54. Made brethren (1 John 3:14–18)
55. Became an heir (Rom. 8:16–17)
56. Made a sheep in the Shepherd's fold (John 10:1–16; John 27–28)
57. Made salt (Matt. 5:13)
58. Made light (Eph. 5:8)
59. Became a part of a holy nation (1 Pet. 2:9)
60. Received citizenship in heaven (Phil. 3:20)
61. Made righteous (Rom. 3:22)
62. Made acceptable (Eph. 1:6; 1 Pet. 2:5)
63. Sanctified positionally (1 Cor. 1:30; 1 Cor. 6:11)
64. Perfected forever (Heb. 10:14)
65. Made fit to be partakers (Col. 1:12)

66. Justified (Rom. 5:1)
67. Received peace with God (Rom. 5:1)
68. Forgiven (Col. 1:14; Col. 2:13; Col. 3:13)
69. Became the object of grace (Rom. 5:1–6)
70. Righteousness of Christ imputed (Rom. 4:1–11)
71. Sins remitted (Matt. 26:28)
72. Delivered from the powers of darkness (Col. 1:13; Col. 2:13–15)
73. Translated (Col. 1:13)
74. Placed on the Rock (1 Cor. 3:11)
75. Part of God's inheritance (Eph. 1:18)
76. Part of God's gift of Christ (John 17:6, 11–12, 20)
77. Circumcised in Christ (Col. 2:11; Phil. 3:3; Rom. 2:29)
78. Made part of the holy priesthood (1 Pet. 2:5)
79. Made part of the royal priesthood (Rev. 1:6)
80. Made part of the chosen generation (1 Pet. 2:9)
81. Made one of God's own people (Titus 2:14)
82. Given access to God (Eph. 2:18)
83. Being washed/cleansed (1 Cor. 6:11)
84. Given a new Advocate (1 John 2:1)
85. Became an object of Christ's prayers (Heb. 7:25)
86. Made one of God's beloved (Eph. 2:4; Rom. 1:7)
87. Made an object of grace of God for salvation (Eph. 2:8)
88. Made an object of grace for keeping (Rom. 5:2)
89. Made an object of grace of God for service (Eph. 2:7)
90. Made an object of grace of God for instruction (Titus 2:12–13)
91. Made an object of the power of God (Eph. 1:9; Phil. 3:13)
92. Made an object of faithfulness of God (Heb. 13:5; Phil. 1:6)
93. Made an object of God's peace (Col. 3:15)
94. Made a part of the body of Christ (1 Cor. 12:27)
95. Made an object of the consolation of the Father (2 Thess. 2:16)
96. Received a new heavenly Father (Matt. 6:19)
97. Guaranteed an inheritance (1 Pet. 1:4)
98. Christ became our life (Col. 3:4; 1 John 5:10, 12)
99. Betrothed to Christ (2 Cor. 11:2)
100. Made a part of the household of God (Eph. 2:19; Eph. 3:15; Gal. 6:10)

101. Made a saint (Rom. 1:7)
102. In God (1 Thess. 1:1)
103. In Christ (John 14:20)
104. In the Spirit (Rom. 8:9)
105. Declared an epistle of Christ (2 Cor. 3:3)
106. Made rich (Eph. 1:3)
107. Baptized with the Holy Spirit (1 Cor. 12:13)
108. Indwelled by the Holy Spirit (Eph. 4:30)
109. Sealed by the Spirit (Eph. 4:30)
110. Given spiritual gifts (1 Cor. 12:7, 11)
111. Develops fruit of the Spirit (Gal. 5:22–23)
112. Received another Comforter (John 14:16–17)
113. Completed in Christ (Col. 2:10)
114. Placed in the heavenlies (Eph. 1:3)
115. Given every spiritual blessing (Eph. 1:3)
116. Became a Christian (Acts 11:26)
117. Qualified for promises of God (2 Cor. 1:20; 2 Pet. 1:3–4)
118. Given eternal life (John 5:24)
119. Received the indwelling faith of God (1 Pet. 1:1)
120. Guaranteed to be secured (John 10:27–29)
121. Given witness of the Spirit (Rom. 8:15)
122. Assured of salvation (1 John 5:13)
123. Received the Spirit of adoption (Rom. 8:15)
124. Led by the Holy Spirit (Rom. 8:14)
125. Qualified for the discipline of the Father (Heb. 12:5–8)
126. Became a partaker of the divine nature (2 Pet. 1:4)
127. Christ became our wisdom (1 Cor. 1:30)
128. Converted (Rom. 6:17)
129. Received the Holy Spirit (Luke 11:13)
130. Given a new understanding of scriptures (1 Cor. 2:13–15)
131. Saved (Rom. 10:13)

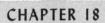

CHAPTER 18

Summary and Analysis

One God, One Faith

There is one God. Faith must be one too. According to the Bible, human beings should only adore and believe in God, the God of Abraham, of Isaac, and of Jacob (Exod. 3:15), the Father of our Lord Jesus Christ (1 Pet. 1:3), the God whom Christians worship. If there are people who believe in a god who is different from the God of the Holy Scriptures, the Bible, we should be clear and say that they are experiencing a false faith.

With the death of Christ, God's holy enmity toward humankind was terminated. Humanity was positionally reconciled to God. However, actual reconciliation occurs when the sinner applies the atoning blood of Christ to his or her life. The doctrine of reconciliation is not an experiential doctrine that works out in a person's lifestyle; reconciliation is a change in the relationship between God and humankind that is enacted in heaven.

Jesus Christ took a penal substitution by offering himself as a sacrifice, by substituting himself for us, actually bearing the punishment that should have been ours. Jesus appeased the Father and effected a reconciliation between God and humanity.

If sinners have faith in God, God will justify them. If the sinned against have faith in God, they can know that God's justice will be done.[264]

Faith, in God's Meaning

To have true faith is to believe in Jesus Christ as Lord and personal Savior. To have faith in him "as Lord" means that a person repents and asks forgiveness for all his or her sins. To have faith in him "as Savior" means that a person recognizes the work of Jesus Christ at the cross and believes that Jesus Christ died for his or her personal sins. The purpose of God's love is to save every one of us. Even if there was only one person on the planet, Jesus Christ would have come and died for that person.

False Faith

A faith that does not believe in Jesus Christ as Lord and Savior, "false faith" means to believe without God's blood being part of the salvation process. It also means to believe in a god who did not become the self-substitute for sinners.

To have false faith also means to exclude Christ's cross from one's beliefs. "For the message about the cross is foolishness to those who are perishing, but to us who are being saved it is the power of God" (1 Cor. 1:18). "Without the shedding of blood there is no forgiveness" (Heb. 9:22; Lev. 17:11).

The Cross

In biblical times, crucifying someone was an extreme punishment of a person who had committed a very serious sin and was sentenced to death.

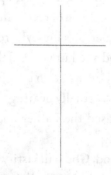

This cross was used in the countries that had Latin as the official language.
The horizontal pole is close to the upper extremity of the vertical pole.

The St. Andrew cross is formed like this.

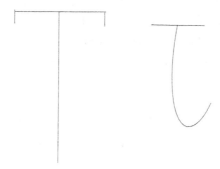

The cross of St Anthony is formed in this way.

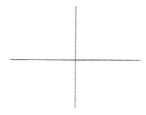

The Greek cross had a vertical and horizontal pole of equal dimensions. The two poles crossed in each's middle.

For the cross of St. Peter, the horizontal pole intersects the vertical pole at the bottom extremity of the vertical pole.

Crucifixion was practiced in times of war by the Phoenicians, the Carthaginians, the Egyptians, the and Romans.

The Cross of Jesus Christ: Place of Reconciliation

Process of Salvation: How True Faith Works

In previous chapters, we talked about the blood of a man that was shed. This perfect man was no other than Jesus Christ: God-man. His blood was shed at the cross of Golgotha. There, on the cross, God was reconciling himself with humankind as Christ paid the price that humankind should pay to God because of their sin.

The process of salvation takes place when a sinner, by faith, fixes his or her eyes on the cross of Jesus Christ and asks forgiveness for all his or her sins. The person must recognize that Christ died on the cross to save him or her.

The blood of Jesus Christ on the cross of Golgotha is the sufficient price for the salvation of all human beings, but everyone must personally believe in Jesus Christ as Lord and Savior for their personal salvation. Salvation is individual, not collective.

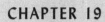

CHAPTER 19

Beliefs' Diagnosis

True Faith

Presence of Jesus Christ's blood	Yes
Presence of Jesus Christ's cross	Yes

False Faith

Presence of Jesus Christ's blood	No
Presence of Jesus Christ's cross	No

Religions and Their Beliefs

Animism

Presence of Jesus Christ's blood	No
Presence of Jesus Christ's cross	No

Buddhism

Presence of Jesus Christ's blood	No
Presence of Jesus Christ's cross	No

Confucianism

Presence of Jesus Christ's blood	No
Presence of Jesus Christ's cross	No

Hinduism

Presence of Jesus Christ's blood	No
Presence of Jesus Christ's cross	No

Islam

Presence of Jesus Christ's blood	No
Presence of Jesus Christ's cross	No

Judaism*

Presence of Jesus Christ's blood	No
Presence of Jesus Christ's cross	No

* According to Romans 11:26, all Israel will be saved.

Marxism

Presence of Jesus Christ's blood	No
Presence of Jesus Christ's cross	No

New Age movement

Presence of Jesus Christ's blood	No
Presence of Jesus Christ's cross	No

Secularism

Presence of Jesus Christ's blood	No
Presence of Jesus Christ's cross	No

Shinto

Presence of Jesus Christ's blood	No
Presence of Jesus Christ's cross	No

Taoism

Presence of Jesus Christ's blood	No
Presence of Jesus Christ's cross	No

Satanism

Presence of Jesus Christ's blood	No
Presence of Jesus Christ's cross	No

Rwandan traditional belief

Presence of Jesus Christ's blood	No
Presence of Jesus Christ's cross	No

Baha'i faith

Presence of Jesus Christ's blood	No
Presence of Jesus Christ's cross	No

Branhamism†

Presence of Jesus Christ's blood	No
Presence of Jesus Christ's cross	No

† Even if there are some different details of the biblical doctrine, the Branhamist belief can be accepted as Christian faith.

Atheism

Presence of Jesus Christ's blood	No
Presence of Jesus Christ's cross	No

Jainism

Presence of Jesus Christ's blood	No
Presence of Jesus Christ's cross	No

Jehovah's Witnesses

Presence of Jesus Christ's blood	Yes
Presence of Jesus Christ's cross	No

Mormonism‡

Presence of Jesus Christ's blood	Yes
Presence of Jesus Christ's cross	Yes

‡ Some details are different from biblical doctrine.

Roman Catholicism§

Presence of Jesus Christ's blood	Yes
Presence of Jesus Christ's cross	Yes

§ Baptism does not give salvation. Faith in Christ alone saves. Also, the principle of "Jesus through Mary" is not correct. There does not need to be someone else between Jesus and you. Direct access to Jesus is available to all. In addition, the place the Catholic Church calls purgatory does not exist. Concerning the dead, there are only two places in the Bible: heaven and hell.

Scientology

Presence of Jesus Christ's blood	No
Presence of Jesus Christ's cross	No

Sikhism

Presence of Jesus Christ's blood	No
Presence of Jesus Christ's cross	No

Unitarian Universalism

Presence of Jesus Christ's blood	No
Presence of Jesus Christ's cross	No

Wicca

Presence of Jesus Christ's blood	No
Presence of Jesus Christ's cross	No

Zoroastrianism

Presence of Jesus Christ's blood	No
Presence of Jesus Christ's cross	No

Christianity

Presence of Jesus Christ's blood	Yes
Presence of Jesus Christ's cross	Yes

How then could God express simultaneously his holiness in judgment and his love in pardon? Only by providing a divine substitute for the sinner so that the substitute would receive the judgment and the sinner the pardon. We sinners still of course have to suffer some of the personal, psychological, and social consequences of our sins, but the penal consequence, the deserved penalty of alienation from God, has been borne by another in our place, so that we may be spared it.

The goal of the mission of Jesus is fulfillment (Matt. 5:17b); according to Matthew 5:17a, this is primarily fulfillment of the law and the prophets, that is, of the whole of the Old Testament (IV, 1058, 15). Jesus has come in order that God's Word may be completely fulfilled, in order that the full measure appointed by God himself may be reached in him.

The demands of the law include total obedience and absolute righteousness (James 2:10; 1 Pet. 1:15–16; Lev. 11:44). Romans 10:4 declares, "For Christ is the end of the law for righteousness to everyone that believeth."

If you believe God self-substituted for you, you are enjoying the true faith. If you believe in a god who did not become the self-substitute for your sins, you are believing and experiencing a false faith, because without the shedding of God's blood (Jesus Christ's blood) there is no forgiveness.

But what must human beings do in order to receive salvation? The answer to this question is found in Romans 10:17: "Consequently, faith comes from hearing the message, and the message is heard through the word about Christ."

Christ died for all persons, but his atoning death becomes effective only when accepted by the individual.

If someone does not have faith, he or she should pray like this: "God, if indeed the Bible is truly your Word, if Christ is really your Son, and if he really died for me, reveal it to me at this moment." God promised that "anyone who chooses to do His will, will find out whether [Jesus's] teaching comes from God" (John 7:17).

Please pray this prayer: "Lord Jesus, I believe in you as Lord and as my personal Savior. I recognize your work at the cross. Forgive me of all my sins and make me become a child of God from this moment. In Jesus's name, amen!"

Conclusion

We have seen that the Bible has met the criteria to support its claim of being the Word of God. These criteria, which could also be applied to a human-authored book, are as follows: the Bible claims to be the Word of God; it is historically accurate; its authors were trustworthy; it is unified amid an amazing diversity; and accurate copies of the original manuscripts have been passed down to us.

With respect to the criteria that only God's Book can be said to meet, the Bible contains scientific statements that predate their discoveries by two thousand to three thousand years; it made accurate predictions that were fulfilled hundreds of years later; its message is unique; its messengers were confirmed by miracles; and the words have a transforming power. There is no other book like the Bible![265]

The necessity of propitiation is found in the holiness of God and the sinfulness of humankind. Salvation became possible only when God became the self-substitute for sinners.

My purpose has been to demonstrate that the problem of sin cannot be resolved without the blood of God himself, based on the following facts:

- "In fact, the law requires that nearly everything be cleansed with blood, and without the shedding of blood there is no forgiveness" (Heb. 9:22).
- All people of earth need a Savior, because all have sinned and all fall short of the glory of God. As it is written, "There is none righteous, no, not one" (Rom. 3:23). In heaven, the angels are not human and are not qualified to be propitiated for sinners. As it is written, "Truly,

he puts no faith in his servants, and he sees error in his angels" (Job 4:18 BEB).

- Only by providing a divine substitute for the sinner could the substitute receive the judgment so the sinner would be pardoned. This substitute was the man Christ Jesus. We are to think of Christ neither as man alone nor as God alone, but rather as the one only God-man who, because of his uniquely constituted person, was uniquely qualified to mediate between us and God. "The fact that it was God's Son, that it was God himself, who took our place on Golgotha and thereby freed us from the divine anger and judgment, reveals first the full implication of the wrath of God, of his condemning and punishing justice." The Son of God, i.e., God himself, took our place on Good Friday. The substitution was effectual and procured our reconciliation with the righteous God. Only God, our Lord and Creator, could stand surety for us, could take our place, could suffer eternal death in our stead as the consequence of our sin in such a way that it was finally suffered and overcome.

So then, God himself is at the heart of our answer to all three questions about the divine propitiation. It is God himself who in holy wrath needs to be propitiated, God himself who in holy love undertook to do the propitiating, and God himself who in the person of his Son died for the propitiation of our sins. Thus God took his own loving initiative to appease his own righteous anger by bearing it his own self in his own Son when he took our place and died for us. Christ's blood at the cross alone has the power to save sinners. But salvation is effective only for those who believe in him as Lord and Savior. This is the true faith spoken of in *True Faith*. The opposite of this faith is a false faith.

The author would like to inform readers that he respects each and every one of you. As God allowed free choice, or freedom, to every creature, starting with the angels even in heaven, the author has no intention of confronting the beliefs of other religions.

According to God, even if he leaves the creatures to do what they want—well, remember what Lucifer and one-third of the angels did in heaven. God pronounces severe punishment upon any creature who precludes his will. Eventually, Lucifer and the angels who helped him were cast out of heaven by an obedient angel of God called Michael. Lucifer and his angels are awaiting the terrible punishment that God has prepared for them because of their disobedience.

The purpose of *True Faith* is to make clear that there is only one true God and that there has been a problem between humankind and God from the time Adam and Eve sinned in the Garden of Eden. This problem must be resolved for a person be saved, as every sinner is assumed to be dead and lost. Human beings seek God through many ways, but God has provided only One way to salvation: Jesus Christ.

According to the scripture—and some world religions seem to understand this—blood is essential to calm the wrath of God. This is why the word *sacrifice* is no stranger in world religions. For those who believe in God's Word, the Bible, the word *blood* and the word *sacrifice* are well-known. As it is written, "In fact, the law requires that nearly everything be cleansed with blood, without the shedding of blood there is no forgiveness" (Heb. 9:22).

As we have seen, animal sacrifices did not manage to erase forever the wrath of God because the blood of animals does not have the ability to save a human being. Only the blood of a man, a perfect man, as God himself, can save humankind. The second person of the Trinity left heaven and descended to earth to be the sacrifice for humanity. He was apparently physically a man. He was a man on the outside, but inside Jesus was God. He was God in human form. He was God-man.

The world religions have adopted different beliefs about how a person is saved and gets to heaven—for those who believe that there is a heaven—but true faith is to believe in Jesus Christ as Lord and Savior, because Jesus Christ alone is the only way, the truth, and the life. As it is written, "I am the way and the truth and the life. No one comes to the Father except through me" (John 14:6).

It is also written, "For God so loved the world that he gave his one and only Son, that whoever believes in him shall not perish but have eternal life" (John 3:16).

Notes

1   Wayne Grudem, *Systematic Theology: An Introduction to Biblical Doctrine* (Leicester: InterVarsity Press, 1994), 490.
2   Gerhard Delling, *Theological Dictionary of the New Testament*, ed. G. Friedrich (Grand Rapids: Eerdmans, 1975), 6:294.
3   Harold Lindsell, *God's Incomparable Word* (Wheaton, IL: Victor Books, 1977), 15.
4   Elmer L. Towns, *Theology for Today* (Harcourt College Publishers, 2001), 47.
5   Ibid., 54.
6   Ibid., 28.
7   Lewis Sperry Chafer, *Systematic Theology* (Dallas: Dallas Seminary Press, 1947), 7:53.
8   Towns, *Theology for Today*, 218.
9   Ibid.
10 Ibid., 220, 221.
11 Westminster Shorter Catechism, question 1.
12 Russell R. Byrum, *Christian Theology* (Anderson, IN: Warner Press, 1976), 184.
13 *West's Analysis*, pp. 17–19, cited in James Petigru Boyce, *Abstract of Systematic Theology* (Philadelphia: American Baptist Publication Society, 1887), 63–64.
14 Ibid., 62.
15 William Newton Clarke, *An Outline of Christian Theology* (New York: Charles Scribner's Sons, 1898), 67.
16 Augustus H. Strong, *Systematic Theology* (Westwood, NJ: Revell, 1907), 252.
17 Boyce, *Abstract*, 58.
18 Strong, *Systematic Theology*, 304.
19 Thiessen, *Introductory Lectures*, 64–66.
20 Ibid., 66–67.
21 Strong, *Systematic Theology*, 90.
22 Edward Burnett Tylor, *Religion in Primitive Culture* (New York: Putnam, 1920), 426–27.
23 Morris Jastrow Jr., *The Study of Religion* (London: Walter Scott Ltd., 1902), 76.

24 George T. W. Patrick, *Introduction to Philosophy*, rev. ed. (New York: Houghton Mifflin, 1952), 221.

25 Robert Flint, *Anti-Theistic Theories*, 4th ed. (Edinburgh and London: Wm. Blackwood and Sons, 1899), 336.

26 Patrick, *Introduction to Philosophy*, 221.

27 Thiessen, *Lectures*, 74.

28 Boyce, *Abstract*, 65.

29 Louis Berkhof, *Systematic Theology* (Grand Rapids: Eerdmans, 1981), 79.

30 Ibid.; Towns, *Theology for Today*, 114.

31 Byrum, Christian Theology, 47.

32 Berkhof, *Systematic Theology*, 47

33 Grudem, *Systematic Theology*, 77, 78, 81–85.

34 Robert Dick, *Lectures on Theology*, cited in Chafer, *Systematic Theology*, 1:283.

35 Clarke, *Christian Theology*, 177.

36 Karl Barth, *The Doctrine of the Word of God* (New York: 1936), 344.

37 Andrew Jukes, *The Names of God in Holy Scripture* (Grand Rapids: Kregel Publications, 1967; reprint of 1888 edition), 19.

38 H. L. Willmington, *The Doctrine of the Father* (Lynchburg: privately printed, 1977), 1.

39 Fitzwater, *Christian Theology*, 90.

40 Mark Allan Powell, *The HarperCollins Bible Dictionary* (New York: HarperCollins, 2011), 397.

41 Grudem, *Systematic Theology*, 440.

42 Chad Brand, Charles Draper, and Archie England, *Holman Illustrated Bible Dictionary* (Nashville: Holman Bible Publishers, 2003), 792.

43 Grudem, *Systematic Theology*, 490.

44 Noel David Freedman, *Eerdmans Dictionary of the Bible* (Grand Rapids: William B. Eerdmans Publishing Company, 2000), 1224, 1225.

45 Erickson J. Millard, *Christian Theology*, 2nd ed. (Grand Rapids: Baker Books, 1998), 579.

46 G. Abbott-Smith, *A Manual Greek Lexicon of the New Testament* (Edinburgh: T. & T. Clark, 1937), 341.

47 C. Ryder Smith, *Doctrine of Sin* (London: Epsworth Press, 1953), 69.

48 Millard J. Erickson, *Christian Theology*, 2nd ed. (Grand Rapids: Baker Books, 1998), 583, 584, 585, 586.

49 Ibid., 16.

50 Francis Brown, S. R. Driver, and Charles A. Briggs, *Brown-Driver-Briggs Hebrew and English Lexicon* (Peabody, MA: Hendrickson Publishers, 1994), 957.

51 Ibid.

52 Ibid.

53 Friedrich Schleiermacher, *The Christian Faith*, vol. 1 (New York: Harper & Row, 1963), 271–73.

54 St. Augustine, *Confessions* ( ), 2.

55 Strong, *Systematic Theology*, 567.

56 Reinhold Niebuhr, *The Nature and Destiny of Man*, vol. 1 (New York: Scribner, 1941), 186–207.

57 Freedman, *Eerdmans Dictionary of the Bible*, 598.

58 Ibid.

59 Ibid., 453.

60 Erickson, *Christian Theology*, 280.

61 Emphasis added.

62 Andrew Sung Park, *From Hurt to Healing: A Theology of the Wounded* (Abingdon Press, 2004), 104, 105, 106.

63 Cf. C. K. Barret, "I Am Not Ashamed of the Gospel," in *Foi et Salut Selon* (St. Paul: Analecta Biblica, 1970), 19–50. Habakkuk 2:4b is quoted (with part of its context) in Hebrews 10:37, where the emphasis is closer to that of the original.

64 Albert Schweitzer, *The Mysticism of Paul the Apostle* (London: E. T., 1931), 219–26; cf. W. Wrede, *Paul* (London:, 1907), 122; W. Heitmuller, *Lutters Stellung in der Religionsgeschichte des Christentums* (Marburg: 1917), 19f.

65 Cf. E. Kasemann, *Perspectives on Paul* (London:, 1971), 60; G. Bornkamm, *Paul* (London:, 1971), 115; R. Y. K. Fung, *The Relation between Righteousness and Faith in the Thought of Paul* (unpublished PhD thesis, University of Manchester, 1975).

66 See p. 188.

67 Rom. 3:21–30.

68 The coincidence of the verb *reckon* in both Gen. 15:6 and Ps. 32:2 suggests a joint interpretation of the two texts, in accordance with the rabbinical exegetical principle of *geizerah shawah* (equal category). (Another instance appears in the two texts linked by the common term *cursed*, adduced in Gal. 3:10–14; see p. 181). On the relation between the two texts quoted in Rom. 4:3–8, see A. T. Hanson, *Studies in Paul's Technique and Theology* (London:, 1974), 52.

69 F. F. Bruce, *Paul, Apostle of the Heart Set Free* (Grand Rapids: William B. Eerdmans Publishing Company, 1977), 325–29.

70 Dean C. Halverson, *World Religions* (South Minneapolis: Bethany House Publishers, 1996), 25, 29.

71 Ibid., 13–16.

72 David A. Noebel, *Understanding the Times* (Irvine: Harvest House Publishers, 1994), 24.

73 Discussed in Stephen P. Goold, *New Age Deception: "No Other Gods,"* part 4 (sermon delivered at Crystal Evangelical Free Church, New Hope, Minnesota, October 4, 1998), message tape #98.

74 Noebel, *Understanding the Times*, 171.

75 Neil T. Anderson, Terry E. Zuehlke, and Julianne S. Zuehlke, *Christ-Centered Therapy: The Practical Integration of Theology and Psychology* (Grand Rapids: Zondervan Publishing House, 2000), 27–35.

76 Ibid., 35.

77 "Religious belief," *Wikipedia*, accessed January 29, 2015, http://en.wikipedia.org/wiki/Religious_belief.

78 Halverson, *World Religions*, 37.

79 Ibid., 37–43.

80 Headings on this page are taken from the lecture notes of Dr. Alvin Low, ACTS, PO Box 62725, Colorado Springs, CO 80962.

81 Halverson, *World Religions*, 54–55.

82 Ibid., 56.

83 "Faith," *Wikipedia*, accessed January 30, 2015, http://en.wikipedia.org/wiki/Faith#Buddhism.

84 Halverson, *World Religions*, 58, 59, 60, 61, 63.

85 Ibid.

86 "Faith," *Wikipedia*, accessed January 30, 2015, http://en.wikipedia.org/wiki/Faith#Hinduism.

87 Halverson, *World Religions*, 87–92.

88 Ibid., 87–108.

89 "Faith," *Wikipedia*, accessed January 30, 2015, http://en.wikipedia.org/wiki/Faith#Islam.

90 Halverson, *World Religions*, 87–108.

91 Ibid., 103–118.

92 Ibid., 121–23.

93 Ibid., 124–26.

94 Ibid., 127.

95 Ibid., 137, 138.

96 "Faith," *Wikipedia*, accessed January 30, 2015, http://en.wikipedia.org/wiki/Faith#Judaism.

97 Ibid.

98 Halverson, World Religions, 144, 145, 147, 157.

99 "New Age Movement," *Wikipedia*, accessed January 30, 2015, http://en.wikipedia.org/wiki/New_Age_Movement.

100 Ibid.

101 Halverson, *World Religions*, 216–222.

102 "Secularism," *Wikipedia*, accessed January 30, 2015, http://en.wikipedia.org/wiki/Secularism.

103 "Shinto," *Wikipedia*, accessed January 31, 2015, http://en.wikipedia.org/wiki/Shinto/.

104 "Taoism," *Wikipedia*, accessed January 31, 2015, http://en.wikipedia.org/wiki/Taoism/.

105 Halverson, *World Religions*, 216–222.

106 Towns, *Theology for Today*, 357.

107 Ibid., 358–60.

108 Chafer, *Systematic Theology*, 30.

109 Ibid., 49.

110 Ibid., 33.

111 G. H. Pember, *Earth's Earliest Ages* (Grand Rapids: Kregel Publishers, 1975), 62.

112 Towns, *Theology for Today*, 360–63.

113 Ibid., 365.

114 F. C. Jennings, *Satan: His Person, Work, Place and Destiny* (Neptune, NJ: Loiseaux Brothers, 1975), 64–65.

115 Towns, *Theology for Today*, 367.

116 J. O. Buswell, *A Systematic Theology of the Christian Religion* (Grand Rapids: Zondervan, 1962), 131.

117 Towns, *Theology for Today*, 367–71.

118 Ibid., 371–73.

119 Ibid., 374–81.

120 Ibid., 381–82.

121 Ibid., 381–83.

122 Marvin R. Vincent, *Word Studies in the New Testament* (New York: Charles Scribner's Sons, 1907), 1:756.

123 Ibid., 1:670.

124 Towns, *Theology for Today*, 381–87.

125 Cf. Al Silvin, *Geography of Rwanda*, ed. A. de Boeck Brussels (Kigali:), 6.

126 "Bahá'í_Faith," *Wikipedia*, accessed January 31, 2015, http://en.wikipedia.org/wiki/Bahá'í_Faith.

127 Ibid.

128 "William M. Branham," *Wikipedia*, accessed February 1, 2015, http://en.wikipedia.org/wiki/William_M._Branham.

129 "How to get to heaven," *Got Questions*, accessed February 2, 2015, http://www.gotquestions.org/how-to-get-to-heaven.html#ixzz3AKjxRoOT.

130 Towns, *Theology for Today*, 843.

131 "How to get to heaven—what are the ideas from the different religions?" *GotQuestions*, accessed February 2, 2015, http://www.gotquestions.org/how-to-get-to-heaven.html#ixzz3AKjxRoOT.

132 Lewis Sperry Chafer, *Major Bible Themes* (Grand Rapids: Zondervan, 1974), 301.

133 Towns, *Theology for Today*, 843.

134 Strong, *Systematic Theology*, 1032.

135 Chafer, *Major Bible Themes*, 304.

136 Thiessen, *Lectures in Systematic Theology*, 517.

137 John Ritchie, Impending Great Events (), 110.

138 Towns, *Theology for Today*, 850.

139 D. L. Moody, *Heaven* (New York: Fleming H. Revell Company, 1887), 3–4, 30–31.

140 Towns, *Theology for Today*, 852.

141 Richard W. DeHaan, *The Heavenly Home* (), 25.

142 Moody, *Heaven*, 57.

143 Powell, *HarperCollins Bible Dictionary*, 373.

144 Freedman, *Eerdmans Dictionary of the Bible*, 573.

145 Strong, *Systematic Theology*, 1033.

146 William L. Pettingill, *The Christian Fundamentals* (Findlay, OH: Fundamental Truth Publishers, 1941), 63–64.

147 James Orr, "Spirits in Prison," in *The International Standard Bible Encyclopedia*, ed. James Orr (Grand Rapids: Eerdmans, 1939), 2457.

148 Alfred H. Joy, "Dark, Darkness," in *The International Standard Bible Encyclopedia*, ed. James Orr (Grand Rapids: Eerdmans, 1939), 789.

149 Barnes, *Notes on the New Testament* (), 2:118–119.

150 *The International Standard Bible Encyclopedia*, 3113.

151 "Jesus," *Wikipedia*, accessed February 2, 2015, http://en.wikipedia.org/wiki/Jesus.

152 Ibid.

153 Ibid.

154 Ibid.

155 Ibid.

156 Ibid.

157 "Christ," *Wikipedia*, accessed February 2, 2015, http://en.wikipedia.org/wiki/Christ.

158 Towns, *Theology for Today*, 155.

159 Cited by Robinson, *Our Lord* (), 115.

160 Kanyabigega Silas, *True Faith* (), 301.

161 C. F. Montefore, *The Synoptic Gospels* (London: MacMillan and Co. Ltd., 1909), 1:361.

162 Karl Scheffrahn and Henry Kreyssler, *Jesus of Nazareth: Who Did He Claim to Be?* (Dallas: Pat Booth, 1968), 9–10.

163 Stevenson, *Titles* (), 120.

164 Pink, *Gospel of John* (), 121.

165 Tenney, *Gospel of Belief*, 62.

166 T. C. Horton and Charles E. Hurlburt, *The Wonderful Names of Our Wonderful Lord* (Los Angeles: Grant Publishing House, 1925). There are 365 names and titles of Christ covered on pp. 1–183.

167 James A. Borland, *Christ in the Old Testament* (Chicago: Ross-shire Christian Focus, 1999), 17.

168 Geisler, *Christ* (), 41.

169 Towns, *Theology for Today*, 155–80.

170 Ibid., 191.

171 Marvin R. Vincent, *Word Studies in the New Testament*, 1:756.

172 See H. E. Dana and Julius R. Mantey, *A Manual Grammar of the Greek New Testament* (Toronto: the Macmillan Company, 1955), 149.

173 Chafer, *Systematic Theology*, 5:8.

174 Leon Morris, "The Gospel According to John," in *The New International Commentary on the New Testament* (Grand Rapids: Eerdmans, 1971), 104.

175 Ibid., 698.

176 Ibid., 114–115.

177 Ibid., 115.

178 G. C. Berkouwer, *The Person of Christ* (Grand Rapids: Eerdmans Publishing Co., 1954), 276.

179 Walvoord, *Jesus Christ Our Lord* (), 116.

180 Ibid.

181 Ibid., 117–118. In the outline, Walvoord uses the definite article *the* before the word *predicate*. However, the seven points aforementioned are explained by the author from his perspective.

182 Ibid., 120–22.

183 Halverson, *World Religions*, 235, 236, 237, 239.

184 For the emphasis on "holy love," see P. T. Forsyth in both *The Cruciality of the Cross* (London: Hodder & Stoughton, 1909), and *The Work of Christ* (London: Hodder & Stoughton, 1910); William Temple, Christus Veritas (London: Macmillan, 1924), e.g., pp. 257 and 269; and Emil Brunner, *Mediator* ().

185 John R. W. Stott, *The Cross of Christ* (Downers Grove, IL: InterVarsity Press, 1986, 2006), 91, 92.

186 Ibid., 92.

187 Ibid., 104.

188 Exod. 3:6; Isa. 6:1–5; Job 42:5–6; Ezek. 1:28; Dan. 10:9; Luke 5:8; Rev. 1:17.

189 Stott, *The Cross of Christ*, 104.

190 E.g., Gen. 14:18–22; Ps. 7:17; Ps. 9:2; Ps. 21:7; Ps. 46:4; Ps. 47:2; Ps. 57:2; Ps. 83:18; Ps. 92:8; Ps. 93:4; Ps. 113:4; Dan. 3:26; Dan 4:2, 17, 24–25, 32, 34; Dan. 5:18–21; Dan. 7:18–27; Hosea 7:16; Hosea 11:7; Mic 6:6; 1 John 1:5; Heb. 12:29 (cf. Deut. 4:24); 1 Tim. 6:16; and Heb. 10:27, 31.

191 Lev 18:25–28; Lev. 20:22–23; Ps. 95:10; Num. 21:5; Rev. 3:16.

192 Stott, *The Cross of Christ*, 107, 108, 109.

193 Brunner, *Mediator*, 152.

194 Gustav Stahlin, "Orge," in *Theological Dictionary of the New Testament*, ed. Gerhard Kittel and Gerhard Friedrich, trans. Geoffrey W. Bromiley (Grand Rapids: Eerdmans, 1967), 5:425.

195 For historical surveys of the different theories of the atonement, see H. E. W. Turner, *The Patristic Doctrine of Redemption* (London: Mowbray, 1952); J. K. Mozley, *The Doctrine of the Atonement* (London: Duckworth, 1915); Robert Mackintosh, *Historic Theories of the Atonement* (London: Hodder, 1920); and Robert S. Franks, *A. History of the Doctrine of the Work of Christ, in Its Ecclesiastical Development* (London: Hodder & Stoughton, 1918).

196 Ibid., 22, 28–29, 36.

197 Ibid., 450, 470, 520.

198 G. C. Berkouwer, *The Work of Christ* (Grand Rapids: Eerdmans, 1965), 277.

199 Berkouwer, *The Person of Christ*, 276.

200 Emil Brunner, *Man in Revolt: A Christian Anthropology*, trans. Olive Wyon (London: Lutterworth, 1939), 187.

201 Forsyth, *The Cruciality of the Cross*, 5–6, 73.

202 Forsyth, *Work of Christ*, 80. He also uses the expression *holy love* in *The Justification of God* (London: Duckworth, 1916), esp. 124–31 and 190–95, William Temple picked it up in *Christus Veritas* (London: Macmillan, 1924), esp. pp. 257–60.

203 James Denney, *The Atonement and the Modern Mind* (London: Hodder & Stoughton, 1903), 82.

204 Thomas J. Crawford, *The Doctrine of Holy Scripture Respecting the Atonement* (Edinburgh: Blackwood, 1871), 453–54.

205 W. P. Paterson, "Sacrifice," in *A Dictionary of the Bible*, ed. James Hastings (Edinburgh: T & T Clark, 1902), 343.

206 B. B. Warfield, "Christ Our Sacrifice," in *Biblical Doctrines* (Oxford: Oxford University Press, 1929), 401–35, esp. p. 411.

207 Ibid., 136.

208 Crawford, *The Doctrine of Holy Scripture*, 237, 241.

209 Karl Barth, *Church Dogmatics*, vol. 4, "The Doctrine of Reconciliation," ed. Geoffrey W. Bromiley and T. F. Torrance; trans. Geoffrey W. Bromiley (Edinburgh: T & T Clark, 1956–57), 165.

210 A. W. F. Blunt, *The Epistle to the Galatians, Clarendon Bible* (Oxford: Oxford University Press, 1925), 96. See the last chapter for a fuller quotation.

211 See Crawford, *The Doctrine of Holy Scripture*, 444–45.

212 Jeremias, *Central Message* (), 36.

213 John Murray, *Redemption Accomplished and Applied* (Carlisle, PN: Banner of Truth Trust, 1961), 77.

214 L. Howard Marshall, *The Work of Christ* (Exeter: Paternoster, 1969), 74.

215 For example, Gen. 39:19; Ex. 32:19; 1 Sam. 11:6; 2 Sam. 12:5; and Esther 7:10.

216 For example, Josh. 7:1; Josh. 23:16; Judg. 3:8; 2 Sam. 24:1; 2 Kings 13:3; 2 Kings 22:13; and Hosea 8:5.

217 For example, Deut. 29:27–28; 2 Kings 22:17; and Ps. 79:5.

218 For example, Jer. 4:4 and Jer. 21:12.

219 For example, Ezek. 36:5–6; Ezek. 38:19; Zeph. 1:18; and Zeph. 3:8.

220 Ps. 78:38. Cf. Isa. 48:9 and Lam. 3:22, and in the New Testament Rom. 2:4 and 2 Pet. 3:9.

221 Jer. 44:22; Ezek. 24:13–14; cf. Exod. 32:10.

222 2 Kings 23:26; 2 Kings 22:17; 2 Chron. 34:25; Jer. 21:12.

223 Deut. 4:24, quoted in Heb. 12:29. Some examples of the portrayal of God's judgment as a devouring fire appear in Num. 11:1; Deut. 6:15; Ps. 59:13; Isa. 10:17; Isa. 30:27; Lam. 2:3; Ezek. 22:31; and Zeph. 1:18.

224 For example, Josh. 7:26; Ezek. 5:13; Ezek. 16:42; and Ezek. 21:17.

225 For example, Jer. 4:4 and Jer. 21:12.

226 Ezek. 5:13; Ezek. 6:12; Ezek. 7:8; Ezek. 13:15; Ezek. 20:8, 21.

227 Ibid., 128.

228 For example, John 10:18; Mark 14:36; and Heb. 10:7 (Ps. 40:7–8).

229 George A. Buttrick, *Jesus Came Preaching* (New York: Scribner, 1931), 207.

230 Dale, *Atonement* ( ), 393.

231 Stott, *The Cross of Christ*, 165, 166.

232 Delling, *Theological Dictionary of the New Testament*, 6:294.

233 F. F. Bruce, *The Epistle of Paul to the Romans* (Grand Rapids: Eerdmans, 1963), 203.

234 Towns, *Theology for Today*, 220, 221, 222.

235 Stott, *The Cross of Christ*, 166.

236 A. T. Hanson, *The Wrath of the Lamb* (London: SPCK, 1959), 192.

237 Forsyth, *The Cruciality of the Cross*, . Compare Calvin's statement: "The work of atonement derives from God's love; therefore, it did not establish it" (*Institutes*, 2:16:4).

238 Barth, *Church Dogmatics*, 398, 403.

239 F. Buchsel, "Hilaskomai," in *Theological Dictionary of the New Testament* (Grand Rapids: Eerdmans, 1972), 37.

240 David F. Wells, *The Search for Salvation* (Downers Grove: InterVarsity Press, 1978), 29.

241 Buchsel, "Hilaskomai," 37.

242 Wells, *The Search for Salvation*, 29.

243 Buchsel, "Hilaskomai," 37.

244 From an article on redemption by B. B. Warfield, first published *in The Princeton Theological Review* 14 (1916), and reprinted in his *The Person and Work of Christ*, ed. Samuel G. Crai (Philipsburg, NJ: Presbyterian & Reformed, 1950), 345, 347.

245 Lev. 25:25–28; Ruth 3–4; Jer. 32:6–8. Cf. Lev. 27 for redeeming land that had been dedicated to the Lord by a special vow.

246 Stott, *The Cross of Christ*, 166–75.

247 Alain M. Stibbs, *The Meaning of the Word "Blood" in Scripture* (London: Tyndale Press, 1948), 10, 12,16, 30. Leon Morris has a chapter titled "The Blood" in his *Apostolic Preaching* (pp. 108–24), and in his *Cross in the New Testament*, in which he writes, "The Hebrews understood 'blood' habitually in the sense of 'violent death'" (219). F. D. Kidner also criticizes Westcott's thesis in his *Sacrifice in the Old Testament* (London: Tyndale Press, 1952), and points out that the prohibition of the use of blood in food "is consistent with the idea of its preciousness, but hardly with that of its potency" (24).

248 Johannes Behm, "Haima," in *Theological Dictionary of the New Testament*, ed. Gerhard Kittler and Gerhard Friedrich, trans. Geoffrey W. Bromiley (Grand Rapids, Eerdmans, 1964), 1:173.

249 Rev. 5:9; cf. Rev. 1:5–6; Rev. 14:3–4.

250 Stott, *The Cross of Christ*, 177–79.

251 James Hope Moulton and George Milligan, *The Vocabulary of the Greek Testament* (Grand Rapids: Eerdmans, 1972), 6.

252 Towns, *Theology for Today*, 219, 220.

253 Ps. 143:2. Cf. Ps. 51:4; Ps. 130:3; and Job 25:4.

254 G. B. Caird, "Justification: The Biblical Basis and Its Relevance for Contemporary Evangelicalism," in *The Great Acquittal*, ed. Gavin Reid (London: Collins, 1980), 16.

255 J. I. Packer, "Justification," in *New Bible Dictionary*, ed. I. Howard Marchall et al., 2nd ed. (Downers Grove: InterVarsity Press, 1982), 647.

256 For example, Rom. 3:28; Rom. 5:1; Gal. 2:16; and Phil. 3:9.

257 From Hooker's "Definition of Justification," in chapter 33 of his *Of the Laws of Ecclesiastical Polity*, which began to be published in 1593. *The Works of Richard Hooker*, ed. John Keble, 3rd ed., 3 vols. (Oxford: Oxford University Press, 1845).

258 Grudem, *Systematic Theology*, 226.

259 Ibid.

260 Ibid.

261 Towns, *Theology for Today*, 115–152

262 Freedman, *Eerdmans Dictionary of the Bible*, 598.

263 Ibid.

264 Ibid., 58, 59, 60, 61, 63.

265 Halverson, *World Religions*, 88.

Sources

Abbott-Smith, G. *A Manual Greek Lexicon of the New Testament.* Edinburgh: T. & T. Clark, 1937.

Anderson, Neil T., Terry E. Zuehlke, and Julianne S. Zuehlke. *Christ-Centered Therapy: The Practical Integration of Theology and Psychology.* Grand Rapids: Zondervan, 2000.

"Bahá'í Faith." *Wikipedia.* Accessed January 31, 2015. http://En.Wikipedia.Org/Wiki/Bahá'í_Faith.

Barret, C. K. "I Am Not Ashamed of the Gospel." In *Foi Et Salut Selon.* St. Paul: Analecta Biblica, .

Barth, Karl. *The Doctrine of Reconciliation.* Vol. 4 of *Church Dogmatics.* Edited by Geoffrey W. Bromiley and T. F. Torrance. Translated by Geoffrey W. Bromiley. Edinburgh: T & T Clark, 1956–57.

———. *The Doctrine of the Word of God.* New York: 1936.

Behm, Johannes. "Haima." In *Theological Dictionary of the New Testament.* Edited by Gerhard Kittler and Gerhard Friedrich. Translated by Geoffrey W. Bromiley. Grand Rapids: Eerdmans, 1964.

Berkhof, Louis. *Systematic Theology.* Grand Rapids: Eerdmans, 1981.

Berkouwer, G. C. *The Person of Christ.* Grand Rapids: Eerdmans Publishing Co., 1954.

———. *The Work of Christ.* Grand Rapids: Eerdmans, 1965.

Blunt, A. W. F. *The Epistle to the Galatians, Clarendon Bible.* Oxford: Oxford University Press, 1925.

Bornkamm, G. *Paul, E. T.* London: 1971.

Boyce, James Petigru. "West's Analysis." In *Abstract of Systematic Theology.* Philadelphia: American Baptist Publication Society, 1887.

Borland, James A. *Christ in the Old Testament.* Chicago: Ross-Shire Christian Focus, 1999.

Brand, Chad, Charles Draper, and Archie England. *Holman Illustrated Bible Dictionary.* Nashville: Holman Bible Publishers, 2003.

Brown, Francis, S. R. Driver, and Charles A. Briggs. *Brown-Driver-Briggs Hebrew and English Lexicon of the Old Testament.* Oxford: Clarendon Press, 1977.

Bruce, F. F. *The Epistle of Paul to the Romans.* Grand Rapids: Eerdmans, 1963.

———. *Paul, Apostle of the Heart Set Free.* Grand Rapids: William B. Eerdmans Publishing Company, 1977.

Brunner, Emil. *Man in Revolt: A Christian Anthropology.* Translated by Olive Wyon. London: Lutterworth, 1939.

———. *Mediator.*

Buchsel, F. *Theological Dictionary of the New Testament.* Grand Rapids: Eerdmans, 1972.

Buswell, J. O. *A Systematic Theology of the Christian Religion.* Grand Rapids: Zondervan, 1962.

Buttrick, George A. *Jesus Came Preaching.* New York: Scribner, 1931.

Byrum, Russell R. *Christian Theology.* Anderson, IN: Warner Press, 1976.

Caird, G. B. "Justification: The Biblical Basis and Its Relevance for Contemporary Evangelicalism." In *The Great Acquittal.* Edited by Gavin Reid. London: Collins, 1980.

Chafer, Lewis Sperry. *Systematic Theology.* Dallas: Dallas Seminary Press, 1947.

———. *Major Bible Themes.*

"Christ." *Wikipedia.* Accessed February 2, 2015. http://En.Wikipedia.Org/Wiki/Christ.

Clarke, William Newton. *An Outline of Christian Theology.* New York: Charles Scribner's Sons, 1898.

Crawford, Thomas J. *The Doctrine of Holy Scripture Respecting the Atonement.* Edinburgh: Blackwood, 1871.

Dana, H. E., and Julius R. Mantey. *A Manual Grammar of the Greek New Testament.* Toronto: the Macmillan Company, 1955.

Delling, Gerhard. *Theological Dictionary of the New Testament.* Edited by G. Friedrich. Grand Rapids: Eerdmans, 1975.

Denney, James. *The Atonement and the Modern Mind.* London: Hodder & Stoughton, 1903.

Dick, Robert. *Lectures on Theology.* Cited in Chafer, *Systematic Theology.*

Erickson, Millard J. *Christian Theology.* 2nd ed. Grand Rapids: Baker Books, 1998.

"Faith." *Wikipedia.* Accessed January 30, 2015. http://En.Wikipedia.Org/Wiki/Faith#Buddhism.

———. *Wikipedia.* Accessed January 30, 2015. http://En.Wikipedia.Org/Wiki/Faith#Hinduism.

———. *Wikipedia.* Accessed January 30, 2015. http://En.Wikipedia.Org/Wiki/Faith#Islam.

———. *Wikipedia.* Accessed January 30, 2015. http://En.Wikipedia.Org/Wiki/Faith#Judaism.

Flint, Robert. *Anti-Theistic Theories.* 4th ed. Edinburgh and London: Wm. Blackwood and Sons, 1899.

Forsyth, P. T. *Cruciality of the Cross.* London: Hodder & Stoughton, 1909.

———. *The Justification of God.* London: Duckworth, 1916.

———. *The Work of Christ.* London: Hodder & Stoughton, 1910.

Franks, Robert S. *A History of the Doctrine of the Work of Christ, in Its Ecclesiastical Development.* London: Hodder & Stoughton, 1918.

Freedman, Noel David. *Eerdmans Dictionary of the Bible.* Grand Rapids: William B. Eerdmans Publishing Company, 2000.

Fung, R. Y. K. *The Relation between Righteousness and Faith in the Thought of Paul.* Unpublished PhD thesis. University of Manchester, 1975.

Goold, Stephen P. "New Age Deception: 'No Other Gods.'" Part 4. Sermon delivered at Crystal Evangelical Free Church. New Hope, Minnesota: October 4, 1998. Message tape #98.

Grudem, Wayne. *Systematic Theology: An Introduction to Biblical Doctrine.* Leicester: InterVarsity Press, 1994.

Hanson, A. T. *The Wrath of the Lamb.* London: SPCK, 1959.

Horne, Charles M. *Salvation.* Chicago: Moody, 1971.

"How to Get to Heaven." *Got Questions.* Accessed February 2, 2015. http://www.Gotquestions.Org/How-To-Get-To-Heaven.Html#Ixzz3akjxroot.

Jeremias. *Central Message.*

"Jesus." *Wikipedia.* Accessed February 2, 2015. http://En.Wikipedia.Org/Wiki/Jesus.

Joy, Alfred H. "Dark, Darkness." In *The International Standard Bible Encyclopedia.* Edited by James Orr. Grand Rapids: Eerdmans, 1939.

Jukes, Andrew. *The Names of God in Holy Scripture.* Grand Rapids: Kregel Publications, 1967; reprint of 1888 edition.

Kasemann, E. *Perspectives on Paul, E. T.* London: 1971.

Kidner, F. D. *His Sacrifice in the Old Testament.* London: Tyndale Press, 1952.

Halverson, Dean C. *World Religions.* Bethany House Publishers, 1996.

Heitmuller, W. *Lutters Stellung in Der Religionsgeschichte des Christentums.* Marburg: 1917.

Hooker, Richard. "Definition of Justification." Chapter 33 of *The Laws of Ecclesiastical Polity.* In *The Works of Richard Hooker.* Edited by John Keble. 3rd ed. 3 vols. Oxford: Oxford University Press, 1845.

Horton, T. C., and Charles E. Hurlburt. *The Wonderful Names of Our Wonderful Lord.* Los Angeles: Grant Publishing House, 1925.

Jastrow, Morris, Jr. *The Study of Religion.* London: Walter Scott Ltd., 1902.

Jennings, F. C. *Satan: His Person, Work, Place and Destiny.* Neptune, NJ: Loiseaux Brothers, 1975.

Laubach, Fritz. "Conversion, Penitence, Repentance, Proselyte." In *The New International Dictionary of New Testament Theology.* Edited by Colin Brown. Vol. 1. Grand Rapids: Zondervan, 1975.

Lindsell, Harold. *God's Incomparable Word.* Wheaton, IL: Victor Books, 1977.

Mackintosh, Robert. *Historic Theories of the Atonement*. London: Hodder, 1920.

Marchall, Howard I. *The Work of Christ*. Exeter: Paternoster, 1969.

Montefore, C. F. *The Synoptic Gospels*. London: Macmillan and Co., 1909.

Moody, D. L. *Heaven*. New York: Fleming H. Revell Company, 1887.

Morris, Leon. "The Blood." In *His Apostolic Preaching*.

———. "The Gospel According to John." In *The New International Commentary on the New Testament*. Grand Rapids: Eerdmans, 1971.

Moulton, James Hope, and George Milligan. *The Vocabulary of the Greek Testament*. Grand Rapids: Eerdmans, 1972.

Mozley, J. K. *The Doctrine of the Atonement*. London: Duckworth, 1915.

Murray, John. *Redemption Accomplished and Applied*. Carlisle, PN: Banner of Truth Trust, 1961.

"New Age Movement." *Wikipedia*. Accessed January 30, 2015. http://En.Wikipedia. Org/Wiki/New_Age_Movement.

Niebuhr, Reinhold. *The Nature and Destiny of Man*. Vol. 1. New York: Scribner, 1941.

Noebel, David. *Understanding the Times*.

Orr, James, ed. *The International Standard Bible Encyclopedia*. Grand Rapids: Eerdmans, 1939.

———. "Spirits in Prison." In *The International Standard Bible Encyclopedia*. Edited by James Orr. Grand Rapids: Eerdmans, 1939.

Packer, J. I. "Justification." In *New Bible Dictionary*. Edited by I. Howard Marchall et al. 2nd ed. Downers Grove: InterVarsity Press, 1982.

Park, Andrew Sung. *From Hurt to Healing: A Theology of the Wounded*. Nashville: Abingdon Press, 2004.

Paterson, W. B. "Sacrifice." In *A Dictionary of the Bible*. Edited by James Hastings. Edinburgh: T & T Clark, 1902.

Patrick, George T. W. *Introduction to Philosophy*. New York: Houghton Mifflin, 1952.

Pember, G. H. *Earth's Earliest Ages*. Grand Rapids: Kregel Publishers, 1975.

Pettingill, William L. *The Christian Fundamentals*. Findlay, OH: Fundamental Truth Publishers, 1941.

Pink, *Gospel of John*.

Powell, Mark Allan. *The HarperCollins Bible Dictionary, Revised and Updated*. New York: HarperCollins Publishers, 2011.

"Religious Belief." *Wikipedia*. Accessed January 29, 2015. http://En.Wikipedia.Org/Wiki/Religious_Belief.

Ritchie, John. *Impending Great Events*.

Scheffrahn, Karl, and Henry Kreyssler. *Jesus of Nazareth: Who Did He Claim to Be?* Dallas: Pat Booth, 1968.

Schleiermacher, Friedrich. *The Christian Faith*. Vol. 1. New York: Harper & Row, 1963.

Schweitzer, Albert. *The Mysticism of Paul the Apostle*. London: 1931.

"Shinto." *Wikipedia*. Accessed January 31, 2015. http://En.Wikipedia.Org/Wiki/ Shinto.

Silvin, Al. *Geography of Rwanda*. Edited by A. De Boeck Brussels. Kigali: .

Smith, C. Ryder. *Doctrine of Sin*. London: Epsworth Press, 1953.

Stahlin, Gustave. "Orge." In *Theological Dictionary of the New Testament*. Edited by Gerhard Kittel and Gerhard Friedrich. Translated by Geoffrey W. Bromiley. Grand Rapids: Eerdmans, 1967.

Stevenson. *Titles*.

Stibbs, Alain M. *The Meaning of the Word "Blood" in Scripture*. London: Tyndale Press, 1948.

Stott, John R. W. *The Cross of Christ*. Downers Grove: InterVarsity Press, 1986, 2006.

Strong, Augustus H. *Systematic Theology*. Westwood, NJ: Revell, 1907.

"Taoism." *Wikipedia*. Accessed January 31, 2015. http://En.Wikipedia.Org/Wiki/ Taoism/.

Temple, William. *Christus Veritas*. London: Macmillan, 1924.

Tenney. *Gospel of Belief*.

Thiessen. *Lectures in Systematic Theology*.

Towns, Elmer L. *Theology for Today*. Harcourt College Publishers, 2001.

Turner, H. E. W. *The Patristic Doctrine of Redemption*. London: Mowbray, 1952.

Tylor, Edward Burnett. *Religion in Primitive Culture*. New York: Putnam, 1920.

Vincent, Marvin R. *Word Studies in the New Testament*. New York: Charles Scribner's Sons, 1907.

Walvoord. *Jesus Christ Our Lord*.

Warfield, B. B. *The Princeton Theological Review* 14 (1916). Reprinted in *The Person and Work of Christ*. Edited by Samuel G. Crai. Philipsburg. NJ: Presbyterian & Reformed, 1950.

———. "Christ Our Sacrifice." In *Biblical Doctrines*. Oxford: Oxford University Press, 1929.

Wells, David F. *The Search for Salvation*. Downers Grove: InterVarsity Press, 1978.

"William M. Branham." *Wikipedia*. Accessed February 1, 2015. http://En.Wikipedia. Org/Wiki/William_M._Branham.

Willmington, H. L. *The Doctrine of the Father*. Lynchburg: published privately, 1977.

Wrede, W. *Paul, E. T.* London: 1907.

Printed in the United States
By Bookmasters